DIGITAL INTERMEDIARIES IN DOMESTIC AND CARE WORK

This edited collection unravels the multiple ways in which digital intermediaries have transformed the domestic and care work sector, and what this development entails for the regulation of digital labour platforms.

Domestic and care work is work like any other – but also work like no other. As a consequence, digital intermediaries in these sectors fulfil partly different functions from other digital labour platforms. Taking a comparative and interdisciplinary socio-legal approach, the book is organised into four parts. The first section describes the different business models used in various geographical areas and analyses the ways in which digital intermediaries reshape these markets. The second section examines how digital intermediaries adapt their structures and organisations to regulatory and institutional frameworks, while also exploiting regulatory gaps and grey zones. The third part of the book highlights the experiences of domestic workers who develop novel forms of platform cooperatives with the potential for better working conditions and a stronger voice. The fourth part of the book looks at the legal and regulatory challenges, discussing the challenge of classifying digital intermediation in care and domestic work not only in relation to employment/ self-employment, but also in relation to the third party in the triangular relationship: the private household. The book analyses cases from South and Central Europe, Southeast Europe, the UK, South Africa and Latin America; its interdisciplinary approach, with sociological, anthropological and legal perspectives, makes the book an important reference in this emerging field of study.

Oñati International Series in Law and Society

A SERIES PUBLISHED FOR THE OÑATI INSTITUTE
FOR THE SOCIOLOGY OF LAW

Recent titles in this series

Contesting Austerity: A Socio-Legal Inquiry
Edited by Anuscheh Farahat and Xabier Arzoz

The Right to the Continuous Improvement of Living Conditions: Responding to Complex Global Challenges
Edited by Jessie Hohmann and Beth Goldblatt

Supporting Legal Capacity in Socio-Legal Context
Edited by Mary Donnelly, Rosie Harding and Ezgi Tascioglu

What Is a Family Justice System For?
Edited by Mavis Maclean, Rachel Treloar and Bregje Dijksterhuis

Combining the Legal and the Social in Sociology of Law: An Homage to Reza Banakar
Edited by Håkan Hydén, Roger Cotterrell, David Nelken and Ulrike Schultz

Criminal Justice and The Ideal Defendant in the Making of Remorse and Responsibility
Edited by Stewart Field and Cyrus Tata

Socio-Legal Trajectories Across Europe: Comparative Perspectives
Edited by Christian Boulanger, Naomi Creutzfeldt and Jennifer Hendry

Parole Futures: Rationalities, Institutions and Practices
Edited by Harry Annison, Nicola Carr and Thomas Guiney

The Socio-Politics of Legal Design and its Epistemic Consequences
Edited by Siddharth Peter de Souza and Joaquín Santuber

Digital Intermediaries in Domestic and Care Work
Edited by Lorena Poblete and Eva Kocher

For the complete list of titles in this series
see www.bloomsbury.com/uk/series/oñati-international-series-in-law-and-society

Digital Intermediaries in Domestic and Care Work

Edited by
Lorena Poblete
and
Eva Kocher

Oñati International Series in Law and Society

A SERIES PUBLISHED FOR THE OÑATI INSTITUTE
FOR THE SOCIOLOGY OF LAW

•HART•
OXFORD • LONDON • NEW YORK • NEW DELHI • SYDNEY

HART PUBLISHING
Bloomsbury Publishing Plc
Kemp House, Chawley Park, Cumnor Hill, Oxford, OX2 9PH, UK
1385 Broadway, New York, NY 10018, USA
Bloomsbury Publishing Ireland Limited, 29 Earlsfort Terrace, Dublin 2, D02 AY28, Ireland

HART PUBLISHING, the Hart/Stag logo, BLOOMSBURY and the Diana logo are trademarks of Bloomsbury Publishing Plc

First published in Great Britain 2026

1

A catalogue record for this book is available from the British Library.

A catalogue record for this book is available from the Library of Congress.

ISBN: HB: 978-1-50999-085-6
ePDF: 978-1-50999-087-0
ePub: 978-1-50999-086-3

Typeset by Amnet

For product safety related questions contact productsafety@bloomsbury.com

To find out more about our authors and books visit www.hartpublishing.co.uk. Here you will find extracts, author information, details of forthcoming events and the option to sign up for our newsletters.

Acknowledgements

This book is the result of a collaboration between legal scholar Eva Kocher (European Universität Viadrina, Frankfurt (Oder), Germany) and sociologist Lorena Poblete (CONICET-Universidad Nacional de San Martín, Argentina), made possible by the Alexander von Humboldt Foundation (Germany). The Georg Forster Research Fellowship, awarded by this foundation, allowed Lorena Poblete to spend 18 months as a visiting scholar at the Centre for Interdisciplinary Labour Law Studies of the Faculty of Law at Europa-Universität Viadrina in Frankfurt (Oder), from 2022 to 2024. We are both grateful for this opportunity for close cooperation and friendship!

The concept of the book started to take shape with the organisation of a workshop entitled 'Domestic Work and the Law', held at European Universität Viadrina in May 2022, followed by the panel session 'The Role of Intermediaries in Shaping Domestic and Care Work in Europe and Latin America', organised at the 6th Conference of the Labour Law Research Network in Warsaw in June 2023. We extend our gratitude to all the participants in these events, namely Kirsten Scheiwe (University of Hildesheim, Germany); Majda Hrženjak (The Peace Institute, Slovenia); Clémence Ledoux (Université de Nantes, France); Franca van Hooren (University of Amsterdam, Netherlands); Nikola Boskovic (Minor – Projektkontor für Bildung und Forschung, Germany); Dominik Schmitz (European Universität Viadrina, Germany); Adelle Blackett (McGill University, Canada); Vera Pavlou (University of Glasgow, UK); Judy Fudge (McMaster University, Canada); Rafael Encinas de Muñagorri (Université de Nantes, France); and Roberto Fragale Filho (Universidade Federal Fluminense, Brazil).

In May 2024, we gathered lawyers and sociologists at the Oñati International Institute for the Sociology of Law (IISL), in Spain, to discuss chapters for this book. We would like to thank all the authors for sharing their thoughts and ideas, and for engaging with us in collective thinking about digital intermediaries in domestic and care work. The cooperation, which included feedback and cross-referencing processes, took place over a period of time, and we are grateful for everyone's persistence and interest. The welcoming atmosphere of the IISL contributed greatly to the success of this collaborative effort. We express our gratitude to Sabine Frerichs, the IISL's Scientific Director in 2024, and Malen Gordoa Mendizabal for hosting and looking after us at the Oñati Institute.

Thanks a lot to Hasna Chatraoui and Vlada Antypenko for their help with editing the chapters. Leire Kortabarri (IISL Publications) and Sasha Jawed (Hart

Publishing) organised the production of this book. Last but not least, this project would not have been possible without our affiliation to public research institutions: Consejo Nacional de Investigaciones Científicas y Técnicas (CONICET), Universidad Nacional de San Martín and European Universität Viadrina Frankfurt (Oder). We cherish public investment in knowledge production and research; these times remind us that it should not be taken for granted.

Contents

PART III
AN ALTERNATIVE MODEL: WORKERS' COOPERATIVES

PART IV
REGULATING DIGITAL INTERMEDIARIES IN EUROPE

Contributors

Antonio Aloisi is an Associate Professor at IE University Law School in Madrid, where he teaches European and comparative Labour Law and guides students through the landscapes of digital regulation. He co-leads the 'Lawtomation' Jean Monnet Centre of Excellence. Antonio held research positions at New York University, Fundação Getulio Vargas, the European University Institute and Saint Louis University. In 2020, he was awarded a Marie Skłodowska-Curie fellowship.

Joe Atkinson is a Associate Professor of Employment Law at the University of Southampton, and Co-Director of the Stefan Cross Centre for Women, Equality and Law. He studied law at the University of Oxford and London School of Economics and received his PhD from University College London. Joe has been a visiting researcher at New York University School of Law and the Surrey Centre for Law and Philosophy. Before academia he worked in the UK Parliament as a Political Advisor and Senior Researcher.

Joanna Bronowicka is a sociologist at the Center for Interdisciplinary Labour Law Studies at the European University Viadrina. She examines novel organisational forms and practices in the platform economy through a socio-legal lens, exploring their significance for labour law and the labour movement. She is completing her PhD at the University of Potsdam.

Milena Franke is a Post-doctoral Researcher working in the Transform group at the Centre for Sociological Research at KU Leuven. She holds a PhD in Sociology Masters' degrees in Sociology and European Policies and Politics. She currently conducts research within the ERC Advanced Grant Project 'ResPecTMe'. Her research focuses on digitalisation and work, labour control and consent, unpaid labour and platform work.

Tish Gibbons is Assistant Professor at the Work & Employment Studies Department, Kemmy Business School, University of Limerick, where she teaches industrial / employment relations, Human Resource Management and research methods. A former Head of SIPTU College, Ireland's only trade union college, she has worked for 35 years in the Irish trade union movement. A graduate of University College Galway, her post-graduate studies include: MA, Keele University, 2004; Post Graduate Diploma Social Research Methods, Open University, 2008; Professional Doctorate in Researching Work, London Metropolitan University, 2014.

Christina Hiessl (Hießl) is Professor of Labour Law at KU Leuven (Belgium), Invited Professor of Social Welfare at Yonsei University (Seoul) and Consulting Expert of the European Commission's Centre of Expertise in the Field of Labour

Law. She has worked and/or studied in eight countries, focusing on comparative social law and policy research. She is associate editor of the *European Labour Law Journal*, scientific advisory board member of the Frankfurt Law Review and managing board member of the honours programme 'KU Leuven Engage'.

Mat Johnson is a Senior Lecturer in employment studies based in the Work and Equalities Institute at the Alliance Manchester Business School. His research interests include wage setting, precarious work and the changing nature of labour market regulation at the local, national, and international levels. Mat currently holds a UKRI Future Leaders Fellowship grant to undertake a comparative qualitative study of work and employment in six cities around the world (2020–27).

Eva Kocher is a Professor for European and German labour law and the head of the Center for Interdisciplinary Labour Law Research (C*LLaS) at the Law Faculty of European University Viadrina Frankfurt (Oder), Germany. She is the chair of the 'Vereinigung für Recht und Gesellschaft' (German Law & Society Association). Among her most recent publication are the books *Digital Work Platforms: At the Interface of Labour Law* (Oxford, Hart Publishing, 2022) and the collection of articles *Das Andere des Arbeitsrecht: Perspektiven feministischen Rechtsdenkens* (Weilerswist-Metternich, Velbrück, 2024).

Claudia Marà is a Post-doctoral Researcher at the Centre for Sociological Research at KU Leuven (Belgium), currently working on the H2020 INTEGRATE-DIALOGUE project on social dialogue for non-standard workers. She holds a PhD in Sociology, and she carried out her doctoral research within the European Research Council project ResPecTMe. Her research interests include working conditions in the digital platform economy, as well as industrial (employment) relations and collective action in the changing world of work.

Caroline Murphy is Associate Professor of Employment Relations at the University of Limerick, Ireland and Associate Research Fellow at the Digital Futures at Work Research Centre, UK. Her research interests include precarious employment, female labour market participation, formal and informal care work and employee representation. She has worked on a variety of research projects relating to precarious work, the impact of technology on work, gender equality in the labour market and care work (formal and informal) funded by the Irish Research Council, European Commission, Higher Education Authority.

Barbara Orth is a Post-doctoral Researcher at the University of Bern. She explores the intersections of migration and digital labour platforms, particularly in the realm of reproductive services. She was awarded her Phd from the Free University Berlin in 2024.

Abigail Osiki is Senior Lecturer in employment law at the University of Canterbury's Faculty of Law and a Research Associate at the Centre for the Transformative Regulation of Work, University of the Western Cape (UWC).

She holds her PhD degree from the University of Cape Town. She has worked as a Senior Lecturer at the UWC Faculty of Law and as a Post-doctoral Researcher at Fairwork. She has also conducted research in collaboration with the International Labour Organisation, and she is an associate editor at the *Canterbury Law Review*.

Ivana Pais is Professor of Economic Sociology at Università Cattolica del Sacro Cuore in Milan, Italy, where she directs the Transformative Actions Interdisciplinary Laboratory (TRAILab). She is a co-editor alongside Elena Esposito and David Stark of *Sociologica. International Journal for Sociological Debate*. Since November 2023, she has been coordinating the project 'ORIGAMI – Home Care Digital Platforms and Industrial Relations', funded by DG Employment, Social Affairs and Inclusion, which ran until October 2025.

Lorena Poblete is a Researcher at the Consejo Nacional de Investigaciones Científicas y Tecnológicas (CONICET) and a full Professor at the Escuela Interdisciplinaria de Altos Estudios en Ciencias Sociales at Universidad Nacional de San Martín. She is researcher at the Inter-University Research Centre on Globalization and Work (CRIMT). She has held various research positions as visiting scholar at Princeton University, McGill University, Freie Universität Berlin, Europa-Universität Viadrina, Université de Lille 1 and Université de Nantes. She was a 2022–24 Alexander von Humboldt fellow and a resident at the Bellagio Rockefeller Center in 2025.

Nastazja Potocka-Sionek is a Post-doctoral Researcher in European and comparative Labour Law at the University of Luxembourg. She holds her PhD degree from the European University Institute in Florence. She has worked as an Adjunct Professor at IE Law School in Madrid and as a Post-doctoral Researcher at Ca' Foscari University in Venice. She has also carried out a research stay at Ewha Womans University and Sogang University in Seoul, and an internship at the International Labour Organization in Geneva.

Valeria Pulignano is Professor of Sociology and Francqui Research Professor of Sociology at KU Leuven. She holds a PhD in Sociology and a scholarly background in socio-economic studies. She is Coordinator of the RN17 Work, Employment and Industrial Relations at the European Sociological Association (ESA) and researcher at the Inter-University Research Centre on Globalization and Work (CRIMT), research fellow at Warwick University (UK) and LISER, Luxemburg. She is Winner of the James G Scoville Award 2015 from LERA and she holds a Chair Jacques Leclerq at UCL.

Luca Ratti is Professor of European and Comparative Labour Law at the University of Luxembourg, where he serves as Director of the Master in European Law (first year). He has held a Jean Monnet Chair in European labour law to research and teach on the Sustainability of the European Social Model (2022–25). He has recently edited (with Elisabeth Brameshuber and Vincenzo Pietrogiovanni)

The EU Directive on Adequate Minimum Wages. Context, Commentary and Trajectories (Oxford, Hart Publishing, 2024) and (with Paul Schoukens) *Working Yet Poor. Challenges to EU Social Citizenship* (Oxford, Hart Publishing, 2023).

Paula Rodríguez-Modroño is a Professor at the Department of Economics and Director of the Interdisciplinary Centre of Women's, Gender and Feminist Studies (CINEF) at Pablo de Olavide University (Seville), Spain. She coordinates the project 'Platformization of the Healthcare Ecosystem. A Feminist and Intersectional Analysis' (CAREFEM, 2024–27). Among her most recent publications are the book *Desigualdades de género en las plataformas digitales de trabajo* (Fundación Centro de Estudios Andaluces, 2024).

Sabri Schumacher holds a Master's degree in Social Sciences as well as a Master's in Management and Law of Non-Profit Organisations. She has extensive experience in project development, campaigning and trade union work. In 2021, together with Jael Bueno, she co-founded the platform cooperative Autonomía in Zurich – a cleaners' cooperative. Since the restructuring of the Center for Care Cooperatives in early 2024, she has been focused on further developing and replicating the Autonomía pilot project.

Natalie Sedacca is Assistant Professor in Employment Law at Durham Law School and previously taught at University College London, Exeter, and Queen Mary University of London. Her research focuses on human rights and labour law, with a particular interest in domestic workers and other marginalised workers, and issues of gender and migration. Natalie is a trustee for the domestic worker NGO Kalayaan and is on the Research Committee of the Society of Legal Scholars.

Jelena Starčević is a Social Sciences and Humanities Research Council (SSHRC) Postdoctoral Fellow at the School of Industrial and Labor Relations at Cornell University. She holds a PhD in Labour Studies from McMaster University, an MA in Peace and Justice from the University of San Diego and an LLB from the University of Belgrade. Her research focuses on comparative employment relations in digital contexts, including platform work, remote work, and AI at work. She has taught at McMaster University, University of Guelph and Tecnológico de Monterrey. She was also a Visiting Fellow at Cornell University's ILR School and the Oxford Internet Institute's Summer Doctoral Programme alumna.

Nicole Teke-Laurent is a PhD in sociology at IDHE.S – Nanterre University and a Post-doctoral Researcher at CNRS – Nantes University. Her thesis is focused on digital platforms providing cleaning services in France. She was a researcher of the ORIGAMI project (2024–25), analysing home care platforms and digital relations in six European countries. Her work has been published in the book edited by Pascal Savoldelli, *Ubérisation, et après?* (Bordeaux, Éditions du Détour, 2021).

Introduction

LORENA POBLETE AND EVA KOCHER

OVER THE LAST 10 years, platform work has been discussed extensively, with sociological studies and legal analyses becoming the basis for new regulations. Following policy discussions in the US and Europe, which often concerned specific sectors such as taxi services and food delivery,[1] the most recent and arguably most significant outcome of these regulatory discussions is Directive (EU) 2024/2831 of 23 October 2024 on improving working conditions in platform work.[2] At its 114th Session in June 2026, the International Labour Conference (ILC) will discuss a binding convention, supplemented by a recommendation, to secure decent work in the platform economy.[3] (Please note that this book's manuscript was completed in July 2025, so the discussions do not include the draft convention published in August 2025.)

Against this backdrop, one might think that the sector has been researched and discussed comprehensively. However, knowledge production is dependent on the visibility or invisibility of workplaces, power structures and gendered social inequalities. Digital intermediaries in care and domestic work, in particular, have only recently received attention. This book brings together sociological, anthropological and economic research, alongside case studies from various regions worldwide, including the Global South and Southeastern Europe, as well as legal research reflecting on policy and regulatory options. Authors come from and have studied in different countries. They are at different stages of their careers. We also present reports from cooperative projects that highlight alternative organisational structures which are often overlooked.

[1] See the overview on https://digitallabour.ilo.org/; see also the analysis in E Kocher, *Digital Work Platforms at the Interface of Labour Law. Regulating Market Organisers* (Oxford, Hart Publishing, 2022).

[2] OJ L, 2024/2831; consolidated text of 11 November 2024 published on https://eur-lex.europa.eu/legal-content/EN/TXT/?uri=CELEX%3A02024L2831-20241111.

[3] Information on www.ilo.org/digital-labour-platforms; the draft for the Convention was published in August 2025 (https://www.ilo.org/sites/default/files/2025-08/ILC114-V%283%29-%5BWORKQ-250714-001%5D-Web-EN.pdf).

This introduction first situates the approach of this book within the academic debate on digital platform work. Second, it outlines the various business models and organisational structures of digital intermediaries in domestic and care work. The term 'labour platform' as it is commonly understood cannot adequately capture all of these. This is why we have chosen to examine domestic and care work through the lens of 'digital intermediaries'. Third, we discuss the complicated interdisciplinary concept of 'formalisation', which only partly captures the ambivalent dynamics of simultaneous precarisation and formalisation that can be observed in digital intermediation in domestic and care work. The final section provides an overview of the book's contributions.

I. DOMESTIC AND CARE WORK IN THE ACADEMIC DEBATES ON DIGITAL PLATFORM WORK

Research on digital platform work started at the beginning of the century with crowdsourcing/crowdworking platforms such as Amazon Mechanical Turk which were shown to organise specific digitalised tasks.[4] Empirical research on crowdworking was often difficult, due to lack of access to workers, mostly working from their private homes. With Uber and other ride-hailing platforms, as well as food-delivery platforms, proliferating in urban centres, platform work became visible to many people, with workers being accessible to researchers. These workers have also been active in creating collectivity, in organising, in protesting against their working conditions, and these protests ultimately lead to regulation and policy discussion. The 'Uberisation' of work became accompanied by a 'Uberisation' of research about digital labour platforms and regulation. We all owe a lot to these workers who took risks when fighting for better working conditions.

On the flipside, however, other types of platform work were less noticed, and less researched.[5] We posit that this is not just an issue of visibility, with the public–private divide coming to be reproduced in the field of research and regulation.[6] It also means that we may overlook the great diversity of work with and on digital platforms, in particular the diversity that domestic and care platforms have been showing.

[4] The article by J Howe, 'The Rise of Crowdsourcing' (2006) 14 *Wired Magazine* has generally been considered the starting point for the debate.

[5] On the challenges of accessing workers, see for example B Orth and F Baum, 'Researching Care Platforms: Methodological and Ethical Considerations in the Broad Field of Domestic Platform Labour' (2024) 0 *Critical Sociology* 1; L Poblete, A Tizziani and F Pereyra, 'La intermediación digital en el trabajo doméstico remunerado en América Latina: una propuesta analítica para su estudio' (2024) 89 *Revista de Estudios Sociales* 3.

[6] E Kocher and J Bronowicka, 'A Blunt Tool for Women in Platform Work? A Feminist Perspective on the Platform Work Directive' (2025) 16 *European Labour Law Journal (ELLJ)* 565.

In many cities across the world, digital platforms have been established that mediate, for example, shopping, cooking, cleaning (domestic work) as well as childcare or elder care (care work). Research on platform work has shown that platforms tend to take advantage of the institutional context made up by welfare regimes and social security systems they operate in.[7] This book contributes to the research aimed at understanding the dynamics of platform capitalism as embedded and conditioned by preexisting institutions. After all, the interventions of digital platforms are tailored according to how a given society understands and organises domestic and caring tasks and responsibilities.

In doing so, the book considers the very specific institutional context of domestic and care work that is different to that of other economic activities. Domestic and care work poses specific problems for regulation precisely because it is a 'job like no other'.[8] As a result, these platforms show specific dynamics that may not be present in other platform sectors. There are several reasons for this.

The first reason has to do with the fact that domestic and care work covers reproductive work activities that have been strongly gendered; rather unsurprisingly, the workforce in these sectors is predominantly female. As is common in digital platform work, workers often have limited employment options, making low-paid and precarious work their only viable means of livelihood – and one of the factors that limits workers' employment options in domestic and care work even more than in others sectors is the fact that female workers are often also burdened by private unpaid domestic and care work to which they dedicate time.[9]

The second reason has to do with the fact that the domestic and care work these platforms organise and/or mediate,[10] do not represent the outsourcing of a company's economic activities, but rather commercialise unpaid private work. At least partly, the platformisation of domestic and care work can be seen as a response to the ongoing crisis of care.[11] This means, very concretely, the services offered through these platforms cater directly and only to private households.

The last factor that contributes to the specific dynamics of the digital intermediation of domestic and care work is evidenced by the claim of some of the founders of domestic and care work platforms (often men in their thirties or

[7] K Thelen, 'Regulating Uber: The Politics of the Platform Economy in Europe and the United States' (2018) 16 *Perspectives on Politics* 938; N Koutsimpogiorgos, K Frenken and AM Herrmann 'Platform Adaptation to Regulation: The Case of Domestic Cleaning in Europe' (2023) 65 *Journal of Industrial Relations* 156; Rodriguez-Modroño, ch 1, Teke-Laurent, ch 2, Johnson et al, ch 3, Starčević, ch 4, Poblete, ch 5, and Pais et al, ch 6, in this book.

[8] See A Blackett, *Everyday Transgressions: Domestic Workers' Transnational Challenge to International Labor Law* (Ithaca, ILR Press, 2019).

[9] See the examples that V Pulignano and M Domecka, *The Politics of Unpaid Labour* (Oxford, OUP, 2025) have gathered.

[10] See below s II on the business models.

[11] Cf N Fraser, 'Contradictions of Capital and Care' (2016) 100 *New Left Review* 99; E Dowling, *The Care Crisis. What caused it and how can we end it?* (London/New York, Verso, 2021).

forties): They advertise their services as a remedy for informal labour markets.[12] And there may be some truth in these assertions: Insofar as domestic and care work had been commercialised before the advent of digital intermediaries, it was usually in a very informal way, by direct contact between a household and a worker. It is therefore possible that the intermediation of platforms in these sectors, contrary to other sectors, contribute to formalisation.

II. ORGANISATIONAL VARIETIES AND BUSINESS MODELS

We have chosen the term 'digital intermediaries' for this book, instead of 'digital platforms', to avoid falling into the trap of limiting our perspective to what has been discussed in relation to other types of platform work.

A. Platform Work and Employment Classification

There have been various attempts at developing typologies for digital work platforms, based on every conceivable variable: the type and scale of the tasks, the level of skills required for the tasks, how workers are matched to tasks (bid-based or contest-based), the type of party that determines the matching or initiates the work, or the type of remuneration.[13] The most important distinction has been the one between offline and online work, that is, distinguishing according to whether the tasks are delivered on-location or online. Domestic and care work platforms serve as examples of on-location work.[14] In general, the research on digital platforms has highlighted a tendency of digital platforms towards institutional isomorphism.[15] When looking at how domestic and care work platforms fit into the typologies that have been developed, we are now asking whether specific typologies are needed. We are interested in a typology that lends itself to an interdisciplinary discussion, or rather, to a discussion with the law and in view of regulation.

[12] P Rodríguez-Modroño, 'A Taxonomy of Business Models of Digital Care Platforms in Spain' (2024) 18 *Sociology Compass* 1; Teke-Laurent, ch 2, in this book.

[13] WP de Groen and others, 'Employment and Working Conditions of Selected Types of Platform Work' (Luxembourg, Eurofound, 2018) 5–6; MC Urzì Brancati, A Pesole and E Fernández-Macías, *New Evidence on Platform Workers in Europe: Results from the Second COLLEEM Survey* (JRC science for policy report, Publications Office of the European Union, 2020); Eurofound, Typology, 6 September 2018, www.eurofound.europa.eu/data/platform-economy/typology.

[14] CEPS et al, *Study to Gather Evidence on the Working Conditions of Platform Workers: Final Report*, 2020; Directorate-General for Employment, Social Affairs and Inclusion; European Commission et al, *Study to Support the Impact Assessment of an EU Initiative to Improve the Working Conditions in Platform Work: Final Report*, 2021; European Commission, Directorate General for Employment, Social Affairs and Inclusion, and CEPS, *Digital Labour Platforms in the EU: Mapping and Business Models: Final Report*, 2021.

[15] P DiMaggio and W Powell, 'The Iron Cage Revisited: Institutional Isomorphism and Collective Rationality in Organizational Fields' (1983) 48 *American Sociological Review* 147.

The legal debate has mostly been focusing on the question of status, ie on the classification as employment or self-employment which came to be the most important legal issue in platform work, and one of the main focuses of regulation. Many platforms have been using civil-law contracts with workers, categorising the relationship as independent contracting and self-employment rather than employment. However, upon closer inspection, this often constitutes nothing more than a strategic approach aimed at minimising costs and reducing employer responsibilities, a disruptive strategy often not in line with the law. Legal analyses in various legal systems and jurisdictions have shown that the contracts drawn up by platforms often merely disguise employment. The basis of such an assessment are definitions of the employment relationship in diverse legal system; nevertheless they all share some common characteristics, which the ILO Recommendation No. 198 on the employment relationship (2006) aptly summarises: An employment relationship would usually be recognised, in particular, if the work 'is carried out according to the instructions and under the control of another party, involves the integration of the worker in the organisation of the enterprise, must be carried out personally by the worker'. According to the principle of the primacy of facts over contract, the legal classification will be guided primarily by the facts relating to the performance of work.[16] In other words: It is the business model in which workers are deployed that serves as the basis and reference of legal classification.

When applying these criteria to platform work, court decisions all over the world have affirmed the employment rights of workers on on-site ride-hailing and food-delivery platforms.[17] Work on such platforms would usually have to be considered employment in legal terms, due the predominant business models in these sectors which rely on close monitoring of workers. As for other types of platform work, the algorithms that platforms use to monitor, coordinate and evaluate work in real time have been an important factor and argument in establishing the existence of employment in the legal sense.[18] The persistent use of rating and review mechanisms has been analysed as a novel form of 'algorithmic management', which has become an object of regulation in its own right.[19]

B. Business Models for Digital Intermediaries in Domestic and Care Work

Digital intermediaries for domestic and care work share some of the characteristics of digital platforms in other sectors. First, these platforms generally present themselves as technological mediators limited to connecting service seekers with

[16] Cf the analyses in Kocher (n 1).

[17] See for example the overview by International Lawyers Assisting Workers Network (ILAW) (ed), *Taken for a Ride: Litigating the Digital Platform Model*, 2021.

[18] For example: German Federal Labour Court (Bundesarbeitsgericht), judgment of 1 Dec 2020 – 9 AZR 102/20.

[19] See, in particular, the Directive (EU) 2024/2831 on improving working conditions in platform work; Aloisi and Potocka-Sionek, ch 11, in this book.

service providers. Second, they structure their intervention using control mechanisms and reputation systems based on arbitrary criteria, thereby promoting an 'audit culture'[20] that pushes workers to accept demands that go beyond what has been agreed in the contract. Third, they mostly hire workers as self-employed, thereby evading employment status and employers' obligations regarding social security contributions and labour rights.

Nevertheless, research on domestic and care work platforms reveals a wider variety of business models,[21] which is why we opted for the term 'digital intermediaries' in this book. These platforms promote a range of services, including live-in and full-time work, as well as part-time and hourly assignments. While most platforms work with self-employed workers, others use employment contracts. Most importantly, while some domestic and care work platforms – similar to ride-hailing, food-delivery and crowdworking platforms, which have served as the blueprint for regulatory discussions – implicitly offer the services they claim to mediate, others occupy an ambiguous position between intermediary and service provider.

In some cases, the platforms are constituted as an app through which employers and workers can post job demands and offers. In this instance, the digital intermediary does not offer anything beyond a matching service. Other models include services for managing formalities related to an employment relationship, such as legal registration of the employment contract, or payment of employer contributions and salary. As platforms mediate workers to work in others' homes, some offer a higher level of trustworthy, reliable workers, and often commit to verifying criminal records and references.

So far, the socio-economic literature on care and domestic work platforms has identified four organisational and business models: on-demand platforms, marketplaces, digital placement agencies and digital labour agencies. These models often appear in various combinations: a company may offer services under different models to adapt to a specific context or attain a dominant position in a particular market.[22]

[20] N van Doorn, 'Platform Labor: On the Gendered and Racialized Exploitation of Low-Income Service Work in the "On-Demand" Economy' (2017) 20 *Information, Communication & Society* 898; K Gruszka, A Pillinger, S Gerold and H Theine, '(In)visible by Desing: An Analysis of a Domestic Labor Platform' (2024) *Critical Sociology* 1.

[21] See the typologies developed in Rodríguez-Modroño (n 12); O Blanchard, 'Digital Labour Platforms in Highly Feminised Sectors: Home Care in Spain' in O Blanchard, C Lopes and P Devaney P (eds), *Global Perspectives on Women, Work, and Digital Labour Platforms: A Collection of Articles from around the World on Women's Experiences of Digital Labour Platforms* (Madrid, Digital Future Society, 2022); F Pereyra, L Poblete and A Tizziani, *Plataformas digitales de servicio doméstico y condiciones laborales. El caso de Argentina* (Buenos Aires, OIT, 2023); F Bonifacio and I Paris, 'How Platformisation is Shaping the Future of Domestic Work. A Mapping of Home Care and Cleaning in Six EU Countries', Future of Work Series, working paper 2025.08. Brussels, ETUI.

[22] Rodríguez-Modroño, ch 1, Starčević, ch 4, and Poblete, ch 5, in this book; L Poblete, F Pereyra and A Tizziani, 'Digital Intermediation in Paid Domestic Work in Argentina: An Analysis of Ambivalent Effects on Working Conditions' (2024) 0 *Critical Sociology* 1; Rodríguez-Modroño (n 12); P Rodríguez-Modroño, 'The Platformization and Marketization of Care: Business Models and Competitive Strategies of Care Platforms' (2025) 29 *Competition & Change* 554.

The on-demand model operates using principles similar to those of digital labour platforms in the delivery and transportation sectors:[23] On-demand intermediaries in the domestic and care work sector offer short-term, and casual services,[24] often without concluding employment contracts with workers.[25]

In contrast, digital intermediaries organised according to the marketplace model focus on connecting supply and demand. They provide their clients with access to a pool of workers and jobs only. Clients can use customisable filters to select the most suitable job or worker. While this model is similar to the on-demand model in that it primarily focuses on short-term, casual, hourly jobs, the digital intermediary plays no part in the matching process per se.[26]

The model of digital employment agencies exhibits different features depending on the region of the world and the regulatory context.[27] These digital intermediaries select workers and match them with suitable job offers. In some countries, these intermediaries play an active role in negotiating contracts, working conditions and wages.[28] Some of them offer staff management services, including registering domestic workers with the social security system, paying wages and preparing payrolls.[29] However, these agencies often promote precarious jobs, with workers accepting long-term contracts involving only a few hours of work per week. Furthermore, the level of formalisation is often inadequate because it depends on employers' complying with legal obligations.

Last, there are business models that resemble digital labour agencies employing workers to provide services to multiple households. In this case, the intermediary explicitly acts as employer.[30] This means that the platform undertakes to comply with legal employer obligations, such as registering workers, paying

[23] A Tandon and A Rathi, 'Care in the Platform Economy: Interrogating the Digital Organisation of Domestic Work in India' in B Dolber, M Rodino-Colocino, C Kumanyka and T Wolfson (eds), *The Gig Economy: Workers and Media in the Age of Convergence* (New York, Routledge, 2021); J Ticona and A Mateescu, 'Trusted Strangers: Carework Platforms' Cultural Entrepreneurship in the On-Demand Economy' (2018) 20 *New Media & Society* 4384.

[24] A Tandon and A Rathi, *Fault Lines at the Front Lines: Care Work and Digital Platforms in South and Southeast Asia* (Singapore, Friedrich Ebert Stiftung, 2021).

[25] Rodríguez-Modroño (n 22); Rodríguez-Modroño, ch 1, in this book; W Sibiya and D du Toit, 'Sweeping up Decent Work: Paid Domestic Work and Digital Platform in South Africa' (2022) 30 *Gender & Development* 637.

[26] Tandon and Rathi (n 23); Rodríguez-Modroño (n 12); Johnson et al, ch 3, in this book.

[27] Tandon and Rathi (n 24); Rodríguez-Modroño (n 12); F Teixeira, '¿Más de lo mismo? Condiciones laborales de las trabajadoras del hogar en las plataformas digitales en México' (2024) 89 *Revista de Estudios Sociales* 43; R Fragale Filho and M dos Santos Lima, 'Alguém se meteu no meio: modelos de intermediação digital do trabalho doméstico no Brasil' (2024) 89 *Revista de Estudios Sociales* 81.

[28] Tandon and Rathi (n 23).

[29] Poblete et al (n 22).

[30] JL Posso Quiceno, SE Castiblanco Moreno and JA Pineda Duque, 'Plataformas digitales del trabajo de cuidado doméstico remunerado en Colombia: el caso de Hogarú' (2024) 89 *Revista de Estudios Sociales* 101; I Pais and A Marcolin, 'Digital Platforms in the Italian Domestic Care Sector: The Emergence of an Unprecedented Corporate Logic and Its Implications for Workers' Social Protection' (2024) 31 *International Labour Review* 397; LC Mantilla-León, I Jaimes Rodríguez and OJ Maldonado Castañeda, 'The Digital Boss: Algorithms, Housekeeping Apps, and the Digitalization of Domestic Work in Colombia' (2024) *Critical Sociology* 1.

monthly social security contributions, respecting working time limits and protections and paying the legal minimum wage. Even if working hours are fragmented into several short shifts, working conditions in this type of company can be less precarious than in the other cases.[31]

In addition to the four organisational and business models identified in various empirical studies, a fifth model remains under-explored: the worker cooperative. Currently, there are few examples of domestic and care workers' cooperatives around the world that have adopted digital technologies comparable to those used by for-profit companies.[32]

The chapters in this book examine how all of these models adapt and operate in different national contexts and what this means for legal analysis. Due to the legal methodology of employment classification, business models are crucial. Thus, the heterogeneity of organisational and business models in this sector can result in different labour relationship outcomes, leading to varying working conditions, employment statuses and levels of worker protection. The relationship with the customer is particularly important in this sector, unlike in ride-hailing or food-delivery services, where it is clear that it is the platform that would have to take on employer responsibilities. Due to the triangular nature of business models of care and domestic work intermediaries, classification is not only about employment or self-employment, but also about the role of the intermediary as an employment agency, temporary work agency or employer.[33]

Last, the triangular relationship between the intermediary, the worker and clients raises another issue that suggests that general policy and regulatory debates on labour market intermediation may need to be reconsidered: The end users of the work and services are usually private households; holding companies accountable for employers' responsibilities is completely different to holding private households accountable.

III. THE DEBATE AROUND FORMALISATION

In an attempt to understand the impact of digital intermediaries in the domestic and home care work sector, where most jobs have traditionally been informal,[34] the literature has focused on the informality/formality dichotomy. From Fudge

[31] Posso Quiceno et al (n 30).

[32] See Osiki, ch 7, and Bronowicka et al, ch 8, in this book; D Kasparian, A Súnico, J Grasas and J Cófreces, 'Socio-Labour Inclusion of Low-Income Women in the Digital Economy: A Comparison Between Corporate and Cooperative Domestic Work Platforms' (2023) 12 *Social Sciences* 1.

[33] Hießl, ch 9, and Ratti, ch 10, in this book.

[34] According to the ILO, 81.2 per cent of domestic workers worldwide remain in informal employment. ILO, *Making Decent Work a Reality for Domestic Workers: Progress and Prospects Ten Years after the Adoption of the Domestic Workers Convention, 2011 (No 189)* (Geneva, ILO, 2021), 189.

and Hobden's[35] pioneering work to more recent publications,[36] the debate has centred on whether intermediaries in these sectors contribute to the formalisation of domestic and care work or perpetuate informal labour relations. However, as formality is not simply a matter of whether or not there is a legal employment relationship,[37] it cannot be answered with a simple 'yes' or 'no'. The question of formalisation through intermediation actually raises the issue of the impact of intermediaries on working conditions.

Historically, domestic and home care work has been characterised by precarious working conditions due to the specific nature of this work relation, which is based on a personal relationship. The workplace (the employer's home) and the assigned tasks (cleaning and caring for members of the employing household) involve different degrees of intimacy. Literature on paid domestic work emphasises the importance of this personal relationship[38] which is primarily governed by informal norms such as tradition, community rules,[39] and the 'law of the household workplace'.[40] The roots of this occupation can be traced back to colonialism and the master-servant model.[41] Consequently, the employer–worker relationship is highly asymmetrical, as the undervalued position of workers relates to their

[35] J Fudge and C Hobden, *Conceptualizing the Role of Intermediaries in Formalizing Domestic Work* (Geneva, ILO, 2018).

[36] L De Vita and A Ciarini, 'Still Informal? Care Platforms in a Loosely Regulated Context, the Italian Case' (2025) 0 *Critical Sociology* 1; AK Korn, 'Informal Home Care in the Digital Transformation: Platform Design and Work Ethics of Care' (2025) 14 *Social Sciences* 225; D Arcidiacono, F Bonifacio and I Pais, 'Transparent Informality: The Ma(s)king of Professionals in Childcare Service Platforms' (2024) 0 *Critical Sociology* 1.

[37] In most countries, national surveys are able to estimate the number of informal workers. The ILO's harmonised definition of informal employment is statistically defined and measured using a combination of approaches. According to the ILO, an employee is considered to be informally employed if their employer does not contribute to social security on their behalf or if they do not benefit from paid annual or sick leave, either because there is no contributory social security scheme in the country or because the household survey provides no answer to this question. Domestic workers who are classified as self-employed are considered to be in informal employment if they work for a non-incorporated private enterprise that is not registered with the relevant national authorities. (ILO (n 34), 189). From a sociological perspective, the formalisation of the labour relationship is used as a proxy for working conditions. However, empirical research has shown that there is no clear correlation between the legal form of the contract and the respect for labour and social security rights in the domestic and care work sector. See K Jaherling, F Pereyra and L Poblete, 'Introduction: The Formalization of Paid Domestic Work – Current Trajectories and Challenges Ahead' (2024) 163 *International Labour Review* 159, and the articles included in this Special Issue.

[38] J Brites, 'Domestic Service, Affection and Inequality: Elements of Subalternity' (2014) 46 *Women's Studies International Forum* 63; C Chan and R Fernández-Ossandon, 'Compañerismo: Care and Power in Affective Labor Relations' (2023) 49 *Critical Sociology* 707.

[39] J Rollins, *Between Women: Domestics and Their Employers* (Philadelphia, Temple University Press, 1985).

[40] Blackett (n 8).

[41] E Kuznesof, 'A History of Domestic Service in Spanish America' in E Chaney and M Garcia Castro (eds), *Muchachas No More: Household Workers in Latin America and the Caribbean* (Philadelphia, Temple University Press, 1989); Blackett (n 8).

socio-economic, racial, ethnic and migrant backgrounds.[42] Based on the notion that domestic workers are 'like family',[43] this labour relationship is guided by a kind of 'maternalism' that conceals various forms of subordination.[44]

In this asymmetrical labour and personal relationship, the two parties constantly negotiate working conditions and arrangements face-to-face in the context of market changes. As Mary Romero[45] pointed out, novel working arrangements such as live-out jobs and 'job work' (ie working for multiple employers on an hourly basis) result in less personalised labour relationships than traditional live-in jobs. Various changes in modern societies have 'modernised' domestic and care work by transforming family-like labour relationships into market-based relationships,[46] consumer/service provider relationships[47] or 'bureaucratic' relationships involving intermediaries that provide services to households.[48] These changes have contributed to the depersonalisation of the employment relationship by reducing workers' dependence on their employers.

Digital intermediaries have emerged as new players in this process of decoupling personal and working relationships. They have been advertising themselves as means of providing domestic and care work in a more flexible, detached and autonomous way.[49] Insofar as they mediate mostly hourly work or casual labour, they allow employers[50] and workers[51] to avoid or limit emotional labour on the personal level. Also, they position themselves as a neutral third party, offering interventions in various ways. Most importantly, they incorporate new digital and management technologies into a working relationship that usually remains invisible because it takes place behind closed doors.

[42] M Romero, 'Sisterhood and Domestic Service: Race, Class and Gender in the Mistress-Maid Relationship' (1988) 12 *Humanity & Society* 318; D Gorbán and A Tizziani, 'Inferiorization and Deference: The Construction of Social Hierarchies in the Context of Paid Domestic Labor' (2014) 46 *Women's Studies International Forum* 54; Blackett (n 8).

[43] BJ Anderson, *Doing the Dirty Work: The Global Politics of Domestic Labor (London/New York,* Zed Books, 2000); A Barbič and I Miklavčič-Brezigar, 'Domestic Work Abroad: A Necessity and an Opportunity for Rural Women from the Goriška Borderland Region of Slovenia' in JH Momsen (ed), *Gender, Migration and Domestic Service* (London, Routledge, 1999).

[44] Rollins (n 39); P Hondagneau-Sotelo, *Doméstica: Immigrant Workers Cleaning and Caring in the Shadows of Affluence* (Berkeley, University of California Press, 2001); J Arnado, 'Maternalism in Mistress-Maid Relations: The Philippine Experience' (2003) 4 *Journal of International Women's Studies* 154.

[45] M Romero, 'Chicanas Modernize Domestic Service' (1988) 11 *Qualitative Sociology* 319.

[46] SA Radcliffe, 'Race and Domestic Services: Migration and Identity in Ecuador' in JH Momsen (ed), *Gender, Migration and Domestic Service* (London, Routledge, 1999).

[47] Romero (n 45).

[48] FX Devetter and S Rousseau, 'The Impact of Industrialization on Paid Domestic Work: The Case of France' (2009) 15 *European Journal of Industrial Relations* 297; J Bickham Mendez, 'Of Mops and Maids: Contradictions and Continuities in Bureaucratized Domestic Work' (1998) 45 *Social Problems* 114.

[49] See Rodriguez-Modroño, ch 1, Teke-Laurent, ch 2, Johnson et al, ch 4, Poblete, ch 5, in this book.

[50] D du Toit and L Heinecken, 'Is Outsourcing Better? Clients' Views on Contracting in Domestic Cleaning Services' (2021) 43 *Employee Relations: The International Journal* 1147.

[51] Pereyra et al (n 21).

In fact, one of the most significant effects of these technologies is that they make the labour relation visible through digital devices. Therefore, the first research on this emergent field of studies[52] linked this visibility with the formalisation,[53] as well as the standardisation, normalisation and institutionalisation of various aspects of working conditions. A divide between studies from the Global North and the Global South crystallised then. Studies focusing on the former showed that digital intermediaries can create informal work even in highly regulated labour markets.[54] In contrast, studies centred on the latter underlined the potential of digital intermediaries to formalise jobs in an already highly informal sector.[55] The latest studies now reveal a more nuanced picture, showing that digital intermediaries can contribute to both the formalisation and informalisation of jobs in this sector,[56] or produce hybrid effects[57] such as 'selective formalisation',[58] 'precarious formalisation'[59]and 'transparent informality'.[60]

Thus, the concept of formalisation became blurred over time because it came to encompass a great variety of impacts of digital intermediaries on domestic and care work. While most studies of formalisation focus on the legal status of the labour relationship, highlighting that digital intermediaries can facilitate the use of less protected labour statuses (such as self-employment,[61] third categories[62] or forms of under- and undeclared work[63]), they also mention other forms of 'formalisation' of working conditions. Digital intermediaries have provided technical and managerial tools allowing the tracing of working

[52] This field of study is relatively new. A non-exhaustive review of the literature that we undertook shows that around 10 publications were dedicated to digital intermediaries in domestic and care work between 2016 and 2019. Ten more articles or reports were published in 2020, and this figure increased further to just over 20 per year between 2021 and 2023. The number of articles and reports then rose to 40 in 2024 and around 30 in 2025.

[53] J Ticona and A Mateescu, 'Trusted Strangers: Carework Platforms' Cultural Entrepreneurship in the On-Demand Economy' (2018) 20 *New Media & Society* 4384; A Hunt and F Machingura, 'A Good Gig? The Rise of On-Demand Domestic Work' (2016) *ODI Working paper* 7.

[54] V Pulignano, C Marà, M Franke and K Muszyński, 'Informal Employment on Domestic Care Platforms: A Study on the Individualisation of Risk and Unpaid Labour in Mature Market Contexts' (2023) 29 *Transfer: European Review of Labour and Research* 323; S Kalla, 'Hacking Platform Capitalism: The Case of Domestic Workers on South Africa's SweepSouth Platform' (2022) 30 *Gender & Development* 655.

[55] K Dattani, 'Platform "Glitch as Surprise": The On-Demand Domestic Work Sector in Delhi's National Capital Region' (2021) 25 *City* 37; Pereyra et al (n 21); A Tandon and A Rathi, 'Sustaining Urban Labour Markets: Situating Migration and Domestic Work in India's "Gig" Economy' (2022) *EPA: Economy and Space* 1.

[56] Poblete et al (n 22); Fragale Filho and dos Santos Lima (n 27).

[57] I Dimitriadis and D Coletto, 'Digital Labour Platforms in the Italian Domestic Sector: Approaching (In)Formalisation Processes from the Other Way Round' (2024) 0 *Critical Sociology* 1.

[58] N Van Doorn, 'Platform Capitalism's Social Contract' (2022) 11 *Internet Policy Review* 1.

[59] Fragale Filho and dos Santos Lima (n 27).

[60] Arcidiacono et al (n 36).

[61] See Teke-Laurent, ch 2, Starčević, ch 4, Poblete, ch 5, in this book; T Nhleko, 'The "Platformisation" of Domestic Work in South Africa: A Shift Towards Marginal Formalization and Deepening Informalization of Domestic Work Employment' (2023) 96 *The Thinker* 87.

[62] See Johnson et al, ch 3, in this book.

[63] See Teke-Laurent, ch 2 and Poblete, ch 5, in this book.

time, the standardisation of services, the standardisation and automation of payments and the institutionalisation of systems of evaluation.[64]

Depending on the context, the impact of these tools can be both positive and negative. While they can provide a clearer, more visible overview of working conditions, they can also lead to new dynamics of precarisation. For example, the use of specific tools, such as digital calculators or tracing devices, makes it easier to determine and visualise working time. However, they can also enable a more fragmented working day, leading to increased commuting time and more intense labour, since service slots are often too short to complete the required tasks.[65] Tracking devices can serve as a control mechanism of the time used to complete the requested tasks or as a tool to protect workers.[66] Digital intermediaries sometimes also provide tools for categorising services, distinguishing between cleaning, care and ironing or other specific services, and between normal and deep cleaning services. Even if this categorisation creates a false idea of professionalisation,[67] it can provide visibility of the tasks included in the service and allow workers to refuse certain demands from employers.[68] Last, the fact that most of the intermediaries process payments via bank transfer or digital wallets, also has ambivalent effects. On the one hand, the automation and bankarisation of payments can secure the payment of wages.[69] On the other hand, it can introduce uncertainty regarding the timing and amount of payments, particularly in cases where intermediaries charge a fee for each service.[70] Finally, the reputation systems have transformed traditional control mechanisms into a gamified evaluation of workers' performance. These systems undoubtedly have significant performative effects.[71] Even when workers are uncertain about the consequences

[64] See J Muldoon, N Sedacca and P Apostolidis, 'Matchmakers: Placement Agencies and Digital Platforms in the UK Childcare Market' (2025) 5 *Work in the Global Economy* 6. These authors propose a classification of these effects.

[65] B Lesala Khethisa, P Tsibolane and JP Van Belle, 'Surviving the Gig Economy in the Global South: How Cape Town Domestic Workers Cope' in RK Bandi, S Klein, S Madon and E Monteiro (eds), *The Future of Digital Work: The Challenge of Inequality*, 601 *IFIP Advances in Information and Communication Technology* (Cham, Springer, 2020).

[66] LC Mantilla-León and OJ Maldonado Castañeda, 'Nosotras de robot no tenemos nada': arreglos intersubjetivos tecnosociales en el trabajo doméstico mediado digitalmente' (2024) 89 *Revista de Estudios Sociales* 61, Teixeira (n 24); Sibiya and du Toit (n 25).

[67] N Teke-Laurent, 'Travailler comme aide ménagère via une plateforme de services à domicile. La professionnalité en question' (2025) 177-178-179 *Travail et Emploi* 45; Arcidiacono et al (n 36).

[68] Poblete et al (n 22).

[69] F Ustek Spilda, A Bertolini, A Badger, A Oguz and M Graham, 'The Strategic Unknowns of Business Models of Digital Care Work Platforms' (2025) *Critical Sociology* 1; Teixeira (n 24).

[70] Fragale Filho and dos Santos Lima (n 27).

[71] F Teixeira, 'Reconfiguring Control and Perpetuating Exploitation: Digital Labour Platforms and Domestic Work in Mexico' (2025) 35 *Labour and Industry* 99; F Flanagan, 'Theorising the Gig Economy and Home-Based Service Work' (2019) 61 *Journal of Industrial Relations* 57; K Floros, 'Rethinking Algorithmic Management in Minor Key: The Case of Housecleaning Platform Labour in Denmark' [2024] *Platforms & Society* 1; F Macdonald, '"Personalised Risk" in Paid Care Work and the Impacts of "Gig Economy" Care Platforms and Other Market-Based Organisations' (2021) 5 *International Journal of Care and Caring* 9.

of negative feedback, they still feel the daily pressure of being evaluated by their employers and monitored closely by the intermediary.[72]

Thus, through digital and managerial tools, intermediaries position themselves as a third party in the labour relationship, with the ability to set new rules for organising domestic and care work.[73] Digital intermediaries are therefore often more than just intermediaries; they actively participate in defining working conditions. Their intervention creates new dynamics that exacerbate the precariousness of working conditions. Furthermore, while the use of these tools represents a step forward in terms of depersonalising domestic and care work by limiting face-to-face negotiations with household members and reducing dependence on individual employers, this does not translate into greater bargaining power for workers. In fact, workers have almost no bargaining power against digital intermediaries as they increasingly depend on them for access to the labour market.

IV. OVERVIEW OF THE BOOK

The book is organised into four parts. It begins with an analysis of the different organisational and business models developed in various geographical areas, such as South and Central Europe, Southeast Europe, the UK, South Africa and Latin America, before moving on to identify the challenges of regulating digital intermediaries in Europe.

The first two Parts, 'Emerging Models at a National Level' and 'Adaptations to Legal Frameworks from a Comparative Perspective', examine how digital intermediaries adapt their structures, organisations and operations to regulatory and institutional frameworks, while also exploiting regulatory gaps and grey zones. The insertion of digital intermediaries into labour markets occurs within specific normative landscapes, but also at the intersection with policies concerning the provision of care in ageing societies – policies that rely on both social security benefits and tax incentives, often with the goal to strengthen an underdeveloped sector. The specific framework of these labour markets sometimes includes employment policies that seek to reintegrate low-skilled workers – especially women and migrant workers – into the labour market. While the first part of the book focuses on cases in Europe – Spain, France and Belgium – the second part addresses the same question from a comparative perspective (covering countries in Southeast Europe, in Latin America and two countries in Europe).

[72] E Fetterolf, 'It's Crowded at the Bottom: Trust, Visibility, and Search Algorithms on Care.com' (2022) 40 *Journal Digital Social Research* 49; K Ettarfi, 'Professionalization from Above in Domestic Work: Accessing Work on Marketplace Platforms' (2024) *Critical Sociology* 1.

[73] L Poblete, 'When Digital Platforms Intrude into the Regulation of Paid Domestic Work: The Case of Formalization in Argentina' (2025) 45 *Comparative Labor Law and Policy Journal* 175.

In the case of Spain, Paula Rodríguez-Modroño analyses in chapter 1 how digital intermediaries operating under different business models are reshaping the provision of domestic and care work. Paula Rodríguez-Modroño identified three organisational and business models among digital platforms operating in Spain: digital agencies, marketplaces and on-demand platforms. This taxonomy is key to understanding the various outcomes in terms of job creation, control mechanisms and strategies for reaching a dominant market position. Given that each type of intermediary has a specific degree of embeddedness in the institutional landscape in which it operates, these three types of digital intermediaries develop different adaptation strategies and use distinctive business logics. According to Rodríguez-Modroño, by interacting with the care and migrant labour regimes, and taking advantage of the discriminatory labour regulation on reproductive activities, these digital intermediaries are blurring the boundaries between formal and informal work, perpetuating the casualisation and informalisation of labour in this sector.

In the case of France, Nicole Teke-Laurent examines in chapter 2 how digital intermediaries offering cleaning services to households have succeeded in establishing themselves within the highly regulated, but very fragmented Personal Services for Households (PSH) market. This study demonstrates how digital intermediaries have exploited public policies that facilitated their development, such as those promoting household services through tax credits and encouraging self-employment by using the category of 'micro-entrepreneur'. In light of the well-established PSH sector, digital platforms have encountered significant challenges in gaining legitimacy as intermediaries. In this regard, they employed two rhetorical strategies to capture both its potential clientele and service providers. Initially, the focus was on the informal sector, with these actors positioning themselves as pivotal in the 'fight against undeclared work'. Now, the focus is on flexibility as a fundamental aspect of their organisation model. As Nicole Teke-Laurent points out: 'Digital platforms are presented as an alternative to the perceived rigidity of formal employment'. Nonetheless, the study demonstrates that digital intermediaries have not delivered on their promise to provide jobs that are more protected than informal ones and less rigid than formal employment.

In the case of Belgium, Mat Johnson, Valeria Pulignano, Claudia Marà and Milena Franke analyse in chapter 3 how the two largest multi-service marketplace platforms adapt their strategies and develop by exploiting tax exemptions, cash-for-care schemes and the 2016 legislation on the 'collaborative economy' and the subsequent amendments. They base the development of their company on the use of a third category of worker: 'peer-to-peer', situated between employees and the self-employed. The aim of this category is to provide flexible working opportunities for those who are excluded from the labour market, such as young people, students and women. Hence, the impact of these marketplace platforms is mixed. While they can facilitate entry into the formal labour market and provide an opportunity to earn additional income, particularly for young workers, they also normalise low wages and precarious work, contributing to the 'de-professionalisation' of care and domestic work. As the authors show, this form of 'peer-to-peer' precarity operates in a legal and social grey zone. Nevertheless, for clients and workers, it appears to be preferable to entirely informal or undeclared work.

In chapter 4, which opens the second Part of the book, Jelena Starčević examines the emergence of digital intermediaries in Southeast Europe, with a focus on companies operating in Slovenia, Croatia and Serbia. These countries provide an interesting case study because, although they share a socialist legacy, their trajectories towards capitalism have been different. Each country inherited a system that promoted legal equality for women, as well as a comprehensive set of labour rights and protections for domestic workers, however, conservative conceptions of gender roles remain in place. After the transition period, these countries adopted various strategies to adapt to new market realities, including different approaches to labour market flexibility, policies regarding women's participation in the labour market and ways of regulating domestic work. As Jelena Starčević points out, digital intermediaries 'adjust their discourse, legal positioning and operational features in response to local regulatory environments and cultural expectations'. This results in the development of hybrid business models that combine the characteristics of marketplaces and on-demand platforms. Therefore, these companies provide varied and often fragmented forms of intermediation, as well as a variety of work arrangements ranging from self-employment, under-declared work to completely informal jobs. The study shows that these platforms selectively reinterpret the legal framework to present themselves as legitimate market actors while evading regulatory obligations. Thus, the presence of digital intermediaries in the domestic work sector in these Southeast European countries has reinforced the informality that characterised domestic and care work.

Lorena Poblete, in chapter 5, observes similar outcomes when studying the development of digital intermediaries in Latin America, with a focus on Argentina, Brazil, Chile and Mexico. A distinctive feature of these countries is the simultaneous emergence and establishment of these companies alongside legislative reforms concerning paid domestic work following the adoption of ILO Convention 189 in 2011. Consequently, as these companies strive to establish themselves in the market, they navigate the evolving legal landscape. Lorena Poblete shows that, although the number of digital intermediaries in the domestic and care work sector increased significantly in all the countries under study between 2022 and 2025, their development followed different paths depending on the legislation of paid domestic work and its level of implementation. These cases range from operating exclusively in the informal market to presenting themselves as allies of the state in promoting labour formalisation, while also exploring the grey areas at the margins of the law.

In chapter 6 Ivana Pais, Caroline Murphy and Tish Gibbons analyse the impact of the emergence of digital intermediaries and in particular the challenges this creates for trade unions in Italy and Ireland. The study shows that the development of care platforms in the two countries is conditioned not by the industrial relations regime, but by the care regime and, specifically, the manner in which care is funded. Despite its stronger industrial relations regime, power of trade unions and existence of detailed labour codes, Italy has seen a proliferation of care platforms. In Ireland, the industrial relations system is voluntarist and union power is largely absent outside the public sector. Nevertheless, care platforms are much less prevalent in Ireland than in Italy. That could be explained by the fact that Italy is more liberal in how funding is allocated, giving individuals greater control over how they access care. In Ireland, although the home care funding system is not means-tested, client and consumer choice is tightly controlled. Ultimately, examining these countries reveals the role of the state as a funder, rather than a regulator, in relation to the emergence of care platforms and their impact on working conditions and union responses.

The third Part of the book highlights the experiences of domestic workers who reinterpret the role of intermediary: Platform cooperatives are seen as offering the potential for better working conditions and a stronger voice.[74] Both of the contributions in this part have been developed by or with the support of actors who report their experiences with organising cooperatives in domestic work – in South Africa, and in Switzerland.

In chapter 7, Abigail Osiki draws on the experiences of the Digital Platform Cooperative Project (DPCP) at the University of the Western Cape in South Africa. Initially an academic research project, it evolved into *WeCare*: an association of domestic workers and a digital platform cooperative. The chapter vividly describes the specific challenges of this ongoing transition, which began in 2022 and is expected to conclude by the end of 2025. By examining the practical challenges faced by the platform in detail, the chapter illustrates how the success of platform cooperatives depends on regulatory and institutional contexts. As digital platforms enter the market as new actors, they bring new technological and financial barriers, exacerbating existing inequalities in South Africa's domestic work sector and shifting power dynamics to the detriment of workers. Against this backdrop, the domestic workers' cooperative must find solutions to issues of legal form, capital mobilisation, worker training and governance. Due to the low income of domestic workers, the cooperative cannot rely on collective pooling of members' resources and requires external funding. The chapter also describes the challenge of equipping domestic workers with the entrepreneurial and management skills required to run a platform cooperative.

In chapter 8, Joanna Bronowicka, Barbara Orth and Sabri Schumacher report on the experiences of Switzerland's first platform cooperative for cleaners, *Autonomía*, which was launched in Zurich in December 2021. Their findings demonstrate the opportunities and advantages of operating in this market, as

[74] ILO, *Decent work and the social and solidarity economy* (Geneva, ILO, 2022).

evidenced by the high demand from clients. Within three years, the organisation had become financially sustainable, providing cleaners with formal employment contracts and offering wages above the legal minimum. The chapter also demonstrates how the cooperative enhanced the visibility and recognition of cleaning work within the Swiss socio-economic and legal framework. The tension between economic sustainability and democratic participation, which is typical of cooperative organisations, added to the difficulty of finding an organisational structure that can empower workers to govern the cooperative. In a predominantly migrant workforce with diverse sociodemographic backgrounds and unequal time resources for community work, building trust, solidarity and a sense of belonging among cleaners proved challenging. The chapter also elaborates on *Autonomía*'s digital infrastructure, which contrasts with for-profit platforms in prioritising human decision-making over automation and in using generic, free or paid digital tools that are open and allow workers to participate in decisions about their implementation.

The fourth Part of the books looks at the legal and regulatory challenges that digital intermediaries in care and domestic work sectors present. In particular, it shows the challenge of classifying digital intermediation in care and domestic work not only in relation to employment/self-employment, but also in relation to the third party in the triangular relationship, the household. Issues of working time and algorithmic management are discussed on the background of EU law. Last, the debate on formalisation is revisited in view of new regulatory models of universal protection, independent of employment status.

In chapter 9, Christina Hießl discusses the challenges involved in legally classifying specific multiparty relationships in the context of domestic work. Here, private households assume the role that commercial actors would typically play on other digital platforms. Hießl demonstrates how administrative and judicial bodies across Europe have categorised these relationships as self-employment, employment by the household, employment by the platform, or temporary agency work, depending on the business model and jurisdiction. The author also points out that, in some legal systems at least, workers could benefit from agencies being considered the employer rather than the household. One advantage of this would be that existing special regimes for households hiring workers (ie exemptions from protection) would not apply. In her discussion of how responsibilities in these multiparty relationships should be allocated, she proposes 'chain agency work' as a model for shared employer functions in some cases, and temporary agency work as the most promising concept for achieving a balanced outcome and enabling a solid classification as an employment relationship. However, in most legal systems, reliance on the concept of temporary agency work would not currently lead to adequate results, as it burdens the end user with responsibilities that a private household should not usually carry. This is one of the regulatory loopholes that this chapter identifies. In most countries, targeted legislative interventions would be needed to ensure adequate protection for workers in these multiparty relationships.

In chapter 10, Luca Ratti takes the cue and examines the triangular relationship created by digital care platforms as labour market intermediaries. With a focus on the EU Temporary Agency Work Directive 2004/104, he explores the potential of this legislation in the context of international and EU law. The author retraces the development of international employment intermediation law since the ILO abandoned its policy goal of progressively abolishing private employment agencies. Today, the free-of-charge principle, as set out in ILO Conventions Nos 181 and 189 on private employment agencies and domestic work respectively, has become the most important aspect of international law. Regarding EU law, the chapter analyses Court of Justice of the European Union (CJEU) jurisprudence as the legal framework for private employment intermediation and the liberalisation of temporary work agencies. Ratti concludes that, in certain instances, digital care platforms can be classified as 'digital' temporary agency work according to the EU Temporary Agency Work Directive 2008/104. However, this categorisation cannot serve as a universal solution for safeguarding workers' rights. In particular, applying the Directive's principle of equal treatment to private households would be challenging. The chapter ends by highlighting the intersections between the EU Platform Work Directive (2024/2831) and the Temporary Agency Work Directive, identifying the main legal uncertainties that remain unresolved.

In chapter 11, Antonio Aloisi and Nastazja Potocka-Sionek examine the impact of algorithmic management systems on domestic work, as well as issues of working time regulation, particularly in the context of digital intermediaries. They demonstrate how algorithms play a pivotal role in not only the recruitment and onboarding phases, but also in matching workers to clients. However, the authors also conclude that the findings of literature on digital platforms' algorithmic management are not necessarily valid for digital intermediaries in domestic work, where human and non-human management practices are intertwined rather than algorithms fully assuming managerial functions. With regard to the non-linear, fragmented and irregular working patterns typical of domestic work, the chapter evaluates the suitability of the EU Working Time Directive (2003/88) and the Transparent and Predictable Working Conditions Directive (2019/1152). In both cases, the analysis criticises the possibility for Member States to exclude domestic work from the scope of the Directives' protection. The EU Platform Work Directive 2024/2831 is shown to be capable of closing some gaps, particularly through the employment presumption. However, the chapter acknowledges the difficulty of establishing 'direction and control' of domestic work platforms. Although the Platform Work Directive makes significant progress for domestic workers on digital platforms, compared to traditional domestic workers, the chapter also highlights the urgent need for comprehensive regulation to address the unique complexities and challenges of domestic work, and, among other issues, empower workers to control their working schedules.

Finally, in chapter 12, Natalie Sedacca and Joe Atkinson revisit the debate surrounding the formalisation of domestic and childcare work on digital platforms. They describe platform domestic work as 'compound non-standard work', highlighting the combination of marginalised domestic work with the risks associated with the platform model. Against the backdrop of widespread informality in domestic work, the authors note that platforms present themselves as formalising the sector by adopting a selective understanding of formalisation as essentially record-keeping and registration with the relevant authorities. A 'thicker' normative conceptualisation of formalisation would have to centre the implementation of labour regulation and social protection, including in the context of employment relationships with end users. Given the diversity of domestic work platforms, the chapter also criticises regulatory approaches that depend entirely on classifying workers as employees. It argues instead for a universalist approach that would provide decent conditions, collective bargaining and job security for everyone involved in personal service work, including solo self-employed individuals. The EU Platform Work Directive (2024/2831) is assessed as representing partial progress towards a universalistic approach. The chapter expresses hope that the ILO's discussion of a platform work convention will maintain the universalistic approach of the summer 2025 draft, which defines 'digital platform workers' regardless of their employment status.

Part I

Emerging Models at National Level

1

The Emergence of Platforms in Care and Domestic Services in Spain: An Exploration of Their Business and Growth Models

PAULA RODRÍGUEZ-MODROÑO*

I. INTRODUCTION

ONE OF THE industries where digital platforms are rapidly expanding is care and domestic services, both in European Union (EU) Member States and in other societies currently experiencing significant ageing.[1] For decades, the global care crisis has transformed care work into a rapidly growing economic sector. In the EU, for example, the number of older people with long-term care needs is expected to increase from about 30.8 million in 2019 to 33.7 million in 2030. As the demand for care grows in a context of financialisation of marketised care, digital platforms have entered this industry and have grown exponentially due to their ability to attract significant capital looking for a home.[2]

Digital care platforms (DCPs) are digital labour platforms that mediate transactions in domestic or home-related services, including, but not limited to, cleaning/ housekeeping, babysitting, childcare, eldercare and household tasks. Therefore, DCP work is very broad and diverse, comprising on-location platform work, mostly low-skilled, but also high-skilled specialised healthcare work, sometimes only online. DCPs create value by quickly and easily

* This research was supported by Grants PID2019-105835RB-I00 and PID2023-146669OBI00 funded by MICIU/AEI/10.13039/501100011033 and by ERDF A way of making Europe.

[1] A Hunt and F Machingura, 'A Good Gig? The Rise of On-demand Domestic Work' (2016) *ODI Working paper* 7.

[2] MG Jacobides and I Lianos, 'Regulating Platforms and Ecosystems: An Introduction' (2021) 30 *Industrial and Corporate Change* 1131.

facilitating transactions between users seeking health and social care services and domestic and care workers offering those services, whether directly or by supporting individuals with the necessary paperwork, and capture value by taking commissions.

Despite the rapid development of platforms in the care sector and the increasing volume of care work mediated through them, we still know very little about the configuration of care platforms and their impact on the industry due to the invisibility and informality of home care and domestic work and the opacity of platforms. Research on digital platforms in care and domestic services is still emerging, but it is already bringing to light different organisational models of platforms, as well as racialised and gendered layers of platformisation. Extant research on DCPs has mainly focused on analysing the new forms of work and their impacts in terms of access, visibility, and formalisation of work,[3] precariousness of working conditions,[4] and gender or intersectional inequalities.[5] But we still know very little about how DCPs operate and their impacts on the care sector. Our research attempts to fill this gap by examining the modus operandi and growth strategies of digital platforms in the care industry, trying to discern how they create value and govern users and what is transformative or continuous in platforms' effects in processes of capital accumulation.[6]

The techniques that enable these platforms to exert control over a contingent workforce marked by superfluity and fungibility rely on the longstanding historical, structural and institutional factors that produce a cheap labour force.[7] Platforms benefit from legislation, currently in force in many countries, which allows households to hire domestic workers without any professional healthcare qualification directly, under worse conditions and with less social protection. The research of Koutsimpogiorgos et al on a domestic cleaning

[3] J Ticona and A Mateescu, 'Trusted Strangers: Carework Platforms' Cultural Entrepreneurship in the On-Demand Economy' (2018) 20 *New Media & Society* 4384; N Van Doorn, 'Platform Capitalism's Social Contract' (2022) 11 *Internet Policy Review*; Starčević, ch 4 and Sedacca and Atkinson, ch 12, in this book.

[4] P McDonald, P Williams and R Mayes, 'Means of Control in the Organization of Digitally Intermediated Care Work' (2021) 35 *Work, Employment and Society* 872; P McDonald, P Williams, R Mayes and M Khan, 'Income Generation on Care Work Digital Labour Platforms' (2024) 62 *British Journal of Industrial Relations* 358; Johnson et al, ch 3, in this book.

[5] JB Schor, W Attwood-Charles, M Cansoy, I Ladegaard and R Wengronowitz, 'Dependence and Precarity in the Platform Economy' (2020) 29 *Theory and Society* 833; P Rodríguez-Modroño, A Agenjo and P López 'Platform Work in the Domestic and Home Care Sector: New Mechanisms of Invisibility and Exploitation of Women Migrant Workers' (2022) 30 *Gender & Development* 619; R Castel-Branco and HJ Dawson, 'The Remaking of Working Classes: Digital Labour Platforms and Workers' Struggles in the Global South' (2023) 3 *Work in the Global Economy* 109.

[6] A Piletić, 'Continuity or Change? Platforms and the Hybridization of Neoliberal Institutional Contexts' (2023) 31 *Review of International Political Economy* 438.

[7] N van Doorn, 'Platform Labor: On the Gendered and Racialized Exploitation of Low-Income Service Work in the "On-Demand" Economy' (2017) 20 *Information, Communication & Society* 898; P Rodríguez-Modroño, A Pesole and P López, 'Assessing Gender Inequality in Digital Labor Platforms in Europe' (2022) 11 *Internet Policy Review* 1.

platform operating in five European countries shows that the platform pursued different trajectories under different institutional arrangements but always tried to benefit from those that exempt the company from having to take on statutory employer responsibilities.[8] This, therefore, perpetuates the historical undervaluation of reproductive work and female and migrant workers.

In the same sense, research on migration and platform labour also posits that migration is not just a side aspect of the platform economy but central to its functioning, as platform companies rely on ever-new workers to come in and take on seemingly unskilled, platform-mediated jobs.[9] As Yin's study in Canada suggests, platform care work should be located in the continuous formal subsumption of reproductive labour and the class immobility of migrant domestic workers.[10] The power asymmetry between platforms and on-demand labour is further intensified by the lack of national labour laws and transnational governance to protect platform workers' rights and regulate platforms' practices, as well as by the declining power of trade and labour unions, and the reconstitution of the international labour market.[11]

In particular, this study aims to contribute to answering this research question. How are digital platforms positioning themselves and reconfiguring care provision? To answer it, our empirical research is based on a case study of 44 digital care and domestic platforms in Spain, combining desk-based research on these platforms with 26 interviews with female workers, company representatives and key stakeholders. We use Spain as a case study because familialistic care regimes with a historically large informal care sector, such as the Southern European migrant-based care model,[12] perfectly epitomise how platforms are emerging as important actors in the political economy of migration,[13] and provide a greater scope for global platforms to commodify reproductive labour.[14] However, the reality of care work in Spain is certainly similar to most countries affected by the global care crisis. In many countries, such as those analysed in

[8] N Koutsimpogiorgos, K Frenken and AM Herrmann, 'Platform Adaptation to Regulation: The Case of Domestic Cleaning in Europe' (2023) 65 *Journal of Industrial Relations* 156.

[9] B Orth, 'Stratified Pathways into Platform Work: Migration Trajectories and Skills in Berlin's Gig Economy' (2023) 56 *Environment and Planning A: Economy and Space* 476.

[10] S Yin, 'Situating Platform Gig Economy in the Formal Subsumption of Reproductive Labor: Transnational Migrant Domestic Workers and the Continuum of Exploitation and Precarity' (2024) 48 *Capital & Class* 119.

[11] M Graham, I Hjorth and V Lehdonvirta, 'Digital Labour and Development: Impacts of Global Digital Labour Platforms and the Gig Economy on Worker Livelihoods' (2017) 23 *Transfer: European Review of Labour and Research* 135.

[12] B Da Roit, A González Ferrer and FJ Moreno-Fuentes, 'The Southern European Migrant-based Care Model: Long-term Care and Employment Trajectories in Italy and Spain' (2013) 15 *European Societies* 577; B Le Bihan, B Da Roit and A Sopadzhiyan, 'The Turn to Optional Familialism through the Market: Long-term Care, Cash-for-Care, and Caregiving Policies in Europe' (2019) 52 *Social Policy & Administration* 579.

[13] N van Doorn and D Vijay, 'Gig Work as Migrant Work: The Platformization of Migration Infrastructure' (2024) 56 *Environment and Planning A: Economy and Space* 1129.

[14] U Huws, 'The Hassle of Housework: Digitalisation and the Commodification of Domestic Labour' (2019) 123 *Feminist Review* 8.

this book,[15] this crisis forces households to resort to low-cost and low-quality care services, which are often performed under the heading of domestic work.

Since recent research has shown that the platform economy cannot be analysed as a homogeneous economic model, as platforms adapt to the different industries and institutional contexts and operate in different ways,[16] our analysis examines key indicators of the three business models of DCP operating in Spain. In a previous study, we constructed a taxonomy of three platform models – marketplace platforms, on-demand platforms and digital agencies and examined the specific features of each DCP model and their differentiated impacts on working conditions in terms of access to tasks, remuneration, flexibility and means of control.[17] This differentiation has provided us with insight into what is continuous or transformative in the precarisation or formalisation of care work on platforms and the working conditions of carers, mainly women and migrants. In this chapter, we follow up on the investigation and delve into the business and growth models of the platforms, examining how the emergence and evolution of DCP changes and reconfigures the provisioning of domestic care work in Spain. Each business model has its differentiated outcomes in terms of labour control and reorganisation of care and reproductive work.[18] Therefore, our research contributes to the literature on care platforms through an in-depth analysis of the characteristics of business models of all platforms active in Spain, taking also into account their main service (childcare, eldercare, cleaning, or domestic services), and how they interact with the Spanish institutional context and regulatory system.

The rest of the chapter is structured as follows. The next section explains the Spanish care system and how recent institutional developments and regulations of care and domestic services affect the nature of the private care market, in this case by encouraging the proliferation of intermediary companies and, among them, digital labour platforms. The findings are structured by platform model, comparing the variances in operational models, as well as growth and competitive strategies of platforms, and discussing the outcomes regarding work, services and the market. The final section discusses the implications of the findings on the impact of digital platforms in the care and domestic work sector.

[15] France (Teke-Laurent, ch 2), Belgium (Johnson et al, ch 3), Slovenia, Croatia, and Serbia (Starčević, ch 4), or Ireland and Italy (Pais et al, ch 6, in this book).

[16] A Mateescu and J Ticona J, 'Invisible Work, Visible Workers: Visibility Regimes in Online Platforms for Domestic Work' in D Das Acevedo (ed), *Beyond the Algorithm: Qualitative Insights for Gig Work Regulation* (Cambridge, Cambridge University Press, 2020); K Gruszka, A Pillinger, S Gerold et al, '(In)visible by Design: An Analysis of a Domestic Labor Platform' (2024) 0 *Critical Sociology 1*.

[17] P Rodríguez-Modroño, 'A Taxonomy of Business Models of Digital Care Platforms in Spain' (2024) 18 *Sociology Compass* 1.

[18] P Rodríguez-Modroño, A Agenjo and P López, 'A Social Reproduction Analysis of Digital Care Platform Work' (2024) 29 *New Political Economy* 616.

II. THE EMERGENCE OF DIGITAL CARE PLATFORMS IN THE SPANISH CARE SYSTEM

Care is a booming market in all ageing societies, also in Spain, which digital platforms are also taking advantage of. The provision of care for older adults has been universal in Spain since 2007, with the Law on the Promotion of personal autonomy and care for dependent persons, which established the System for Autonomy and Care for Dependency (SAAD). The care sector in Spain was born weak and, although Spain is one of the European countries that exhibit the largest expansions in long-term care (LTC) in the last two decades,[19] it has never been equipped with sufficient funding – only 0.7 per cent of GDP per year on average. As a result, less than one in four potentially dependent persons is receiving care services or cash-for-care allowances from the public care system.[20]

Cash-for-care allowances have been the preferred option by regional administrations as well as families in a system characterised by its underfunding since the beginning.[21] Over the past few years, following recommendations across most developed welfare states, there has been a steady shift to home care to support independent living for as long as possible and prioritisation of in-kind (service) benefits over financial benefits for informal care. However, home care provided directly by the public LTC system is very limited in terms of time, on average 60 hours per month for those persons with the highest level of dependence.[22] Therefore, families may still prefer to receive cash allowances that help them at least to directly hire some hours of home care. Given the insufficient number of benefits, the limited amount of cash and the long delays in their resolution, the Spanish LTC system still relies heavily on informal care. This means that care remains in the hands of families. Families who can afford it resort to hiring care workers under the domestic work contract.

Studies show that cash-for-care allowances are being used to pay informal care workers hired as domestic workers in Spain.[23] In fact, the hiring of migrant domestic care workers has become the most important resource that sustains the LTC system in Spain.[24] According to labour force survey statistics, the

[19] J Costa-Font, S Jimenez-Martin, C Vilaplana-Prieto and A Viola, 'Universalizing the Access to Long-term Care: Evidence from Spain' (2023) *National Bureau of Economic Research Working Paper* 31825.

[20] https://imserso.es/el-imserso/documentacion/estadisticas.

[21] P Rodríguez-Modroño and M Matus-López, 'Childcare and Long-term Care Policies. Evolution and Pro-market Conditioning' (2016) 66 *Revista del CLAD Reforma y Democracia* 99.

[22] M Flores, 'Case Study: Spain' in *Pricing Long-Term Care for Older Persons* (Geneva, OECD and World Health Organization, 2021).

[23] P Rodríguez-Modroño and M Matus-López, 'Tendencias a largo plazo en la financiación de los cuidados a la infancia y a la población dependiente en Europa' (2018) 65 *Zerbitzuan* 29; R Martínez-Buján, 'Migration, Domestic Care Work and Public Policies on Long-Term Care in Spain' (2022) 30 *Revista Interdisciplinar da Mobilidade Humana: REMHU* 73.

[24] L Oso L and R Martínez-Buján, 'Welfare Paradoxes and Interpersonal Pacts: Transnational Social Protection of Latin American Migrants in Spain' (2022) 10 *Social Inclusion* 194.

number of domestic workers reached almost 600,000 in 2024, and 45 per cent are migrants.[25] Domestic service is the biggest sector of employment for female migrant workers; particularly for Latin American women in their first years of arrival in the country.[26]

Traditionally, families have found carers via informal channels such as word of mouth and referrals from public services, third-sector organisations and the Catholic Church, and increasingly more through private companies such as placement agencies.[27] Authorised agencies are public or private entities that act as employment intermediaries between job seekers and employers. Despite the intermediation of an agency, the family continues to be the employer under the Special Social Security System for Domestic Workers. As Spanish legislation stipulates that domestic workers cannot be self-employed or employed by a company, it is cheaper for households to hire domestic workers directly rather than using the services of a company. The creation of these placement agencies has multiplied in Spain during the last two decades and particularly since 2015, due to several institutional changes. First, the SAAD has promoted the 'service-linked financial benefit', a subsidy granted directly to families to acquire the care they consider necessary on the private market, which already represents 11 per cent of the benefits.[28] One of the conditions of this aid is that the personal care services provided to households must be acquired from a specialised service company, which will handle the necessary administrative procedures. This has also attracted many intermediaries into the provision of home care services. Second, Spain has finally ratified Convention 189, which extends the rights of domestic workers, and issued Royal Decree 16/2022, whose main measure is the entitlement of domestic workers to unemployment benefits. These measures are increasing the number of legal hires and improving their working conditions, but it is also likely that families will turn to intermediary agencies for assistance with the required administrative procedures.[29]

In summary, the configuration and development of an underfunded LTC system have contributed to the spread of traditional intermediary agencies and also of digital platforms specialising in home care services during the last 20 years.[30] Against this backdrop, care and domestic workers are increasingly hired through service providers, including digital platforms. For our empirical study, we compiled a list of 44 platforms that have been operating in Spain since

[25] www.ine.es.

[26] UGT, *Mujeres Migrantes en Ocupaciones Precarias* (Madrid, Union General de Trabajadores, 2025).

[27] O Blanchard, *Home Care and Digital Platforms in Spain* (Barcelona, Digital Future Society, 2021).

[28] https://imserso.es/el-imserso/documentacion/estadisticas.

[29] R Martínez-Buján and P Moré, 'Home Care for Profit: Intermediary Agencies and Digital Platforms Brokering Migrant Women's Labour in Spain' (2024) 73 *Current Sociology 1036.*

[30] O Lenzi, 'Plataformas digitales y empleo doméstico en España' (2023) 13 *Lex Social* 1; P Rodríguez-Modroño, A Agenjo and P López, 'A Feminist Political Economic Analysis of Platform Capitalism in the Care Sector' (2023) 55 *Review of Radical Political Economics* 629.

2004. In addition to care platforms, our study includes platforms that provide domestic and cleaning services due to the blurry line between domestic, care and medical services and because in Spain most care workers are hired under the domestic work regime. Of the 44 platforms examined, half provide care and domestic services; nine are specialised in cleaning and domestic services; and the remaining 13 are multiservice platforms offering care, domestic, and other personnel services (Table 1.1). Each platform business model generates revenue streams in different ways.

1. Marketplace platforms: 12 platforms list workers' data in their profile, provide certain filters for automated selection of a pool of workers, and charge a fee to clients and/or workers to access contact details. This is a subscription-based model that monetises access to information.
2. On-demand platforms: 17 companies provide services or gigs, withholding a certain amount for each transaction, controlling all information, negotiations and conditions.

Table 1.1 Typology of digital care platforms in Spain by business model and main service provided

Service provided	**Business model**		
	Marketplace	*On-demand*	*Digital agency*
Care	Aupair.com, Auxiliatus, Babysits, Sitly	Cuidelia, Familiados, Joyners, Nannyfy	Aiudo, Cuidabi, Cuideo, Cuidum, CuoreCare, Depencare, Lady Helper, Loreka, Mimocare, Qida, Senniors, Ubikare, Wayalia, Weli
Domestic services	Doméstico24	Cleanzy, Eslife, Getyourhero, Helpling, Limpiu, MyPoppins, Tidy, Wayook	
Multiservice	Care.com, Confio, Cronoshare, Familiafacil, Habitissimo, Topayuda, Yocuido	Clintu, Taskia, Trabeja, Webel, Yoopies	Helpycare

Source: Own elaboration.

3. Digital agencies (DA): 15 platforms operate in a similar way to traditional agencies, where families make an initial payment for the candidate search and intermediation services and then a monthly fee for all administrative formalities.

We first analysed data on the DCP, including marketing and recruitment materials, app- and web-based tools, public statements, terms and conditions documents and other company-produced discourses, as well as market and financial research reports (CB Insights, Crunchbase, einforma, SABI, etc). The analysis was completed by conducting 26 in-depth interviews with workers, platform chief executive officers (CEOs) and key stakeholders in Spain. The interviews comprised 15 workers (two women from Spain and 13 from eight Latin American countries), along with interviews with six CEOs and five interviews with representatives of trade unions, public agencies for LTC and digitalisation and national associations of domestic workers.

III. THE GROWTH AND EXPANSION OF DIGITAL CARE AND DOMESTIC PLATFORMS

In this section, we examine in detail the operational models and growth strategies of the three different types of DCP. All platforms are private companies, and the most widespread legal form is that of limited liability companies.[31] Almost three out of four platforms were founded in Spain, where they have their headquarters. The most common profile among the founders of these platforms is that of a 30- to 40-year-old man with an MBA. Generally, they have experience in the field of consulting and business, and a few in computing or engineering, but none in the healthcare sector. Most DCPs emerged as technological start-ups that went through different private investment rounds to start and develop their business. These platforms have been growing rapidly, thanks to considerable cash injections, with the incorporation of national and international venture capital funds that see this sector as a high growth potential industry.

In addition to these features common to all platforms, this main section analyses essential indicators of the three platform business models, trying to discern the differentiating elements regarding their organisational and growth strategies. Table 1.2 summarises the main features of each type of platform, comparing their operational models with respect to key analytical variables: service provided, recruitment process, management of the matching process, employment status and social protection, price setting and payment, ratings and supervision, worker profile and value capture. By comparing the three

[31] There are no platform cooperatives in the care sector in Spain, unlike other countries, such as Italy (L Ratti, ch 10) South Africa (Osiki, ch 7), or Switzerland (see Bronowicka et al, ch 8, in this book).

Table 1.2 Main organisational features of business models of digital care platforms

Model	Marketplace	On-demand	Digital agency
Value capture	Commissions or membership fees to workers &/or clients. Unpaid working time (profiles, searching).	Commissions, punitive penalties and wage theft. High unpaid work (commuting, profiles, searching).	Households pay one-time fee before placement, and a recurring monthly fee.
Type of work	Short-term gigs and regular (part- or full-time) jobs across all care and domestic tasks.	Short-term gigs in domestic work, childcare and elderly care.	Regular (part- or full- time) employment, mainly for elderly care. Some live-in.
Workers' profile	National and migrants with legal status & work permit, some qualified professionals.	Migrant women without work permit nor care responsibilities.	Migrant women with legal status but without care responsibilities.
Pre-screening	No control.	Only a questionnaire, unchecked assumption of legal residence and self-employment.	Legal residents, interviews, informal experience, no qualifications required.
Matching	Workers are algorithmically shortlisted based on the requirements of employers. Employers contact shortlisted workers. Workers can also directly contact if they paid for the premium subscription.	Workers are algorithmically matched with employers according to their requirements. Workers only have the option to digitally accept or decline jobs.	Workers are algorithmically and manually shortlisted on the basis of the requirements of employers. Selected workers are interviewed by households, which have the final decision.
Employment status & Social protection	None or self-employed.	None. Only a standard term of service and health insurance.	Special regime of domestic workers with households.

Table 1.2 (*Continued*)

Model	**Marketplace**	**On-demand**	**Digital agency**
Price setting & payment	Workers set and list their wage expectations; some platforms mandate a minimum wage or suggest a range of competitive prices. Platforms provide the payment method.	The pricing mechanism, invoicing and payments are controlled and managed entirely by the platform.	Minimum wage. Households pay, though platforms manage workers' payments if this extra service is hired by the household.
Ratings, supervision & training	One-way rating system with workers rated by the platform and clients. Inexistent training nor conflict solving mechanisms.	One-way rating system with workers rated by clients. No training.	None.
Growth strategies	Product differentiation based on quick access to professional / freelancers. Internationalisation and diversification.	Price-and-size strategy. Mergers & acquisitions. Data monetization.	Product differentiation. Adding services and providers of public homecare. Geographical expansion (some through franchising).

Source: Adapted from Rodríguez-Modroño.[1]

[1] P Rodríguez-Modroño, 'The platformization and marketization of care: Business models and competitive strategies of care platforms' (2025) 29 *Competition & Change* 554.

business models of care platforms, we examine in detail how each operational and growth model interacts with the institutional framework and shapes power dynamics between workers, clients and platforms and, consequently, employment and working conditions.

Besides, DCPs develop through different growth and competitive strategies depending on their business model.[32] Following the framework of competitive strategies of platforms proposed by Friederici et al, platforms may compete through three different types of competitive strategies: price-and-size, differentiation strategies and/or expansion strategies.[33] When pursuing the price-and-size strategy, a platform tries to position itself as serving users the same platform product, but at a lower price. With respect to differentiation strategies, platforms try to offer something 'similar but different', thereby appealing to different user groups. There are several variants of the differentiation strategy: product/distinctive positioning, sustainability niche, technological architecture and geographical differentiation. Regarding expansion strategies, platforms can opt for different variants. One way is geographical expansion; entering a country that a platform is not yet active in. Another pathway to expand is to widen the scope of transactions that the platform mediates by incorporating different services – a strategy that is referred to as platform envelopment. A third variant is mergers and acquisitions.

A. Marketplace Platforms

Marketplace platforms generate revenue by implementing a subscription model, charging clients/households, and/or workers/carers to become members who can use the full functionalities of the platform for a certain period. For example, the multiservice marketplace platform *Cronoshare* charges a fee to both customers and workers. Workers, many of them self-employed, pay an upfront fee to be able to contact their potential customers. This is materialised through the purchase and usage of a virtual coin called *cronos*. Each service request has a specific amount of *cronos* associated with it and, in order to access the information on customers and job demands, the workers need to redeem the corresponding amount. Then, once the information is disclosed, the workers negotiate directly with the customers.

This marketplace model is based on generating a large pool of workers and offering matching services tailored to the needs of employers. Their systems are therefore designed with simple registration processes to maximise their reach, as

[32] P Rodríguez-Modroño 'The platformization and marketization of care: Business models and competitive strategies of care platforms' (2025) 29 *Competition & Change* 554.

[33] N Friederici, G Reischauer and V Lehdonvirta, '*The Business of European Platforms. How Digital Intermediaries in E-Commerce, Food Delivery, Health and Care, and Social Networking Manage Value and Compete*' (2022) Alexander von Humboldt Working Paper, DOI: 10.5281/zenodo.7318958.

they seek to emphasise quick access to a wide range of professionals. The platform provides standard templates to create profiles and task lists and to establish a set of criteria to compare workers before recruitment, but there is a considerable amount of unpaid labour in creating and updating profiles and negotiations to reach an agreement.[34]

Marketplace platforms do not intervene or control the negotiating process, nor do they monitor the service, but they have a significant influence on matching and recruitment processes because they use a one-way rating system where workers are evaluated by both platforms and clients with the power to determine the success or failure of workers in their job search. However, the platforms do not control the quality of the work, and their objective is to bring together the largest volume of supply and demand in the industry in an attempt to maximise their value capture. There is no employment contract with the client or the platform, but many workers are self-employed or professionals. Workers set and list their price, some platforms mandate a minimum wage or suggest a range of competitive prices, and they also provide the payment tool.

The marketplace model is the least developed in the domestic and care sector in Spain. It is more typical of large multiservice and childcare platforms, and foreign or international companies that operate in different countries. In marketplace care work, we find young Spanish students and older women, some of them Spanish, who want to earn some income by working as hourly childcare workers. In these cases, working on platforms allows them the possibility of choosing and controlling the schedules that best allow them to balance work and family life, although this entails a loss of the most basic labour rights since there is no labour contract.

Since workers are usually self-employed, freelancers or informal workers, they are less affected by national labour legislation, and their operating model is easy to export. Therefore, marketplace platforms try to grow through geographical expansion to other countries. Babysits started in Rotterdam in 2008 and is present in almost 100 countries; *Sitly*, also from the Netherlands, is active in 14 countries. *Aupair.com* is an online matching platform focused on providing au pair services within the childcare sector. It was founded in 1999 and operates in six European countries, North America and Japan. Care.com offers a wide range of services in 20 countries. Doméstico24 provides domestic services in four European countries as a brand of the Swiss Lemonfrog AG, which operates 15 placement platforms in the areas of domestic help, care and dating.

These platforms need to sustain themselves until they reach a sufficient volume of users, but in today's highly financialised capitalism, it is very easy for platforms to obtain public or private funding. For example, *Cronoshare*, a

[34] V Pulignano, C Marà, M Franke and K Muszyński, 'Informal Employment on Domestic Care Platforms: A Study on the Individualisation of Risk and Unpaid Labour in Mature Market Contexts' (2023) 29 *Transfer: European Review of Labour and Research* 323.

multiservice platform, was founded as a start-up in Valencia in 2012 by three entrepreneurs with the financial support of the business accelerator BBooster Ventures, with the support of two public investors, the *Institut Valencià de Finances* and ENISA (a public company actively involved in the funding of viable and innovative technological projects in Spain). It began by providing services in all major cities in Spain, and in 2016 expanded its business to other countries (Italy, Brazil and Mexico) with the support of the European Fund for Regional Development and XPANDE Digital, a programme launched by the Valencia Chamber of Commerce to improve the competitiveness of small and medium-sized companies. This backing helped improve its search engine rankings and increase its number of users. Additionally, the company's expansion strategy allowed the acquisition of Reformayuda.com in 2018. Therefore, public funds that promote the digitalisation of the business sector are also facilitating the growth of platforms in the care sector.

To capture more value from their client database, many marketplace platforms are also adding extra services to their basic ones. The French platform *TopNanny* started out as a platform with a focus on babysitting, but now it has created *TopAyuda* and offers domestic services, elderly care, tutoring and pet sitting.

B. On-demand Platforms

On-demand platforms charge commissions for each transaction from the amount paid by clients. They work in the same way as platforms like *Uber* or *Glovo*; that is why some researchers refer to their expansion as the 'uberisation' of the care industry.[35] This model has developed greatly in the field of cleaning and domestic services because no specialised training is required, and the selection process is very basic. Their presence is growing in Spain, and they account for almost 40 per cent of the platforms analysed.

This model features minimal pre-screening (only a basic online questionnaire). Workers are algorithmically matched with employers based on few criteria (place, time and tasks required) and can only digitally accept or decline jobs. On-demand platforms do not provide formal employment contracts, social protection or training. Between the platform and the workers, there is no formal relationship beyond the registration form that the workers need to fill in to publicise their services on the platform. The majority of costs, risks and responsibilities are shifted from the platform to workers. Since most of the jobs are of very short duration, they involve a lot of time online searching and travelling,

[35] A Trojansky, *Towards the 'Uber-isation' of Care? Platform Work in the Sector of Long-term Home Care and its Implications for Workers' Rights* (Brussels, European Economic and Social Committee, 2020).

the cost of which is borne entirely by the workers. Platforms only provide carers with insurance cover for personal accidents.

Despite this lack of formal labour relations and the claims of platforms that they are mere intermediaries, on-demand platforms monitor the time of arrival and departure from the place where they are required to provide their services. It is the platform that sets the hourly rates per service, the workers cannot negotiate their working conditions, and they can only apply for the jobs after they have been posted on the platform. For instance, in the case of *Clintu*, a large Spanish on-demand platform, workers are paid weekly or fortnightly through a payment gateway managed by the platform, which charges an 8–15 per cent commission depending on the type of service provided. Cancellation of a service by workers with less than 24 hours of notice implies an economic penalty and a temporary or permanent expulsion from the platform. *Clintu* allows customers to assess worker performance after each service (on a scale of one to five). Low ratings may lead to deactivation or temporary suspension of the worker profile on the platform.

Therefore, these platforms exercise a strong control, not to monitor the quality of the services, but to control the matching process, the establishment of prices and the payment. Platforms manage all invoicing and payments, taking substantial commissions from workers' earnings. In this sense, the use of mobile devices, algorithmic management (AM) and apps is a form of labour organisation and control that allow the platforms to appropriate as much as they can of the workers' salary. The technology used also makes it possible for the companies to exclude workers who are problematic or have reached an agreement with some client outside the platform, and to make those who are better qualified more visible for potential customers. Indeed, in Spain, there have been three trials involving almost 700 female workers that have found evidence of an employment relationship between the workers and the on-demand platforms.

These information and power asymmetries allow platforms to pay workers less than outside the platform, since they lose negotiating power over working conditions and payments. Furthermore, as platforms grow, the bargaining power of workers diminishes. In the first stage of their operations, platforms offer a higher income to workers because they need to attract workers to expand their database and supply of workers. But these platforms can quickly grow and increase their supply of workers, as they easily access migrant women with no qualifications and scarce employment opportunities. In on-demand work, we find mostly young women, mainly migrants in their first stage of entry into the country. Since Spanish migration legislation imposes many requirements to obtain residence and a work visa, migrants enter on the lowest level of the occupational structure. This is the case of many of the workers interviewed, who highlight their entry into informal care work as one of the few employment opportunities upon their arrival in Spain. On-demand platforms allow newly arrived migrant women to quickly gain access to job offers, but this work is informal and the most precarious. Hence, this model benefits from Spanish discriminatory migration and labour policies that restrict migrants' employment opportunities for many years upon arrival, until they obtain legal status as workers. And once they have a sufficient supply of labour, they use their bargaining power to be more competitive by reducing workers' payments.

As on-demand platforms provide very basic services, such as cleaning or domestic tasks (cooking, laundry, ironing, pet walking, etc) on an hourly basis, many of them try to pursue the price-and-size strategy, trying to position themselves as serving users a common basic service at a lower price. However, their limited capacity to differentiate their services makes them more vulnerable to competition from national and international platforms and increases the number of mergers and closures in this model. But they usually manage to survive through several investment rounds while growing their user database, and then sell their company to other platforms.

For example, *Clintu* was founded in 2014 as a tech platform by a young consultant in Barcelona. This private limited company started its activity by providing one-time and short-term cleaning services to households. Initially, it received the support of the *Empresa Nacional de Innovación* (ENISA), the *Institut Català de Finances* (ICF) and FFF (Family, Friends and Fools). Later, other private investment groups like Dozen, Seaya Ventures and Media Digital Ventures joined in. *Clintu* has raised a total of EUR 1.74 million in three investment rounds. With this capital, the platform has pursued a strategy of expansion and growth through mergers with and acquisitions of other firms in the industry: *Getyourhero* in 2017 (which, in turn, had previously acquired the operations of *Helpling* in Spain), and *Wayook* in 2019. It subsequently expanded its supply to companies and diversified its services (household renovations, removals, plumbing, pet care, etc). Today, *Clintu* owns a database of over 800,000 professionals and operates in all major Spanish cities.

Despite the ease in obtaining investors, some platforms have had to shut down because of the increased competition they face due to the ease of entry of new national or foreign platforms in the provision of basic domestic services under this business model of on-demand platforms. *Eslife* only survived three years (2012–15), while *Joyners*, created in 2014, closed in 2021. Others had to completely modify their business: *Nannyfy* used to specialise in babysitting and now provides online lessons for children under the new brand *ApoloKids*.

C. Digital Agencies

Digital agencies constitute the predominant model in the eldercare industry in Spain, because the older population usually requires longer-hours, ongoing and long-term services where it is harder to avoid the formalisation of a labour contract. They mediate in the recruitment of carers by families in a similar way to traditional agencies. Families make an initial payment for the candidate search and intermediation services, and then a monthly fee for all administrative formalities (payroll management, search of substitutes during holiday periods). Workers are often manually shortlisted based on employer requirements and undergo more rigorous pre-screening, including legal residency verification, and interviews, compared to on-demand care platforms. Algorithmic matching is used in the selection process, though not promoted as a marketing asset, and is complemented by manual matching by the platform and a final decision among two-three candidates by the client.

Although digital agencies are favouring the recruitment of carers under the special domestic work regime, thereby reducing informal work, this mechanism does not guarantee the quality of the employment generated, but, on the contrary, it helps to reproduce the low-cost care model that relies on families rather than the professionalised public care service model. Digital agencies tend to recruit older migrant women, who have residence permits, some of whom have dual nationality and can aspire to formal and more stable contracts, but not outside the domestic and care sector.[36]

Many of these companies are Spanish, as they are more embedded institutionally, and like traditional intermediaries, they benefit from discriminatory labour policies that allow households to hire care work disguised under the category of domestic work, as well as from the cash-for-care allowances provided by the Spanish LTC system to beneficiaries. Digital agencies try to differentiate themselves from traditional agencies by emphasising their agility and quality of their selection procedures due to their use of technology. They also emphasise the high professionalisation of their care services, focusing on a single and specific service; for example, *Aiudo*, *Cuideo*, *Cuidum*, *Qida* and *Wayalia* focus on home care for elderly and dependent people. However, interviews with carers showed recruitment procedures were very basic, and workers lacked any formal qualifications.

Some platforms are also expanding to other countries, particularly those with cash-for-care allowances in the LTC sector. *Cuideo* was created in 2016 in Barcelona and is now operating in all major cities in Spain and France. *Aiudo* has entered the United Kingdom market. *Senniors*, a healthcare Spanish platform, is expanding to the United Arab Emirates. *Aiudo* and *Senniors* have also incorporated cross-sales of care materials and complementary health and social services, including teleassistance or telemonitoring.

Since their growth is more complex, they try to grow through several strategies, including their entry into the public system and alliances with insurance companies and healthcare funds. After the COVID-19 pandemic, with the new impulse to home-care provision, some of these digital agencies, such as *Cuideo*, *Cuidum*, *Depencare*, *Qida* or *Senniors*, have started to operate as authorised providers of public home care services, either recruiting health or social care professionals directly under the general Social Security regime or acting as

[36] Rodríguez-Modroño et al (n 5).

digital labour agencies providing carers to elderly people's homes as temporary workers. The integration of *Felizvita* in 2022 allowed *Cuideo* to consolidate the direct provision of care with its own caregivers on staff. These home care services for the public LTC system currently account for 18 per cent of *Cuideo*'s turnover.

Finally, some of the platforms have signed collaboration agreements with insurance or health companies in order to widen their pool of clients and/or subsidise or cover the costs of a treatment or care service. For instance, *Cuideo* has joined forces with several insurance companies (*Catalana Occidente, Plus Ultra Seguros*, and *Seguros Bilbao*) to expand services aimed at seniors. Customers of these insurance companies can now receive advice on dependency through *Cuideo*. In 2024 *Cuideo* bought the insurance company Dpen-D. Adapted home care, telecare or legal procedures are some of the services that the group will offer to its more than 500,000 policyholders. It also provides a home pharmacy service and assistance in the search for residences.

IV. CONCLUSION

This chapter analyses the growth and expansion of digital platforms in the care and domestic work sector, making four important contributions to the emerging literature. First, our study helps to show how digital platforms insert themselves into neoliberal transformations of labour markets and care systems, taking advantage of recent trends towards de-institutionalisation of LTC, coupled with under-investment in public care services, and the financialisation of the healthcare sector. Our findings reveal that platforms interact with the care and migrant labour regimes in which they operate, benefitting from a discriminatory labour regulation on reproductive activities, while further blurring the boundaries between formal and informal work and accentuating the existing power imbalance. Aware that they operate in a sector characterised by informality, poor working conditions and exploitable workers, composed mainly of migrant and racialised women with limited agency and access to formal employment, platforms take advantage of these circumstances. The shift from a two-actor relationship to a triangular one opens new ways for existing power imbalances and inequalities to be amplified.[37] Despite the extent of platforms' command and control over domestic workers varies considerably, the three platform models operating in Spain (marketplace, on-demand and digital agencies) use AM to generate significant information asymmetries, retain more power and capture more value from the participants, as it has happened in other economic

[37] L Wiesböck, J Radlherr and ML Angelique, 'Domestic Cleaners in the Informal Labour Market: New Working Realities Shaped by the Gig Economy?' (2023) 11 *Social Inclusion* 262.

activities.[38] Also in the care sector, AM is a feature that permeates all categories of digital platforms influencing both organisational practices and worker experiences,[39] and reinforcing some of the gendered elements of care work, and its precarity. Although platforms argue that their intervention improves the formalisation of the sector, our research illuminates how platforms exploit welfare systems by perpetuating the casualisation and informalisation of labour.[40] In fact, the employment management practices of the three business models of platforms are undermining the legislative and de facto advances achieved in relation to the formalisation of employment in the care and domestic sector.

Second, in this interaction with the institutional framework, platforms develop different operational models and competitive strategies. These operational differences reflect both their strategic adaptations to distinct institutional and market contexts and platforms' business logics.[41] Each business model has its differentiated outcomes in terms of the type of work created, the degree of formalisation and their distinct mechanisms of control and working conditions. Marketplace platforms do not provide a labour contract, but they do not manage the matching process either, giving clients and workers more autonomy and bargaining power in negotiating prices and conditions. On-demand platforms directly manage the matching process, controlling the price and all negotiations, but they are very loose in the pre-screening process and do not promote job contracts, facilitating informal low-cost care and domestic work. Digital agencies are characterised by stronger and more centralised management of the services they mediate through direct management of the matching process and the contractualisation of workers. These platforms help to formalise care work, but only under the devalued contractual relation of domestic work, instead of promoting the professionalisation of care work under a regular work contract.

Third, since each platform model has a different degree of embeddedness in the institutional context in which it operates, it develops different growth and expansion strategies. The marketplace model is usually adopted by multiservice platforms, many of which are foreign and/or operate in different countries. Marketplace platforms generate revenue by implementing a subscription model, charging clients and workers to become members who can use the platform's full functionalities for a given period. On-demand platforms capture value by charging commissions whereby they withhold a certain percentage for each transaction from the amount paid by one platform side. They usually operate in the domestic sector, offer a more basic service and are more capable of

[38] M Kenney, P Rouvinen, T Seppälä and J Zysman, 'Platforms and Industrial Change' (2019) 26 *Industry and Innovation* 871; M Kenney, D Bearson and J Zysman, 'The Platform Economy Matures: Measuring Pervasiveness and Exploring Power' (2021) 19 *Socio-Economic Review* 1451; D Cutolo and M Kenney, 'Platform-dependent Entrepreneurs: Power Asymmetries, Risks, and Strategies in the Platform Economy' (2021) 34 *Academy of Management Perspectives* 584.

[39] Aloisi and Potocka-Sionek, ch 11, in this book.

[40] See also Teke-Laurent, ch 2, and Sedacca and Atkinson, ch 12, in this book.

[41] Also in this book, Starčević, ch 4, and Pais et al, ch 6.

easily increasing their supply of workers, growing and expanding to other countries. However, their limited capacity to differentiate their services makes them more vulnerable to competition from national and international platforms and increases the number of mergers and closures in this sector. These two types of platforms emphasise their role as technological intermediaries whose advantage is the rapid access to a large database of users and usually resort to financing through tech venture capital. Contrary, digital agencies in the care sector are more embedded institutionally and try to differentiate themselves by emphasising the quality and professionalisation of their care services. They pursue different growth strategies, including operating as authorised providers of public home care services in Spain and abroad, and partnering with other companies that offer complementary services to create a more comprehensive and attractive service portfolio.

Fourth, despite these differences between the operational and growth models, we contend that all models are enabling a further expansion in the commodification of reproductive activities.[42] Our results confirm previous studies arguing that none of these platforms promotes the professionalisation of care work. By limiting the bargaining position of workers, and removing the distinction between professional and non-professional labour, platforms are increasing competition between carers and domestic workers.[43] Consequently, our results confirm that platforms are not merely intermediaries, on the contrary, they can and do amplify the power imbalance between platforms and workers.[44] DCPs are a perfect example of how platforms are transforming and reconfiguring labour relations, production and markets at an unprecedented speed, scale and scope,[45] and how they are expanding their activities to penetrate traditional and informal sectors with high growth potential. Although platforms are not yet the dominant player in the market of domestic and home care services, they are beginning to hold a significant share of the market, thanks to their capacity to attract venture capitalists interested either in technological start-ups or in the high growth potential of the healthcare industry.

[42] P Rodríguez-Modroño et al (n 18).

[43] S Shibata, 'Gig Work and the Discourse of Autonomy: Fictitious Freedom in Japan's Digital Economy' (2020) 25 *New Political Economy* 535.

[44] M Montalbán, V Frigant and B Jullien, 'Platform Economy as a New Form of Capitalism: A Régulationist Research Programme' (2019) 43 *Cambridge Journal of Economics* 805.

[45] D Bearson, M Kenney and J Zysman, 'Measuring the Impacts of Labor in the Platform Economy: New Work Created, Old Work Reorganized, and Value Creation Reconfigured' (2021) 30 *Industrial and Corporate Change* 536.

2

Between Formal and Informal Work? Analysing Insertion Strategies of Digital Platforms in the French Domestic Services Market

NICOLE TEKE-LAURENT

I. INTRODUCTION

IN FRANCE, HOME services have been developing through an institutional commodification strategy since the end of the 1980s, following two concomitant objectives: first, meeting the social needs of care, and second, creating new jobs in a sector perceived with high potential for it. The latest progressively became the priority and led to the emergence in 2005 of the 'Personal and household services sector' (PHS, *services à la personne*) through an important public policy named *plan Borloo*.[1] This policy involved several public measures aiming at making it easier to purchase these services, particularly through strong socio-fiscal benefits. This newly created sector included workers intervening in people's home, for activities going from care to cleaning tasks, but also other activities such as gardening or school support at home.

Home service digital platforms emerged in the second half of the 2010s in this already favourable environment in terms of French public policies. On the one hand, they benefitted from socio-fiscal measures aimed at developing personal services.[2] On the other hand, they enjoyed a facilitated insertion by public policies dedicated at promoting the digital platform model and independent work,

[1] FX Devetter, F Jany-Catrice, 'L'invention d'un secteur et ses conséquences socio-économiques: les politiques de soutien aux services à la personne' (2010) 27 *Politiques et management public* 75.

[2] C Carbonnier and N Morel, *Le retour des domestiques* (Paris, Le Seuil, 2018).

especially through the *micro-entrepreneur status*.[3] The competitive asset for these digital intermediaries is thus multiple. As home service providers, they benefit from socio-fiscal policies: platforms could use a 50 per cent tax cut to promote their services at half price. They also benefit from assets based on their business model relying mainly on self-employement, giving them the possibility to be exempted from the employer responsibilities and the social security contributions that it entails.

As in other sectors, home service platforms manage the matching of services, the organisation of work through algorithmic management and customer ratings, mostly operating on the margins of salaried employment. A mapping of digital platforms[4] shows that in 2024, there were 14 platforms providing cleaning and/or care services in France. Most of these platforms provided exclusively cleaning services, three of them provided both kind of services, care and cleaning, and three platforms were dedicated only to care services towards the elderly or disabled people. The French-based platforms are besides mainly on-demand or marketplaces.[5] Only a few digital placement agencies exist, mostly providing care services as it is the model that suits the most to the national regulations, although recent public policies have shown a strong political will to open the care sector to these economic actors.[6] We can thus expect a growing number of this kind of platforms to offer care services in the coming years.

As new actors in the home services market, digital platforms legitimate their position using a rhetoric that places them in a strategic position, in between formal and informal work. This is not new, when analysing intermediaries of domestic work, whose variety of employment arrangements make it possible to talk about a 'continuum of formalization'.[7] Yet what is new, is that these actors promote their model as a way to solve two identified problems: by fighting the black market on the one hand, and by offering a more flexible system than salaried employment, judged too rigid, on the other hand. This chapter aims therefore at questioning this strategic positioning: do these platforms actually

[3] One of the main measures digital platforms benefitted from is the creation in 2008 of the *auto-entrepreneur* status promoting self-employment, by the Secretary of State Hervé Novelli. Even if the term *auto-entrepreneur* is still often used, both *auto-entrepreneur* and *micro-entrepreneur* statuses have merged in 2016. Legally speaking, the *micro-entreprise* is the only term recognised in France nowadays. See S Abdelnour, *Moi, petite entreprise: Les auto-entrepreneurs, de l'utopie à la réalité* (Paris, Presses Universitaires de France, 2017).

[4] In the context of the European research project ORIGAMI, with Lorena Poblete, we did a mapping of digital platforms in France, see: https://origamiproject.it.

[5] P Rodríguez-Modroño, A Angenjo-Calderón and P López-Igual, 'A Social Reproduction Analysis of Digital Care Platform Work' (2024) 29 *New Political Economy* 616; P Rodríguez-Modroño, ch 1, in this book.

[6] On November 2023, the French Ministry of the Economy and Finance published a decree amending the specifications for personal services approval. One of the main objectives was to open the care sector to 'digital platforms and other innovative actors', as the Minister for Small and Medium-Sized Companies stated it.

[7] J Fudge and C Hobden, *Conceptualizing the Role of Intermediaries in Formalizing Domestic Work* (Geneva, ILO, 2018)

get to formalise informal work in the sector, while at the same time offering more flexible working conditions?

In order to answer this question, we will analyse digital platforms' self-legitimisation processes and insertion strategies as newcomers to a highly structured, but at the same time, highly fragmented market. For this purpose, we will draw on an empirical work, focusing on cleaning services provided through three platforms: *Wecasa*, *Lulu dans ma rue* and *Yoojo*. Seeking to understand the way these platforms have built their legitimacy, by presenting themselves as the solution to pre-existing issues in the PHS market, we will present the empirical data, before looking at how home service platforms entered in a strongly regulated market (Section II) and benefitted from public policies that facilitated their entry and development in the PHS sector (Section III). This legitimation rhetoric enabled them to develop differentiated settlement strategies (Section IV) and to get different shares of this market: as an actor involved in the 'fight against black market' while at the same time offering more flexible working arrangements that in formal employment, in a position between formal and informal work (Section V).

II. METHODOLOGY

As the literature on care and domestic work platforms has shown, workers in this field constitue a 'hidden population' difficult to contact due to the context in which they operate: stong isolation and therefore invisibility of their work, no physical place to reach them and few of them knowing some of their colleagues, making snowball sampling difficult.[8] That is why this sociological survey, as most reasearch in this field, is based on a mixed method, mobilising a diversity of material:

- Semi-structured interviews (47) with service providers (20), customers (12), platform representatives and employees (11) and social actors (four);
- Participatory observation by registering as a provider of cleaning services on one of the platforms, and as a customer on another platform;
- Analysis of discourse, including articles and interviews with the founders, published on the platforms' websites or in the media.

This study is focused on three home service platforms based in France: one *marketplace* and two *on-demand* platforms. The first platform, *Yoojo*, functions as a *marketplace*, with lower control and intermediation. Founded in 2012, it describes itself as 'Europe's No.1 of jobbing platforms', offering a wide range

[8] L Poblete, F Pereyra and A Tizziani, 'Digital Intermediation in Paid Domestic Work' (2024) 0 *Critical Sociology* 1; B Orth and F Baum, 'Researching Care Platforms: Methodological and Ethical Considerations in the Broad Field Of Domestic Platform Labour' (2024) 0 *Critical Sociology* 1.

of services at some of the lowest rates on the market. In 2024, the platform counted 24,000 active jobbers, 19 employees, 855,000 customers, and carried out almost 80,000 services every month. It does not seem to have obtained any public or private fundings, contrary to the other two platforms studied, thus relying mainly on its activity. As a marketplace, clients publish a request for a gig and workers can apply for it, letting them negotiate the price by themselves. *Yoojo* enables the payment by Chèque emploi service universel (CESU) vouchers, which means their their home service providers can either choose to be *micro-entrepreneurs* (self-employed) or, when they use CESU vouchers, they can be employed by the household (*salariés du particulier employer*, SPE). In the latest case, the platform may be associated with a *mandataire*[9] structure, that is to say an intermediary between clients and salaried employees.[10] However, if the payment is online and does not include CESU vouchers, *Yoojo* also makes it possible to register without any work status, promoting small services amongst individuals, therefore contributing to the informalisation of work. As a marketplace, Yoojo enables thus a diversity of work arrangements, which is not the case for the two other platforms, *Wecasa* and *Lulu dans ma rue*, that are on-demand platforms, exclusively based on self-employment under the *micro-entrepreneur* status.

Lulu dans ma rue was created in 2015. It offers a wide range of services, going from cleaning to handiwork or gardening, and stands out from the two others by its approach, presented as social: it is inserted in an experimental public scheme initiated in 2018, entitled *Entreprise d'insertion par le travail independent* (EITI, 'Insertion company through independent work') aiming at helping long-term unemployed people going back to the job market through self-employment. This platform has been the main driving force of this pilot in France, enabling it to receive public subsidies from the French government and Paris City Council, in particular. *Lulu dans ma rue* is also distinguished by its physical presence in neighbourhood kiosks, so the users can interact with members of the platform. In 2024, it counted 35 employees, 17,000 customers and nearly 400 service providers.

Wecasa is specialised in well-being and beauty services, created in 2017. It insists, in its communication, on the professionalism of its service providers. This *on-demand* platform counted 100 employees, 10,000 self-employed workers and 300,000 customers in 2024. Since its creation, more than a million services have been carried out. The structure reached profitability in 2024, and raised important funds from the part of venture capitalists, up to 39 million euros between 2018 and 2024.

[9] Similarities of such mixed economic models of platforms combining both a marketplace and a more formalised *on-demand* system exist in other national contexts, as it is the case for example of the Argentinian platform *Zolvers*. See Poblete et al (n 8).

[10] On Yoojo's website, it is specified: 'As the only accredited personal services platform [mandataire], we manage your relationship with your service providers'. See https://yoojo.fr/qui-sommes-nous.

As on-demand platforms, both *Wecasa* and *Lulu dans ma rue* manage the demand of services and organise the matching. They also set the prices and follow closely the activity of their workers, even though they are independent workers. As authorised service providers in the PHS, *Wecasa* and *Lulu dans ma rue*'s clients automatically provide the 50 per cent tax credit when paying for home services. This enables these platforms to sell these services at half price, constituting therefore a major promotional argument. The tax credit is indeed an example of the way digital platforms have benefitted from an institutional context promoting the commodification of the PHS sector.[11]

III. A FRAGMENTED BUT REGULATED MARKET

According to French public data from the Ministry of Labour,[12] more than one million people – amongst whom 89 per cent of women – were employed in the PHS sector in 2019. This represented 4 per cent of the total salaried employments in France, placing these jobs amongst those that have seen the strongest expansion since 1990.[13] The home service sector is in fact structured and regulated by a diversity of actors within a formal labour framework that has contributed to the expansion of jobs in the sector. If they have not directly aimed at regulating platforms, this institutional context has paved the way for their development in this market.

Domestic services are regulated by the French Labour Code: the decree D7231-1 establishes a list of 26 activities in the sector, including household and family chores, childcare and assistance to the elderly and disabled. Amongst those 26 activities, some of them are related to priority social needs (long-term care, childcare) while others are more assimilated with everyday services, sometimes referred to as 'comfort' services, such as cleaning or gardening.[14] Households using these services benefit from social and fiscal assets (tax credit, exemption from employer contributions, reduced VAT rates).

The PHS sector is indeed regulated but also fragmented in various statuses related to the type of employer: the worker can be employed directly by the household, or by a provider (public or private agency).[15] There are accordingly different recruitment models: direct employment on the one side, and *mandataire*

[11] Johnson et al, ch 3, in this book.

[12] *Direction de l'Animation de la Recherche, des Études et des Statistiques* (DARES). See M Beltzung, M Lefebvre, G Borey and J Warmoës, 'Les salariés des services à la personne en 2019' (2024) *DARES Résultats* 1.

[13] Carbonnier and Morel (n 2).

[14] FX Devetter, T Ribault and F Jany-Catrice, *Les services à la personne* (Paris, La Découverte, 2010).

[15] C Ledoux and R Krupka, 'Negotiating in a Highly Feminised Sector: The French Domestic Work and Home-Based Care Sector' in A Elomäki, J Kantola and P Koskinen Sandberg (eds), *Social Partners and Gender Equality: Change and Continuity in Gendered Corporatism* (London, Palgrave, 2021).

or *prestataire* models on the other side, when the domestic worker is hired through an intermediary agency. In the case of direct employment, that is to say when the household hires directly the worker, the contractual relationship can be facilitated through the payment by CESU vouchers. In the *mandataire* model, clients are employers of workers, but they delegate administrative formalities related to the working relations to an agency. As for the *prestataire* model, it is the agency that employs the worker. In this case, the household is the client of the *prestataire* agency, which invoices for the service provided. The employment relationship is thus different, if the customer is the employer (known as a *particulier employeur*), or if it goes with an intermediary agency.

Regulations depend on whether the worker is employed by a household, by a service provider or if she/he is a micro-entrepreneur (self-employed). The sector is covered by three main collective agreements, depending on the employer, whether it be private households, non-profit associations or for-profit companies. In the case of direct employment, the workers are covered by the collective agreement for private domestic employers (SPE), even though many protective provisions in the Labour Code do not apply to them.[16] When workers are employed by a service provider, so under the *prestataire* model, the employment statuses differ according to whether the organisation is public or private. In the public sector, domestic workers are covered by civil-service law, whereas employees from non-profit organisations are covered by the common provisions of the Labour Code and by specific collective agreements (mainly the *branche de l'aide, de l'accompagnement, des soins et des services à domicile*, BAD). In the case of employees from for-profit organisations, they are covered by the collective agreement of the *entreprises de services à la personne* (SAP). The two main collective agreements of the non-profit (BAD) and for-profit providers (SAP) have been extended branch-wide, which means that they apply to all personnel working in their fields and not only to members of the signatory organisations.[17] Thus, the same worker may therefore be covered by three different collective agreements if in the same day, he or she works for different kind of employers. In the case of digital platforms, some of them use the *mandataire* model, and enable the payment by CESU vouchers implying that they are under the SPE collective agreement. When they work as *micro-entrepreneurs*, many of which go through digital platforms, their self-employed status means that they are not covered by any collective agreement. In some cases (observed on *Yoojo*), additionnaly, some workers may even not be registered under any work status, as it is the case for some markeplaces.[18]

The PHS sector is, therefore, due to the fragmentation of the collective agreements and rights related to the employer type, also fragmented when it comes to

[16] C Ledoux, A Dussuet, P Caillaud and N Teke-Laurent, 'ORIGAMI Report - Home Care Employment Conditions and Industrial Relations before and after the Covid-19 in France' (2024) https://origamiproject.it.

[17] ibid.

[18] J Deauviau (ed), C Didry, M Plault, and M Snape, 'Le Jobbing - Une Enquête Sociologique Sur Le Travail de Plateformes', (2022) *Rapport d'études* DARES.

industrial relations.[19] Trade-unions involve different federations within national confederations, according to the collective agreement. For instance, CFDT Services and CGT Commerce negotiate the collective agreement for SPEs, whereas CFDT Health & Social Services and CGT Social Action negotiate the agreement in the non-profit home-help sector (BAD). On the employers' side, the mode of representation is directly related to the number of affiliates. The *Fédération des Particuliers Employeurs de France* (FEPEM) represents householders and is the sole private households employers' organisation, whereas there are four trade-unions representing the workers, giving them a major power of negotiation.[20] *USB Domicile* confederation represents non-profit service providers while for-profits are represented by four federations, amongst which the largest one is the *Syndicat des Entreprises de Services aux Personnes* (SESP). The SESP is a member of the larger federation representing the interests of a larger number of agencies active in home services, the *Fédération du Service au particulier* (FESP), which is also a member of the main national business federation, the MEDEF (*Mouvement des entreprises de France*). These social partners have been able to negotiate collective agreements that, in spite of this important fragmentation, have still introduced minimum rights, regulation and protection where previously there were none.[21]

Thus, home services are heteroclite, as well as their employment modalities (direct employment, *mandataire*, *prestataire* providers, public organisations, private companies, associations, micro-entrepreneurship), covered by a variety of legal regimes. Yet, these regulations seem to have evolved aside the development of digital platforms, a model based (for cleaning services) on self-employment or even sometimes without labour status, which means that they are not covered by any collective agreement. Also, the complexity of industrial relations has not prevented digital platforms from breaking into this fragmented but already structured market, as both employers organisations as well as trade-unions have shown up to now, few interest in this work arrangement.[22] Actually, the institutional context in the PHS sector has facilitated platforms' insertion in the home service market, with public policies aiming at the commodification of home services, especially through financial incentives.

IV. PUBLIC POLICIES FACILITATING THE ENTRY OF PLATFORMS INTO THE HOME SERVICES MARKET

Home service platforms have thus benefitted from public policies favourable to their development. These public policies are twofolds: some of them intended

[19] Devetter, Ribault and Jany-Catrice (n 14).
[20] Ledoux and Krupka (n 15).
[21] ibid.
[22] Pais et al, ch 6, in this book.

to promote personal and household services, while others aimed at encouraging self-employment.

On the PHS side, public policies initiated in the 1980s intended to promote the commodification of homecare services.[23] These measures were extended to all groups in 1991, with the creation of the *particulier employeur* status in the 'family employment' law, offering a 50 per cent tax cut of expenses incurred, regardless of age, needs or income level. Other incentives were subsequently introduced, such as the simplified declaration of employment with the introduction of the declaratory *chèque emploi service* (CES) in 1994.

Later on, a bill passed in 2005, known as the *plan Borloo*, named after the Minister in charge of social cohesion at the time, Jean-Louis Borloo, constituted a turning point in this commodification strategy. The plan framed more widely the PHS sector, encompassing three main professions: domestic workers, in-home carers (*aides à domicile*) and childminders (*assistantes maternelles*). It also expanded the scope of former policies by social and fiscal measures as well as simplified payment modalities, such as a 50 per cent tax credit or the possibility to pay by universal employment service voucher (CESU, formerly CES), which facilitates the declaration and payment of home service workers. This voucher may be bought, either directly by the household (*déclaratif*), through a service provider, or it may be prefunded (*préfinancé*) entirely or partially by a company, an employee representative committee or providers of social benefits (departmental councils, pension funds, mutual insurance companies, communal social action centres (or CCAS). For companies distributing prefunded CESU vouchers, this aid granted to their employees is not subject to social security contributions and is eligible for a tax credit of 25 per cent of the amount.

The *plan Borloo* was promoted as a policy dedicated to fighting unemployment and informal work, but also to meeting the growing needs of an ageing population, as well as the growing demand for 'comfort services'[24] such as cleaning work. It also introduced a reduction in social security contributions for individual employers, the establishment of a 5.5 per cent VAT rate,[25] as well as the creation of a dedicated national agency (*Agence nationale des services à la personne*, ANSP[26]). By 2007, the tax cut became a 50 per cent tax credit enabled for the payment of home services. In 2020, the 'CESU +' system was implemented as part of a reform of withholding tax, enabling, through the social security organisation responsible to collect social contributions, the URSSAF (*Union de*

[23] Carbonnier and Morel (n 2).

[24] Devetter, Ribault and Jany-Catrice (n 14).

[25] Home services can be subject either to the standard VAT rate of 20 per cent, or it can be reduced by 10 per cent or 5.5 per cent, depending on the employment mode and the kind service.

[26] The ANSP was placed under ministerial supervision, both from the Ministry of Labour, Employment, Training and Social Dialogue as well as the Ministry of Crafts, Trade and Tourism. The agency was eventually shut down in 2014.

recouvrement des cotisations de sécurité sociale et d'allocations familiales), the payment of tax-deductible wages to domestic workers.

The tax credit as well as the CESU system have been advantageous for platforms, as they benefitted from these socio-fiscal assets like any other company. But some specific policies have also focused more precisely on these actors. In October 2023, the Minister for Small and Medium-sized Companies, Olivia Grégoire, announced two major measures presented as a way of favouring 'digital platforms and other innovative actors' entry in the home services market.[27] First, the removal in January 2024 of the condition to have premises in all the *départements* (counties) where companies intervene. Before this change, the service providers operating under the *mandataire* scheme needed to have physical premises in order to by authorised to intervene in the sector. As this obligation was considered as an obstacle to fully digitalised intermediaries it was consequently removed.[28] Second, the 'clause of exclusivity', that imposed workers to work solely in the home service sector – making it impossible to work at the same time in other sectors – to be able to propose the tax credit to their clients, was made more flexible. Micro-entrepreneurs and companies with fewer than 10 employees whose main activity is home service, are since January 2025 able to carry out an extra activity in another professional sector without losing their benefits, especially the possibility to offer the 50 per cent tax credit to their clients.[29]

We have seen that public policies aiming at promoting the development of the PHS sector have been favourable to digital platforms' insertion in the market, especially through socio-fiscal assets but also by alleviating some constraints such as the condition to have premises or the obligation to work exclusively in the PHS sector to be able to propose the 50 per cent tax credit. Also, some other public policies dedicated at facilitating self-employment have also played a key role in this facilitated insertion. Since the 1970s, policies supporting business creation have been implemented in line with a liberal interpretation of the crisis and unemployment. This was the rationale behind the creation of the ACCRE scheme (*Aide aux chômeurs créateurs et repreneurs d'entreprise*) in 1977, which aimed at addressing unemployment with an entrepreneurial answer, as the Prime Minister of that time, Raymond Barre, explained: 'The unemployed could try to create their own business, instead of just collecting social benefits'.[30] In 2020, the ACCRE becomes ACRE (*Aide à la création ou à la reprise d'entreprise*), offering a 50 per cent tax exemption for the first year of activity.

Following the same trend, the year 2008 marked a turning point with the creation of the *auto-entrepreneur* labour status by the Secretary of State, Hervé

[27] 'Services à la personne: Olivia Grégoire annonce la levée de "barrières à l'entrée" pour exercer auprès de publics fragiles', *Banque des territoires*, 28 November 2023.

[28] Ledoux and Teke-Laurent, 'Social dialogue and home care platforms', ORIGAMI report, 2025 https://origamiproject.it.

[29] ibid.

[30] Abdelnour (n 3).

Novelli. The micro-enterprise regime is a simplified tax and social regime that allows the creation of businesses with relatively low annual profits (up to 77,700€ per year in 2024). It aims to simplify administrative formalities, and the calculation and payment of social security contributions and income tax.[31] The income gained could then be combined with other sources of income, for example from salaried employment or social benefits. This system happens to be particularly successful, as according to the French national statistical institute, the INSEE, there were 4.5 million micro-entrepreneurs by 2020. However, this is a poorly protected and precarious status: in 2012, only half of all *auto-entrepreneurs* declared any profits, and 90 per cent of them were earning less than the minimum wage after three years.[32] Their social rights are also less protective than salaried employment, especially when it comes to access to sick or maternity leave, retirement or unemployment rights.

Digital platforms thus emerged in France in this context of promotion of self-entrepreneurship. Their regulation has been relatively accommodating and surrounded by a political support, with successive governments under the presidency of Emmanuel Macron (since 2017) that positioned themselves in favour of a 'presumption of independence' more than of 'presumption of employment', as evidenced by the negotiations about the European Directive on the status of digital platform workers. While a national regulatory authority known as the *Autorité des relations sociales des plateformes d'emploi* (ARPE) has been set up in order to improve digital platforms regulation and establish the premises of a social dialogue – yet being criticised by several unionists for its lack of representativity – it is important to point out that the debates on these issues focus only on mobility platforms (delivery workers and drivers), leaving a clear path for home service platforms to develop their activity, with few regulatory constraints.[33]

This section has shown how digital platforms have benefitted from public policies favourable to their development, as actors part of the PHS sector, and also as compagnies organising the work of independent workers, mainly under the *micro-entrepreneur* status. If these policies have been largely favourable for these home care platforms, if we look more into details the platforms studied in this research, we can also notice different market entry strategies from their part, according to their business model.

V. DIFFERENT MARKET ENTRY STRATEGIES

As favourable public policies are not sufficient to legitimise their place in the PHS market, and given the already structured sector organised by different work arrangements, digital platforms have developed differentiated marketing strategies, according to their business model. The three platforms studied here give

[31] L Poblete and N Teke-Laurent, ORIGAMI report, 2025, https://origamiproject.it.
[32] ibid.
[33] Aloisi and Potocka-Sionek, ch 11, in this book.

us a scope of those strategies deployed in order to remain competitive in this already structured market. Some platforms, like *Wecasa*, emphasise the quality of the services offered by professionals whose expertise is highlighted. Others, such as *Yoojo*, will focus on the multiplicity of services provided, offering a wider range of low-cost gigs and promoting their simplicity of use with a very low level of control from the part of the platform. The third kind of platform studied, *Lulu dans ma rue*, has invested in a social strategy, positioning itself as an actor of the sector of Integration through self-employment (*Insertion par le travail independent*, IAE), by helping long-term unemployed people getting back on the job market and benefitting this way from additional public subsidies.

First, let's take a look at *Wecasa*'s 'professional' strategy. This platform insists on the professionalism of its workers as a major commercial asset. As one of its founders states it:

> You have to understand that in our business, the quality of the service depends exclusively on the quality of the professional. It's very different, if I take the example of delivery, for instance. For meal delivery, whether the delivery worker is A, B, C, D or F, it makes absolutely no difference as for your customer experience. While I can guarantee you that whether it's A, B, C, D or F, for a cleaning worker, it changes everything in your customer experience. So, in fact, the well-being of the professional, their skills, their willing to work, is just the basic point, if we want to succeed. I've always said: If the professionals are happy, then the customers will be happy too. There's no secret.[34]

This qualitative approach, which seeks to highlight the professional nature of the service providers, brings them closer to 'traditional' agencies where workers are formally employed, while at the same time seeking to distinguish themselves from them:

> You have the actors . . . I call them 'traditional', which are the agencies that were set up when personal services were created in the 90s, for which the biggest companies are O2 and Shiva . . . They're going to offer a service based on commitment, estimates and so on. In any case, it's a way of providing the service . . . to put it politely, that doesn't fit in with the codes that our core target market is seeking. In other words, our clients want to book easily, with their phone. Whereas these companies are more like: I request an estimate, then a sales rep comes to my house, I'm committed, if I want to cancel I'll need . . . a cancellation letter . . . in any case something a little more . . . binding. While we wanted to make it easy and accessible'.[35]

The simplicity of use is one of all platforms' major selling argument: in the case of Wecasa, the centrality of their algorithmic management makes it all the more possible to promote their services quickly and easily, with no commitment, 'in two clics'. For *Lulu dans ma rue*, their smaller scope of intervention and the possibility to have human interactions directly in their physical implantations in

[34] P André, co-founder of Wecasa, interview 16 November 2023.
[35] ibid.

several parts of Paris, make it easier for the users to exchange about their needs. In the case of *Yoojo*, this simplicity is all the more of a selling argument as the platform has based its business model on connecting as many – and different kinds of – gigs as possible at the lowest possible price. Unlike the other two platforms studied, *Yoojo* being a *marketplace,* the price is determined by the customer (with a suggestion of price range by the platform), and the service providers can then negotiate. However, the competition amongst workers is important. Therefore, this pricing system automatically leads to social dumping, with lower rates compared with the rest of the market. In addition, the difficulties encountered sometimes in obtaining assignments make the use of this platform a way to earn a little extra money, but prevents it from becoming the main activity:

> We have quite a few professions – I won't name them all, because some of them are not allowed to work [through the platform]. But they do it to earn a little extra money. We have people who need to get married, who need to save money, who want to buy a ring, and all.[36]

Multiactivity is particularly prevalent on this type of *marketplaces*, which are more focused on small and unskilled services between private individuals. The simplicity to register with this platform should therefore be seen in the light of the number of missions that are actually obtained, and the relative income that can be generated with them. For instance, in the context of the participatory observation done on *Yoojo*, after having registered on this platform as a cleaning worker and applying for over 200 assignments, I was only selected for seven of them. As other digital platforms, *Yoojo* works by building up a large reserve army of workers,[37] who can be *micro-entrepreneurs*, companies or individuals. A web scraping also carried out on this platform also revealed that out of the 32,000 jobbers' profiles found on their site, only 12.4 per cent had worked at least once.

On a different note, *Lulu dans ma rue* has chosen a social strategy that brings together a smaller number of workers (around 1,000), but with personalised support for their professional career. As an EITI, since 2018, which is a pilot that the platform directly helped to develop, aiming to turn long-term unemployed persons into independent workers, *Lulu dans ma rue* gets public subsidies to develop this economic model, from the part of the State and the City council of Paris. This has raised some criticism, due to the lack of clarity of this scheme, whose results are yet to be confirmed. In a report submitted to the French Social Affairs Inspection Authority (IGAS), the Federation of Integration Enterprises

[36] B Tournier, founder of Yoojo, radio interview 6 February 2024.

[37] N van Doorn, 'Platform Labor: On the Gendered and Racialized Exploitation of Low-Income Service Work in the "On-Demand" Economy' (2017) 20 *Information, Communication & Society* 898; S Bernard, *Uberusés: Le Capitalisme Racial de Plateforme à Paris, Londres et Montréal* (Paris, Presses universitaires de France, 2023).

(*Fédération des Entreprises d'Insertion*, FEI) pointed out the risks posed by the EITI's model, as this scheme may in some cases reveal issues assimilated to disguised salaried employment:

> Depending on the circumstances, the EiTI structures that accompany independent workers may run the risk of seeing the 'commercial' relationship between two professional and independent structures degenerate into an employment relationship. When, for example, independent workers do not have the freedom to set their own price or working hours, or when they work with an equipment that does not belong to them and that they do not rent, or when they are subject to various obligations that could be otherwise subject of penalties akin to disciplinary sanctions, then a judge may be led to consider that the independent worker is in fact placed under a relationship of dependence and subordination that characterises the employment contract.[38]

These three ways of entering the home service market – either by promoting the professionalism of the workers, or the multiplicity of low-cost gigs, or the potential to help long-term unemployed to access to the labour market through independent work – are therefore interesting as they reveal different business models, which are sometimes based on grey areas at the margins of labour law. Yet, in spite of differentiated models to find a specific place in this already structured marked, these platforms also show that their commonality is their simplicity of use and their flexibility. All the more, what home service platforms have in common is that they built their legitimacy on a relatively harmonised discourse, aimed at highlighting the issues of the PHS sector, in particular the problems raised by undeclared work and the identified constraints of salaried employment.

VI. MORE PROTECTION THAN IN THE BLACK MARKET BUT MORE FLEXIBILITY THAN IN FORMAL EMPLOYMENT?

Due to this already complex and relatively well-structured ecosystem in the service economy, breaking into this market has constituted a major strategic positioning challenge for platforms, let alone their business models. In response, they used two major rhetorical arguments, towards both their (potential) clients and service providers: on the one hand, by attacking head-on the informal sector, and positioning themselves as key players in the 'fight against undeclared work'. On the other hand, by promoting the flexibility of their model, enabling workers to define their own schedules and workload. Digital platforms are presented as an alternative to the perceived rigidity of formal employment. It is thus interesting to focus on these two issues home service platforms propose to tackle,

[38] Fédération des Entreprises d'Insertion, 'Contribution au rapport IGAS – évaluation de l'expérimentation EiTI' (2023).

and analyse the effectiveness of these arguments as well as the capacity of these actors to actually solve them.

A. Joining 'the Fight Against the Black Market'

By the 1980s, commodification policies in the PHS sector had not only promoted jobs creation, but also the 'whitening' of the black market, as it is in fact difficult to distinguish one from another. The introduction in 1991 of the 50 per cent tax reduction aimed specifically at lowering the cost of declared work compared with undeclared work:[39] socio-fiscal benefits were thought as a way to make it more profitable to buy domestic services in the formal way. Informal work in home services is indeed tackled by public policies as a major issue that needs to be solved, as stated later on, in a report from the Ministry of Economics:

> The use of undeclared work is all the easier in these activities because the barriers to entry are low: little or no equipment . . . and technical skills accessible to the greater number. In addition, direct work relations can encourage the use of informal contacts.[40]

The *Cour des comptes* (National Court of Audit) also considers that partially declared work ('grey work') is observed in the sector, considering that it 'enables to benefit from a social security coverage in the event of occupational accidents, while evading part of their contributions'.[41] Another reason explaining this phenomenon is that the perception of the risks of control and sanction is very low.

Having said this, the extent of undeclared work has yet been diminishing since the establishment of socio-fiscal measures lowering the price of home services. The amount of undeclared work in the PHS sector has been declining since the 1990s, and reached approximately 20 per cent in 2017, compared with 25 per cent in 2011.[42] It is also important to point out that informal work within the cleaning sector, more specifically, is below the European average, with 10 per cent in France, compared with 16 per cent at European level in 2020.[43] This gradual reduction in the share of informal work can be explained by the socio-fiscal incentives, which make it more advantageous to declare domestic work, both for customers, who benefit from a generous 50 per cent tax credit up to a basic ceiling of €12,000 per year, and for workers, who benefit from social protection.

However, even if informality is losing ground, the sector still lacks attractiveness and the job creation strategy aimed by the *plan Borloo* was only partially

[39] C Marbot and D Roy, 'Évaluation de la transformation de la réduction d'impôt pour l'emploi de salariés à domicile en crédit d'impôt en 2007'(2014) 1–2 *Économie & prévision* 53.

[40] Direction Générale du Trésor, 'La Politique de Soutien Aux Services à La Personne' (2016).

[41] Cour des Comptes (2024) 46.

[42] M Beltzung and L Malard, 'Services à la personne – Baisse du travail non déclaré en 2017' (2021) 70 *DARES Résultats* 1.

[43] European Commission, 'Special Eurobarometer 498: Undeclared Work in the European Union' (2020).

achieved, facing today a stagnation in the activity. In 2017, 12.6 per cent of households employed someone at home, slightly fewer than in 2011 (13.2 per cent), even if more and more households declare hiring a domestic worker in the formal sector.[44] Those who make most use of these services are high-income households: 34 per cent amongst the 10 per cent wealthiest, compared with 6 per cent amongst the 10 per cent poorest, qualified by the *Cour des comptes* as a 'windfall effect'.[45] Given the stagnation of the activity and the failure to create more jobs in spite of the importance of public financial support to the sector (4.4 million users received €8.8 billion in 2022), which ultimately benefitted the most to the highest incomes, the *Cour des comptes* has recommended that government subsidies should be reduced.

This recommendation has triggered strong opposition from the part of home service companies and employers' organisations, claiming that such decision would lead to a massive return to undeclared work by domestic workers.[46] The structures of the sector have indeed identified informal work as one of the major issues of the sector. In this context, digital platforms not only place themselves in the continuity of this discourse about the dangers of informal work, they also present themselves as key players against it. The 'fight against the black market' is in fact one of the main arguments for home service platforms, particularly present on their websites and widely taken up by their founders in the media. For example, *Batmaid*'s website states: 'Join the fight, help us put an end to undeclared work!' Fighting undeclared work is indeed a slogan shared widely amongst home service platforms. It is based on a moral rhetoric of informal work, pointing out the dangers of illegality and precariousness. This is also what the founder of *Yoojo* said in a radio interview, defending the interest of the model, which would provide a form of protection thanks to the platform's insurance:

> All services are insured by Axa [insurance company]. The insurance covers breakage, personal injury and material damage . . . Those who decide to work illegally take ill-considered risks, all this to save a few euros a month . . . It's not worth it at all.[47]

There would thus be an advantage in terms of protection for domestic workers who register on a platform, justifying the intermediation relationship and thus also the income deductions that this entails. However, the economic issue is also raised by some workers who sometimes consider bypassing the platform to avoid this loss of income:

> For the jobber . . . but that for sure is not legal (laughs)! From the point of view of the application, it's not right, but . . . the clients, when my job is finished, you must know

[44] Beltzung and Malard (n 9).
[45] Cour des Comptes (2024) 96.
[46] 'Des salariés vont replonger dans le travail au noir: la mise en garde des particuliers employeurs face à la remise en cause du crédit d'impôt' (Le Figaro, 27 March 2023).
[47] B Tournier, founder of *Yoojo*, interview 6 February 2024.

> that I still have their number. I can tell them, well, if you've got another job for me, you can send me a message, and then we can settle it hand to hand. And in fact, by doing this, you avoid paying additional fees, because you must know that the application takes five per cent, at least for me, of what I receive. And they also take . . . well I don't know the percentage for the client. But you save money, and obviously from the application's point of view it's illegal, but it can also be an advantage for the jobber.[48]

On *Yoojo*, service charges amount to 5 per cent for the workers and 20 per cent for the customers[49] (except when paid by CESU, in which case the platform deducts 6 per cent from the amount of the voucher). In other words, for a service that costs €10, the customer will pay €12 and the service provider will receive €9.5. For the worker, this fee remains lower than on the other platforms surveyed (25 per cent at *Wecasa*, 29 per cent at *Lulu dans ma rue*). Therefore, while the fight against informal work is presented as one of the main commercial assets of home service platforms, as well as one of the major incentives for public policies, the temptation to go in direct, once the first contact is established, remains particularly strong, for both workers and customers. The reason is not only economic, as the tax credit, when applicable, may diminish considerably the cost of the service. It can also be explained by a willingness to keep things simple, or by immediacy effects:

> With this system, I think it's easy to slip into undeclared work. Once you're in contact with the person. Because it's really easy, it's easier to say: I'll make you a transfer, or I'll leave you an envelope. And that's tempting. Then, you can't get tax deductions, but I think it's cheaper.
>
> Even with the tax credit?
>
> I don't know . . . Well yes, in the end it comes down to the same thing. But there's a psychological effect to paying less at a given moment, I guess.[50]

Justine used *Yoojo* as a client but was confronted with the complexity of having to calculate the 'right price' for her domestic worker. The fact that she had to do it by herself seemed particularly complicated to her, which explains her temptation to opt for an informal work arrangement. Attractive socio-fiscal measures happen therefore to be insufficient to avoid bypassing platforms and can sometimes constitute a psychological brake by being perceived as administrative complexity. Informal work can thus not be entirely avoided, which weakens platforms' 'formalisation' commercial argument.

Even if digital platforms legitimise their insertion in the market as a way of formalising the black market, there still remains a part of informality, especially because some users tend to bypass the platform once the first contact is done. If the formalisation argument needs thus to be nuanced, we can also question

[48] Ahmed, 19 years old, worker at *Yoojo*.
[49] Information found in the general terms and conditions on *Yoojo*'s website.
[50] Justine, 33 years old, client at *Yoojo*.

the other argument put forward, that is the one of a model that would be more flexible than in formal employment.

B. 'Workers Want To Be Free!' Promoting the Flexibility of Work

Home service digital platforms present their model as a way to fight informal work, but also as a way to have a more flexible system than in formal employment, as the founder of *Wecasa* states:

> From the client's point of view, it's the simplicity of use. If we look at the cleaning market in France today, what does it represent? First, it's direct employment. And for a good part of it, undeclared, historically. Against which the public authorities have successfully fought. Which is terrible for the undeclared part of it. And for the declared one, it also means a lot of constraints for the people who want to make use of it, because they end up as employers, with all that means in terms of legal and regulatory obligations. And for people who aren't necessarily trained for it, or ready for it. And so . . . with a lot of people who don't want to be employers legally speaking, and who . . . direct employment is for some people and not for others.[51]

To justify their insertion, home service platforms position themselves as the middle ground, in between the illegality of informal work and the perceived 'rigidity' of salaried employment, in order to promote non-salaried, intermediated work:

> From the workers' point of view, what they want is to manage their time, to work whenever they want, not be forced to . . . not be constrained. . . . The sector is hiring everywhere, so if all these people who work for us wanted to have a permanent contract with a cleaning agency tomorrow, they could. Why don't they? Well, that's because they want to be free! To work whenever they want. And because it is not always the kind of sectors where working conditions are those of a permanent contract as you and I imagine them. Rarely the nice, well-paid 35-hour week, etc.[52]

The platforms, and above all their founders, who regularly defend their model in the media and through lobbying actions in the institutions, justify their position as newcomers to this market. Yet, to do so, they have to demonstrate that they are not acting head-on against salaried employment, but rather 'alongside' it, in vacant spaces that intermediated self-employment could fill, as *Lulu dans ma rue*'s founder, Charles-Edouard Vincent explained, at a conference organised by the platform at the French National Assembly in February 2024: 'We talk a lot about independent work, but we're not ayatollahs of independent work! We're

[51] P André, co-founder of *Wecasa*, 16 November 2023.
[52] ibid.

very happy when [workers] find their way back into the employment market, because what is important is finding your rightful place in society'.

For these platforms, upholding their place as structures based mainly on self-employment, places them at the heart of several contemporary debates on 'uberisation'. They are confronted with criticisms addressed mainly towards mobility platforms (drivers and delivery workers), stating that working conditions may sometimes be assimilated with bogus employment. To distance themselves from this, they seek to position themselves as an 'anti-model to Uber', as one of *Wecasa* founders put it during an interview. But also, because the very nature of the services they offer, in particular with cleaning work, raises questions about domesticity, for which they also have to defend themselves against accusations of 'modern slavery':[53]

> They take control of their destiny, they're anything but slaves. Because in fact they work whenever they want, so I don't know what could be less of a slave! If anything, an employee is more of a slave, because they have to do what they're told to.[54]

To distance themselves from 'uberisation' accusations or other forms of exploitation, the freedom assertion is all the more important as it is used in opposition to salaried employment. Some people, according to the platform founders, may not be suited to this work environment, and would never fit in. For this reason, one of the main demands of home service platforms today is that public policy should give independent workers access to social protection, which in France is closely linked to the status of salaried employment:

> But the real challenge is that today, in terms of protection, when you're an independent worker, you're not as protected as when you're an employee. And today, that's our next challenge. So, rather than trying to kill self-entrepreneurship: no, the tool is good, but it's incomplete. We need to build a society, I'd like to say, where this protection is consistent. Whether you're a salaried employee or self-employed, there's no longer this two-speed society, because let me remind you, for some people, becoming a salaried employee is out of question![55]

The platform model would thus be the alternative to the overly rigid framework associated with salaried employment, which is often criticised by workers for not giving the possibility to choose their time or locations of work, with agencies that often make them do long distances between two homes, for a time that is not paid. The flexibility provided by the platforms therefore makes it possible to improve certain working conditions that domestic workers did not find in salaried employment, in particular the possibility to choose their working

[53] P André, 'Travailleurs de plateforme: de l'esclavage moderne?' (*Medium*, 23 May 2018).

[54] P André, co-founder of *Wecasa*, 16 November 2023.

[55] Charles-Edouard Vincent, founder of *Lulu dans ma rue*, conference at the National Assembly, 1 February 2024.

hours and distances.[56] However, the model also makes this work more precarious in other respects, particularly in terms of risk management: once a problem occurs, domestic workers often realise that they face an important individualisation of risks, with few support from the part of the platforms.[57] Working as *micro-entrepreneurs* also means not benefitting from the main protective social rights associated with salaried status. To protect themselves, these workers have thus to take out professional insurance, on their own account[58] and often realise, only once they are confronted to a serious issue, that they have to deal with it on their own.

VII. CONCLUSION

The strategies adopted by digital platforms to establish themselves in the home service economic market appear to be convincing, as public policies – through legislation and public subsidies – have facilitated their insertion. We have seen in this chapter that the French institutional context in the PHS sector was already structured prior to the arrival of platforms in this market, contrasting with other national contexts presented in this book.[59] Yet, these regulations have not prevented them to develop their activity. On the contrary, they benefitted from public policies favourable to their arrival, as PHS companies, and as digital platforms. Still, they needed to distinguish one from another, in order to occupy a specific place in this already structured market. *Wecasa* highlighted the professionalism of its workers, while *Yoojo*, as a marketplace was more into promoting the great diversity of small gigs at a very low price. As for *Lulu dans ma rue*, the platform developed a social strategy by being part of a pilot helping long-term unemployed to get back into the job market by being self-employed. If they tried to distinguish one from another according to their business models, these platforms also have in common a public rhetoric towards their users (both clients and workers) that is to say that their model helps to formalise informal work while at the same time provide more flexibility that in formal salaried employment. In this context, the workers are keen to embrace the ideology of flexibility and autonomy, while customers are seduced by the accessibility and simplicity of the services. Yet, in this fight against informal work and in favour of self-employment, the formalisation claimed by home service platforms,

[56] K Uysal and C Boyraz, 'Autonomy and Control in the Gig Economy and Platform Work: Domestic and Home Repair Workers in Turkey' (2023) 26 *Journal of Balkan and Near Eastern Studies* 23.

[57] V Pulignano, C Marà, M Franke and K Muszyński, 'Informal Employment on Domestic Care Platforms: A Study on the Individualisation of Risk and Unpaid Labour in Mature Market Contexts' (2023) 29 *Transfer: European Review of Labour and Research* 323.

[58] F Gallot and A Koechlin, 'Analyse Sociologique de l'appréhension de La Protection Sociale Par Des Travailleuses de Plateformes: Une Analyse Par Le Prisme Du Genre' in *Réinventer La Protection Sociale Des Travailleurs de Plateformes Numériques* (Paris, Mare&Martin, 2023).

[59] Rodriguez-Mondroño, ch 1 and Starčević, ch 4, in this book.

remains unfulfilled. Workers are kept in the grey areas of a model that fails to be fully formalised, having to take charge of their own protection and risks' anticipation by themselves, with relative support from these digital intermediaries when problems actually arise. This formalisation also remains incomplete, as the bridges with informal work are still very much present.

In more practical terms, it is yet important to take into account the problems raised by home service platforms, as they are indicators of the reality of working conditions in the PHS sector, whether it be the precariousness of informality, even though the share of the black market is steadily diminishing, or the constraints of rigid employment conditions in the formal sector. There are also other important problems in the sector more widely, as highlighted in the report by the *Cour des comptes*,[60] that need to be taken into account, such as the precarious nature of the profession, unpaid commuting and heavy workloads, which contribute to the sector's lack of attractiveness.

[60] Cour des Comptes, 'Le Soutien de l'Etat Aux Services à La Personne' (2024).

3

*Peer-to-Peer Precarity: The Role of Multi-Service Platforms in Shaping Wages and Working Conditions in Belgium**

MAT JOHNSON, VALERIA PULIGNANO,
CLAUDIA MARÀ AND MILENA FRANKE

I. INTRODUCTION

THE EXPANSION OF digital platforms from consumer markets such as transportation and food delivery into health and personal care services is recognised as presenting a range of opportunities and challenges. On the one hand, digital platforms are arguably a response to the growing unmet demand for at-home support associated with an ageing and increasingly geographically dispersed population,[1] and platforms promise more flexible and personalised services when compared with traditional 'bureaucratic' state welfare systems.[2] Platforms may also reduce the burden of unpaid care within the extended family unit[3] while also creating formal job opportunities for marginalised groups in the labour market.[4] On the other hand, digital platforms potentially intensify

* This research received funding from the European Research Council (ERC Advanced Grant) under the European Union's Horizon 2020 research and innovation programme (grant agreement n_ 833577—Project ResPecTMe—Resolving Precariousness: Advancing the Theory and Measurement of Precariousness across the Paid/Unpaid Work Continuum) and the FWO–Flemish Research Council—Grant/Award Number G073919N (PI: Valeria Pulignano).

[1] M Franke, V Pulignano and C Marà, 'Workers' Contentions Over Unpaid Labour Time in Food Delivery and Domestic Work Platforms in Belgium' (2023) 3 *Work in the Global Economy* 6.

[2] F Macdonald, '"Personalised Risk" in Paid Care Work and the Impacts of "Gig Economy" Care Platforms and Other Market-based Organisations' (2021) 5 *International Journal of Care and Caring* 9.

[3] J Berg, M Furrer, E Harmon, U Rani and MS Silberman, *Digital Labour Platforms and the Future of Work: Towards Decent Work in the Online World* (Geneva, ILO, 2018).

[4] F Pereyra, L Poblete, C Poggi and A Tizziani, 'Precarisation or Protection? The Impact of Digital Platform Labour on Argentinean Domestic Workers in Times of Pandemic' (2022) AFD Working Paper 235.

competition between workers for low paying and short-term care 'gigs' which particularly affects women and migrants.[5] There are also growing concerns about the spread of algorithmic management techniques into high-touch roles such as care and domestic work, with the attendant risks of task standardisation, reduced autonomy and worker surveillance.[6]

But while there are concerns about the potential 'Uberisation of care', this is not an inevitable product of technological innovation, but rather is shaped by the structure, financing and market dynamics of welfare provision. For example, the specific business and employment models of platforms vary by country, sector and service area,[7] and platforms have also expanded on the back of particular institutional modes of welfare financing such as personal support vouchers and 'cash-for-care' schemes.[8] Similarly, while platforms are often seen as 'regulatory disruptors' in some cases governments have accepted their position as a legitimate part of the 'collaborative economy' which operates largely outside of existing systems of regulation, taxation and social security.[9] The question now is whether platforms (and platform work) should be treated as a novel feature of the modern economy or whether more inclusive and reflexive systems of labour market regulation and social protection would reduce the incentives for clients and workers to use platforms in the first place.[10]

The current study explores the recent, and relatively rapid, growth of multi-service platforms in Belgium that offer (among other things) care and personal services for those with disabilities, domestic work, childcare, tutoring, home maintenance and handiwork and pet sitting. By analysing the business and employment models of the multi-service platforms *Helpper* and *RingTwice* we reveal how platforms have been quick to respond to changing patterns of supply and demand in the market, while at the same time exploiting various institutional grey zones around the collaborative economy in Belgium. We consider the implications of 'platformisation' for individual workers across a number of dimensions including job availability, wages, working conditions, social security and performance management.

We find that there are some similarities between platforms such as *Helpper* and *RingTwice* and on-demand consumer platforms such as Uber and Deliveroo

[5] J Meijerink, M Boons, A Keegan and J Marler, 'Algorithmic Human Resource Management: Synthesizing Developments and Cross-disciplinary Insights on digital HRM' (2021) 32 *The International Journal of Human Resource Management* 2545.

[6] A Glaser, 'Uberized Care: Employment Status, Surveillance, and Technological Erasure in the Home Health Care Sector' (2021) 42 *Anthropology of Work Review* 24.

[7] P Rodríguez-Modroño, A Agenjo-Calderón and P López-Igual, 'A Social Reproduction Analysis of Digital Care Platform Work' (2024) 29 *New Political Economy* 616.

[8] V Pulignano, C Marà, M Franke and K Muszyński, 'Informality of Employment in Digital Domestic Care Platforms: A Study on the Individualization of Risk and Unpaid Labour in Mature Market Contexts' (2023) 29 *Transfer: European Review of Labour and Research* 323.

[9] JB Schor and W Attwood-Charles, 'The "Sharing" Economy: Labor, Inequality, and Social Connection on For-profit Platforms' (2017) 11 *Sociology Compass 1*.

[10] M Johnson and A Martín-Caballero, 'Platform Capital and the City: Governing Uber in Buenos Aires and Manchester' (2025) 45 *Comparative Labor Law & Policy Journal 201*.

namely in respect of the reliance on individual worker profiles, ratings and quick response times in determining work opportunities. Furthermore, the low barriers to entry for workers ensure a large pool of standby labour which in turn intensifies competition between individual workers and keeps rates of pay low. However, we also observe that marketplace platforms allow clients and workers to negotiate tasks, working patterns and hourly rates of pay 'offline'. Rather than the highly centralised model of technological control and labour exploitation leveraged by Uber, marketplace platforms combine notions of entrepreneurial freedom with normative mechanisms of control that legitimise low paid and, in some cases, voluntary labour, as part of a collaborative and local community network. This form of 'peer-to-peer' precarity operates in a legal and social grey zone, but for all of the problems it creates appears to be preferable (in the eyes of clients and many workers) to wholly informal or undeclared work.

The chapter is structured as follows. The next section summarises emerging literature on the expansion of digital platforms from consumer services into health and care services, and the attendant challenges created in terms of precarious work. It then outlines the research design and methods, focusing on the specific case of marketplace care platforms in the context of Belgium, which is a mature, but relatively inflexible, welfare state. It then presents the findings which are analysed in respect of the steady normalisation of casual care and domestic work in Belgium, and the role of platforms in facilitating 'peer-to-peer precarity'. We then discuss the findings and offer some conclusions.

II. THE 'UBERISATION' OF WORK AND CARE

A key transformation in the world of work in recent years has been the growth of digital service platforms. Although they are often grouped together, platforms can be web-based where work is outsourced through an open call to a geographically dispersed crowd ('crowdwork'), or location-based applications (apps) which allocate work to individuals in a specific geographical area.[11] And while digital platforms remain only a modest proportion of the overall economy in many countries outside of the US, there are growing concerns about the influence of platform management strategies on the world of work.[12]

For example, the ride hailing platform Uber initially claimed to be simply a technology provider that facilitated local 'peer-to-peer' interactions between drivers and customers as part of the emergent 'sharing economy'.[13] In the wider public discourse platforms were keen to emphasise the economic 'win-win'

[11] Berg, Furrer, Harmon, Rani and Silberman (n 3).

[12] A Aloisi and V De Stefano, *Your Boss is an Algorithm: Artificial Intelligence, Platform Work and Labour* (Oxford, Hart *Publishing, 2022).*

[13] Schor and Attwood-Charles (n 9).

that simultaneously fulfilled the unmet demand for affordable transportation, delivery services, odd-jobs and short-term accommodation, while also creating additional earning opportunities for 'micro-entrepreneurs' with spare time, skills, a vehicle or property that could be 'put out' to the market.[14] However, the ability of platforms to offer cheap services has been subsidised by high volumes of venture capital,[15] the avoidance of existing regulations and the (mis) classification of platform workers as self-employed contractors.[16] Similarly, an extensive body of work has shown how algorithms control the labour process of individual workers through job allocation mechanisms, digital surveillance and performance metrics[17] and influence the earnings of workers through opaque 'dynamic pricing' mechanisms.[18]

There are also concerns about the spillover of algorithmic management into labour intensive 'high touch' services such as health and social care.[19] As with platform ride hailing and food delivery services that have gradually become part of the legitimate transportation system,[20] health, home care and domestic work platforms have grown rapidly over the last decade or so, particularly after the COVID-19 pandemic.[21] The 'platformisation of care' is not just a product of individual customer choice, but is driven by the changing structure, financing and market dynamics of welfare provision. For example, at a macro-level, austerity pressures and an ageing population have resulted in the increased 'rationing' of care services in many countries, which has been compounded by the growing corporatisation and marketisation of welfare services through outsourcing and supplementary private health insurance.[22] Fundamentally, the thinning of state provision combined with a shift away from unpaid care within families, particularly as more women enter the paid labour force, has led to the expansion of alternative forms of care and home support such as through platforms.

[14] M Bartosz, 'Digital "Putting-out System": an Old New Method of Work in Platform Economy' (2020) 211 *Polish Sociological Review* 265.

[15] D Howcroft and A Leaver, 'Unstable Platforms: Uber's Business Model and the Challenge of Organisational Legitimacy' (2024) 49 *In Accounting Forum 369*.

[16] K Thelen, 'Regulating Uber: The Politics of the Platform Economy in Europe and the United States' (2018) 16 *American Political Science Association* 938.

[17] A Shapiro, 'Dynamic Exploits: Calculative Asymmetries in the On-demand Economy' (2020) 35 *New Technology, Work and Employment* 162.

[18] U Rani, V Pulignano, N Gobel and K Muszynski, 'Challenging Boundaries: Exploring Pricing Strategies, and Unpaid Labour Time to Explain Earning Disparities in Online Labour Markets' (2024) 30 *New Political* Economy 342.

[19] A Glaser, 'Uberized Care: Employment Status, Surveillance, and Technological Erasure in the Home Health Care Sector' (2021) 42 *Anthropology of Work Review* 24.

[20] Johnson and Martín-Caballero (n 10).

[21] U Rani, RK Dhir and N Gobel, 'Digital Labour Platforms and Their Contribution to Development Outcomes' in WM Moore, C Scherrer and M van der Linden (eds), *The Elgar Companion to Decent Work and the Sustainable Development Goals* (Cheltenham, Edward Elgar Publishing, 2025).

[22] SR. Farris and S Marchetti, 'From the Commodification to the Corporatization of Care: European Perspectives and Debates' (2017) 24 *Social Politics: International Studies in Gender, State & Society* 109.

However, this apparent 'care fix'[23] also creates new possibilities for profit and financial value creation which increasingly relies on extractive business models and high volumes of informal and semi-formal work.[24]

For example, the expansion of cash-for-care schemes in many countries provides individual clients with greater control over the type, frequency and duration of care that they receive and can improve the affordability and flexibility of services.[25] But at the same time, the individualisation of care budgets effectively makes clients 'micro-employers' who hire from a local spot market on an hourly, daily or weekly basis.[26] This spot market is increasingly made up of care agencies and platforms who compete for small packages of care usually on the basis of cost and flexibility, which requires a large pool of cheap and available labour. In many countries, this labour pool has been expanded as a result of government policy to try and reduce rates of unemployment and inactivity, particularly among migrants and women.[27] However, the vulnerable position of these workers can mean they are in a weak position to resist low wages and poor working conditions.[28]

Rather than providing a 'care fix', platforms have arguably contributed to the ongoing care crisis in a number of countries by perpetuating a precarised commodification of socially reproductive activities.[29] Clearly there is a paradox in that by embedding themselves into markets and social relations, platforms steadily build infrastructural, institutional and political power but they may remain 'dis-embedded' from the regulatory structures and mutual obligations that historically bound together employers, employees and the state.[30] Indeed, while platforms may continue to grow market share in an increasingly diverse range of industries, they often remain 'free-riders' or 'parasitic organisations' that draw more from individuals and society than they return.[31] Platforms also contribute to the simultaneous formalisation and informalisation of work among precarious and marginalised groups.[32] For example, in respect of domestic work, platforms can regularise the contracts and working patterns of highly informalised workers who typically work in private homes.[33] At the same time, platforms

[23] E Dowling, *The Care Crisis: What Caused It and How Can We End It?* (London, *Verso Books,* 2022).

[24] Pulignano et al (n 8).

[25] B Orth and F Baum, 'Researching Care Platforms: Methodological and Ethical Considerations in the Broad Field of Domestic Platform Labour' (2024) 0 *Critical Sociology 1.*

[26] Macdonald (n 7).

[27] Rodríguez-Modroño, Agenjo-Calderón and López-Igual (n 7).

[28] N van Doorn, 'Liminal Precarity and Compromised Agency: Migrant Experiences of Gig Work in Amsterdam, Berlin, and New York City' in D Das Acevedo (ed), *The Routledge Handbook of the Gig Economy* (London, Routledge, 2022) 158.

[29] Rodríguez-Modroño, Agenjo-Calderón and López-Igual (n 7).

[30] PD Culpepper and K Thelen, 'Are we all Amazon Primed? Consumers and the Politics of Platform Power' (2020) 53 *Comparative Political Studies* 288.

[31] Schor and Attwood-Charles (n 9).

[32] Meijerink et al (n 5).

[33] Pereyra et al (n 4).

can also further normalise the low pay and short hours working typically faced by women and migrant workers in a precarious economic and social position.[34]

There are however differences between more conventional 'on-demand' care platforms and 'marketplace' care platforms. Whereas in the former, job allocation and fees are generally set by platform algorithms, in the latter workers and clients negotiate fees and working arrangements directly.[35] The role of marketplace platforms is particularly interesting as they are arguably closer to the original notion of a 'peer-to-peer' platform within the sharing economy rather than the current iterations of Uber, Lyft and Deliveroo that rely heavily on technology to monitor and control a highly atomised workforce. Recent years have seen a marked growth in multi-service platforms that offer help with a wide range of domestic tasks such as personal care, childcare, pet sitting, tuition and cleaning services on an as-and-when basis.[36] These platforms have sought to formalise 'neighbourhood' job adverts and informal 'word of mouth' recommendations for childminders, domestic workers and carers, by handling job postings, displaying worker ratings and references, and giving clients reference points for typical hourly fees. Again, the argument is that marketplace platforms can efficiently utilise idle assets such as spare time, skills and previous caring experience (paid and unpaid), but the trade-off is that multi-service platforms blur the boundaries between different occupational specialisms and reinforce the general low valuation of what remains highly feminised labour.[37] The individual negotiation of working time, rates of pay and work tasks also creates significant risks of exploitation and inappropriate requests that the platforms have little or no control over.[38]

III. RESEARCH DESIGN AND METHODS

In this study, we explore the growing platformisation of care in Belgium and the role of multi-service platforms in meeting various care and domestic support needs. We do this by comparing two of the largest multi-service marketplace platforms currently operating in Belgium, *Helpper* and *RingTwice*. These platforms are market leaders and digitally link individual workers as self-employed 'service providers' with clients in the local area, who need assistance with a range of tasks including home care and nursing support, domestic duties and childcare.

[34] ibid.

[35] P Hopwood, E MacEachen, I Bourgeault, C McAiney, B Yanar and A Davis, 'On-Demand and Marketplace Platforms: Gig Care Work Conditions on Two Digital Labour Platform Care Models' (2024) 0 *Critical Sociology* 1.

[36] Schor and Attwood-Charles (n 9).

[37] Rodríguez-Modroño et al (n 7).

[38] Pulignano et al (n 8)

RingTwice was founded in 2013 and has grown steadily in recent years with an estimated 50,000 clients and more than 35,000 workers across Belgium.[39] The platform provides a wide range of domestic and care services such as babysitting, elderly care, gardening, house repairs, IT services, administrative support. *Helpper* was founded in 2017 and has been so far particularly active in the Flemish region of Belgium where it has successfully mediated between more than 5,000 clients and workers[40] and is increasingly expanding to the regions of Brussels and Wallonia.

Through interviews with platform managers, individual workers and worker representatives, we explore different perspectives on 'platformisation' in terms of providing both a 'care fix' (for families and wider society) and a 'work fix' (for those looking for part-time and flexible work opportunities). Furthermore, narrative biographies collated by individual workers reveal the contradictory dynamics of working via multi-service platforms in terms of formalising work opportunities (particularly for those with limited labour market experience) set against the challenges of individual negotiations with clients around rates of pay, working time, work tasks and performance ratings and reviews. This multi-strand analysis allows us to explore the ways in which platforms have established, and legitimised, themselves within the emerging semi-privatised' care market, while at the same time analysing the role of marketplace platforms, as well as individual clients, in shaping wages and working conditions.

The research draws on 41 qualitative narrative interviews with workers, and seven semi-structured interviews with platform management and non-profit organisations management (see Appendix).

IV. CASUALISED CARE AND THE GROWTH OF PLATFORMS IN BELGIUM

Since the mid-2000s Belgium has sought to formalise and regulate care and domestic services through a combination of social policy reform, the expansion of private health and home care provision and the restructuring of labour market institutions. This was partly in response to demographic changes that led to increasing demands on health services and long-term care for elderly citizens, as well as a perceived need to increase, and formalise, employment opportunities for marginalised groups, particularly women and migrant workers. Increasing the labour supply has also become a regional policy objective that in turn may shape employment outcomes. For example, the current regional

[39] https://ringtwice.be/fr.

[40] www.helpper.be/nl/home.

Flemish government has adopted measures to push low-wage workers, jobseekers and economically inactive people towards self-employment.[41]

The rapid growth of platforms has certainly been facilitated by the creation of specific tax and social security exemptions, but it is also the 'rigidity' of formal welfare provision that has created demand for 'on-demand' services that do not incur the high costs associated with regular contracts of employment and collectively agreed pay and conditions. In common with many European countries, informal care within families and neighbourhoods has always taken up some of the slack, but mobility and migration patterns have changed the availability and norms of inter-generational care, and rural areas are particularly underserved in respect of personal care and support. The Belgian voucher system, and subsequently care and domestic help platforms, were an attempt to increase 'choice' in the market, while also encouraging providers to adapt to changing family and household needs. However, vouchers can only be used for specific domestic services (ie, cleaning, cooking, ironing and laundry services) as the provision of services more closely related to personal assistance remains within state social care structures. The voucher system is organised around a 'triangular' scheme that connects domestic service agencies, clients and workers.[42] Clients use vouchers to purchase domestic services through state-accredited domestic service agencies, which then assign workers to perform tasks. The agency acts as an employer, mediating and organising the provision of services to clients and hiring workers as regular full- or part-time employees. Cash-for-care schemes are designed to benefit people with disabilities or in conditions of non-self-sufficiency, such as the PVB/PAB budget (Personal Assistance Budget or *Persoonlijke-assistentiebudget/budget d'assistance personnel*) from the regional government (*Budgethouders/ Détenteurs de budget*). The PVB/PAB was first introduced in Flanders in 2001, a few years later in Wallonia in 2009 and then in the Brussels region. For example, *Helpper* specifically targets recipients of cash-for-care benefits for children and adults with disabilities (through PVB and PAB schemes who can use the platform to purchase specialist care or to reimburse family members who provide care and support), as well as those who are looking for generic support services (eg not professionally licensed health and care roles). For example, the *Helpper* website[43] states:

> Through Helpper, PVB/PAB become budget holders and care organizations that are looking for help with daily tasks such as transport, shopping, company, etc. connected with flexible & enthusiastic assistants from the neighbourhood.[44]

[41] ETUC, Platform Reps. Belgium Country Report 2022 (2023) <www.etuc.org/sites/default/files/page/file/2023-05/ETUC_country%20report_Belgium-EN.pdf>.

[42] A Safuta and B Camargo, 'The More Things Change, the More They Stay the Same? The Impact of Formalising Policies on Personalisation in Paid Domestic Work: The Case of the Service Voucher in Belgium' (2019) 7 *Comparative Migration Studies* 14.

[43] www.helpper.be/nl/home.

[44] Translated from original.

In tandem with reforms to the care and support system, a number of legal and tax reforms have also contributed to the growth of platforms, as well as the growth of a third category of 'peer-to-peer' worker that falls between regular employees and the self-employed. Whereas the legal basis of employment in Belgium is labour law and with it the entitlement to minimum wages, social security, trade union representation and collective bargaining, the legal basis of self-employment is civil law which excludes workers from minimum wages, trade union representation and collective bargaining, and workers are responsible for making their own social security contributions. Peer-to-peer (P2P) workers have an ambiguous legal position in that they are similarly exempted from minimum wages and collective bargaining, they can make their own social security contributions (although this is not required) but they are theoretically eligible to be represented by a trade union.[45]

The De Croo Law passed in 2016 to regulate the 'collaborative economy' (*économie collaborative/deeleconomie*) specifically allowed for the provision of 'extra' domestic and care support carried out in a P2P form, although many food delivery and other consumer platforms took advantage of the P2P exemptions. For example, P2P workers are exempt from tax and social contributions on earnings up 7,000€ (as of 2024), which was designed to formalise and legitimise platform work as a source of supplementary income (eg, seasonal work or part-time work while studying). However, around a quarter of platform workers earned the majority of their income from platforms, and there is some evidence that platforms simply 'switch workers off' once they have reached the €7,000 threshold.[46] There are also other exemptions for categories of workers who are not part of the voucher system such as babysitters, who cannot work for more than eight hours per week without a formal contract of employment. The appeal for platforms is that they do not have to make social security contributions (as an employer would), and the appeal for workers is that they do not have to register as self-employed for the purposes of VAT payments and social security contributions.

The Royal Decree of 2017 followed shortly after De Croo's Law and established a system of official accreditation for platforms that wish to use the P2P tax regime. The criteria for accreditation mostly concern the registration of companies within the EEA for the purposes of tax and VAT at a rate no less than would be applied within Belgium.[47] No specific provisions are made for the type of service, the number of workers or the volume of transactions. Platforms are not obliged to apply for accreditation to operate in Belgium, although the

[45] ETUC, Platform Reps. Belgium Country Report 2022 (2023) <www.etuc.org/sites/default/files/page/file/2023-05/ETUC_country%20report_Belgium-EN.pdf>.

[46] ETUC, Platform Reps. Belgium Country Report 2022 (2023) <www.etuc.org/sites/default/files/page/file/2023-05/ETUC_country%20report_Belgium-EN.pdf>.

[47] Eurofound, *Loi De Croo (Belgie programmawet 2016021055) (Initiative), Record number 2971, Platform Economy Database* (2021, Dublin) <https://apps.eurofound.europa.eu/platformeconomydb/loi-de-croo-belgie-programmawet-2016021055-103167>.

number of accredited firms nearly doubled between 2019 and 2020, from 68 to 127.[48] Accredited firms include food delivery companies such as *Deliveroo* and *UberEats*, along with a number of 'miscellaneous' platforms, such as *Helpper* and *RingTwice* (which was the first accredited platform). Most of these larger platforms utilise the P2P arrangement for at least 80 per cent of their workforce.

In 2021, it was estimated that 42,618 people worked under this regime (including over 20,000 in the transport sector and almost 12,000 in 'miscellaneous services to persons', such as care services).[49] Thus, a significant share of workers engaged in platform work are beyond the system of collective bargaining and social protection.[50] And while a 10.7 per cent tax rate now applies to P2P workers this is still far below the regular 33 per cent rate for employees, and workers are still exempt from mandatory social security contributions.[51] In February 2022, the Belgian government introduced a 'new labour deal' that establishes a legal presumption of employment for platform workers as of 1 January 2023 and obliges platforms to provide accident insurance to self-employed workers as of 1 January 2026. This measure addresses the heightened risk of workplace accidents for platform workers, who are more likely to face task-related risks compared to the average worker. For example, the new law will ensure that all platform workers will receive compensation for accidents occurring during work or commutes. Compensation will be based on the incapacity benefit for a single self-employed person, typically exceeding the earnings of most platform workers. A separate fund will provide coverage in cases where platforms fail to secure the required insurance. Recent debates on the Belgian approach refer to the EU platform Directive and stress that the law will serve as a 'complementary' and not a 'substitutive' safeguard of platform workers' rights, extending protections to all platform workers, including those who genuinely operate as self-employed. However, at the time of writing these rules still do not apply to P2P workers, and weak enforcement of the rules means that very few (if any) self-employed or P2P workers have been converted into regular employees. This suggests that platform workers regardless of their employment status will still lack protection in the future.

V. PEER-TO-PEER PRECARITY

As discussed above, the specific Belgian P2P arrangement is central to the operation of both *Helpper* and *RingTwice*, which brings with it a number

[48] ETUC, Platform Reps. Belgium Country Report 2022 (2023) <www.etuc.org/sites/default/files/page/file/2023-05/ETUC_country%20report_Belgium-EN.pdf>.

[49] ETUC, Platform Reps. Belgium Country Report 2022 (2023) <www.etuc.org/sites/default/files/page/file/2023-05/ETUC_country%20report_Belgium-EN.pdf>.

[50] V Pulignano and W van Lancker, 'Digital Cleavages and Risk in the Platform Economy in Belgium' (2021) 159 *Sociologia del lavoro* 71.

[51] Franke et al (n 1).

of contradictions. On the one hand, platforms have created flexible earnings opportunities in the formal economy for those with limited work experience, or who wish to earn a small supplementary income without the administrative burden of registering as self-employed. On the other hand, platforms have also arguably further normalised low paying and precarious work, by blurring the boundaries between different occupations and tasks, and transferring risks onto individual workers.

Platforms have been keen to leverage the apparent legitimacy of the 'collaborative economy' and emphasise the mutual benefits to both service users and workers of highly tailored but also flexible support at home. For example, the *RingTwice* website points to the ready availability of 'talented neighbours' to help with specific tasks, whereas for workers the website emphasises the opportunities to 'monetise skills'. The added value of the platform is to facilitate easy connections between clients and workers that comply with the relevant laws and regulations. For example, *Helpper* charges a 2€ fee from clients for every transaction and subtracts the 10.7 per cent taxes for P2P workers. The website makes explicit reference to the €7,000 tax free limit, and the easy handling of payments via the platform. *Helpper* also offers an additional service to beneficiaries of PVB and PAB, setting up the paperwork to report on these expenses under the two budget schemes.

Both *Helpper* and *RingTwice* also ensure workers' compliance with the P2P regulation by filing, 'in accordance with the legislation, your income to the FPS finance. . . . So that's another reassurance'.[52] As they do so, they relieve workers of significant administrative work, which raises workers' appreciation in that 'all the administrative stuff is taken care of anyway. You don't have to start dealing with contracts or insurance anymore'.[53]

In this way the platform provides a sense of safety: 'You normally, in nearly all cases, stay on the platform so that you can have guarantees, of the insurance and of the fact that your work is declared'.[54] In addition, clients attach value to the insurance provided through the platforms as well: 'Families want to go through the platform because there is insurance. Even though they have to pay for a subscription, they do it because it's insured, and that's important'.[55]

For clients, *RingTwice* has a detailed evaluation system, classifying workers in five 'experience levels' based on clients' ratings, number of jobs performed via the platform, seniority on the platform, recurrent clients and steps taken in the platforms' identification procedure. This acts as an additional element of trust-creation, especially from the client's perspective in that 'it is often based on the reputation that a client chooses the person who has more experience, more

[52] *Helpper* worker, female, age 32, cooking and IT support for disabled clients.
[53] *Helpper* worker, female, age 22, support and assistance to elderly and disabled clients.
[54] *RingTwice* worker, male, age 35, cleaning, gardening and handiwork.
[55] *RingTwice* worker, female, age 47, babysitting and domestic tasks.

clients, etc. And this [good rating] obviously gives us more chances to be hired by clients through the platform'.[56]

Ring Twice 'gamifies' the application procedure by limiting to six the number of prospective providers who can apply for one job which spurs competition to 'be the first' to reply. More broadly, the large pool of standby workers keeps response times short and rates of pay low: 'Talented neighbours, just around the corner from you! Request a service and choose the best offer from 50,000 individuals and self-employed people!'[57]

There is clearly significant heterogeneity within the P2P platform workforce in terms of age, gender and nationality (see Appendix), but for many, working via the platform was an important alternative to regular employment, either as a direct employee within the public sector, or via employment agencies where qualifications and experience requirements were typically higher. Workers reported being able to: 'take small jobs, something easy, and that interests me. So I am not forced to do it, I just apply for what I want' and 'it's usually 3–4 hours, and that's a little top-up, and then you see a different place and meet different people. That's fun'.[58]

RingTwice also promotes platform work as a good opportunity for self-employed workers to start up their own business: 'for starting young independents, it could be a nice springboard to look for some work there'.[59]

The low rates of pay on offer within the P2P structure could also incentivise workers to go fully self-employed:

> those [platform] prices are a lot lower than a self-employed person should charge. I sometimes see the prices and I'm shocked because I think: there are self-employed people, they can't survive.[60]

In theory P2P workers are free to set a tariff themselves (hourly or fixed-rate per job) however, *RingTwice* also suggests pay minima (and maxima) per job category and highlights to workers where rates of pay are above the market average. Interestingly, while some categories that require a degree of physical strength or basic technical skills such as 'small jobs around the hours', 'interior works' or 'transport' have a recommended price range of around €15–25 per hour, other tasks requiring caring and domestic skills such as 'housekeeping', 'pet sitting' and 'babysitting' command a suggested fee of just €8–15 per hour. Services on *Helpper* are typically advertised at lower rates than *RingTwice* (generally below €18 per hour) and *Helpper* also offers the possibility to recruit volunteers which strongly relies on notions of altruism:

> I want to contribute society, and if I can work less individually, I'd engage in volunteer work . . . I also wanted to earn something on the side, even if it's not a lot. That's how I ended up with Helpper. It's a truly great initiative . . . it is a gift.[61]

[56] *RingTwice* worker, female, age 75, babysitting and ironing.
[57] Translated from original.
[58] *RingTwice* worker, male, age 35, cleaning and gardening.
[59] *RingTwice* worker, male, age 48, gardening and handiwork.
[60] ibid.
[61] *Helpper* worker, male, age late 30s, support and assistance to elderly and disabled clients.

In some case jobs undertaken via the platform were being used to top up health insurance payments while on long-term sick leave:

> I'm on [long-term] sick leave now, paid by the health insurance. So I could apply for that, too . . . Because Helpper is not really an employer. That falls under the collaborative economy. . . . So, after your work. Or now my case, after the insurance.[62]

For many, the opportunity to contribute to society was as important as the additional income:

> The greatest act of kindness is found in caring for others, for in nurturing those in need, I discover the true essence of humanity . . . I think there are other ways to earn more, but I see a lot of purpose in doing this job which helps someone. In reality, it's not the kind of hard work I feel burdened by.[63]

Given the multiple problems arising with P2P work through digital platforms, trade unions have lobbied to have the De Croo exemption revoked and have pushed for a stronger enforcement of the 2023 law that presumes regular employment for platform workers (ETUC, 2023). However, the dispersed nature of the P2P workforce, and the largely private domestic settings within which work takes place, are major barriers to worker organising and collective action.

Moreover, it was argued that closing the P2P 'loophole' via the platform would simply drive more work into the offline informal economy:

> I would blame our government if they were to stop this system, I'd say that it would a big mistake. Because I am convinced that more than half of Ring Twice workers will continue to work in black.[64]

VI. DISCUSSION AND CONCLUSIONS

This chapter has explored the growth of multi-service marketplace platforms in Belgium that offer an increasingly wide range of domestic services to families and households, and the implications for work opportunities and earnings. The relatively rapid growth of such platforms, in a historically well-regulated welfare and labour market context, is a response to the increasing demand for flexible and affordable support within the home that is typically not available through the regular system of health and social care in Belgium. This demand includes non-medical care and personal assistance (particularly for those with disabilities and specific care needs) and childcare, along with various forms of handiwork, gardening and cleaning.

Our analysis shows how the expansion of platform mediated provision has been enabled, and legitimised, by the peculiarities of the Belgian labour market, welfare and taxation system. The voucher system introduced in 2001

[62] *Helpper* worker, male, age 45, support and assistance to elderly and disabled clients.
[63] *Helpper* worker, female, age 50, admin support to elderly and disabled clients.
[64] *RingTwice* worker, male, age 74, cooking, tutoring, house repair.

was designed to introduce a degree of choice and flexibility into the market for domestic support and assistance, and a number of reforms since 2016 were explicitly intended to stimulate the growth of platform businesses, including food delivery and support to households as part of the burgeoning 'collaborative economy'. Since 2017, companies that have received Royal Accreditation, are allowed to offer 'peer-to-peer' (P2P) work and to take advantage of various tax and social security exemptions, while also avoiding full employment protections and collectively agreed standards. Unsurprisingly many food delivery and miscellaneous platforms (including *Helpper* and *Ring Twice*) make extensive use of the P2P system. The intermediate category of P2P work exists in something of a grey zone between regular employment (which is protected by various labour and social rights) and self-employment (which is largely exempt from core labour rights and social protection). The P2P system was designed to create flexible labour market opportunities for younger workers, students, and others who were potentially excluded form 'regular' employment opportunities, and who did not want to register as fully self-employed. The findings show that P2P platforms can provide an important additional source of supplementary income for those with other commitments, or with a desire to help out in their local community. At the same time, the 'labour of love' argument compounds the subordinate position of workers (vis a vis clients and platform managers) as they are expected to accept unpaid and underpaid work for the greater good.[65] As with food delivery and other on-demand platforms, care platforms also rely on a large pool of flexible labour competing to be exploited,[66] and the P2P earnings threshold, combined with low hourly rates of pay means that workers (and their families) cannot rely on platform work to meet their subsistence needs.

Platforms also potentially contribute to work standardisation and de-professionalisation within care and domestic work through simplistic customer ratings and the blurring of occupational boundaries. In the case of *Helpper*, the offer of support from 'flexible and enthusiastic assistants' allows clients to choose from a menu of generic domestic and family support tasks but with no reference to the professional or occupational experience of workers, nor the specific qualifications required to be able to provide a high-quality service. Indeed, the main criteria for matching clients to workers are proximity, availability and price. In contrast, *RingTwice* preserves a degree of occupational specialism but also reinforces embedded patterns of gender segmentation in the labour market by organising, and pricing, tasks and services along the lines of supposedly distinct *technical* and *physical* skills (that are generally positioned as male jobs and are priced higher) and *caring* skills (that are generally positioned as female jobs

[65] GJ Whitfield, 'The Organising Model of Trade Unionism in England's Social Care Sector' (Doctoral dissertation, University of Sheffield, 2020); V Pulignano and M Domecka, *The Politics of Unpaid Labour. How the Study of Unpaid Labour Can Help Address Inequality in Precarious Work* (Oxford, Oxford University Press, 2025).

[66] van Doorn (n 28).

and are priced lower). More broadly, while multi-service platforms simplify the administrative process for both clients and workers, they also introduce additional complexity in that they require individuals to become micro-employers by negotiating hourly rates, work tasks and working patterns.[67]

While platform capitalism is not necessarily the future of work,[68] it is the current reality of work for those with few alternative opportunities such as younger workers, migrants and those with family caring responsibilities. Clearly the potential 'care fix' and 'work fix' offered by platforms brings a number of risks for clients, workers and the state, and the continued growth of multi-service platforms in the institutional grey zone of the 'collaborative economy' may require governments to rethink the rules around platform businesses and the precarious P2P relationships that they increasingly rely upon.

[67] Macdonald (n 2).

[68] D Azzellini, I Greer and C Umney, 'Why Platform Capitalism is Not the Future of Work' (2022) 2 *Work in the Global Economy* 272.

VII. APPENDIX: INTERVIEWS WITH KEY ACTORS

Number	Interview code	Gender	Age	Worker/ Manager	Platform/ organisation	Task performed
1	BEMFRT04	M	48	Worker	Ring Twice	Gardening and door installations
2	BEMFRT20	M	43	Worker	Ring Twice	Event planning
3	BEMFRT21	M	64	Worker	Ring Twice	House repair work
4	BEMFRT22	M	35	Worker	Ring Twice	Cleaning, help with moving, gardening, etc.
5	BEMFRT23	M	39	Worker	Ring Twice	House repair work
6	BEMFRT24	M	36	Worker	Ring Twice	IT support
7	BEMFRT25	F	55	Worker	Ring Twice	Hairdressing
8	BEMFRT26	M	74	Worker	Ring Twice	Cooking, tutoring, house repair work
9	BEMFRT28	M	62	Worker	Ring Twice	House renovation work
10	BEMFRT29	M	Early 60s	Worker	Ring Twice	House repair work (including electro-mechanical reparation)
11	BEMFRT31	F	47	Worker	Ring Twice	Babysitting and other domestic tasks
12	BEMFRT32	F	75	Worker	Ring Twice	Babysitting and ironing
13	BEMFRT33	M	38	Worker	Ring Twice	Gardening
14	BEMFRT34	M	54	Worker	Ring Twice	House repairing and IT support
15	BEMFRT50	F	59	Worker	Ring Twice	Babysitting, helping the elderly/people with disabilities, cooking, etc
16	BEEDRT01	M	21	Worker	Ring Twice	IT support

17	BEEDRT02	F	55	Worker	Ring Twice	Cooking, babysitting, support activities for people with disabilities
18	BEEDRT03	M	65	Worker	Ring Twice	Support activities and assistance to people with disabilities
19	BEEDRT04	F	47	Worker	Ring Twice	Babysitting and gardening
20	BEGTRT01	F	60	Worker	Ring Twice	Babysitting, tutoring, gardening, clothing repair
21	BEGTRT02	M	45	Worker	Ring Twice	Tutoring
22	BEGTRT03	M	28	Worker	Ring Twice	House repair work (including electro-mechanical reparation)
23	BEEDHE01	F	25	Worker	Helpper	Support activities and assistance to the elderly/people with disabilities (e.g. cooking, accompanying, transport, etc.)
24	BEEDHE02	F	62	Worker	Helpper	Support activities and assistance to the elderly/people with disabilities
25	BEEDHE03	F	70	Worker	Helpper	Support activities and assistance to the elderly/people with disabilities
26	BEEDHE04	F	23	Worker	Helpper	Support activities and assistance to the elderly/people with disabilities
27	BEGTHE01	M	45	Worker	Helpper	Support activities and assistance to the elderly/people with disabilities

Continued

(*Continued*)

Number	Interview code	Gender	Age	Worker/ Manager	Platform/ organisation	Task performed
28	BEGTHE02	M	Late 30s	Worker	Helpper	Support activities and assistance to the elderly/people with disabilities (children in particular)
29	BEGTHE03	F	45	Worker	Helpper	Support activities and assistance to the elderly/people with disabilities, babysitting
30	BEGTHE04	F	50	Worker	Helpper	Admin support to elderly/people with disabilities
31	BEGTHE05	F	57	Worker	Helpper	Support activities and assistance to the elderly/people with disabilities
32	BEGTHE06	F	27	Worker	Helpper	Support activities and assistance to the elderly/people with disabilities
33	BEGTHE07	F	28	Worker	Helpper	Support activities and assistance to the elderly/people with disabilities
34	BEKLHE01	F	28	Worker	Helpper	Support activities and assistance to the elderly/people with disabilities
35	BEKLHE02	F	22	Worker	Helpper	Support activities and assistance to the elderly/people with disabilities
36	BEKLHE03	F	32	Worker	Helpper	Cooking (for people with disabilities) and IT support
37	BEKLHE04	F	24	Worker	Helpper	Support activities and assistance to the elderly/people with disabilities

38	BEKLHE05	M	48	Worker	Helpper	Support activities and assistance to the elderly/people with disabilities
39	BEKLHE06	F	23	Worker	Helpper	Babysitting (mostly children with disabilities)
40	BEKLHE07	F	33	Worker	Helpper	Support activities and assistance to the elderly/people with disabilities
41	BEKLHE08	F	-	Worker	Helpper	Support activities and assistance to people with disabilities
42	BEMFEX04	M	-	Manager	Ring Twice	-
43	BEMFEX10	M	-	Manager	Ring Twice	-
44	BEMFEX14	M	-	Manager	Helpper	-
45	BEMFEX12	M	-	Manager	Mobilant vzw (no-profit care organisation)	-
46	BECMEX06	M	-	Manager	Alin vzw (no-profit care organisation)	-
47	BEMFEX13	M	-	Manager	Exxtra (no-profit care organisation)	-
48	BEMFEX09	M	-	Manager	Federgon Vlaanderen	-

Part II

Adaptations to Legal Frameworks from a Comparative Perspective

4

Business as Usual? Strategic Adaptation and Effects on Labour Formalisation in Domestic Work Platforms in Southeast Europe

JELENA STARČEVIĆ

I. INTRODUCTION

OVER THE PAST decade, the paid domestic work sector has witnessed a significant surge in the number of digital labour platforms offering domestic work.[1] Digital labour platforms are credited for bringing innovation in recruitment and reconfiguring the concept of intermediaries in the domestic work sector, positioning themselves as next-generation placement agencies.[2] Entering a particularly vulnerable and unprotected sector,[3] digital labour platforms are seen as potentially playing an important role in fostering formalisation and improving working conditions. Features of the platform business model, such as transparency of pay rates, digitised transactions and establishment of formal communication channels, contribute to increased visibility and

[1] International Labour Organization, *Making Decent Work a Reality for Domestic Workers – Progress and Prospects Ten Years After the Adoption of the Domestic Work Convention, 2011* (Geneva, ILO, 2021).

[2] A Hunt and T Machingura, 'A Good Gig? The Rise of On-Demand Domestic Work' (2016) *Policy File*. Overseas Development Institute.

[3] According to the ILO, there are 75.6 million domestic workers globally, of which 76.2 per cent are women; this sector is also characterised by high informality, as 81.2 per cent of all work is performed informally. Informal work includes a lack of legal status and/or access to labour and social rights and a lack of some elements of formal employment (for example, having a formal contract but not being registered on social insurance or not benefitting from paid annual leave or sick leave).

(selective) formalisation of domestic work.[4] However, the characteristics of the platform business model, which focus on empowering customers and avoiding responsibilities for workers, cast doubts that they are able to contribute to the meaningful formalisation of domestic workers or the improvement of working conditions.

Rather than viewing digital labour platforms as either vectors of formalisation or as mechanisms of precarisation, recent scholarship has increasingly turned to examining how features of the national institutional framework shape the intervention of digital labour platforms and their impact on workers' labour status and protection. Many authors advance the idea of different embeddedness, showing how domestic service platforms adapt across different national contexts.[5] Other scholars have examined the variety of work arrangements found on digital labour platforms for domestic work, highlighting how these are closely shaped by the incentives and constraints imposed by national regulatory frameworks. In some countries, platforms are willing to hire workers directly if they can take advantage of public funds,[6] whereas in other countries, regulations can effectively exempt platforms from assuming statutory employer responsibilities.[7] Highly regulated labour markets for domestic and care work can also generate informality.[8] This chapter builds on this scholarship by examining how platform business models in the domestic work sector in Southeast Europe are shaped by institutional settings and, in turn, how these models influence the labour status and working conditions of domestic workers.

Countries in Southeast Europe are no exception to the growing presence of digital intermediaries in the domestic work sector. While their emergence follows the broader expansion of platform labour in sectors such as ride-hailing and food delivery, the platformisation of domestic services in this region has remained modest and is primarily driven by local start-ups rather than transnational actors. The three countries focused on in this chapter – Slovenia, Croatia and Serbia – also present a distinct institutional context for exploring the impact

[4] See N van Doorn, 'Stepping Stone or Dead End? The Ambiguities of Platform-Mediated Domestic Work under Conditions of Austerity. Comparative Landscapes of Austerity and the Gig Economy: New York and Berlin' in D Baines and I Cunningham (eds), *Working in the Context of Austerity: Challenges and Struggles* (Bristol, Policy Press Scholarship Online, 2021); CE Weber, M Okraku, J Mair and I Maurer, 'Steering the Transition from Informal to Formal Service Provision: Labor Platforms in Emerging-Market Countries' (2021) 19 *Socio-Economic Review* 1315; J Ticona and A Mateescu, 'Trusted Strangers: Carework Platforms' Cultural Entrepreneurship in the on-Demand Economy' (2018) 20 *New Media & Society* 4384.

[5] N Koutsimpogiorgos, K Frenken and AM Herrmann, 'Platform Adaptation to Regulation: The Case of Domestic Cleaning in Europe' (2023) 65 *Journal of Industrial Relations* 156.

[6] P Rodríguez-Modroño, A Agenjo-Calderón and P López-Igual, 'A Feminist Political Economic Analysis of Platform Capitalism in the Care Sector' (2023) 55 *The Review of Radical Political Economics* 629.

[7] N van Doorn, 'Platform Capitalism's Social Contract' (2022) 11 *Internet Policy Review* 1.

[8] V Pulignano, C Marà, M Franke and K Muszynski, 'Informal Employment on Domestic Care Platforms: A Study on the Individualisation of Risk and Unpaid Labour in Mature Market Contexts' (2023) 29 *Transfer* 323.

of digital labour intermediaries on domestic work, shaped by common socialist legacies and divergent trajectories of transition to capitalism. Each country inherited a system that promoted legal equality of women and a full set of labour rights and protections for domestic workers; however, the legal equality of women and domestic workers in employment did not translate into equality in the family and households as it coexisted with conservative conceptions of gender roles; more so, the ideological and cultural norms contributed to the stigmatisation of domestic work.[9] Following the transition period, each country pursued distinct approaches to adapting to new market realities, including varying strategies for labour market flexibility, different policies on women's labour market participation, and distinct approaches to regulating domestic work.

Today, Slovenia is an advanced capitalist country with low unemployment and a stable, formalised labour market, characterised by high female labour force participation and residual informality concentrated among the solo self-employed.[10] Croatia, still in the late stages of economic convergence, is characterised by a fluctuating labour market due to its tourism-driven demand for part-time and seasonal work as well as widespread undeclared and under-declared work among both self-employed and wage employees.[11] Female labour force participation declined during the 1990s state-building period but has gradually increased since EU accession. Serbia is a mixed-market economy with an incomplete transition, characterised by low wages, a low-skilled workforce and limited labour protections, especially among women. Informal employment remains widespread, particularly in agriculture, construction and domestic work, largely due to limited opportunities in the formal sector. These varied institutional conditions are expected to shape how domestic work platforms operate across the region and the extent to which they reinforce or reshape existing patterns of labour informality.

The chapter is based on a comparative analysis of three platform companies – *Beeping*, *Siterice* and *Uradi-Zaradi* – operating in the selected countries over the past decade.[12] *Beeping* is a local Slovenian start-up founded in 2015, which primarily offers cleaning services for private households and commercial clients; it later expanded its business to include elderly care. In less than three years, it has been recognised as the Slovenian Start-up of the Year as a successful model of data-driven business operations. It still operates in four major cities in Slovenia and has over 200 cleaners. Beeping also expanded to neighbouring Croatia in 2017; however, while it remains active in the business register, it seems to have withdrawn from the market. *Siterice* is a Czech platform that provides cleaning

[9] V Tomšič, *Ženska v razvoju socialistične samoupravne Jugoslavije* [*Women in the Development of Socialist Self-Governing Yugoslavia*] (Ljubljana, Delavska enotonost, 1980).

[10] C Williams and IA Horodnic, 'Horizon scanning: early warning signals of future trends in undeclared work', European Platform Tackling Undeclared Work, Brussels, June (2020): 26 per cent of all self-employed without employees in Slovenia are considered to be in bogus self-employment.

[11] Williams and Horodnic (n 10).

[12] While some platforms have since ceased or suspended operations, their models remain analytically valuable for understanding platform adaptation and labour regulation dynamics in the region.

and babysitting services. It started operating in Croatia toward the end of 2023, in 10 major cities and has 289 cleaners on its roster. *Uradi-Zaradi* is a Serbian start-up founded in 2016, initially as a multi-service platform; it has focused on providing only cleaning services since 2018, with more than 200 active cleaners. The platform operations are currently on hiatus due to unresolved issues related to its payment processing model; however, the platform's founder remains active in policy debates on platform work and labour regulation.

Data collection on the platforms' operations was primarily based on desk research gathered from publicly available information on their websites and terms of service. For a more in-depth understanding of platforms' operations, desk research was expanded in two ways: first, I created accounts on each platform and conducted basic interactions; second, I conducted informational interviews with one platform co-founder and five platform workers. The analysis employed a comparative qualitative approach, incorporating discursive, thematic and legal analysis, which specifically examined organisational discourse, legal positioning and core business model features. These elements are analysed and compared across national institutional conditions, with the aim of understanding how platforms adapt their strategies to local contexts and how these adaptations shape the labour status and protections of domestic workers. The findings show that platforms operating within the domestic work sector adapt their strategies and business models to local institutional and regulatory contexts, resulting in varied interventions. Furthermore, the findings demonstrate that the impact of digital platforms on labour status and protection in the domestic work sector also varies, as platforms engender different work arrangements spanning the (in)formality continuum, from (bogus) self-employment, under-declared work, to informal work.[13]

This chapter is structured as follows: first, I examine the strategic positioning of platforms through their organisational discourse and legal classifications. The following section assesses the intervention of digital platforms by examining their core functions and operational adaptations. The final section discusses how the interplay between the institutional framework and platform business models impacts labour status and labour protection of domestic workers.

II. STRATEGIC POSITIONING: LEGITIMACY NARRATIVES AND LEGAL CLASSIFICATION

To understand how digital intermediaries intervene in the domestic work sector, it is essential to begin by examining how platforms present themselves and define their role. This includes analysing the organisational discourse they deploy to

[13] J Fudge and C Hobden, *Conceptualizing the Role of Intermediaries in Formalizing Domestic Work* (Geneva, ILO, 2018) conceive formality and informality as a continuum, with one pole marked by no employee status and no minimum rights, and the other by full registration, written records and social-security coverage, while most arrangements fall somewhere in between.

frame their role and gain legitimacy, and how they position themselves in relation to existing legal frameworks. These elements not only reflect how platforms seek to distinguish themselves from traditional employers or agencies but also reveal how they adapt to, navigate or contest institutional conditions in different national contexts.

A. Organisational Discourse

Digital platforms in the domestic work sector employ organisational discourse similar to that of their counterparts in the transportation and food delivery sectors, emphasising the ease of obtaining services and their convenience. This is most pronounced in the case of *Beeping* in Slovenia. The platform promises users the ability to 'enjoy a clean and tidy home' and have 'extra free time for more pleasant things in life' in just '60 seconds'.[14] Such a narrative resonates strongly in Slovenia, addressing the high demand for domestic work from dual-income households. With the female employment rate among the highest in the European Union,[15] the growing dependence on the labour market and increased work demands have made domestic services essential, particularly for middle- and higher-income dual-career couples with children, who are the primary users of domestic services, such as cleaning and ironing.[16] *Beeping*'s discourse directly taps into the broader neoliberal logic of time optimisation and consumer empowerment, portraying domestic work not as labour to be valued but as a service to be seamlessly integrated into one's lifestyle.[17]

In addition to this broad narrative of convenience, *Beeping* (SLO) also draws on a normative discourse aimed at legitimising itself as a formalising agent in a sector marked by informality. Such strategic positioning responds to the characteristics of the labour supply in Slovenia, primarily performed by women in economically vulnerable positions, such as unemployed women, women in low-paid jobs or immigrant women, who often turn to informal arrangements as a survival strategy.[18] It also responds to government efforts to combat informality in this sector. Namely, in efforts to combat undeclared work, in 2014, the Slovenian government introduced a new legal form of personal supplementary work, under which households can hire domestic workers without establishing employment relationships, provided they pay social security contributions in the

[14] Beeping.si, House cleaning, www.beeping.si.

[15] Eurostat, Employment and Activity by Sex and Age - Annual Data, 2024. https://doi.org/10.2908/LFSI_EMP_A.

[16] M Hrženjak, 'Hierarchization and Segmentation of Informal Care Markets in Slovenia' (2012) 19 *Social Politics* 38.

[17] N van Doorn, 'Platform Labor: On the Gendered and Racialized Exploitation of Low-Income Service Work in the "On-Demand" Economy' (2017) 20 *Information, Communication & Society* 898.

[18] Hrženjak (n 16).

form of vouchers.[19] This solution has been criticised for being overly costly and imposing complicated bureaucratic procedures.[20] Relying on a legally ambiguous category of self-employed cleaners, *Beeping* (SLO) responds to these institutional frictions by inviting customers to 'end the black market together', positioning itself as a modern, user-friendly and ethical alternative to both informal arrangements and the voucher system.

However, in markets where paid domestic work remains uncommon and socially obscured, such as the case of Croatia, platforms adopt a discourse of normalisation, primarily oriented toward increasing trust and adoption among hesitant clients. Notably, *Beeping*, which in Slovenia promoted itself as a formalising agent, adjusted its discourse in Croatia, branding itself instead as the 'Uber for cleaning'. This discourse emphasises technological familiarity and lifestyle convenience over formalisation, reflecting the different barriers to market uptake in each country. In Croatia, where outsourcing domestic work is not widespread, this discursive shift positions domestic work platforms as part of a modern, aspirational way of life, rather than a corrective to informality. This can be further linked to characteristics of the labour market and cultural norms. In contrast to Slovenia's strong support for female labour market participation, the Croatian post-socialist transition was marked by retraditionalisation and religious revival, which promoted a new pronatalist agenda and reasserted traditional patriarchal family and gender norms.[21] Despite a recent rise in dual-income households and a steady increase in female labour force participation (from 54 per cent in 2014 to 66 per cent in 2023),[22] recent surveys show that 90 per cent of Croatian households have never used paid domestic help.[23] Cultural expectations continue to assign household labour primarily to women, with 67 per cent reporting that they carry out domestic tasks entirely or mostly by themselves.[24] Assistance is more commonly sought through informal networks, such as grandmothers, neighbours or friends, and typically goes undeclared, reflecting how social norms obscure paid work.[25] Similarly, *Siterice* adopts an explicitly client-oriented normalising discourse.

[19] *Zakon o preprečevanju dela in zaposlovanja na črno* [Prevention and Detection of Undeclared Work Act], *Uradni list RS* [Official Gazette of the Republic of Slovenia], no 32/2014.

[20] I Selišnik, 'Experiences from the Past: Domestic Help Workers and Legal Solutions' (2021) 29 *Acta Histriae* 947.

[21] T Pavasović Trošt and K Slootmaeckers, 'Religion, Homosexuality and Nationalism in the Western Balkans: The Role of Religious Institutions in Defining the Nation' in K Slootmaeckers, H Touquet and P Vermeersch (eds), *Religious and Sexual Nationalisms in Central and Eastern Europe* (Leiden, Brill, 2015) 154.

[22] Eurostat, *Employment and Activity* (n 15).

[23] Odjel za sociologiju Sveučilišta u Zadru, *Ispitivanje javnog mišljenja i potreba roditelja maloljetne djece: Istraživački izvještaj* [University Department of Sociology, University of Zadar, *Survey on Public Opinion and the Needs of Parents of Minor Children: Research Report*] (July 2022).

[24] European Institute for Gender Equality (EIGE), *Gender Equality Index: Croatia, 2022*. www.eige.europa.eu/gender-equality-index/2022/country/HR.

[25] C Williams, M Radvansky and M Stefanik, *The Extent and Nature of Undeclared Work in Croatia* (2017) SSRN Working Paper 2944950, www.ssrn.com/abstract=2944950.

It emphasises that 'every cleaner at Siterice.hr is insured', appealing to users' concerns about safety and trust, while also highlighting the ability for clients to choose a cleaner according to their own ideas.[26] This narrative builds legitimacy through risk mitigation and customisation, addressing the need to normalise paid domestic work without directly challenging social and family norms.

A third discursive strategy observed across platforms is differentiation, employed to distinguish the platform from existing intermediaries in a market where outsourcing is already more common. Among the three countries, Serbia reports the highest share of households using paid domestic help (2.3 per cent) and the largest proportion of domestic workers employed through intermediaries (27.8 per cent).[27] Despite this, most domestic workers in Serbia continue to operate informally, regardless of intermediary involvement; traditional agencies are often viewed unfavourably, as even through agencies, work is commonly performed based on verbal agreement and uncertainties regarding working conditions and payments.[28] As a result, *Uradi-Zaradi* does not focus on normalising domestic work, nor does it position itself as a formalising agent, but rather employs organisational discourse to differentiate itself from social norms and existing intermediaries, while at the same time responding to characteristics of labour supply and demand. For example, by referring to cleaners as 'associates', the platform tries to differentiate itself from traditional stigmas associated with the use of paid domestic work and its traditional undervaluation. This narrative is specifically tailored to appeal to employed women from urban areas with high levels of education, who are the primary target audience. Reframing domestic labour as comparable to other forms of legitimate work also aims to rebrand the character of labour supply, which is predominantly filled by women from rural areas with lower education, women working in low-wage jobs, or beneficiaries of social assistance.[29] At the same time, *Uradi-Zaradi* employs a discourse that differentiates it from traditional agencies by emphasising that domestic workers on their platform have the ability to earn a living wage, enjoy fair management practices and equality, and an environment free of discrimination.[30] Through framing domestic labour as professional and socially valuable work, *Uradi-Zaradi* tries to position itself within Serbia's informal and segmented domestic economy.

[26] Siterice.hr, *Home Cleaning*, www.siterice.hr.

[27] ILO (n 2).

[28] ASTRA, *Position and Challenges of Women Workers in Cleaning and Care Services in Serbia – Rapid Assessment* (Belgrade, ASTRA, 2024).

[29] I Đorđević, *Ex Ante Analiza Proširenja Sistema Pojednostavljenog Angažovanja Radnika na Privremenim i Povremenim Poslovima* [*Ex Ante Analysis of Expanding the Simplified System of Engaging Workers for Temporary and Occasional Jobs*] (Belgrade, GIZ, 2020).

[30] Fairwork, *Fairwork Serbia Ratings 2022: Labour Standards in the Platform Economy* (Belgrade, Serbia; Oxford, United Kingdom, 2022).

B. Legal Positioning

Beyond symbolic strategies and organisational discourse, platforms also engage in legal positioning, actively defining their legitimacy and role within existing institutional frameworks. This primarily involves classifying their legal status in relation to business and labour regulation. Traditionally, intermediaries in the domestic work sector can be private enterprises that directly employ workers (where households are only consumers), or recruitment and employment agencies that act as labour brokers, matching households and workers, or serving as direct employers.[31] Unlike these traditional intermediaries, digital platforms strategically position themselves as a distinct category that operates outside the regulatory frameworks typically applied to labour intermediation or service provision.

All observed platform companies are registered as private, limited liability companies within the respective national business registers. As their primary business activity, all observed platforms listed some digital services, such as web solution development (*Beeping* Slovenia), IT services (*Beeping* Croatia), web portals (*Uradi-Zaradi* Serbia) or providing space for communication with other users (*Siterice* Croatia). This type of legal registration falls within a broader pattern of regulatory evasion, where digital platforms intentionally classify themselves as information society services to avoid more stringent, high-barrier sectoral regulation, whether it relates to care work or taxi services.[32] However, its application in the domestic work sector is particularly notable, given that cleaning is a low-barrier field with no formal licensing or professional requirements. Even in the lightly regulated sector of domestic cleaning, platforms do not want to bear the costs or risks of service provision. As *Uradi-Zaradi*'s terms of service clearly state, the platform is 'not responsible for the quality and improper performance of obligations' arising from services facilitated through the platform.[33]

This legal classification also shapes another important aspect of platform positioning: the application of labour and employment regulation. Although platforms register as IT service providers, their functional role often resembles that of regulated intermediaries. In Slovenia, Croatia and Serbia, both recruitment and employment agencies are subject to licensing and employment agencies, which assign workers to user firms, are treated as legal employers and are responsible for contracts, social security contributions and employment rights. Platforms, by contrast, avoid these classifications by presenting themselves as neutral facilitators merely connecting 'visitors of the website and professional cleaners'[34] and distancing themselves from any contractual

[31] Fudge and Hobden (n 13).

[32] F Macdonald, 'Care Work, Individualisation and Risk' in S Rangel and U Pape (eds), *Individualising Risk: Paid Care Work in the New Gig Economy* (Singapore, Springer Singapore, 2021) 135.

[33] *Uradi-Zaradi*, Terms of Service, www.uradi-zardi.rs/terms.

[34] *Beeping.si*, Terms of Use, www.beeping.si.

obligations in respect to workers and clients in their terms of service. For example, *Siterice*'s terms of use state that users (customers and cleaners) are 'solely responsible for the correct identification of the legal relationship' between them and 'for the fulfilment of all obligations that the legal regulations associate with such a relationship'.[35]

It is interesting to note that *Beeping* (SLO) does not fully exclude itself from the contractual relationship: its terms of use specify that cleaners perform work 'in the name and on behalf of the platform'.[36] This suggests a higher degree of involvement in organising and supervising service provision, potentially bringing *Beeping* closer to the legal definition of an employer or labour intermediary under national labour laws. Despite this, *Beeping* is still able to avoid such classification by relying on a self-employment model in which cleaners are engaged as independent contractors. Crucially, this legal distancing is made possible not only through contractual arrangements but also through the company's classification in the business register as a web solution development, illustrating the importance of both business and labour regulation in defining the role of digital intermediaries.

III. PLATFORM FUNCTIONS AND BUSINESS MODEL ADAPTATIONS

Although digital platforms in the domestic work sector adopt remarkably similar legal strategies and present themselves as mere technical intermediary, their actual operations reveal significant variation. Their core functions, such as registration procedures, matching and selection systems, pricing structures, quality control, payment models and labour status of workers, showcase different levels of platform involvement in the labour process. These operational differences reflect not only the platforms' business logics but also their strategic adaptations to distinct institutional and market contexts. By comparing these functional features, this section demonstrates how domestic work platforms selectively blend elements from on-demand and marketplace models to construct hybrid business models that both manage risk and shape labour conditions.

A. Access and Selection

Across all platforms, registration is free, but access to certain features often requires memberships, subscriptions or premium status. These features shape both the supply and demand sides of the market and are part of how platforms manage and control participation in the labour process. For example, *Beeping*'s

[35] *Siterice*. Hr. Terms and Conditions, www.siterice.hr.
[36] *Beeping.si* (n 34).

subscription plan allows clients to choose permanent cleaners. Similarly, membership status on *Siterice* allows users to contract workers directly. By layering access through paid tiers, platforms do not merely act as technical intermediaries, but as active market-making agents that shape who can participate and under what conditions.

On the supply side, platforms similarly construct a layered system of visibility and access through profile requirements, premium features and selection process. On platforms that support user-driven selection, such as *Siterice*, domestic workers are expected to present themselves through photos, skill descriptions, languages spoken, education and other personal details aimed at attracting clients. The platform aggregates these profiles into a pool of workers and uses an algorithm to suggest specific profiles to clients based on criteria such as responsiveness and verification status. Furthermore, workers are incentivised to pay for premium profiles to gain greater visibility and prominence in search results, increasing their chances of being hired. This model illustrates a system of asymmetric visibility, in which clients provide minimal information, while workers bear the burden of self-promotion and compliance with the platform's presentation logic.

Uradi-Zaradi, by contrast, combines elements of marketplace visibility with more centralised control over matching. While workers still have to create profiles, the platform handles the matching process internally. Workers' profiles form a roster from which the platform identifies the appropriate worker for the requested task. Communication between the worker and the customer is enabled only after a match is made, and exclusively through the platform's chat system. On the other end of the spectrum, when matching is entirely centralised and managed internally by the platform, as with Beeping, cleaners are rendered invisible to clients and are only required to provide basic information about their location, availability and the duration of services. These matching and access structures illustrate how platforms exercise varying degrees of control over entry into the labour process and visibility within the marketplace.

B. Tasks and Remuneration

Across the three platforms, there are significant differences in how the terms of work are defined and how remuneration is determined. While most on-demand platforms in sectors like ride-hailing or food delivery are designed for short-term, hourly-paid tasks, *Beeping* diverges from this model by structuring services around recurring, fixed-price packages that incentivise long-term engagement between clients and cleaners. Although one-off tasks are available (within a 48-houring window), the platform incentivises clients to subscribe to recurring cleaning packages through price discounts and continuity features, such as the ability to retain the same cleaner for a premium. This operational adaptation, while aimed at reinforcing customer loyalty and increasing client retention, also redefines the transactional logic of on-demand models and introduces a degree of job security for workers by building continuity in a client-worker relationship.

Similarly, *Uradi-Zaradi* encourages recurring service through bundle packages and fostering stable client-worker relationships; the operational practice is to assign the same cleaners to returning clients. In terms of remuneration, the platform retains the hourly rate payment system. Although this piecework structure reflects typical on-demand pricing, *Uradi-Zaradi* guarantees a minimum payment of three euros per hour, regardless of the package, providing a floor for income security.[37] This hybrid approach blends on-demand operational control with elements that gesture toward improved working conditions.

By contrast, *Siterice* plays no role in defining the scope of work or remuneration. There is no pre-determined pricing or task structure; clients and cleaners are free to define their own conditions. This model affords greater formal autonomy to workers but also increases exposure to uncertainty, fluctuating expectations and informal arrangements. This approach aligns well with the marketplace model, which intensifies competition among workers, especially in the labour market with limited alternative employment opportunities.

C. Fees and Payments

The platforms also differ in how they structure fees and manage payment systems, key mechanisms through which they extract value and allocate responsibility in the labour transaction. These arrangements reflect the platforms' underlying business models and their broader strategies for managing financial and legal risk.

Beeping and Uradi-Zaradi both charge service fees to workers, deducted directly from their earnings. On *Beeping*, these fees can reach up to 25 per cent, while *Uradi-Zaradi* applies a slightly lower rate of 18 per cent. In both cases, the fee structure reflects a broader pattern of cost externalisation, where platforms monetise access to clients and shift the financial burden onto workers. In contrast, *Siterice* does not charge direct service fees to workers. Instead, it monetises platform use through premium profile subscriptions, which cleaners can purchase to enhance their visibility. This model avoids taking a share of workers' income but still introduces indirect costs for those seeking better access to clients.

Payment handling further distinguishes these platforms. *Beeping* manages all transactions internally, processing payments between clients and cleaners through the platform. This centralised approach not only facilitates fee collection but also reinforces *Beeping*'s position as an active intermediary, despite its legal classification as a mere technological intermediary.

[37] For a reference the cheapest package is five euros per hour.

Uradi-Zaradi and *Siterice* do not handle payments, but there is a significant difference between these two platforms. On *Siterice*, users are responsible for negotiating and executing payments independently, reinforcing the platform's self-identification as a marketplace. *Uradi-Zaradi* outsources payment processing to a third-party financial provider. This arrangement enables the platform to integrate into the financial exchange and capture revenue while maintaining its position as a pure marketplace.

D. Quality Assurance and Control

All three platforms deploy user ratings as the primary mechanism for monitoring service quality. However, they differ in the intensity and structure of their quality assurance practices. Beeping employs different strategies to ensure quality of service, including extensive verification checks that include criminal background checks, identity verification and interviews. It also offers formal training to ensure service quality and compliance with platform rules. Control through ratings is supplemented by occasional mystery shopper assessments.

Uradi-Zaradi also offers training, though less formalised, covering basic topics such as health and safety, communication and task-specific procedures. New workers undergo a probationary period, during which they must complete three trial tasks. Verification is more limited than on Beeping, including only an ID check and a phone interview.

Siterice, consistent with its marketplace model, takes a lighter-touch approach. Verification includes ID and background checks, but the responsibility for assessing service quality is left mainly to the clients. The platform does not provide training, but adjusts worker visibility in search results based on client ratings and verification status.

E. Labour Status of Domestic Workers

Finally, one of the most direct implications of platform model choices is how they determine the legal status of domestic workers, thereby affecting their access to employment rights and protections. *Beeping* (SLO) requires domestic workers to register as sole proprietors or limited liability companies as a prerequisite to becoming '*beepers*'. Moreover, *Beeping* actively encourages the formalisation of domestic work through self-employment by offering mentorship and assistance to workers in setting up their own firms. While self-employment status shifts all costs to workers and deprives them of labour protection, in Slovenia, self-employed individuals enjoy almost the same set of social security rights as employees, including pensions and disability insurance, health insurance, sickness benefits and parental care.

It is interesting to observe that, upon entering the Croatian market, *Beeping* modified its requirements regarding the legal status of cleaners by adding an option of using an intermediary. Namely, the platform relaxed its requirement of allowing access only to registered domestic workers as solo self-employed to allow domestic workers to work through other individual entrepreneurs or companies owned by someone workers know. This adaptation to local conditions was driven primarily by cleaners who do not wish to open their own firms because they are looking for flexible earning opportunities in addition to their regular employment.[38] It also mirrors the widespread practice of platforms operating in transportation and food delivery sectors, which overwhelmingly subcontract work to third parties – aggregators.[39] The use of third parties further distances platforms from any responsibility for workers and work arrangements in subcontracting chains; there is no evidence that *Beeping* supervises work arrangements between intermediaries and workers. Additionally, using third parties creates space for misappropriation and informality, as workers are usually denied their labour rights, and their wages and hours are underreported.[40] The consequences of such under-declared work are significant reductions in the amount of paid social contributions, which result in reduced future benefits and increased risk of poverty.

In contrast, *Siterice* and *Uradi-Zaradi* do not impose any requirements regarding the legal status of domestic workers. All responsibilities for formalising the relationship are transferred to households and workers, and the platform does not supervise compliance with local regulations. In the absence of any official data or empirical research about *Siterice*, the legal status of domestic workers cannot be verified, while limited data obtained from interviews with *Uradi-Zaradi* workers indicate that tasks are predominantly performed informally, with no contract with either platform or household.

Taken together, these functional differences reveal how domestic work platforms strategically blend and recalibrate elements of on-demand and marketplace models to manage risk, respond to institutional constraints and shape labour arrangements. These functional variations are summarised in Table 4.1, which highlights key differences in how the three platforms handle matching, labour status and work conditions, quality control and payment systems.

[38] D Kucinac, 'Uber za čišćenje. Platformski rad u Hrvatskoj: prekarnost skrivena iza online aplikacija', *Bilten*, 25 November 2021.

[39] See P Bejaković and P Gladoić Håkansson, 'Platform Work as an Important New Form of Labour in Croatia' (2021) 24 *Zagreb International Review of Economics & Business* 159; A Bilić and V Smokvina, 'What Lessons Could Croatia Learn from a Comparative Perspective Regarding the Labour Market Status of On-Demand Platform Workers?' (2022) 9 *InterEULawEast: Journal for the International and European Law, Economics and Market Integrations* 51; J Starčević, 'Platform Work in Croatia and Serbia: Varieties of Organizational Models and Work Arrangements' (2022) 2 *Hungarian Labour Law E-Journal* 58.

[40] B Predrag and P Gladoić Håkansson, 'Platform Work as an Important New Form of Labour in Croatia' (2021) 24 *Zagreb International Review of Economics & Business* 159.

Table 4.1 Overview of the main functions of digital platforms operating in the domestic work sector

Platform	Matching and Selection	Terms of Work	Quality control	Fees and Payments	Legal status
Beeping	Direct control – platform selects workers	Cleaning packages with a pre-determined price per package	Clients' rating Mystery shopper Verification Training	Charges fee to workers in the amount of 25% Handles all payments	Self-employment (SLO)/ Self-employment and subcontracting (CRO)
Siterice	Algorithmic curation of the pool of workers – clients choose workers	Clients and workers determine the terms of work	Clients' rating Verification	No direct fees Does not handle payments; clients and workers handle payments	No requirements
Uradi Zaradi	Direct control – platform selects workers	Cleaning packages with a pre-determined price per hour; guaranteed wage per hour	Clients' rating Verification Training Probation period	Charges fee to workers in the amount of 18% Does not handle payments; Outsources payment to third-party	No requirements

IV. STRATEGIC ADAPTATION AND THE REPRODUCTION OF VULNERABILITIES

This chapter analysed the intervention and adaptation of domestic work platforms in Southeast Europe. Digital labour platforms do not emerge in a vacuum – they interact with pre-existing institutional configurations that shape both the supply and demand for domestic work. As the cases of Slovenia, Croatia and Serbia illustrate, platform companies adjust their discourse, legal positioning and operational features in response to the local regulatory environment and cultural expectations. In doing so, they not only reflect existing institutional logics but also actively interpret, exploit and reshape them.

Looking at organisational discourse, three distinct discursive framings were observed: user-friendly formalisation, normalisation and differentiation. The variety of discursive framing reflects adaptations to distinct structures of the labour market supply and demand, as well as institutional and social norms surrounding domestic work. In Slovenia, user-friendly formalisation discourse is used in the effort to portray digital intermediaries as a solution to local institutional frictions and shortcomings. Normalisation discourse is evoked by digital intermediaries in Croatia, as they attempt to carve out their place within prevailing cultural norms that shape domestic work. In contrast, in Serbia, platforms employ a differentiation strategy to occupy a space in a market already heavily intermediated by traditional actors. While symbolic, these narratives play a constitutive role in reframing domestic work as modern, safe and professional work legitimised through the platform's role as a necessary market actor.[41]

At the same time, such discourses serve as a tool to shift attention from platforms as subjects of regulation reinforced by their legal positioning, where all three observed platforms strategically avoid being classified as service providers or labour intermediaries. Legal distancing, as evident in disclaimers within terms of service, reinforces the narrative that platforms are not parties to the contractual relationship between workers and clients. These strategies reflect broader institutional failures across observed countries to adapt regulatory categories to the realities of digitally mediated domestic work. In particular, there remains a notable absence of legal recognition of digital intermediaries as either sectoral service providers or as labour intermediaries subject to employer obligations, posing a few (if any) regulatory barriers to the way platforms organise domestic work.[42] As the findings show, platforms actively use this legal ambiguity as their strategic resource to avoid assuming responsibility for domestic work.

While outside the scope of this chapter, the introduction of a new regulatory framework for platform work in Croatia, effective as of January 2024, may signal shifts in how platforms in the region are classified and operated.[43] The new rules introduce the presumption of employment between platform companies and workers, thereby providing a legal basis for identifying platforms as employers. Whether and how this regulatory shift will be enforced, particularly in domestic work sectors, remains unclear, as neither *Beeping* nor *Siterice* (as of 2024) has been registered within the new register of digital labour platforms.

Lastly, the findings presented in this chapter demonstrate how, in interaction with national institutional systems, platforms adapt their primary business

[41] See also Teke-Laurent, ch 2, in this book on the use of rhetoric as market entry strategies of domestic work platforms in France.

[42] See Ratti, ch 10, in this book for discussion on legally treating platforms as labour market intermediaries.

[43] *Zakon o izmjenama i dopunama Zakona o radu* [Law Amending the Labour Act], *Narodne novine* [Official Gazette] 151/22.

features, resulting in substantial differences across countries and established business models.[44] The types of work arrangements promoted by platforms also result from interactions between business models and local institutional frameworks.

Beeping (SLO) exemplifies a hybrid model, blending features of the on-demand model and functions of traditional employers. It manages access to work, assigns tasks, sets pricing and payments, exercises controls through training, ratings, mystery shoppers and has the capacity to discipline and exclude workers from the platform. These features mirror a high degree of managerial control.[45] Moreover, it fosters stable client-worker relationships, diverging from the one-off task orientation characteristic of many on-demand models. Despite highly centralised control, the platforms promoted self-employment, as is typical of on-demand platforms.

The reliance on self-employed workers is reinforced by the structure of domestic work in Slovenia, which privileges the use of self-employed workers over direct employment and a broader institutional and cultural landscape where bogus self-employment serves as a regulatory workaround, enabling companies to sidestep employment liabilities while still exercising substantial control over workers. Slovenia's high female labour market participation rate drives demand for flexible and accessible domestic work, typically filled by women with fewer economic resources or lower-paying jobs. Such a structure of demand and supply creates favourable conditions for digital intermediaries offering easy, on-demand services. The personal supplement work regime further effectively shifted domestic workers from employees under general labour regulations toward self-employed individuals, exempting households from establishing employment relationships with domestic workers in return for paying discounted social security contributions. Under such structural conditions, *Beeping* is able to offer more convenient service to households by eliminating the administrative burden associated with the voucher system and shifting all the costs to domestic workers, who are now fully self-employed. Thus, *Beeping* established itself as a safe, easy and on-demand alternative to the informal market while relying on self-employed workers. In conclusion, *Beeping*'s model illustrates how digital labour intermediaries in domestic work in Slovenia can perpetuate informal employment structures, rebranded as self-employment.

Similarly, *Uradi-Zaradi* combines features of highly centralised, employer-like, on-demand platforms and marketplaces. The platform exercises a high degree of control in the selection process by imposing probation periods and terminating workers. It determines price in a piecemeal fashion and charges commission as an on-demand platform, but provides greater visibility and

[44] Compare Rodríguez-Modroño, ch 1, in this book.

[45] V De Stefano, 'The Rise of the "Just-in-Time Workforce": On-Demand Work, Crowd Work and Labour Protection in the "Gig-Economy"' (2016) 37 *Comparative Labor Law and Policy Journal* 471; J Prassl, *The Concept of the Employer* (Oxford, Oxford University Press, 2015).

does not handle payments as a marketplace. Most importantly, mimicking the features of marketplaces, it poses no requirements regarding the type of work arrangements. In the context of Serbian weak labour law enforcement and widespread informality, this results in high instances of informal work through the platform. The lack of legal regulation of platform companies and their role vis-à-vis workers has reinforced platforms' ability to renounce any responsibilities for workers, while the general regulation of domestic work does not incentivise households to formalise work relationships. The structure of labour supply, predominantly comprised of women from vulnerable backgrounds and driven by economic necessity, contributed to informality as they tend to prioritise higher take-home pay over formalising their work as self-employed individuals. In such conditions, digital intermediaries like *Uradi-Zaradi* become an attractive alternative for those groups that cannot rely on informal networks and personal recommendations, such as younger clients who embrace technological innovation and are unburdened by social stigma,[46] and cleaners who want to expand their pool of clients or transition to digital platforms from working through traditional agencies.[47] In conclusion, intervention brought about by digital intermediaries in the domestic sector in Serbia remains limited to the application of digital technologies, whereas domestic work continues to be characterised by informality, reinforced by a lack of effective supervision and enforcement of laws and the social construction of domestic work as gendered and unproductive work performed as a survival strategy by already economically vulnerable women.

Among the observed platforms, *Siterice* retains most of the features of a marketplace; clients choose workers from algorithmically curated roasters. Once the matching is complete, clients and workers agree on the terms of work and pay and handle all payments. The platforms have no occupational requirements or requirements regarding the formalisation of work relations, leaving most workers outside formal protections.

Another particularity observed across cases that merits attention is the introduction of an additional layer of intermediation by the platforms in the domestic sector. In an effort to diffuse responsibility and adapt to local conditions, *Beeping* in Croatia resorted to using subcontractors, while *Uradi-Zaradi* outsourced its payment processing. The subcontracting arrangement distances the platform from any responsibility for employment relationships, while subcontractors (and workers) bypass formal registration, social security contributions, or tax compliance through various means, including the misappropriation of employment contracts (eg, underreporting hours or wages). Similarly, the outsourced payment structure allows the platform to appear as though they have no role in the intermediation, despite controlling key aspects of the labour exchange, and complicates the traceability of income and employment relationships. In both

[46] ASTRA (n 28).
[47] Djordjevic (n 29).

cases, platform strategies result in a reconfiguration of intermediation that fragments responsibility, reduces transparency and facilitates under-declared or informal work.

V. CONCLUSION

This chapter has examined how digital labour platforms intervene in the domestic work sector in Slovenia, Croatia and Serbia, focusing on their organisational discourse, legal positioning, operational functions and impacts on labour formalisation. A comparative analysis of three domestic work platforms revealed that the way digital intermediaries intervene in domestic work is deeply shaped by national regulatory frameworks, labour market structures and cultural norms. Platform strategies – including discursive framings, legal classification, business functions and fee structures – are not just operational choices but strategic responses to regulatory gaps, normative expectations and opportunities to minimise liability. In doing so, platforms construct new forms of labour intermediation that often reproduce informal work arrangements, such as bogus self-employment, under-declared labour and informal work.

The chapter highlights that even in a shared regional context marked by socialist legacies and gendered constructions of care, there is no single model of platform adaptation. *Beeping*'s use of centralised control and formalised rhetoric in Slovenia contrasts with its subcontracted model in Croatia, while *Uradi-Zaradi*'s hybrid approach in Serbia reflects a calculated navigation of weak enforcement and normalised informality. These variations underscore the importance of attending to institutional conditions in understanding how digital platforms shape labour outcomes.

Ultimately, the emergence of digital intermediaries in the domestic work sector reveals more about the persistence and reinvention of informality than about innovation and disruption. Platform companies often harness digital tools to refine and entrench exploitative arrangements in ways that are difficult to detect and regulate. This calls for a rethinking of regulatory approaches – ones that are attuned to the specificities of the domestic work sector, capable of addressing multi-layered intermediation, and sensitive to the gendered, informal and often invisible nature of domestic work.

5

Within and Without the Margins of the Law: Digital Intermediaries in Domestic and Care Work in Latin America[*]

LORENA POBLETE

I. INTRODUCTION

PAID DOMESTIC WORK is a highly relevant occupation in Latin American countries, as it is one of the main sources of labour for low-income women, as well as migrant workers. According to the International Labour Organization (ILO), this sector represents 6.8 per cent of the workforce and 11.3 per cent of working women. As a region, Latin America account for almost 20 per cent of worldwide domestic work.[1]

The traditional understanding of paid domestic work as a servile labour exposes domestic workers to different forms of discrimination based on gender, ethnicity, race and social inequalities that structure Latin American societies.[2] Domestic workers usually experience precarious working conditions due to

* This research was funded by the Consejo Nacional de Investigaciones Científicas y Técticas (CONICET) Project PIP11220200100664CO and the Alexander von Humboldt Foundation. The chapter was written during a residency at the Rockefeller Foundation's Bellagio Center.

[1] ILO, Making Decent Work a Reality for Domestic Workers: Progress and Prospects Ten Years after the Adoption of the Domestic Workers Convention, 2011 (No 189) (Geneva, ILO, 2021).

[2] E Kuznesof, 'A History of Domestic Service in Spanish America' in E Chaney and M Garcia Castro (ed), *Muchachas no More: Household Workers in Latin America and the Caribbean* (Philadelphia, Temple University Press, 1989); J Brites, 'Domestic Service, Affection and Inequality: Elements of Subalternity' (2014) 46 *Women's Studies International Forum* 63; D Gorbán and A Tizziani, 'Inferiorization and Deference: The Construction of Social Hierarchies in the Context of Paid Domestic Labor' (2014) 46 *Women's Studies International Forum* 54; M Garcia Castro, 'Trabajadoras domésticas en el Brasil: ¿sujetas o sujetadas en la clase, en el género y en la raza? Descolonizando cuidados' in E Masi de Casanova, L Acciari, J Brites, E Hutchison, R Fernández Ossandon, L Pérez and L Poblete (eds), *Mujeres, trabajadoras y ¡mucho más! Los desafíos del trabajo del hogar en América Latina* (Lima, Fondo Editorial de la Universidad del Pacífico, 2025).

frequent violations of their rights, as their workplace is their employer's home and the state has limited resources to enforce the law.[3] Since the adoption of the ILO Convention 189 (C189) in 2011, 14 countries in the region have ratified it and amended their legislation to ensure decent working conditions. However, the access to rights remains challenging due to the high level of informality, which affect 72.3 per cent of domestic workers in the region.[4]

The literature has shown that, apart from the persistence of informality, the definition of working conditions largely depends on recruitment mechanisms because intermediaries (both public and private) play a fundamental role.[5] To date, intermediaries are still underdeveloped in Latin America because recruitment and direct hiring by households through personal relationships and proximity networks remain the main strategy.[6] In Argentina, for example, jobs involving intermediaries represents less than five per cent, and in Brazil less than one per cent,[7] although there has been a clear upward trend over the past years.

This chapter analyses how these intermediaries enter and develop within the domestic and care work sector in Latin America. Our focus is on how the legal framework has conditioned their development. Literature on digital intermediaries in various sectors, including domestic and care work, has shown that these companies use different strategies to establish and consolidate their position in the market. Some develop in areas where there is little or no legislation, gradually imposing their own rules,[8] while others grow in grey areas, partially complying with legislation by adapting their strategies to the legal context.[9] Thus, a distinctive feature of Latin American countries is the simultaneous emergence and establishment of these companies alongside legislative reforms concerning paid domestic work. Therefore, as they attempt to secure a position in the market, these companies must adapt to the evolving legal landscape.

[3] ML Vega Ruiz, 'L'administration et l'inspection du travail dans le domaine du travail domestique: les expériences de l'Amérique latine' (2011) 23 *Canadian Journal of Women and the Law* 341.

[4] ILO (n 1).

[5] J Fudge and C Hobden, *Conceptualizing the Role of Intermediaries in Formalizing Domestic Work* (ILO, Geneva, 2018).

[6] M Cebollada Gay, *Mecanismos de intermediación laboral en el trabajo del hogar remunerado en la Ciudad de México* (México, OIT, 2021); M Krislane Andrade and AB Araujo, 'Un análisis de agencias, empresas y aplicaciones para trabajadoras del hogar' in *Themis, Estudio de mercado - Brasil: ¿Nuevos actors, Viejas cuestiones? Un análisis de agencias, empresas y aplicaciones para trabajadoras del hogar* (Rio de Janeiro, Themis, 2020).

[7] OIT, *El trabajo doméstico remunerado en América Latina y el Caribe a diez años del Convenio núm.189* (Lima, OIT, 2021) 9.

[8] K Thelen, 'Regulating Uber: The Politics of the Platform Economy in Europe and the United States' (2018) 16 *Perspectives on Politics* 938; N Koutsimpogiorgos, K Frenken and AM Herrmann 'Platform Adaptation to Regulation: The Case of Domestic Cleaning in Europe' (2023) 65 *Journal of Industrial Relations* 156; Starčević, ch 4 and Pais et al, ch 6, in this book.

[9] P Dieuaide and C Azaïs, 'Platforms of Work, Labour, and Employment Relationship: The GreyZones of a DigitalGovernance' (2020) 5 *Frontiers in Sociology* 1; V Pulignano, C Marà, M Franke and K Muszyński 'Informal Employment on Domestic Care Platforms: A Study on the Individualisation of Risk and Unpaid Labour in Mature Market Contexts' (2023) 29 *Transfer: European Review of Labour and Research* 323; Teke-Laurent, ch 2, in this book.

Adopting a qualitative approach to study the outcomes of these parallel processes, this chapter focuses on four Latin American countries: Argentina, Brazil, Chile and Mexico. These countries have adopted different approaches to reforming the legal framework for paid domestic work. In Argentina and Brazil, legal reforms were triggered by the adoption of C189 and the social movement that accompanied the standard-setting process during 2010 and 2011. Although the ratification of C189 plays an important role in Chile, normative reforms started in the late 1990s and have gradually aligned domestic work legislation with the general labour regime. By contrast, Mexico's reform was the latest, taking place in 2019 after the ratification of C189.

This research is based on the analysis of three types of empirical material: (1) a corpus of regulations concerning paid domestic work; (2) statistical data on these labour markets; and (3) a database of digital platforms for domestic and care work operating in Latin America. This database was created using information collected from websites, apps and blogs in 2022[10] and later updated in 2024 and 2025. Thus, to understand their development, the landscapes of 2022 and 2025 will be compared. The search was keyword-based, focusing on the common terms used to refer to domestic workers in each country, such as 'nana' and 'asesora del hogar' in Chile, 'empleada doméstica' in Argentina and Mexico, and 'babá', 'faxineira' or 'diarista' in Brazil. We focused on the 'Terms and Conditions' section when it was available, as this is not a mandatory requirement in all countries under study. We also used press articles and blogs to supplement information missing from their websites or apps. As nothing dies on the internet, we gathered information from various media to ascertain whether these digital intermediaries were still operating. Additionally, in order to gain a better understanding of how these companies function, we relied on case studies.

The chapter is structured into two further sections. The first focuses on legal reforms relating to paid domestic work. The second analyses how these companies have adapted their operations in the face of the changing legal landscapes in recent years.

II. THE REGULATORY REFORMS

In Latin America, the creation of the Confederation of Domestic Workers' Unions in 1988 marked a significant milestone in the recognition of domestic workers' rights. Since then, domestic workers' trade unions in the region have been campaigning alongside NGOs, feminist groups and international organisations – such as the ILO – to raise awareness of the poor working conditions

[10] F Pereyra, L Poblete and A Tizziani, *Plataformas digitales de servicio doméstico y condiciones laborales. El caso de Argentina* (Buenos Aires, OIT, 2023).

in the sector.[11] As a result of this movement, progress has been made in several countries. Peru and Bolivia, both in 2003, and Uruguay in 2006 have completely changed the regulatory framework for the sector.[12] By contrast, Argentina, Brazil, Chile and Ecuador introduced limited amendments in their legislations at that time.

It was not until 2011 that a large number of countries undertook more comprehensive regulatory reforms following the ILO C189 framework. The participation of various groups of domestic workers was crucial in the years leading up to the drafting of C189, as well as during the 2010 and 2011 conferences.[13] Thus, during the preparation period for the Convention (2008–10), there was a wave of new legislation at the regional level,[14] and after the adoption of C189, 11 countries in the region reformed their legislation. The C189 acted as a catalyst for the recognition of domestic workers' rights, a process that had been underway in the region since the 1990s.[15] Among the countries under study, three have been pioneers in regulating paid domestic work: Argentina, Brazil and Chile have included domestic workers in their legal frameworks since the 1950s, albeit in a partial and limited way. However, the processes of reforming the legal framework differ from country to country.

In Chile, reforming the regulatory framework of the sector was a progressive process that took place over a longer period of time. The first amendments to the Labour Code were made at the end of the 1990s, to give domestic workers the right to maternity leave.[16] Since 2008, regulatory changes intensified, with the introduction of a minimum wage[17] and the inclusion of domestic workers in the pension system.[18] Then, these changes were reinforced when a specific law[19] for the sector was approved in 2014, accompanying the ratification of C189. This law included domestic workers in the general working time regime, while establishing the possibility of an additional 15 hours per week, paid at 50 per cent more. It also prohibited the deduction of food and lodging from salary and

[11] R Rojas Scheffer, 'Same Work, Same Value? Paid Domestic Workers' and Housewives' Struggles for Rights in Uruguay and Paraguay' (2021) 69 *Current Sociology* 843; M Goldsmith, 'Los espacios internacionales de la participación política de las trabajadoras remuneradas del hogar' (2013) 45 *Revista de Estudios Sociales* 233.

[12] MR Goldsmith Connelly, RB Canedo, A Ferrari and MC Vence, *Hacia un fortalecimiento de derechos laborales en el trabajo de hogar: algunas experiencias de América Latina* (Montevideo, Friedrich-Ebert-Stiftung, 2010); L Poblete, 'The ILO Convention 189 as a Catalyst for the Domestic Workers' Rights Movement in Latin America' (2024) 4 *Revue de droit comparé du travail et de la sécurité sociale 58*.

[13] A Blackett, *Everyday Transgressions: Domestic Workers' Transnational Challenge to International Labor Law* (Ithaca, ILR Press, 2019); E Boris and JN Fish, 'Slaves No More': Making Global Labor Standards for Domestic Workers' (2014) 40 *Feminist Studies* 411.

[14] H Valiente, *Regímenes jurídicos sobre trabajo doméstico remunerado en los estados del Mercosur* (Montevideo, Articulación Feminista Marcosur – OXFAM, 2010)

[15] Poblete (n 12).

[16] Law 19591/1998.

[17] Law 20279/2008.

[18] Law 20255/2008.

[19] Law 20786/2014.

made it compulsory to sign a written contract and register it with the Labour Ministry, and it banned the wearing of uniforms in public spaces to prevent discriminatory behaviour. As a consequence of the Covid-19 pandemic, amendments were introduced to allow domestic workers to be included in general unemployment regime,[20] and latter into the new working time regime (40 hours per week).[21] Thus, Chile represents a case of a long trajectory of incremental changes, deployed either through successive amendments to the Labour Code and through legislation establishing timetables for the gradual incorporation of changes that would eventually lead to full recognition of rights. Regarding the minimum wage, for example, a three-year timetable was established whereby, in the first year, the salary of domestic workers would reach 83 per cent of the minimum wage, 92 per cent in the second year, and 100 per cent in the third year. These gradual and incremental changes, which accelerated and intensified after the ratification of C189, enabled domestic workers to be included in the general labour regime.

In Argentina, prior to the introduction of a new labour regime for the domestic work sector in 2013,[22] working conditions were regulated by the Special Regime approved in 1956.[23] This regime provided a narrow definition of domestic work, covering only individuals who performed domestic work for at least four hours, four days a week, for a single employer, excluding other labour arrangements. In 1999, a special social security regime[24] was introduced to cover a larger number of domestic workers, however it did not change the exclusion from labour rights. Under this new social security regime, any domestic worker who worked at least six hours per week for a single employer was entitled to social security benefits – health insurance and pension. The scheme provided for mandatory social security contributions to be paid by the employer, as well as voluntary contributions from workers. These voluntary contributions were essential for accessing social security benefits, as the employer's contribution only covered part of the minimum amount required.[25] Additionally, in 2004, those excluded from this special regime – meaning those working less than six weekly hours for the same employer – were authorised to register themselves as self-employed workers.[26] In that sense, the labour regime approved in 2013 was crucial because it granted all domestic workers the same rights as those established in the general labour regime, regardless of their working hours. However, social security rights remained segmented by working time arrangements in line with the special social security regime for domestic workers introduced in 1999,

[20] Law 21269/2020.
[21] Law 21561/2023.
[22] Law 26844/2013.
[23] Law Decree 326/1956.
[24] Law 25239/1999.
[25] L Poblete, 'Decent Work for Domestic Workers in Argentina: Institutional Innovations within the Same Framework' (2021) 24 *Journal of Labor and Society* 187.
[26] Presidential Decree 804/2004.

until 2023 when domestic workers were covered by the general social security system, including unemployment insurance.[27]

Similarly in Brazil, some legal protections were established prior to the adoption of C189, including the optional registration of workers in 'Fundo de Garantia do Tempo de Serviço' in 2001,[28] and the recognition of one-month annual leave, as well as the prohibition of salary deductions for in-kind payments and termination due to pregnancy, both in 2006.[29] Nevertheless, the main advancement in terms of the expansion of rights took place in 2013,[30] when Constitutional Amendment 72 granted domestic workers most of the rights included in Chapter 7 of the Federal Constitution.[31] These rights include a minimum wage, an annual bonus, a weekly rest day on Sundays, overtime compensation, public holidays, maternity leave, 30 days' notice and compensation for unfair dismissal. The amendment also incorporated domestic workers into the general system of working time and of social security. Additionally, in 2015, a specific law for the sector[32] introduced new provisions, mainly related to part-time work like the calculation of salary and paid vacations according to the number of hours worked, the mandatory registration of workers within 48 hours of the first day of work, and a probationary period of a maximum of 90 days. Regarding working hours, this law recognised a weekly rest period of 36 hours and 11 hours of night rest. It also established the payment of overtime at 50 per cent of the normal hour and an additional 25 per cent if the worker accompanies the employer on a trip. As in Argentina, this specific legislation for the sector introduced a definition of domestic workers based on the working time arrangements. However, the Brazilian reform took the opposite direction, defining legally as domestic worker all individuals who work more than two days a week for the same employer. Therefore, the law explicitly excludes those working in hourly basis, called 'diaristas' (because they are paid by the day). This exclusion is significant due to the fact that the diaristas represent almost half of all domestic workers.[33] Diaristas do not have access to labour and social security rights granted to domestic workers legally recognised as such, nevertheless, they can register as micro-entrepreneurs and access social benefits like public health insurance, a basic pension and subsidies for illness and maternity.[34] Thus, despite exhibiting similar trajectories in terms of timing and the recognition of rights, the approaches adopted by Argentina and Brazil differ

[27] Presidential Decree 90/2023.

[28] Law 10208/2001.

[29] Law 11324/2006.

[30] See AV Moreira Gomes, 'La réglementation du travail domestique' (2018) 1 *Revue de droit comparé du travail et de la sécurité sociale* 132.

[31] Constitutional Amendment 72/2013.

[32] Supplementary Law 150/2015.

[33] Departamento Intersindical de Estatística e Estudos Socioeconômicos (DIESSE), Brazil, 2025, www.dieese.org.br/infografico/2025/trabalhadorasDomesticas.html.

[34] OIT, *Políticas para la formalización de las micro y pequeñas empresas en Brasil* (Lima, OIT-FORLAC, 2014).

significantly in terms of the law's coverage. While Argentina's 2013 law seeks to include all domestic workers, Brazil's 2015 law explicitly excludes those working on a daily basis.

Mexico's trajectory of normative reform is completely different. Although Mexico had made some regulatory progress prior to 2019, the delayed nature of its reforms sets it apart from the other three countries. In 2012, the Federal Labor Law was amended,[35] establishing a rest period (nine hours at night and three hours during the day) for workers who work in live-in arrangements, as well as a weekly rest of one and a half days (preferably Saturdays and Sundays); and the obligation to provide a 'comfortable and hygienic' room, as well as 'healthy and sufficient' food. Similarly, in 2015, another reform to the Federal Labor Law[36] limited the value of the provision of food and a room to 50 per cent of the minimum wage and stipulated that the National Minimum Wage Council would be the body responsible for setting wages in the sector. It also established a 30-day trial period. Following the Supreme Court ruling,[37] in 2019, both the Federal Labor Law and the Social Security Law were amended by decree,[38] establishing a maximum daily working day of six hours and a maximum weekly working day of 36 hours. In the case of live-in domestic workers, the on-call time is considered overtime. There is a requirement that the contract must be in writing. In addition, protection against dismissal on the grounds of pregnancy and severance pay have been introduced. The law stipulates that domestic workers must be included in the mandatory social security system, recognising their right to holidays, paid vacations, rest day pay and an annual bonus. It also establishes an eight-day notice period for both parties. Finally, in 2022, a decree reforming the Social Security system[39] established that the worker must be registered from the first day of work and that those who perform sporadic tasks may register as independent workers.

When these regulatory reforms are all aligned with the provisions of C189 and therefore share similar characteristics, the way they have been designed and implemented has produced very different outcomes. In Chile, where normative reform began earlier and incremental changes have been introduced over time accompanied by various enforcement mechanisms, as a result, nearly half of domestic workers now have a formal labour contract.[40] Even though Argentina and Brazil adopted very different definitions of domestic work when new legislation was adopted a decade ago, less than a quarter of domestic workers in these

[35] Decree 30 November 2012.

[36] Law 12/06/2015.

[37] Amparo Directo 9/2018. The Supreme Court established that the exclusion of domestic workers from the social security regime is unconstitutional and recommend the State to introduce a new legislation on that matter. The Supreme Court ruling: www.scjn.gob.mx/derechos-humanos/sites/default/files/sentencias-emblematicas/sentencia/2020-01/Sentencia%20AD%209-2018%20PDF.pdf.

[38] Decree 2 July 2019.

[39] Decree 11 November 2022.

[40] Instituto Nacional de Estadísticas Chile, Boletín Estadístico: Informalidad laboral 30 (5 de mayo de 2025).

countries have formal employment contracts[41]. In Argentina, 77 per cent[42] are informal workers and in Brazil, 76.4 per cent.[43] In both cases, formal contracts are concentrated in full-time working arrangements. For example, in Argentina, 40 per cent of those working more than 24 hours per week have a legal contract, in contrast with the 18 per cent of those who work less than 18 hours per week,[44] or in Brazil, those who work 40 hours per week and more represent 82 per cent of all formal positions in the sector.[45] In contrast, in Mexico, where the regulatory reform is very recent and enforcement mechanisms have not yet proven their effectiveness,[46] almost all domestic workers work without a legal contract (96.3 per cent[47]). Therefore, in order to gain a share of the market, digital platforms develop different strategies.

III. THE DEVELOPMENT OF DIGITAL INTERMEDIARIES

To grasp the relevance of labour intermediaries in domestic and care work, the ILO proposes classifying them into three types: (a) 'traditional companies', which provide services from a physical location; (b) 'hybrid companies', using a physical location as well as a website or platform; (c) 'digital platform companies', operating exclusively through a website or platform. As the ILO survey shows, the number of hybrid intermediaries began to grow from 2000 onwards, as digital technologies became more widely accessible, with their participation in the sector increasing in 2008 and particularly since 2014. For their part, digital platform companies started operating in the sector in 2006 but only became relevant a decade ago.[48] While this classification is useful for highlighting changes over the time, it does not capture transitions between categories brought about by the introduction of digital technologies into everyday life. The widespread use of these technologies over the last decade has led to most traditional intermediaries becoming hybrid companies or more generally digital platforms. As the CEO of an international platform pointed out: 'Companies that don't have

[41] *See* F Pereyra and L Poblete, 'The Persistence of Informality in Paid Domestic Work in Argentina' (2024) 163 *International Labour Review* 435; R Fragale Filho, '¡Un día va a funcionar! La interminable jornada por la efectivización de los derechos laborales de las trabajadoras domésticas' in Masi de Casanova et al (eds) (n 2) 221.

[42] Instituto Nacional de Estadísticas y Censos Argentina. Trabajo e ingresos 9, Mercado de trabajo. Indicadores de informalidad laboral.

[43] Departamento intersindical de Estadística e Estudos Socioeconómicos (DIEESE), Boletim Especial (27 de abril de 2025).

[44] A Tizziani, L Poblete and F Pereyra, 'Modalidades de contratación a medida. La intermediación digital en el trabajo doméstico en Argentina' (2024) 89 *Revista de Estudios Sociales* 119.

[45] Ministério do Trabalho e Emprego, Governo Federal Brasil. RAIS/eSocial TRABALHO DOMÉSTICO FORMAL Anos-base 2015 a 2024.

[46] Cebollada Gay (n 6).

[47] Data México, Encuesta Nacional de Ocupación y Empleo, Trabajadores Domésticos, 2025.

[48] ILO (n 1).

a platform today or rather a website where you can do much more than just see what services the company offers before having to call them, cannot operate'.[49]

Thus, all labour intermediaries are therefore affected by distinct but simultaneous process, known as digitalisation and plataformisation. The first one involves the introduction of digital technologies into traditional companies, modifying some of their structural features in the process. Nowadays, for example, most companies use digital payment methods and web forms to handle requests for their products and services. The second one – plataformisation – implies that the organisation of labour is built around a digital infrastructure that acts as an intermediary between different actors – clients, service providers and workers.[50] The existence of this infrastructure presupposes a certain degree of automation and algorithmic management for organising labour and assigning tasks and jobs. Drawing on experiences from different countries, the literature identifies four models of digital intermediaries at the intersection of these two processes: (a) digital labour agencies; (b) digital placement agencies; (c) marketplaces; and (d) on-demand platforms.[51] The first two models show, mostly, how digitalisation is affecting traditional intermediaries because they offer services traditionally provided by private employment agencies. By contrast, the latter two demonstrate the impact of platformisation by highlighting the new business and organisational models that have emerged as result of the development of digital infrastructures.

Like traditional temporary work agencies, digital labour agencies hired workers as employees of the agency to provide cleaning or care services to several households. However, they used digital technologies to process the households' requests and to organise the workers schedules and payments.[52] The source of income is a percentage of each service. In this case, the workers are employed by the agency but provide services to households. They can be hired for permanent positions, short-term contracts or as temporary workers. For their part, digital placement agencies also focus on services traditionally provided by private employment agencies,[53] such as selecting workers and matching them

[49] Interview with the CEO of a cleaning company operating in the EU, conducted by Nicole Teke-Laurent in October 2024.

[50] M Zukerfeld, 'Bits, plataformas y autómatas. Las tendencias del trabajo en el capitalismo informacional' (2020) 7 *Revista Latinoamericana de Antropología del Trabajo* 1.

[51] A Tandon and A Rathi, 'Care in the Platform Economy: Interrogating the Digital Organisation of Domestic Work in India' in B Dolber, M Rodino-Colocino, C Kumanyka and T Wolfson (eds), *The Gig Economy: Workers and Media in the Age of Convergence* (New York, Routledge, 2021); P Rodríguez-Modroño, 'A Taxonomy of Business Models of Digital Care Platforms in Spain' (2024) 18 *Sociology Compass* 1; P Rodríguez-Modroño, 'The Platformization and Marketization of Care: Business Models and Competitive Strategies of Care Platforms' (2025) 29 *Competition & Change* 554; P Rodríguez-Modroño, ch 1, in this book.

[52] JL Posso Quiceno, SE Castiblanco Moreno and JA Pineda Duque, 'Plataformas digitales del trabajo de cuidado doméstico remunerado en Colombia: el caso de Hogarú' (2024) 89 *Revista de Estudios Sociales* 101.

[53] Pereyra et al (n 10).

with job offers.[54] Additionally, some intermediaries offer an innovative service: staff management. This means that they are in charge of the bureaucratic side of the labour relationship, like wage payment, preparation of payslips, and, in some cases, enrolment of the domestic worker in the social security system and payment of the mandatory monthly contributions.[55] It is worth noting that even when digital platforms offer staff management services, the labour relationship remains one between the household – as the employer – and the domestic worker. These two types of intermediaries could be hybrids, or they could have become completely digitalised over time. Generally, employers pay for the service of selecting and matching, however, some companies also charge workers to be able to candidate for a job.

For their part, the process of platformisation gives rise to new business and organisational models such as marketplaces and online platforms, initially developed in sectors such as delivery and transportation. Marketplaces seek to connect supply with demand for cleaning and care services by providing clients with a pool of workers displayed virtually according to their personal characteristics and client ratings. Then, the clients select the 'perfect' worker for the job from that pool by using filters designed to customise their search.[56] Sometimes, the digital intermediary will suggest a restricted number of workers to the client, so that the client can make a choice. Most marketplaces rely on workers labouring as independent contractors, but most workers are not legally registered as such.[57] Nevertheless, marketplaces can also be used to recruit permanent employees. In such cases, it is presumed that an employment relationship will be established with the household. In this model, both workers and employers pay to enter the marketplace, to be able to post their job offer or their job search. Finally, on-demand platforms, mirroring digital work platforms in the delivery and transportation sectors, offer irregular short-hour gigs and one-off jobs.[58] Given the nature of the service, a labour contract is not expected. The matching of workers to gigs is done using algorithms that filter by specific characteristics, such as location, worker rating, availability and personal features. Generally, both parties pay for intermediation services. For

[54] SR Farris, 'The Business of Care: Private Placement Agencies and Female Migrant Workers in London' (2020) 27 *Gender, Work & Organization* 1450; S Grover, 'Placement Agencies for Care-Domestic Labour: Everyday Mediation, Regimes of Punishment, Civilizing Missions, and Training in Globalized India' (2022) 56 *Modern Asian Studies* 1901.

[55] A Tandon and A Rathi, *Fault Lines at the Front Lines: Care Work and Digital Platforms in South and Southeast Asia* (Singapore, Friedrich Ebert Stiftung, 2021).

[56] Johnson et al, ch 3, in this book.

[57] K Gruszka and M Böhm, 'Out of Sight, Out of Mind? (In)visibility of/in Platforms-Mediated Work' (2022) 24 *New Media & Society* 1852.

[58] A Trojansky, *Towards the "Uber-isation" of Care? Platform Work in the Sector of Long-term Home Care and Its Implications for Workers' Rights* (Brussels, European Economic and Social Committee, 2020); D Kavita, 'Platform "Glitch as Surprise": The On-demand Domestic Work Sector in Delhi's National Capital Region' (2021) 25 *City* 376; F Baum, 'Platforms Don't Care – Qualified and Experienced Women Do: A Case Study on Self-Employment and On-Demand Platforms in Eldercare' (2024) 0 *Critical Sociology* 1.

workers, this often takes the form of a percentage of each gig. These last two models only exist in digital form.

Despite the coexistence of these four models and the utilisation of various models within the same company, or even in mixed versions,[59] all digital intermediaries in domestic and care work have adopted features typically found on digital platforms in other sectors, like the use of gamification to increase engagement among clients and workers[60] and control mechanisms based on reputation systems for monitoring workers' performance.[61] In their narratives, they emphasise the importance of choice and flexibility.[62] Embedded in the gig economy, these intermediaries tend to promote jobs characterised by short hours, although they also mediate traditional full-time positions.

As in other regions, digital intermediaries in these four countries used three principal narratives to advertise their services. The first focuses on the possibility of having tailored services. Digital intermediaries' websites include slogans such as: 'Find the caregiver that best suits your needs';[63] 'Your accomplice for a clean and disinfected home';[64] 'Find the perfect domestic worker for you'.[65] The second narrative highlights the simplicity of access: 'Click and cleaning now';[66] 'The easiest way to hire a cleaner for your home or office'.[67] The third narrative emphasises the professionalism and trustworthiness of the workers: 'Looking for reliable and skilled help?';[68] 'Find trustworthy help';[69] 'Childcare you can trust';[70] 'Qualified and verified domestic professionals'.[71] To demonstrate their trustworthiness, most of these companies offer a satisfaction guarantee on their services. This guarantee may include replacing the worker within the first two or three months, with or without limits on the number of replacements.[72]

Between 2022 and 2025, the number of digital intermediaries in the domestic and care work sector has significantly increased in all the countries under study. Brazil accounted for ten companies in 2022, doubling their number over the last

[59] L Poblete, F Pereyra and A Tizziani, 'Digital Intermediation in Paid Domestic Work in Argentina: An Analysis of Ambivalent Effects on Working Conditions' (2024) *Critical Sociology* 1.

[60] A Tizziani and L Poblete, 'La intervención de plataformas digitales en el trabajo doméstico remunerado en Argentina' (2022) 25 *Sociedade e Cultura* 1.

[61] K Floros, 'Rethinking Algorithmic Management in Minor Key: The Case of Housecleaning Platform Labour in Denmark' (2024) 1 *Platforms & Society* 1; R Fragale Filho and M dos Santos Lima, 'Alguém se meteu no meio: modelos de intermediação digital do trabalho doméstico no Brasil' (2024) 89 *Revista de Estudios Sociales* 81.

[62] Teke-Laurent, ch 2, and Starčević, ch 4, in this book.

[63] Cuidarlos (Argentina).

[64] Aliada (Mexico).

[65] Ahoyapp (Brazil).

[66] Twoclean (Chile).

[67] Donamaid (Brazil).

[68] Housekeeping (Argentina).

[69] Zolvers (Argentina).

[70] Babysits (Argentina, Brazil, Chile, Mexico).

[71] Famyle (Brazil).

[72] See Nanas Chile, PideTuNana and Asesoras Chile in Chile, Zolvers and Housekeeping in Argentina and Aliadas de la limpieza in Mexico.

three years, while in Mexico the number of digital intermediaries increased threefold. In Argentina, where these companies were not previously well established, their number has more than doubled during the same period. Chile is the only country where the number of digital intermediaries has remained stable, having the largest number of companies operating in 2022. In total, in 2025, Brazil, Chile and Mexico account for 20 or 21 digital intermediaries, while Argentina accounts for 10. Still many companies disappeared during that period, while others emerged and some changed their business model. Thus, our analysis reveals country-specific trends associated with the opportunities and limitations set out by the legal frameworks.

A. Chile: The Digitalisation of Existing Intermediaries

Of the four countries studied, Chile is the only one that has maintained a consistent number of digital intermediaries over the past three years. This suggests that this type of intermediary emerged earlier than the period covered by our analysis, developing in Chile before other countries in the region. This is because existing intermediaries underwent a digitalisation process. Digital placement agencies accounted for over half of the digital intermediaries identified in 2022, and digital labour platforms were widespread. By 2025, intermediaries had diversified to include marketplaces. Additionally, there has been a trend towards mixed-models, whereby the same company offers both recruitment services and the option to select from a pool of workers, depending on the type of service chosen by the client (basic or premium).

In Chile, these companies offer a wide range of services, with most providing cleaning and care work under the 'nana' category (traditionally the person responsible for both tasks in the home) or cleaning services exclusively. In fact, many of these companies include the word 'nana' in their name, such as NanasChile, PideTuNana, Nanamanía and Chilenanas. Nevertheless, in 2025, intermediaries offering care services for children and the elderly were also identified. Most companies proposed all types of working arrangements in 2022; whereas currently, half of the companies only offer hourly and sporadic work.

Compared to the other countries under study, Chile has a high number of digital labour platforms. This can be explained by the fact that cleaning companies providing household services have been developing since the mid-twentieth century.[73] Additionally, there is a long-standing tradition of domestic work intermediation services specialising in staff recruitment. On their websites, many companies highlight their long experience in recruiting domestic workers. Many of these companies are hybrid, in that they have a physical space and also sell

[73] M Greene Núñez, *Estudio sobre el trabajo doméstico remunerado desde la perspectiva de género: sistematización y análisis para la política pública en Chile* (Santiago de Chile, Dirección del Trabajo, 2024).

services through their website or mobile application. During the pandemic, movement restrictions prompted the use of digital devices for conducting pre-selection interviews, although many companies still conduct interviews in person. When it comes to recruitment services, all companies provide detailed information on their websites about how the recruitment process works. Although they emphasise the efficiency and simplicity of digital devices,[74] they highlight that the selection process is carried out by multidisciplinary teams of professionals, including psychologists, human resources specialists and social workers.[75] The pre-selection process includes verifying the accuracy of personal details (address, identity document, immigration status), criminal records and references from previous employers. In many cases, companies offer a premium service in which workers undergo a series of psychological tests. No digital intermediary offers this service in the other three countries under study, even those operating under the digital placement agency model.

These companies specialise in permanent, full-time employment, including live-in arrangements and their fees depend on the type of contract. Many also offer advice on drawing up employment contracts or provide staff management services. As they emphasise their expertise in selecting workers, these companies offer different types of worker replacement guarantee in the event of customer dissatisfaction. These two- or three-month guarantees create an overlap between labour regulations and the rules of digital intermediaries, acting sometimes as a barrier to the formalisation of labour relations.[76]

Given the relative high level of compliance with domestic work legislation, it is expected that digital intermediaries will seek to establish themselves within the formal sector, focusing on jobs involving longer working hours per week, which are more likely to be formalised. However, they have also increased their participation in the informal sector. This is due to an expansion of digital intermediaries offering sporadic or short-hour jobs, which are more likely to be informal, under the marketplace and on-demand models.

B. Argentina: Promoting Formalisation and Facilitating Informal Work

Of the four companies operating in Argentina in 2022, two offered a wide range of services to households, including cleaning, care and repairs, while the other two exclusively offered cleaning services. All of them were organised as marketplaces, except Zolvers, which began operations in 2014 as the first digital

[74] N Rodríguez-Conarrubias and F Álvarez-Figueroa, 'Digital Platforms for (Female) Domestic Workers in Chile: Precarization, Invisibilization, and Mercantilization' (2024) 32 *Gender, Work and Organization* 868.

[75] See LaNana.CL, Nanas Chile, Nanamanía, Chilenanas, Nanas Perú, TeLoCuido.

[76] The same was observed in Argentina, see L Poblete, 'When Digital Platforms Intrude into the Regulation of Paid Domestic Work: The Case of Formalisation in Argentina' (2025) 45 *Comparative Labor Law & Policy Journal* 175.

intermediary and remains the most significant today. Zolvers started as a digital placement agency before incorporating the on-demand model. All four companies were fully digital. They offered a variety of working arrangements, including full-time, part-time, short-hours and occasional jobs.

The increase in the number of platforms in 2025 compared to 2022 is partly due to the emergence of companies specialising in care services for the elderly or children. The specialisation of childcare has coincided with the recent establishment of two multinational companies, Sytly and Babysits. While the marketplace model remains dominant (six out of 10 platforms operate as such), there is currently greater diversification in business and organisational models. Although all digital intermediaries offer various work arrangements, including full-time, part-time, hourly and occasional positions, their websites tend to promote short-hour jobs. This type of jobs has grown in importance, becoming highly significant by the beginning of the twenty-first century. Those working fewer than 20 hours per week represented 40 per cent of all domestic workers in 2003, rising to 46.5 per cent by 2022.[77] Currently, 14.4 per cent of workers are employed by two employers, while 14.7 per cent are employed by three or more.[78] Consequently, digital intermediaries are focusing on this part of the market.

In Argentina, the growth of digital intermediaries has coincided with the implementation of a new domestic labour regime accompanied by various and creative implementation strategies.[79] Initially, some of these companies advertised themselves as allies of the state in reducing informal work. For instance, one of Zolvers' founders stated in several interviews that the company's primary goal is to 'transform the landscape of domestic employment in Latin America'.[80] This involves promoting formal jobs that are paid in accordance with the provisions of the collective labour agreement. To this end, Zolvers offers two services: free worker enrolment in social security and a paid staff management service, called 'Zolvers Pagos'. The latter implies taking care of everything related to the management of the employment relationship. This platform operates in Chile and Mexico, but it only offers this service in Argentina.

A survey of 300 workers conducted between December 2020 and January 2021 showed that the level of formalisation among those working in positions mediated by Zolvers is significantly higher. Of the positions managed by Zolvers Pagos, which represent 37 per cent of the total, 66 per cent are legally registered. Among the positions mediated by Zolvers (but not using Zolvers Pagos),

[77] Tizziani et al (n 44).

[78] Ecofeminita, Las trabajadoras de servicio doméstico en Argentina. Datos de la Encuesta Permanente de Hogares (2025) https://ecofeminita.com/wp-content/uploads/2025/08/informe.nb_.html.

[79] L Poblete, 'The Different Meanings of Formalisation. Experiments from the South: The Case of Argentina' in D Ashiagbor (ed), *Re-Imagining Labour Law for Development: Informal Work in the Global North and South* (Oxford, Hart Publishing, 2019).

[80] Pereyra et al (n 10).

32 per cent are registered.[81] This higher registration rate is due to the company constantly promoting formalisation through its app and blog. Also, employers are aware that using digital intermediaries leaves a digital trace of the employment relationship, which makes formalisation more convenient.[82] Despite expressing an interest in promoting formalisation, digital intermediaries are still exploiting informal labour. This part of the labour market is too important to be ignored. Zolvers also operates under an on-demand model, offering one-off cleaning services that, by their nature are not covered by law. Additionally, the digital companies organised as marketplaces do not make recommendations or references to formalising the employment relationship, as the decision to register the worker is assumed to be at the household's discretion.

C. Brazil: Exploiting the Margins of the Legal Framework

Since 2016, there has been growth in the number of digital intermediaries in Brazil, increasing from five companies in 2015 to 13 in 2016.[83] This growth is mainly due to the process of platformisation, whereby all companies emerge as completely digital companies that use applications in most cases. Of the digital intermediaries identified in 2022, all were local companies, most of which adopted the marketplace and on-demand models, focusing on the cleaning sector. These intermediaries primarily offer services that last a few hours and/or are sporadic, making use of the category 'diaristas'. In fact, many companies present themselves as intermediaries between households and daily workers. According to the 2015 law, the use of this category allows households and companies to avoid being considered employers, as the workers are treated as self-employed. In 2025, the trend towards the fragmentation of the working time and the almost exclusive use of the 'diarista' category is intensifying. Most of the companies identified focus on sporadic cleaning services lasting a few hours. Some are dedicated to cleaning private homes, while others provide services to both households and commercial establishments. Nevertheless, there has also been an increase in companies using digital labour platforms and digital placement agency models, confirming the variety and diversity of digital intermediaries in the domestic and care work sector. As Fragale Filho and dos Santos[84] point out, the effects of this heterogeneity of intermediaries range from precarious formalisation to the reinforcement of informality.

[81] ibid.

[82] Pereyra and Poblete (n 41).

[83] AC Andrada, AC Moreira Cardoso, N Araujo Guimaraes, R Moreno and MJ Tavares Pereira, 'Plataformas digitais de cuidado no Brasil: acesso e controle do trabalho no entrecruzamento de múltiplas crises' (2023) 35 *Tempo Social* 5.

[84] Fragale Filho and dos Santos Lima (n 61).

A survey of 99 employers conducted between April and August 2020 found that 83 per cent[85] had used a digital intermediary to hire 'diaristas'. The increase in the hiring of domestic workers on a daily basis is not a phenomenon induced by the entry of digital intermediaries, but rather a trend that has been observed since the beginning of the 21 first century. Daily workers represented 16 per cent[86] of all domestic workers in Brazil in 1992, rising to 26.5 per cent in 2008,[87] 30 per cent in 2011, 37.5 per cent[88] in 2013 and 43.6 per cent in 2022.[89] By 2024, this figure had increased to 45.4 per cent. Additionally, 'diaristas' outnumber permanently employed domestic workers when performing cleaning tasks, representing 53 per cent.[90] This trend towards hourly work is driven by several factors, including smaller family sizes, the introduction of technologies that facilitate domestic tasks, and the cost of domestic work.[91] In this sense, digital intermediaries introduce the possibility of finding short-hour jobs more easily.

While some workers claim that they work as daily labourers out of necessity, others argue that working by the hour or day helps to limit their emotional involvement with employers. At the same time, having fewer employers means they are less likely to experience discrimination, both racial and class-based, because the cost of leaving employers who normalise these practices is much lower.[92] However, as the literature has shown, reputation systems reconfigure the experience of discrimination by shifting it to the digital realm. There, it manifests itself in the selection of workers based on their profile photos[93] or gamified reviews[94] organised around characteristics advertised by companies, such as 'dedication', 'commitment' and 'efficiency'.[95] Some companies implement blocking mechanisms when workers receive a high number of negative evaluations or have not been active on the app for several months.[96]

Similarly, the cost of intermediation significantly impacts the income of daily workers because companies set the rates and also charge a monthly subscription

[85] Themis (n 6).

[86] OIT (n 34).

[87] J Brites, 'Trabajo doméstico en Brasil: transformaciones y continuidades de la precariedad' (2013) 15 *Trayectorias* 3.

[88] OIT (n 34).

[89] www.dieese.org.br/infografico/2023/trabalhoDomestico2023.html.

[90] Departamento intersindical de Estadística e Estudos Socioeconómicos (DIEESE), Boletim Especial 27 de abril de 2025. Dia do Trabalhador Doméstico. https://www.dieese.org.br/boletimespecial/2025/trabalhoDomestico.pdf.

[91] OIT (n 34).

[92] C Bezerra de Melo, 'A diariização do trabalho doméstico e o processo de tornar-se diarista' *SciELO Preprints*.

[93] C Cardoso Pelegrini and AP Motta Costa, 'Trabalho, emprego e renda na era da plataformizaçao digital: o caso dos trabalhos de cuidado' (2022) 18 *Liinc em Revista* 1.

[94] Fragale Filho and dos Santos Lima (n 61).

[95] G Ferreira Vale, 'Prescriçoes de comunicação e empresas de plataforma digital: um enfoque na discursividade da Parafuzo sobre o trabalho doméstico' (XVIII Congresso Brasileiro Científico de Comunicação Organizacional e Relações Públicas, Curitiva, 2024)

[96] B Gonsales de Souza, 'Reflexões sobre a precarização de disaristas: uma análise a partir dos termos de uso de plataformas de trabajo' (2025) 28 *Cuadernos de Psicología Social do Trabalho* 1.

in cash or in company tokens to access job offers,[97] as well as a percentage of each gig – typically between 15 and 30 per cent of the payment.[98] As companies primarily seek to attract customers, they offer households the possibility of cancelling scheduled services, which contributes to the irregularity of workers' income because most of these cancellations do not involve payment for the service not provided. In this sense, the economic risks are transferred entirely to the workers, considered as self-employee.[99]

D. Mexico: The Normalisation of Operating Outside the Law

In 2022, the first digital intermediaries were established in Mexico using the four organisational and business models identified in the literature. As in Brazil, these companies focused almost exclusively on cleaning private homes. In its early stages, the Mexican market included local, regional and multinational intermediaries offering all types of contracts, mainly short-term and sporadic ones. While multinational companies offering care services (especially childcare) have entered the market, the exponential growth of intermediaries in Mexico over the past three years (from six in 2022 to 21 in 2025) is primarily due to the proliferation of local digital intermediaries providing cleaning services to households.

In terms of organisational and business models, Mexico has maintained its initial profile, with digital labour platforms and marketplaces predominant, alongside a significant number of digital placement agencies and on-demand platforms. Half of the companies offer all types of working arrangements, and the other half only offer short-term or casual jobs. This is related to the fact that the Mexican domestic work sector is divided almost equally between those who work fewer than 20 hours per week, those who work between 20 and 34 hours, and those who work between 35 and 48 hours.[100] Furthermore, as the sector is almost entirely informal due to the fact that the implementation mechanisms of the recent legal reform have yet to yield results,[101] digital intermediaries offer services without considering the possibility of formalising employment relationships. Companies highlight the trustworthiness and professionalism of

[97] M Carvalho Sampaio Oliveira, AD Menezes Cardoso, RH de Souza Lopes, SH Coelho Gomes, 'O trabalho na plataforma digital GetNinjas: vitrine de pessoas, moedas virtuales e leilão reverso' (2021) 6 *Teoria jurídica contemporánea* 1.

[98] R Cuoto de Acevedo de Oliveira, 'Analise crítica do discurso das falas das diaristas no vídeos da plataforma de serviços domésticos Parafuzo' (XI Encontro de Estudos Organizacionais da ANPAD, online, 2022).

[99] M Libralon Kosaki Ponchio and PT Martins Berolin, 'Trabalho doméstico realizado por meio de plataformas digitais: gig economy da servidão?' (2024) 27 *Revista da Faculdade Mineira de Dereito* 358.

[100] OIT (n 7).

[101] IA Salas Durazo and FG Ordóñez de la Cruz, 'Las condiciones laborales de las empleadas domésticas. ¿Dignificación o precariedad?' (2023) 58 *La Ventana* 148.

their workers on their websites.[102] However, there is no information on what the worker selection process entails. According to the information provided on the websites and apps, only households pay for the intermediation service. The cost varies according to the number of hours requested and how frequently the services are required.

An empirical study of two intermediaries – an on-demand company and a marketplace company – shows that the fragmentation of working time caused by digital intermediation can manifest in different ways, thereby affecting working conditions differently. According to Teixeira,[103] the on-demand platform requires a minimum of three hours per service but offers much more fragmented schedules than the marketplace platform, where the most common service blocks are eight hours on the same day. In the former case, the working day is very long because travel time between jobs is added to service time. This can be considerable when working in Mexico City, where distances are long and public transport is unreliable. On top of this, the work is intensified by the fact that families expect domestic workers to complete tasks that would normally take a full day in just three or four hours. In the latter case, although commuting is reduced, workers report an increase in workload as households hire a worker to do the work previously done by a full-time worker, once or twice a week. In all cases, workers emphasise that it is their employers' unrealistic expectations of what can be achieved within the agreed timeframe that cause them to work quickly, compromising the quality of their work. This results in negative reviews and low ratings, which jeopardise their ability to attract new clients.[104]

A relevant factor in the Mexican case is that digital intermediaries set hourly rates that are higher than those of traditional contracts, which incentivises workers. However, when payments are not mediated by companies, workers experience the same difficulties getting paid the agreed price for the hours worked as they do when working without intermediation. In all cases, income is also variable because it depends on demand, which can fluctuate from week to week.[105] The simplicity of cancellation mechanisms and the lack of penalties for last-minute cancellations suggest that rescheduling of working hours is a very common practice. Studies on these intermediaries in Mexico reveal the persistence of precarious working conditions in the sector. In this sense, digital intermediaries seem to exacerbate this precariousness or at least undermine the

[102] F Teixeira, 'Reconfiguring Control and Perpetuating Exploitation: Digital Labour Platforms and Domestic Work in Mexico' (2025) 35 *Labour and Industry* 99.

[103] F Teixeira, '¿Más de lo mismo? Condiciones laborales de las trabajadoras del hogar en las plataformas digitales en México' (2024) 89 *Revista de Estudios Sociales* 43.

[104] Teixeira (n 102).

[105] A Santiago Páramo and C Piñeyro Nelson, 'Aliada and Alia: Contrasting for-profit and non-profit platform for domestic work in Mexico and the United States' in J Drahokoupil and K Vandaele (eds), *A Modern Guide to Labour and the Platform Economy* (Cheltenham, Edward Elgar Publishing, 2021).

possibility of improvements relating to labour and social security rights recognised since the 2019 normative reform.

IV. CONCLUSION

Despite the rapid growth of digital intermediaries in recent years, labour intermediation in the domestic and care work sector in Latin America is still in its early stages. While these digital intermediaries seem to perpetuate the trend of short-hour, sporadic jobs without social protections, how they develop in each country depends on the domestic work regulatory framework, even when it remains partially or inadequately enforced. The legal reforms, which resulted from two converging movements – bottom-up and top-down – sought to bring about a cultural change focused on socially recognising this work as entitled to rights. Thus, as well as establishing a regulatory framework, these reforms reshaped the labour market by shifting the expectations of workers and employers, as well as by creating spaces on the margins of the law. The four countries studied here show different paths in terms of the implantation and development of digital intermediaries. These cases range from operating exclusively in the informal market to presenting themselves as allies of the state in promoting labour formalisation, while also exploring the grey areas at the margins of the law.

Mexico is at one of the extremes of this spectrum. Where regulatory reform is more recent and significant changes in terms of rights recognition have not yet occurred due to limited implementation, the development of digital intermediaries takes place exclusively outside the law. These intermediaries promote precarious jobs that are very similar to those outside of the digital platform economy. The only difference is that they facilitate the temporary recruitment and the interchangeability of workers. At the other end of the spectrum is Chile. Over the last quarter of a century, this country has gradually recognised domestic workers' rights. While it is challenging to measure the respect for labour rights closed doors – at the employer's home, the fact that half of domestic workers have legal employment contracts is indicative of a certain level of compliance with the law. This explains why digital intermediaries are interested in defining their sphere of influence in both the formalised and informal segments of the labour market.

Argentina and Brazil are somewhere in the middle of this spectrum. Although they have similar levels of compliance with the law, with only one in four workers having a legal employment contract, their situations differ depending on what their regulatory frameworks allow. In Argentina, the domestic labour regime covers all domestic workers without exception, and the formalisation of the sector has been a priority objective of information campaigns since 2013. This has led digital intermediaries to develop in a borderline space. Even though they mostly mediate short-term jobs, they need to echo the campaigns in order to gain legitimacy. Consequently, it is common to find mechanisms that facilitate formalisation, ranging from providing staff management services to advertising how to formalise the employment relationship and comply with basic rights such as paid holidays, leave, public holidays and salary increases. Thus, within the framing of the recognition of rights, they promote temporary and flexible employment relationships. In contrast, digital intermediaries in Brazil are almost exclusively located within the exclusion zone defined by the regulatory framework, which classifies work performed for the same employer for more than two days a week as regular work – 'occupational basis' work. This space outside the labour regime of the sector does not exclude workers from rights, but recognises an alternative employment status: that of independent workers or micro-entrepreneurs. However, due to the poor working conditions, low and irregular incomes, very few domestic workers working as 'diaristas' are actually registered under this regime.

Thus, these different paths challenge the common assumption that digital intermediaries always make labour relations in this sector more precarious, regardless of the organisational or business model they adopt. These trajectories demonstrate that the impact of these intermediaries can be ambivalent; they can facilitate both protected employment and labour relations that fall outside of the law.

6

*Care Regimes and Industrial Relations: A Comparison of the Factors Shaping the Emergence of Digital Care Platforms and Trade Union Responses in Ireland and Italy**

IVANA PAIS, CAROLINE MURPHY AND TISH GIBBONS

I. INTRODUCTION

ACROSS EUROPE, COMMONALITIES are evident in the challenge when it comes to providing care, particularly that provided in the context of the private home. These challenges span four areas: ensuring access to an adequate supply of care, quality of care provided, financial sustainability of care models and the employment of carers.[1] This chapter focuses on the latter area from an employment relations perspective. Despite extensive rhetoric regarding the value of care in society, particularly during the onset of Covid-19, conditions for care workers remain characterised by low pay, precarious working arrangements and limited development opportunities. Domestic care is performed in the private sphere, which is precisely where regulation and formalisation of working arrangements face the challenges. The risk of exploitation increases with live-in arrangements, particularly for migrant workers.[2] The European Institute for Gender Equality (EIGE) estimates that about nine out of 10 paid

* The authors would like to acknowledge funding from the Friedrich-Ebert-Stiftung Competence Centre on the Future of Work which supported this research.

[1] S Spasova, R Baeten, S Coster, D Ghailani, R Peña-Casas and B Vanhercke, 'Challenges in Long-Term Care in Europe' (2018) 24 *Eurohealth* 7.

[2] A Rogalewski and K Florek, *The Future of Live-in Care Work in Europe* (2020), www.eesc.europa.eu/sites/default/files/files/qe-03-20-090-en-n.pdf.

care workers are women, with one in four having a migrant background.[3] Employees in the care sector earn less than employees with comparable qualifications and work experience in other sectors as cost-containment underpins the system.[4] An absence of regulation is linked to stimulation of private sector provision and informal arrangements.[5] A distinctive feature of domestic care work is that it is comprised of tasks classified as both family work and market work, performed in both private and public spaces, and can take place in both the formal and informal economy.[6] While professionalisation of domestic care has not progressed significantly despite calls for this, it is argued that wherever public funding has been provided for care, working conditions for domestic care workers have become more formalised over time, particularly where the state acts as the direct employer.[7]

In many European contexts however, publicly provided care services are declining, with the state instead taking on the role of funder or commissioner of care. Intermediaries have entered the care market, creating digital marketplaces where clients and care workers can arrange the provision of care services at the client's home. Trojanksy argues that it is reasonable to assume that such intermediaries will follow the trend set by other platforms in areas such as transport or domestic services, and increasingly become more pervasive in the market.[8] For this reason alone, their development is worthy of investigation from a trade union perspective, which is the aim of this chapter.

Different countries, however, face different challenges. In the case of Italy and Ireland we examine how the business models adopted by the digital intermediaries in each country are conditioned by different institutional settings (the care and industrial relations regime in which they operate). We examine how these new intermediaries reconfigure the domestic and care sector and then suggest possible actions which trade unions can take to address this phenomenon. The content that follows is based on secondary analysis of key policy documents and submissions made to a public consultation on reforms in the care sector. This is then combined with data from semi-structured interviews with key stakeholders

[3] European Institute for Gender Equality, *Gender inequalities in care and consequences for the labour market*. (2021), https://op.europa.eu/cs/publication-detail/-/publication/64766cd9-643c-11eb-aeb5-01aa75ed71a1/language-en.

[4] MJ Budig and J Misra, 'How Care-Work Employment Shapes Earnings in Cross-National Perspective' (2010) 149 *International Labour Review* 441; F Macdonald and S Charlesworth, 'Cash for Care under the NDIS: Shaping Care Workers' Working Conditions?' (2016) 58 *Journal of Industrial Relations* 627.

[5] C Murphy and T Turner, 'Formal and Informal Long Term Care Work: Policy Conflict in a Liberal Welfare State' (2017) 37 *International Journal of Sociology and Social Policy* 134.

[6] J Fudge, 'Global Care Chains: Transnational Migrant Care Workers' (2012) 28 *International Journal of Comparative Labour Law and Industrial Relations* 63.

[7] S Charlesworth and J Malone, 'Re-imagining Decent Work for Home Care Workers in Australia' (2017) 27 *Labour & Industry: A Journal of the Social and Economic Relations of Work* 284.

[8] A Trojansky, *Towards the 'Uber-isation' of Care? Platform Work in the Sector of Long-term Home Care and Its Implications for Workers' Rights* (Brussels, European Economic and Social Committee, 2020).

including the trade unions, workers in the sector, inspection agencies and carer representatives to identify what actions unions can take to address the emergence of platforms.[9]

II. SHAPING CARE WORK: CARE REGIMES AND INDUSTRIAL RELATIONS IN IRELAND AND IN ITALY

Care regime typologies classify the institutional design of policies (eligibility criteria, levels and types of support) and the underlying cultural values embedded within distinct mixtures of state and family responsibilities in different countries.[10] Policy reforms and changes however, have gradually called into question the capacity of these typologies to classify care regimes in selected countries into distinct types.[11] There is growing consensus that welfare regimes, in themselves, are an incomplete classificatory mechanism to comparatively analyse low-status work in care and domestic services.[12] An understanding of the institutional context in which labour regulation is developed is also important. Therefore, we examine both the care regime and the industrial relations context (particularly important regarding platform work) in Ireland and Italy. We begin with a comparison of the care regime, before examining industrial relations in each country.

A. Care Regimes

Italy and Ireland show different demographic patterns: according to 2022 data, citizens aged over 65 accounted for 23.8 per cent of the population in Italy, compared to just 15 per cent in Ireland. Italy has the fastest population

[9] For Ireland, interviews were conducted with the main trade unions active in the care sector, SIPTU and Forsa as well as with a representative of main labour standards enforcement agency the Workplace Relations Commission. Interviews were also held with representatives of the migrant works and the main body representing family carers. As for Italy, the following interviews were conducted by Ivana Pais: two interviews with care platform founders (one in March 2023 and one in May 2023); one interview with a labour inspectorate officer in May 2023; three interviews with carers working in platforms in July 2023 (a 59-year-old woman from Morocco; a 54-year old woman from Nigeria; a 56-year old woman from Italy); seven interviews with trade unionists carried out between January and May 2023 (two with Nidil CGIL trade unionists, one with Anolf CISL, one with Fisascat CISL, two with Felsa CISL, one with CISL confederale di Milano). The interviews with trade unionists were conducted in collaboration with Arianna Marcolin.

[10] H Theobald and M Luppi, 'Elderly Care in Changing Societies: Concurrences in Divergent Care Regimes – a Comparison of Germany, Sweden and Italy' (2018) 66 *Current Sociology* 629.

[11] ibid.

[12] N Lightman, 'Comparing Care Regimes: Comparing Care Regimes: Worker Characteristics and Wage Penalties in the Global Care Chain' (2021) 28 *Social Politics: International Studies in Gender, State & Society* 971.

ageing among EU countries while outside Europe it is second only to Japan.[13] Projections, however, suggest that the number of people over 65 in Ireland will grow by 33.3 per cent between 2022 and 2050, compared to a 25.9 per cent increase in Italy over a similar period. Thus, the comparison is between a country like Italy, already dealing with the challenges of an ageing population, and Ireland, which still needs to adapt its welfare system in anticipation of the demographic transition. These two countries also differ significantly in the way long-term care (LTC) is delivered. Ireland is typically classified as following a liberal care regime,[14] whereas Italy is considered to follow a familistic model.

In Ireland, the care regime is characterised by a minimal level of state provision of welfare, modest benefits and the enforcement of strict entitlement criteria where welfare recipients are means-tested.[15] Alongside the other Mediterranean countries, the Italian LTC system is sustained by informal care, with few economic resources allocated by the state. The 'familistic' care regime leaves most of the care arrangements to families that have relied on the 'migrant-in-the-family' model to care for their oldest members.[16]

In Ireland, the workforce employed in the care sector numbers only 135,000, with 66.4 per cent working in non-residential assistance, 29.7 per cent in residential assistance, and just 3.9 per cent employed directly by families as domestic workers. In contrast, Italy counts 1,213,600 workers in the care sector, with more than half (53.9 per cent) employed as domestic workers by families, 29.7 per cent in residential assistance, and 21.9 per cent in non-residential assistance. In 2000, public social spending per capita was €11,213 in Ireland compared to €9,276 in Italy.[17]

Ireland, much like other European countries, faces challenges in providing LTC to support independent living in private domestic settings amid a high rate of population ageing and increasing dependency ratio. Currently, publicly funded domestic care is allocated on the basis of a care needs assessment, and while there is currently no statutory right to home care, a process is being developed, though delays have been ongoing. For many, therefore, the state is a funder rather than a provider of care as private and non-profit care agencies are commissioned to provide care on behalf of the state.[18] Thirty-eight per cent of care is

[13] Eurostat, *Ageing Europe - Statistics on Population Developments* (2004); United Nations, *World Population Prospects 2022*, Department of Economic and Social Affairs (New York, United Nations, 2022).

[14] Murphy and Turner (n 5).

[15] TA Eikemo and C Bambra, 'The Welfare State: A Glossary for Public Health' (2008) 62 *Journal of Epidemiology and Community Health* 3; M Richter, K Rathman, SN Nic Gabhainn, A Zambon, W Boyce and K Hurrelmann, 'Welfare State Regimes, Health and Health Inequalities in Adolescence: A Multilevel Study in 32 Countries' (2012) 34 *Sociology of Health & Illness* 858.

[16] F Bettio, A Simonazzi and P Villa, 'Change in Care Regimes and Female Migration: The "Care Drain" in the Mediterranean' (2009) 16 *Journal of European. Social Policy* 271.

[17] www.domesticworkobservatory.com/.

[18] J Mercille and N O'Neill, 'The Growth of Private Home Care Providers in Europe: The Case of Ireland' (2021) 55 *Social Policy & Administration* 606.

provided directly by public provision, with 62 per cent delivered through indirect provision.[19] Families also can choose to pay private organisations directly for domestic care services.[20] A 2018 report by the Health Service Executive (HSE), which coordinates domestic care, acknowledged that the greatest barrier to the provision of services in some regions is the inability to source staff.[21] A significant proportion of those providing domestic support are themselves older, with around 42 per cent being aged 60 and over, while the sector is not seen as attractive to workers given the associated pay and conditions. State cash-for-care programmes or vouchers instead of services-in-kind to people who need care, which allows for a varying level of freedom in their allocation are relatively limited in Ireland, with instead the state commissioning or providing care directly.[22] Similar to Italy and other Mediterranean countries – Greece, Spain – Ireland also exhibits a tendency to intensively resort to informal care, which is not unexpected given the cohesion and importance that the family still retains.[23] The Irish welfare state has neo-liberal features in its low level of expenditure and the heavy reliance on the family as caregivers.[24] Timonen et al[25] predicted that Home Care Grants would stimulate private-sector care and potentially lead to an unregulated market in home-care services with little or no employment protection, social security rights or professional development and training. Such predictions did largely ring true with a subsequent proliferation of private care provider and increased reliance on international migrant workers in the sector.

As regards Italy, although overall life expectancy is high, the number of years expected to be lived in good health remains lower than in many other EU countries: over 28 per cent of those aged over 65, and over 64 per cent of those over 85 years, are not self-sufficient and need daily care, corresponding to 3.9 million people. [26] The care needs expressed by this substantial portion of the population are met only minimally by the public welfare system: 2.8 million elderly people in conditions of dependency do not receive any public LTC service.[27]

The overall public expenditure for LTC was 1.7 per cent of GDP in 2022, of which approximately three-quarters was for people aged 65 or older: it corresponds to €32.4 billion, of which €24.4bn was destined for totally disabled

[19] Department of Health, *Report of the Strategic Workforce Advisory Group on Home Carers and Nursing Home Healthcare Assistants* (2022).

[20] M Pierce, F Keogh and E O'Shea, *The Impact of COVID-19 on People Who Use and Provide Long-term Care in Ireland and Mitigating Measures* (2020) Country report available at LTC covid. org, International Long-Term Care Policy Network, CPEC-LSE, 13.

[21] Health Service Executive, *Review of Role and Function of Health Care Assistants*, HSE (2018).

[22] V Timonen, J Convery and S Cahill, 'Care Revolutions in the Making? A Comparison of Cash-for-Care Programmes in Four European Countries' (2006) 26 *Ageing & Society* 455.

[23] F Bettio and J Plantenga, 'Comparing Care Regimes in Europe' (2004) 10 *Feminist Economics* 85.

[24] Timonen et al (n 22).

[25] ibid.

[26] Domina, *Quinto Rapporto Annuale sul Lavoro Domestico* (Roma, Osservatorio Nazionale sul Lavoro Domestico, 2023).

[27] G Fosti, E Notarnicola and E Perobelli, *Il personale come fattore critico di qualità per il settore Long Term Care: 5° Rapporto Osservatorio* Long Term Care. Egea, Milano (2023).

older adults.[28] According to Domina - the National Domestic Work Employers Association – half (50.3 per cent) is allocated to public subsidies given to beneficiaries without specific restrictions; 33.5 per cent is allocated to subsidised residential care; only 16.2 per cent concerns in-kind provision of home care.[29]

Since the 1990s, LTC policies have mainly consisted of cash transfers to citizens: Italy is one of the very few EU countries that invest more than half of the total LTC national spending in cash-for care schemes (Cfc) for the purchase of private care. Moreover, the provision of subsidies is far from covering a significant part of the population. Italian families spend almost €8 billion for regular domestic workers (housekeeper and care workers) and €7 billion for irregular ones.[30]

Currently, women represent 86.4 per cent of domestic workers and migrants 69.5 per cent. Focusing on their composition, workers from East Europe represent 35.4 per cent, those from Asia 17.2 per cent, Latin America 9.9 per cent and those from Africa total 6.7 per cent. The main nationalities are Romania (21.1 per cent), Ukraine (14.7 per cent), Philippines (10.6 per cent), Peru (6.0 per cent) and Moldova (5.6 per cent).[31]

Italy's migration regime appears particularly restrictive for those seeking to enter to work legally, while being quite tolerant towards undocumented migrants.[32] Even if the number of regular employments has risen in the last 20 years, especially for live-in care workers, undeclared work is still dominant: of more than 1.85 million domestic workers in Italy, 48.2 per cent are regularly employed and 51.8 per cent are irregular.[33] According to recent estimates, domestic care work is responsible for 37.8per cent of the overall undocumented workers in Italy.[34]

The number of agencies and companies that provide home-care services or intermediate care services has grown in recent years, especially from the first decade of the 2000s but labour market intermediaries are not automatically drivers of domestic work's formalisation.[35] Moreover, obtaining a job as a care worker in an agency is quite difficult for migrants, as this requires them to hold a professional qualification and a good level of linguistic skills in Italian.[36]

[28] F Pesaresi, *La spesa pubblica per long-term care in Italia*. Online Publications. Welforum: Osservatorio nazionale sulle politiche sociali (2023) www.welforum.it/la-spesa-pubblica-per-long-term-care-in-italia/

[29] www.domesticworkobservatory.com/.

[30] ibid.

[31] ibid.

[32] B Da Roit and B Weicht, 'Migrant Care Work and Care, Migration and Employment Regimes: A Fuzzy-set Analysis' (2013) 23 *Journal of European Social Policy* 469.

[33] www.domesticworkobservatory.com/.

[34] Assindatcolf, *Il costo nascosto del lavoro domestico* (2022) Online publication https://assindatcolf.it/scarica-report-il-costo-nascosto-del-lavoro-domestico/.

[35] L Amorosi, 'A Private Business. Labour Brokering and Domestic Work: Opportunities and Challenges' (2023) 129 *Stato e Mercato* 451.

[36] S Marchetti and F Scrinzi, *Gendered and Racialised Constructions of Work in Bureaucratised Care Services in Italy* (2014) European University Institute Working Paper, RSCAS 123; for more details on the care regime in Italy, please refer to F Diodati, I Pais, F Bonifacio and R Lodigiani, *Socio-economic Literature Review Report on Care Regime at Country Level. Italy*, ORIGAMI project, https://origamiproject.it/reports/d2.1-italy.pdf.

B. Industrial Relations Context

Italy and Ireland also differ significantly in terms of their industrial relations systems. While the difference in union density – the percentage of employees who are union members – may be significant but not particularly striking (34 per cent in Italy versus 26 per cent in Ireland), the main distinction lies in the level of collective bargaining coverage. In Italy, this coverage reaches 80 per cent, while in Ireland it is 34 per cent and only a little over a fifth of workers in the private sector are covered by collective bargaining.[37] However, according to Eurofound, the quality of industrial relations – which is measured by an indicator that summarises industrial democracy, industrial competitiveness, social justice and the quality of work and employment – Italy (38.9) is below the EU average (49.9), while Ireland surpasses the average with a score of 58.6. Ireland outperformed Italy, particularly in areas such as social justice (poverty reduction, income inequality, and equality of educational opportunities) and the quality of work and employment (employment security and skills). However, both countries have similar rates when it comes to industrial democracy.[38]

Italy fits within the embedded corporatism model typical of continental Europe, whereas Ireland's position is more difficult to classify. While Irish social partnership did not share all the features of social democratic European corporatist models, it was also substantively different to the neoliberalist approaches evident in New Zealand or the UK.[39] The strength of collective labour power in Ireland has never been weaker than currently. From 1987 to 2008, Irish industrial relations were dominated by a series of centralised, tripartite social partnership agreements.[40] The collapse of social partnership in 2009 amid failure to conclude a new agreement post the onset of the global financial crisis, was anticipated to shift Ireland further towards the UK's liberal market approach, though some collectivist mechanisms have been retained and strengthened.[41]

Although Ireland is currently at full employment, care is still associated with precarious work and casualisation.[42] There remains no statutory route to trade

[37] European Commission (2020) *Commission Staff Working Document: Impact Assessment Accompanying the document- Proposal for a Directive of the European Parliament and of the Council on adequate minimum wages in the European Union*. Brussels: European Commission.

[38] Eurofound, *Measuring key dimensions of industrial relations and industrial democracy (2023 update)* (2023) Publications Office of the European Union, Luxembourg.

[39] C McLaughlin and CF Wright, 'The Role of Ideas in Understanding Industrial Relations Policy Change in Liberal Market Economies' (2018) 57 *Industrial Relations: A Journal of Economy and Society* 568.

[40] V Maccarrone and R Erne, 'Ireland: Trade Unions Recovering after Being Tipped Off Balance by the Great Recession?' in J Waddington, T Müller and K Vandaele (eds), *Trade Unions in the European Union: Picking Up the Pieces from the Neoliberal Challenge* (Bruxelles, Peter Lang Verla, 2023).

[41] T McDonough and T Dundon, 'Thatcherism Delayed? The Irish Crisis and the Paradox of Social Partnership' (2010) 41 *Industrial Relations Journal* 544; McLaughlin and Wright (n 39).

[42] C Murphy and T Turner, 'A World of Unstable Jobs Is Far from the Empirical Trends Displayed in the Irish Labour Market in the 21st Century' (2023) 65 *Journal of Industrial Relations* 734.

union recognition in Ireland, and as union recognition and collective bargaining are linked, collective bargaining coverage outside of the public sector is extremely low. While the European Care Strategy stresses the importance of access to collective bargaining in care work, the options for achieving this at present in Ireland are limited. This in part accounts for the poor employment conditions in some sectors such as care. However, the advent of the Directive on Adequate Minimum Wages in the EU is seen as presenting an opportunity for reform. The Directive aims to improve living and working conditions by strengthening workers access to adequate minimum wage protection, whether through minimum wages, or through collective bargaining. The Directive had been due to be transposed in November 2024 but has been delayed with legal challenges.[43] Regarding the gig economy, regulation in Ireland has been relatively late coming with a seminal case regarding tax and employment rights occurring in 2024.[44] The Health and Safety Authority (HSA) has stated it will target the gig economy as part of its 2022–24 strategy, including increasing inspections in sectors with higher risks.[45] In its programme of work for 2023, the HSA has stated it will consider options for influencing and enhancing engagement with sectors including the health and social care sector, though no explicit reference is made to whether that extends to domestic care.[46]

Trade unions (SIPTU and Forsa) have actively organised domestic care workers over the past two decades achieving improvements in conditions. These include the alignment of pay scales for health care assistants in domestic settings (formerly known as 'home help') with other health care workers; the introduction of written contracts, pay premiums, pension entitlements and travel allowances.[47] However, these improvements have been difficult to replicate beyond the public sector amid the increasing presence of private sector care providers which collective agreements do not cover. Vying to secure HSE tenders has now become highly competitive and increasingly dominated by private sector providers, particularly as the domestic care sector has been identified as a high growth sector, where investors can expect to become profitable within three years.[48]

Italy displays, in many respects, a profile that contrasts sharply with that of Ireland. From the post-World War II era until the late twentieth century, Italian industrial relations were characterised by a strong tradition of centralised collective

[43] E Malone, 'Unions "Appalled" by Advocate General Recommendation Minimum Wages Directive Be Annulled' (2025) *Irish Times*, 15 January 2025, www.irishtimes.com/business/work/2025/01/15/unions-appalled-by-advocate-general-recommendation-minimum-wages-directive-be-annulled/.

[44] C Murphy and L Ryan, 'What Impact on the *Gig Economy* in Ireland? Analysis of the Judgment Karshan Limited v the Revenue Commissioners' (2024) 1 *Revue de Droit Comparé du Travail et de la Sécurité Sociale* 304.

[45] Health & Safety Authority, *Strategy statement, 2022–2024* (Dublin, HAS, 2022).

[46] ibid.

[47] C Murphy and T Turner, 'Organising Non-standard Workers: Union Recruitment in the Irish Care Sector' (2014) 45 *Industrial Relations Journal* 373.

[48] M Mulkeen, 'Going to Market! An Exploration of Markets in Social Care' (2016) 64 *Administration* 33.

bargaining and significant union influence in shaping national policies through their involvement in tripartite negotiations with the government and employers' associations. The global financial crisis of 2008–09 marked a significant turning point for Italian industrial relations. While some feared a shift towards a more liberal market approach, Italy has managed to retain certain collectivist mechanisms. For instance, while union density has partially declined, collective bargaining coverage remains relatively high, especially in the public sector and large firms.

Italy faces ongoing challenges in sectors like care work, where informal labour, precarious employment and casualisation are prevalent. Domestic work was first addressed by the Italian legislature with the Special Law 339/1958, requiring the Italian state to regularise the sector, but focusing only on workers working at least four hours per day. After the abolition of the ban on domestic work collective bargaining in 1969, thanks to a sentence of the Italian Constitutional Court, time was ripe for a national collective contract, which was finally signed in 1974.[49] Since then, things have gradually improved, but some challenges are still open. Given the existence of 21 collective bargaining agreements for domestic work, there is a great risk of contractual dumping and the issue of the effective representativeness of both unions and employers' associations is crucial in determining this reality.[50] The ratification of ILO Convention 189/2011 on domestic work in 2013 occurred in an already institutionalised setting and was not backed by workers' participation, nor by public debates.[51] Moreover, the uniqueness of the Italian unions, which also represent pensioners, creates jurisdictional conflicts since the unions represent workers, but at the same time can also include employers among their members.

The national collective bargaining agreement signed by FIDALDO/DOMINA with Confederazione Generale Italiana del Lavoro (CGIL), Confederazione Italiana Sindacati Lavoratori (CISL), Unione Italiana del Lavoro (UIL) and the Italian Federation of Domestic Workers (FEDERCOLF) is the one that the judicial authorities refer to in identifying the standards to be applied in terms of wages and social security in the event of a dispute. This agreement was recently renewed by social partners in 2023 and introduced some relevant novelties compared to the previous version, signed in 2013. It introduces the single definition of the 'family assistant' for all the different professional figures involved in domestic work and defines new workers' professional classification, articulated in four levels.[52]

[49] R Sarti, 'Casalinghe e colf: gerarchie domestiche o comune oppressione? Tentativi di riforma, mancate sinergie e prospettive future' in B Busi (ed), *Separate in casa, Lavoratrici domestiche, femministe e sindacaliste: una mancata alleanza* (Rome, Ediesse, 2020).

[50] S Borelli, *Who cares? Il lavoro nell'ambito dei servizi di cura alla persona* (Napoli, Jovene Editore, 2020).

[51] S Marchetti, D Cherubini and G Garofalo Geymonat, *Global Domestic Workers: Intersectional Inequalities and Struggles for Rights* (Bristol, Bristol University Press, 2021).

[52] For more details on industrial relations in home care services in Italy, please refer to L Amorosi, I Pais, F Bonifacio and M Faioli, Report on home care services' employment conditions and industrial relations at country level before and after the Covid-19 crisis (2024) ORIGAMI project, https://origamiproject.it/reports/d2.2-italy.pdf.

C. Emergence of Care Platforms

The ORIGAMI project's mapping of platforms for carers and cleaners[53] identified 27 platforms operating in Italy – nine focused on carers, seven on cleaners and 11 serving both groups – and five platforms active in Ireland, including one for carers, two for cleaners and two addressing both categories. With reference to the typology presented,[54] in Italy there are nine marketplaces, eight digital placement agencies, two digital labour agencies and one on-demand platform: in Ireland, three marketplace, one digital labour agency and one on-demand platform.

The low number of platforms in Ireland can be explained by the limited regulation of domestic care provision to date, especially when compared to the more structured oversight of the residential nursing home sector. A new statutory care scheme is currently being developed, which is expected to introduce greater regulation for professional providers of in-home support. This evolving regulatory landscape may help account for the relatively weak presence of platform-based care services in Ireland compared to other European countries such as Italy. Nevertheless, international platforms such as Care.com and Helpling do have a presence in Ireland, though these provide domestic as well as care-based services. On its site, *Care.com* indicates that 'the average hourly rate for elderly carers in Ireland is between €12 and €16' though a review of carer profiles indicates several where a rate of €10 per hour (significantly below national minimum wage rates) is mentioned. As a client, there is an option to undertake a subscription (monthly/yearly) which allows for contacting any providers directly, and according to the site 'save time by hiring from better-matched candidates'. Carers can create a carer profile for free and search for jobs by type of care and location. On the website *Care.com* issue a caveat stating that:

> *Care.com* is not a recruitment or other agency and any screening it does of members is limited and should not be relied upon. Members are solely responsible for selecting an appropriate employer or carer for themselves or their family, and employers are solely responsible for obtaining and reviewing any necessary Garda vetting or other identity, verification, background, or reference checks before hiring a carer. Each employer is also responsible for verifying the age of the carer they select, as well as that carer's eligibility to work in Ireland.

One indigenous care agency has already pivoted to offer services via a platform. Home Care Direct (HCD) was established in 2018 by an existing traditional care agency and focuses on care for the elderly and persons with a disability. While the industry has low levels of regulation regarding qualifications, the

[53] F Bonifacio and I Pais, *The landscape of digital platforms in the home care sector* (2024) ORIGAMI project, https://origamiproject.it/reports/d3.2_report-on-landscaping-of-the-home-care-digital-platform.pdf.

[54] Rodríguez-Modroño, ch 1, in this book.

platform assures clients that 'all carers are interviewed, garda vetted and reference checked'.[55] They also emphasise that care recipients themselves do not need to 'become an employer', while stressing that this is not 'removing any of their control' over the service. Once signed up to the platform, clients are given access to a list of carers based on geographical proximity. One of the goals that HCD promotes is the localisation of care by ensuring carers can build a pool of clients in the same area where they live. While platform working arrangements are not always associated with positive outcomes for workers, the provider highlights how working in this model can lead to better outcomes for workers compared to traditional agencies, where there is a lack of predictable working hours and travel allowances for workers. Providers have pointed to the low rate of funding provided by the government as a contributory factor to this. By working in a platform model, workers can liaise directly with clients to set rates of pay and other conditions such as travel allowances. However, in doing so they forfeit protections associated with having an employee contract.

With one of the highest rural populations in Europe, in Ireland the HSE operates an approved provider list on a regional basis, meaning that public funds can only be directed towards those providers who are approved in each region. Therefore, while platforms have a presence in Ireland, their use by families is currently likely to be more limited to privately purchased care, thus restricting the extent to which they can grow compared to countries with unrestricted cash transfer systems. The introduction of regulation is anticipated to go hand in hand with a statutory right to domestic care provision, thus further accelerating demand for services. An indigenous platform has been vocal about the lack of regulation and statutory entitlement to care, seeing their introduction as 'a real opportunity to ensure home care plays a much fuller role in the health care continuum'.[56] Of concern for the platform is which of the various models of funding and service provision might transpire through regulation. They argue that the Irish system should include a greater use of personal budgets and direct payments, whereby clients can decide on care providers rather than reinforcing existing practice, in which the HSE operates the outsourcing of home care packages[57] to private agencies. They contend that 'increased choice for families is a great driver of quality and efficiencies'.[58] They stress that regulation should not indiscriminately regulate out of existence models or practices that are working successfully, and it must be flexible enough to allow for future innovation.[59]

[55] The vetting process is a statutory requirement under the Children and Vulnerable Persons Acts 2012 for individuals undertaking work on behalf of organisations that work with children or vulnerable adults.

[56] https://blog.homecaredirect.ie/policy-challenges-for-the-introduction-of-regulation-in-home-care/.

[57] Home care packages include additional home help hours, nursing care, respite care, physiotherapy and other supports which, while funded by the state, can be supplied by private companies.

[58] https://blog.homecaredirect.ie/policy-challenges-for-the-introduction-of-regulation-in-home-care/.

[59] ibid.

This illustrates fears that the introduction of regulation may include provisions which limit the ability of platforms to operate in the care market: 'Home care provision in Ireland is hugely lucrative for the limited list of approved corporate providers and will be even more so when regulation and a statutory scheme are introduced'.[60] The platform has also highlighted the informal market for care and suggests that regulation should include generous tax reliefs for individuals availing of formal care provision in order to combat the informal market.

The high number of platforms in Italy reflects a different context where a large number of care agencies operate, even though carers are still predominantly found through informal networks, with 70.8 per cent being hired via word of mouth. Some municipalities make available a register of family assistants which can be consulted by families. The possession of a title or professional qualification relating to care work, as well as a good knowledge of the Italian language, are generally minimum requirements for enrolment in the registers of family assistants. However, just over one in ten carers are registered.[61]

While in general, checks by the state to uncover labour irregularities in this sector are rather limited, platform work does not allow for stronger controls. In 2022, inspections relating to domestic work accounted for just 1.3 per cent of total inspections.[62] The Labour Inspectorate officer interviewed confirmed the limitations of inspections and their implications for platform work:

> If a platform just do the matching of job supply and demand and is registered with the Ministry of Labour, everything is fine; if it is not registered, a minimum penalty is imposed on it, within the range of EUR 1500 . . . We don't have such a timeliness that we can affect these platforms, which we know have only been operating for a couple of years. Furthermore, a family that has an illegal worker cannot be sanctioned for undeclared work because it is not an entrepreneur.[63]

In Italy, so far, the only form of platform work that has been subject to regulatory intervention is food delivery. The Law No 128/2019, often referred to as the 'Riders' Law', focuses on the working conditions and protections for these workers, specifically transparent payments, insurance coverage, compensation for accidents, social security and pensions. Italian courts have ruled on several cases regarding the classification of gig workers, often challenging the autonomy status given to them. From 2022 onwards, trade unions and certain platform companies have negotiated collective agreements to regulate the working conditions of platform workers in the food delivery sector. These agreements aim to provide fairer pay and protections without classifying workers as employees.

[60] https://blog.homecaredirect.ie/corporatizing-of-irelands-home-care-sector/.

[61] Censis-Assindatacolf (2022). *Welfare familiare e valore sociale del lavoro domestico in Italia*, https://assindatcolf.it/scarica-il-quarto-report-censis-assindatcolf/.

[62] Ispettorato Nazionale del Lavoro (2022). Relazione sull'attività svolta dall'Ispettorato Nazionale del Lavoro Anno 2021, www.ispettorato.gov.it/files/2022/12/Relazione-attivita-INL-e-Rapporto-Vigilanza-2021-12082022.pdf.

[63] Labour Inspectorate officer.

D. Trade Union Actions

In Ireland, unions noted that while care platforms are not as yet a major feature of the sector, they are aware that many people in the sector are using social media tools such as Facebook groups to source work and that this could act as a precursor to formal platform work. The unions also noted the level of informality[64] that still exists in the sector despite unions actively organising workers in the past and the fact that Ireland has signed up to the ILO Domestic Workers Convention. The provision of care falls under the criteria of domestic worker and as such the Domestic Workers' Convention applies. The Workplace Relations Commission (WRC), the body responsible for labour standards enforcement in Ireland, sets out clearly the requirements for domestic workers regarding pay and working conditions. Domestic workers who feel that their employment rights have been breached can make a complaint to the WRC's Information and Customer Services, and this will be dealt with either through an inspection or at a hearing by a WRC Adjudicator. However, the vulnerability of such workers may negate their ability to report infringements. Regulations require all employers to keep detailed records for all employees for three years. Failure to do so is a punishable offence. Such records may be required by WRC Inspectors in an inspection. However, regulatory effectiveness in the context of a platform arrangement where there is no formal employment relationship with either the platform or the client receiving care further complicates the capacity to regulate standards, and the effectiveness of the Domestic Workers' Convention.

Trade unions in Ireland continue to actively organise care workers but acknowledge that platforms have not yet been included in that strategy. The complexity and efforts required in organising such a dispersed and difficult to identify group is a concern for organisers. Platform workers have not approached unions. The organisers acknowledged that there 'is no issue organising the directly employed staff' but organising such 'a widespread and far-flung workforce . . . [would be] . . . literally impossible'.[65]

A sectoral approach by unions in Ireland to addressing employment conditions in areas of work with strong vocational elements and feminised workforces has proven relatively successful in the past in sectors like early childhood education. One organiser drew attention to a long-running SIPTU campaign in childcare that bears similarities to domestic care, where a similar strategy of lobbying to create a joint labour committee (a body responsible for negotiating tri-partite agreements in typically low-paid sectors) could have merit. However, for this to happen 'these people need to be employees'.[66] Hence, while such a

[64] See Sedacca and Atkinson, ch 12, in this book, for a more in-depth discussion of the role of informality in this sector and the potential of platforms in enabling processes of formalisation, whether thick or thin.

[65] Trade Union officer 1.

[66] ibid.

strategy may be useful for the care sector in general, it would have little value in terms of addressing platform work.

One of the recommendations emerging from a strategic workforce advisory group established to examine issues in the care sector concerns the creation of an appropriate mechanism to reach agreement in the private and voluntary sector in respect of pay and pensions for domestic-support workers and healthcare assistants. While such a strategy may be useful for the care sector in general, nonetheless it would have limited value in terms of addressing platform work in the current context or where workers are trapped in informality. One organiser from SIPTU recounted the experience of organising migrant domestic workers in the early 2000s, noting that the workers were 'very isolated' and 'treated appallingly', stating that 'I don't believe too much has changed with regard to that'.[67] This is despite changes since then, such as Ireland's passing of the Domestic Workers Convention. This organiser also felt that the sector needed stronger regulation and organised representation, noting that a series of individual referrals to the Labour Court had done little to improve matters: 'A huge amount of the settlements won in the Labour Court had to be confidential . . . because the employers didn't want to be named and shamed. They reneged frequently'.[68]

In Italy, the home care sector has strong resistance to unionisation, which is exacerbated by platform work. Interviews with platform care workers illustrate the difficulties that exist in extending trade union representation in this sector:

> I never went to the union, not even when I worked in a factory. I have never had, even if they treat me in a way that I don't like, instead of going to the union, I say to myself: stop, stop. Because if I go to the union, tomorrow, when I look for work, I can't find it anymore, because it's already marked that you brought the employer to the union. When you are looking for a job they ask you for your reference, the telephone number of the person you recently worked for and if you don't have a reference, it becomes very difficult to find work. Without reference [platform name] won't even let you register.[69]

Trade unionists report that they have never come into contact with platform workers in the care sector, attributing this to invisibility and fragmentation of labour in this field.

> We as a union generally act if there is demand. In the case of riders, even if the demand didn't arrive, you could see them on the street and so we went. Here, on the other hand, no one contacted us, there was no question. Then you don't meet them.[70]

> For us, platform work is a challenge, but we don't quite know what tools to tackle it with. We don't know how to intercept them, but then we don't even know what

[67] Trade Union officer 2.
[68] ibid.
[69] Carer, female, 54 years old, of Nigerian origin.
[70] Nidil, CGIL, territorial level.

> to propose because we can't offer a platform worker what we do in traditional situations.[71]

Among the strategies that could be activated, the importance of raising awareness, both of workers and families, is mentioned most frequently.

> Campaigns should be made to raise awareness among workers; this has been done with riders. In this case the campaign could also involve the pensioners' union, to signal the agencies to avoid, but also to promote the agencies – even the platforms – which instead operate in compliance with the law.[72]

Furthermore, some interviewees draw attention to the traditional levers of trade union action from advocacy to collective bargaining. 'There are different levels. The first is the regulation of platforms. We are witnessing a hyperregulation of rider platforms and a complete absence of regulation of other platforms'.[73]

To improve working conditions, some trade unionists are open to accepting contracts other than for employees.

> From this point of view, if the person who works through the platform at least opened a VAT number, it would certainly be a step compared to the intermediation of undeclared work. This would mean having the courage to promote welfare policies that do not depend on the employment contract and to ensure rights also for the self-employed.[74]

Finally, unions are calling for a strengthening of public intervention in the sector in the form of economic support for families, in the promotion of intermediation tools that favour agencies that adopt ethical behaviour and in the promotion of training courses.

> We should also aim at the state level to introduce training courses in vocational schools to take care of the elderly. Let's start with three years and then later you can get to five, but you have to give this job a value, a professionalism, because our young Italians don't want to do this job.[75]

III. DISCUSSION

In examining the emergence of care platforms, we presented the care regime for both Ireland and Italy. A comparison of the two countries reveals that Ireland, although moving rapidly towards privatisation in the sector, still differs substantially from Italy in regard to the level of involvement by the state in the

[71] Felsa CISL, territorial level.
[72] Nidil, CGIL, territorial level.
[73] Felsa CISL, national level.
[74] Vivace, freelance association, CISL, national level.
[75] Maids and carers office, CISL, territorial level.

provision of care. This is evident when viewed from an employment relations perspective. While in Italy elder care remains primarily the responsibility of the family, although there are some limited mechanisms in place – such as personal budgets and care credits – to support and facilitate this role, the commissioning approach in Ireland still retains a strong level of involvement in regulating how care is provided and by whom through controlling the standards providers must meet. Thus, working conditions in the care sector in Ireland are buffered by the leverage that government can exert through the tendering process, with only limited suppliers being added to the approved providers list.

In presenting the industrial relations regime of each country we also see differences emerge that are of significance when it comes to the presence of digital labour platforms. Trade unions in Ireland are generally in a relatively weaker position than unions in Italy given the lack of collective bargaining coverage, trade union recognition rights and absence of social partnership arrangements that extend to the private sector. However, in looking at the care sector specifically some features exist which are counter intuitive given the power differential which Italian unions hold relative to Irish unions. Membership of unions and union density in Ireland has been in decline largely since the 1980s which means that as a percentage of the overall population, union membership is no longer the substantial representative grouping it once was to support unions lobbying position. In contrast, in Italy, present within the membership is a cohort of individuals who themselves employ care workers. Therefore, while the membership in Italian unions is marginally more substantial than in Ireland,[76] it is also more diverse in its interests. Such diversity can have the effect of diluting the unity and strength of demands that unions can make in relation to the care sector, since decisions that increase the cost of care will be borne by some of the membership. Opposition to models of care provision, i.e. digital labour platforms which provide greater flexibility regarding costs for consumers, are therefore potentially challenged in a less robust manner.

In both Ireland and Italy, digital platforms are now taking their first steps in the care sector, but the strong demand for services in this area and increasing privatisation are facilitators of the diffusion of these infrastructures and related organisational models. Domestic care work is already fragmented and individualised, with little opportunity for interaction among workers, even when employed by the same organisation, thus making it difficult for unions to organise.

Despite the commonalities, platforms have distinctive features in countries with different models of capitalism and of care regimes. While in Ireland platforms are born out of the large international chains entering the market, and the example of digitalisation of existing agencies, in Italy so far, the establishment of new digital native start-ups is prevailing. Both models challenge established

[76] European Trade Union Institute (2025) Available at: www.worker-participation.eu/national-industrial-relations/countries/ireland.

norms in the sector and to a lesser or greater extent introduce new risks for workers, such as the tendency toward fragmentation of labour and the impact on social protection, on which regulation has not yet intervened.

The potential for platform work to increasingly become the model through which domestic care is delivered potentially creates challenges for unions in seeking to raise standards on behalf of workers. Our findings illustrate that care platforms have not been placed high on union agendas to date and that unions are continuing to prioritise the organisation of domestic care workers employed in the public and non-profit sectors and by private agencies, while so far, a clear strategy to actively address the increasing growth of platform-based work is lacking. Therefore, care platforms can be viewed as an area exhibiting a growing representation gap, even relative to the care sector itself which too has low levels of unionisation in the private sector. Unions approach to securing worker protections varies based on their institutional strength or weakness and representation within various sectors. Therefore, the lack of representation within the platform economy and the care sector concurrently combine weaken union strength and legitimacy of voice when it comes to demanding change.

Furthermore, there remains a dearth of union organisation among platform workers more generally speaking in both Ireland and Italy. Many actors in the trade union movement question the fairness of platform-based work and view the gig economy as a threat to working conditions more broadly. We identify a trichotomy of approaches. The first approach is a complete rejection of platform work, whereby unions' attempt to address the emergence of platform work in the care sector through lobbying for broader regulation of work and employment. The second approach is once again regulatory in nature but focused directly on the care sector. This involves unions campaigning for greater regulation in the care sector itself. The interpretation and application of the European Care Strategy is of relevance to this approach. The third option is to accept that platform work is a growing feature of the care sector and adopt active organising strategies in response. The Directive on Platform Work could be an important support for unions seeking fair treatment of workers in line with legislation. Below we examine these options, specifically for Ireland and Italy.

In both countries, an outright rejection of platform work seems unlikely as a viable solution. While in many contexts numerous cases have come before the courts in relation to platform work and the gig economy, the most seminal case to have taken place in Ireland on this issue was in 2023. That case, *Revenue Commissioners v Karshan (Midlands) Ltd t/a Domino's Pizza*, related to the tax rather than employment status of delivery drivers with the Supreme Court concluding that the drivers were employees for tax purposes. SIPTU, the largest trade union welcomed the decision but, while emphasising that there is potential for the effects of the decision to be felt across many sectors of the economy, acknowledged that as a tax case the implications for employment rights are not clearcut.[77] The case essentially has laid bare problems regarding the interpretation of 'mutuality of obligation' (that is an expectation between employer and worker that work will be offered and carried out in the future) that have long been the basis of assessing whether a worker's status is that of an employee or self-employed.

In Italy, too, interventions have focused only on platform work in home delivery. The first cases date back to 2018, and there have since been numerous interventions by various Courts of Appeal, as well as the Court of Cassation and the Labour Inspectorate, which have ruled on the employment status of platform workers. These rulings highlighted the need for companies to ensure fair treatment, including minimum wage and social protections, affirming that these workers should enjoy the same rights as traditional employees. This may become important when it comes to how the EU Directive on Platform Work is transposed at national level.[78] However, for now the first category of action seems unlikely to change the situation regarding care platforms significantly.

Of greater relevance and more related to the second option around regulation of care work, are the proposed changes to funding and commissioning of care. This so far can be seen in Ireland, but not in Italy. In Ireland, in 2024, waiting lists for home care reached record levels, while at the same time the HSE amended the hourly rate paid to care providers in order to guarantee a living wage for carers and to pay them for travel (for the first time ever). Although the rate paid to providers was increased this did not change the overall HSE budget allocated to home care meaning fewer hours of care could be provided.[79] The decision was criticised by the founder of HCD, who called for a revamp of this system, arguing a 'middle man' is often unnecessary and that long waiting lists 'play into the hands of the providers because they can pick and choose the cases they take on and make sure they suit them' instead arguing that the HSE should adopt a personal budget or direct payment model where families 'have the option to take that funding directly themselves and source and self-manage their own care'.[80] This is viewed as a way of increasing efficiency of resources, but traditional care agency providers have criticised such an approach, arguing that there is 'room for abuse' in the system as seen in other countries.[81] With both platforms and traditional agencies critical of the current approach, an opportunity exists for unions to apply pressure on government for changes which reflect

[77] E Malone, 'Supreme Court decision provides "ammunition" to those seeking to challenge contractor status', *Irish Times* (2023) www.irishtimes.com/business/work/2023/10/23/supreme-court-decision-provides-ammunition-to-those-seeking-to-challenge-contractor-status-says-union/.

[78] For a more detailed exploration of the potential implications of the national transposition of the Platform Work Directive, see Aloisi and Potocka-Sionek, ch 11 and Sedacca and Atkinson, ch 12, in this book.

[79] C McGuirk, *Huge regional divide in waiting list for carers* (2024) available at https://extra.ie/2024/08/11/news/waiting-list-hse-home-care.

[80] ibid.

[81] ibid.

the concerns of both regarding system inefficiencies and leverage support for change.

The third option has not yet been adopted either in Ireland or Italy, but has been discussed, especially with the Italian trade unions, where the high and growing number of people in need of care determines a situation that is already urgent, due to a shortage of care facilities and a lack of public funds to cover domestic personal assistance. The burden of care falls almost entirely on families and determines as a consequence the deterioration of working conditions for caregivers. This need, as we have seen, has generated the emergence of numerous digital platforms in this area. The presence of platforms that – without falling into the rhetoric of digital disintermediation – take precisely a third-party role between family and caregiver may represent value but requires a clearer identification of their role, with related rights and duties, as distinct from traditional agencies.

IV. CONCLUSION

What then accounts for the differences between Ireland and Italy in terms of the emergence of platforms in the care sector? From our analysis it appears that it is not the industrial relations regime but rather the care regime and specifically the manner in which care is funded and supported that impacts the development of care platforms in the two countries. In Italy, there is a proliferation of care platforms, despite the stronger industrial relations regime, power of trade unions and existence of detailed labour codes. In Ireland, the industrial relations system is voluntarist, and union power is largely weakened outside of the public sector. Yet the presence of platforms in the care sector in Ireland is much less prevalent than in Italy. Of those that are present in Ireland, the emphasis appears to be more on general domestic work rather than on care which suggests that the funding model of care is a key point of difference between the two countries. Italy, however scarce resources are – or perhaps precisely because of this – is more liberal in how funding is allocated, allowing individuals greater control over how they acquire care. While in Ireland although the system of home care funding is not means-tested, it is tightly controlled insofar as client and consumer choice is concerned. The structures in place to commission care still support outsourcing only to traditional care agencies for most recipients of elder care support. However, those agencies are still employers of the carers working for them, by comparison with placement agencies or platforms where carers are self-employed. Therefore, platforms are more likely to be engaged only by those who are paying directly out-of-pocket for care services since those organisations are not usually part of the commissioning structures. While a tax credit exists for care, the likelihood is that this will not outweigh the financial difference that can be achieved by paying for care through the informal economy. If we look outside the care sector, both countries have shown a similar approach to platforms in the transport sector, where platforms like Uber are not permitted to operate in the usual ride-sharing manner and can only operate as a taxi service. In that case the power of the industry regulator was critical, rather than the power of trade unions and worker representatives. However, that was not a sector in which state funding was a critical factor unlike in care. Ultimately an examination of these countries points to the role of the state as a funder rather than as a regulator in relation to the emergence of platforms in care and the attendant impact on working conditions and union responses. With regard to union actions, in Ireland, it has been noted that Irish unions have neither organised nor campaigned strongly on behalf of platform workers generally and so there has been little pressure on the state to introduce platform-specific regulations.[82]

Future research on digital labour platforms in European care and domestic sectors should focus on several key areas. It is vital to examine how platform models impact workers' rights and job security both within and between different countries particularly as platforms can operate in regulatory grey zones due to the invisibility and vulnerability of the workforce. Moreover, in relation to health and social care provision, investigating the quality of care delivered through these platforms compared to traditional services is essential in order to evaluate the effectiveness and reliability of such models from a consumer perspective. Additionally, exploring the socio-economic implications for clients, including issues of accessibility and affordability, can provide valuable insights into how funding models across different countries impact how care delivery is shaped. Research should also consider technological advancements, such as algorithmic management and its role in shaping care services, assessing whether such innovation can contribute to enhanced care provision and the autonomy of workers in providing that care. Finally, developing an understanding of the long-term sustainability of platforms, factoring in funding models, market demand and regulatory changes, is needed to envision their potential role in Europe's care sector in the future.

[82] J Duggan, M O'Sullivan and M O'Sullivan, 'Essential or Excluded? Union Pressures and State Responses to Platform Work in Three Liberal Market Economies' (2023) 29 *Transfer: European Review of Labour and Research* 491.

Part III

An Alternative Model: Workers' Cooperatives

7

Towards Transition from an Academic Project to WeCare Workers Enterprise: Lessons from the Digital Platform Cooperative Project, South Africa

ABIGAIL OSIKI*

I. INTRODUCTION

DOMESTIC WORK IS an important source of employment, representing 2.1 per cent of overall employment in Africa.[1] According to the International Labour Organization (ILO), when the agriculture sector is excluded, the likelihood that an individual on the continent works as a domestic worker doubles.[2] The domestic work sector overlaps with informality, which manifests in terms of exclusion from labour and social security laws, limited implementation and compliance with these laws and inadequate levels of legal protection. The emergence of digital domestic work platforms has caused a significant shift in the labour markets of many countries in Sub-Saharan Africa.[3] As a result, particularly in South Africa, the domestic work sector has been incorporated into the platform economy, exacerbating precarity for workers while erecting new technological and financial barriers to market entry.[4] The

* This article is based on an academic initiative undertaken by the members of CENTROW, University of the Western Cape. I extend my sincere gratitude to them for allowing me to document their experiences.

[1] *International Labour Organization (ILO), Making decent work a reality for domestic workers: Progress and prospects ten years after the adoption of the Domestic Workers Convention, 2011 (No. 189)* (Geneva, ILO, 2021).

[2] ibid 41.

[3] See also the following chapters in this book, which discuss the emergence of digital domestic work platforms in various regions, Rodríguez-Modroño (ch 1); Starčević (ch 4); Poblete (ch 5); Pais, et al (ch 6).

[4] W Sibiya and D du Toit, 'Sweeping Up Decent Work: Paid Domestic Work and Digital Platforms in South Africa, Gender & Development' (2022) 30 *Gender and Development* 637; *World Employment and Social Outlook: The Role of Digital Labour Platforms in Transforming the World of Work*, ILO Flagship Report (Geneva, ILO, 2022).

power dynamics in this sector have also shifted, as domestic workers now have to negotiate with digital labour platforms in addition to their employers. Within this context, platforms act as intermediaries, while clients specify the location, size and services required for the workplace. These changes have implications for the earnings and job security of domestic workers.

Although there are no official statistics, Fairwork estimates that platform workers, including those on digital domestic work platforms, represent around one per cent of the working population in South Africa.[5] This is primarily driven by the country's high levels of unemployment, its highly developed internet infrastructure, and widespread phone ownership.[6] An example of a digital domestic work platform in South Africa is SweepSouth, which provides a range of domestic services to private households across major cities in the country.[7] However, research shows that digital domestic labour platforms, while presenting income-generating opportunities for workers, do not improve the working conditions and livelihoods of domestic workers in South Africa.[8] These platforms disregard regulatory provisions, such as Sectoral Determination 7, which regulates the working conditions of domestic workers, and have a contractual form that assumes equality between parties in the platform economy. Thereby, reinforcing pre-existing inequalities in the domestic work sector. Despite this, there is limited will on the part of policymakers in the country to regulate digital labour platforms.

An alternative platform model to facilitate decent work for platform workers is emerging globally.[9] This model, known as platform cooperatives, is 'an enterprise that operates through digital platforms for the interaction or exchange of goods and/or services and that is structured in line with the International Cooperative Alliance Statement on the Cooperative identity'.[10] Platform cooperatives have the potential to improve labour market outcomes for digital domestic workers; however, this is dependent on the regulatory and institutional context, which determines the role these cooperatives play in the labour market.

This chapter examines the opportunities and challenges of platform cooperatives, drawing on the experiences of an emerging domestic worker platform

[5] Fairwork, *Fairwork South Africa Ratings 2023: Advocating for Safety, and Dignity in the Platform Economy* (Oxford, United Kingdom; Berlin, Germany, 2023).

[6] ibid.

[7] Apart from *SweepSouth*, other digital platforms which match domestic workers with households are *GetTOD* and *Kandua*.

[8] A Hunt and E Samman, 'Domestic Work and the Gig Economy in South Africa: Old Wine in New Bottles?' (2020) 15 *Anti-Trafficking Review* 102.

[9] ILO, *Platform Labour in Search of Value: A study of Worker Organizing Practices and Business Models in the Digital Economy* (Geneva, ILO, 2021); 'Interview with Trebor Scholz – Connecting Cooperatives to the Future of Work, Digitally' (February 2018) www.ilo.org/global/topics/cooperatives/news/spotlight/WCMS_616775/lang- -en/index.htm; MM Bühler et al, 'Unlocking the Power of Digital Commons: Data Cooperatives as a Pathway for Data Sovereign, Innovative and Equitable Digital Communities' (2023) 3 *Digital* 146.

[10] E Mayo, '¿Democracia digital? Opciones de la Alianza Cooperativa Internacional para avanzar en las cooperativas de plataforma' (2019) *Brussels: Alianza Cooperativa Internacional* cited in D Kasparian et al, 'Socio-Labour Inclusion of Low-Income Women in the Digital Economy: A Comparison between Corporate and Cooperative Domestic Work Platforms' (2023) 12 *Social Sciences* 578.

cooperative in South Africa, the Digital Platform Cooperative Project (DPCP), situated in the University of the Western Cape (UWC), Centre for Transformative Regulation of Work (CENTROW). DPCP began as an academic research project and has evolved into a voluntary association of domestic workers, known as WeCare, a digital platform cooperative serving the domestic work sector. Although the ILO has acknowledged the significance of cooperatives as a means to achieve decent work and gender equality in the platform economy, there are significant practical challenges to this.[11]

This study documents some of these challenges from the experience of DPCP. To unpack this, this article first explores the context and regulatory framework of domestic work and digital labour platforms in South Africa. The following section provides an overview of platform cooperatives as a pathway to achieving decent work for platform workers. Hereafter, the history and context of DPCP are discussed. The final section offers insights into the challenges encountered during the transition from DPCP to WeCare.

II. WOMEN, DOMESTIC WORK AND DIGITAL LABOUR PLATFORMS IN SOUTH AFRICA

The domestic work sector in South Africa is highly feminised, with women constituting the majority of the 876,000 domestic workers as of 2023.[12] Furthermore, the face of the domestic work sector is characterised by black women who are from poor socio-economic backgrounds and many of whom are increasingly migrants from mainly neighbouring African countries such as Lesotho, Malawi and Zimbabwe.[13] Domestic work is historically undervalued, more so in the context of South Africa, where the racial and structural legacies of apartheid have disproportionately impacted this sector.[14] Indeed, under apartheid, domestic workers worked under conditions of isolation, exploitation, discrimination and abuse. This is because they were excluded from the protective scope of laws regulating labour relations for most of this era.[15] Consequently, these workers were disempowered in the socio-political and economic sense.[16]

Following the end of apartheid, comprehensive legal reform led to the inclusion of domestic workers within the scope of labour and social security

[11] ILO, *Decent work and the social and solidarity economy*, Report IV (Geneva, ILO, 2022).

[12] www.statssa.gov.za/publications/P0211/P02114thQuarter2023.pdf.

[13] JN Fish, 'Rights Across Borders: Policies, Protections and Practices for Migrant Domestic Workers in South Africa' in D du Toit (ed), *Exploited, Undervalued – and Essential: Domestic Workers and the Realisation of their Rights* (Johannesburg, Pretoria University Law Press, 2013) 214.

[14] S Ally, 'Domestic Worker Unionisation in Post-Apartheid South Africa: Demobilisation and Depoliticisation by the Democratic State' (2008) 35 *Politikon: South African Journal of Political Studies* 1, 2.

[15] D du Toit and E Huysamen, 'Implementing Domestic Workers' Labour Rights in a Framework of Transformative Constitutionalism' in du Toit (ed) (n 13) 66.

[16] S Ally, *From Servants to Workers: South African Domestic Workers and the Democratic State* (Ithaca, Cornell University Press, 2010).

laws. Domestic workers have the right to fair labour practices, as stipulated in Section 23(1) of the 1996 Constitution. Specifically, primary labour statutes such as the Labour Relations Act 66 of 1995(LRA) and the Basic Conditions of Employment Act 75 of 1997 (BCEA), which give effect to the constitutional right to fair labour practices, grant domestic workers the same protections as other employees in South Africa. Such protections include freedom of association, collective bargaining rights, access to dispute resolution mechanisms, protection against unfair dismissal, remedies for breaches of employment rights and minimum working conditions, among others. Domestic workers are also broadly protected against unfair discrimination under the Employment Equity Act 55 of 1998 (EEA).[17]

Furthermore, in recognition of the uniqueness of the domestic work sector, Sectoral Determination 7: Domestic Worker Sector (SD 7) was introduced by the Minister of Labour in 2002. Together with the provisions of the BCEA, SD 7 aligns with the basic conditions of employment required for domestic workers in terms of the ILO's Domestic Workers Convention, 2011 (No. 189). In this regard, SD 7 applies to all domestic workers, whether they are employees or independent contractors, except those employed on farms, covered by another sectoral determination or collective bargaining agreement.[18] The conditions of employment regulated by SD 7 are wages,[19] written particulars of employment,[20] working hours,[21] leaves[22] and termination of employment.[23] Specifically for live-in domestic workers, item 8(b) of the Determination provides that an employer cannot deduct more than 10 per cent of the worker's wage for a room or other accommodation which must be waterproof, generally in good condition, has at least one window and door which can be locked, and has a toilet and bath or shower, if the worker does not have access to any other bathroom. The sectoral determination also prohibits the employment of a child under 15 years or one who is under the minimum school-leaving age, as defined by any law, as a domestic worker.[24]

Similarly, in terms of protection under social security laws, the Constitutional Court, in *Mahlangu v Minister of Labour* (CCT306/19) [2020] ZACC, has recently extended the scope of the Compensation for Occupational Injuries and

[17] See also National Minimum Wage Act 9 of 2018 (NMWA) which regulates minimum wage and Occupational Health and Safety Act 85 of 1993 (OHSA) addresses health and safety standards in the workplace, among others.

[18] Section 2 Sectoral Determination 7: Domestic Worker Sector (SD 7).

[19] Part B Sectoral Determination 7: Domestic Worker Sector (SD 7); in 2018, the National Minimum Wage Act which prescribes a national minimum wage was enacted. This now regulates the minimum wage of all workers including domestic workers. For domestic workers, this law initially introduced a tiered phase-in wages for domestic workers. However, the wages of domestic workers have been equalised with other workers and now stands at R28.79 per ordinary hour worked.

[20] Item 9 Sectoral Determination 7: Domestic Worker Sector (SD 7).

[21] Part D Sectoral Determination 7: Domestic Worker Sector (SD 7).

[22] Part E Sectoral Determination 7: Domestic Worker Sector (SD 7).

[23] Part G Sectoral Determination 7: Domestic Worker Sector (SD 7).

[24] Section 23 Sectoral Determination 7: Domestic Worker Sector (SD 7).

Diseases Act (COIDA) to domestic workers.[25] This Act aims to protect employees from income shocks resulting from temporary or permanent incapacity and inability to work. Apart from the COIDA, in 2003, the Unemployment Insurance Act 63 of 2001 (UIA) was extended to domestic workers.[26] This Act regulates the payment of unemployment and maternity benefits, among others, to qualifying contributors. However, to gain access to the benefits under this law, domestic workers must be registered by their employers, who must complete and submit certain forms through an online uFiling system or manually.[27]

Notwithstanding the general inclusion of domestic workers in labour and social security regulation in South Africa, there remain four significant challenges in the domestic work sector. First, the asymmetrical power dynamics in this sector, enabled by the intra-household nature of the relationship between domestic workers and their employers, raise issues of compliance with legislative provisions.[28] For example, although the UIA covers domestic workers, a 2019 study shows that only 20 per cent of South Africa's 1.2 million domestic workers were registered for the Unemployment Insurance Fund (UIF).[29] A significant barrier to accessing the UIF is the registration requirement, which is a legal duty of employers of domestic workers.[30] The impact of this non-compliance was further aggravated for domestic workers during the lockdown period of the COVID-19 pandemic.[31]

Second, the regulatory framework does not adequately consider the occupational uniqueness of domestic work, resulting in doctrinal gaps in protection for these workers. As mentioned above, SD7 and the BCEA regulate the minimum working conditions for domestic workers. However, domestic workers who work less than 24 hours for their employer(s) are unprotected under most provisions in the BCEA and SD7, except for clauses 2 and 3, which provide for the payment of the national minimum wage.[32] In reality, many domestic workers work for multiple employers for less than 24 hours per month individually, but collectively could be working 45 hours (full-time) weekly. As a result, many domestic workers are outside the protective scope of the BCEA and SD 7 except in respect of the minimum wage.

[25] See also F Mullagee, C James and A Osiki, 'Domestic Workers in South Africa: Inclusion Under the Compensation of Occupational Injuries and Diseases Act' (2023) 96 *The Thinker 13*; Act 130 of 1993.

[26] D Du Toit and E Huysamen, 'Implementing Domestic Workers' Labour Rights in a Framework of Transformative Constitutionalism' in du Toit (ed) (n 13) 76.

[27] See also, K Malherbe, 'Implementing Domestic Workers' Social Security Rights in a Framework of Transformative Constitutionalism' in du Toit (ed) (n 13) 127.

[28] C Horton and M Vilana, Working Conditions of Domestic and Agricultural workers NALEDI Policy Memo (2001); Q Dawood and M Seedat-Khan, 'The Unforgiving Work Environment of Black African Women Domestic Workers in a Post-apartheid South Africa' (2022) 33 *Development in Practice 1*.

[29] C Skinner, J Barrett, L Alfers and M Rogan, 'Informal Work in South Africa and COVID-19: Gendered Impacts and Priority Interventions' (2021) 19 *WIEGO Policy Brief* 12.

[30] ibid.

[31] GroundUp, 'Covid-19: Open Letter to President Ramaphosa' (2020) www.groundup.org.za /article/COVID-19-open-letter-president-ramaphosa/.

[32] It is important to note that the National Minimum Wage Act now regulates minimum wage of domestic workers.

Likewise, the BCEA and SD 7 are silent on the standard of accommodation to be provided for live-in domestic workers who reside on the employer's premises. Furthermore, the BCEA and SD 7 do not explicitly address the right of domestic workers to be with their family or children while living on the employer's premises.

Third, closely related to the issue of compliance is enforcement, which hinges on labour inspection. Private homes as the workplaces of domestic workers make labour inspection challenging because of the tensions between an employer's right to privacy and the domestic worker's rights. According to a 2017 research by the Department of Labour, access to private households is a major hindrance to labour inspection in the domestic work sector.[33] Many employers either refuse entry to inspectors or threaten their safety while in private homes.[34] This is furthermore aggravated by the cumbersome and time-consuming legal process required to access private homes for labour inspection. In terms of sections 63 and 64 of the BCEA, the Minister may appoint labour inspectors to promote, monitor and enforce compliance with any employment law. However, before an inspector can enter a home, the consent of the owner or occupier must be obtained, or an authorisation in writing from the Labour Court must be obtained to gain entry.[35] To obtain authorisation from the Labour Court, an inspector must complete a written application stating, under oath, the reasons for the need to enter a home to monitor or enforce compliance with any employment law.[36] Consequently, without adequate enforcement measures, the BCEA and SD 7 are merely an exercise in ethics.

Finally, the exercise of the right to collective bargaining is limited in the domestic work sector despite being enshrined in the LRA. Yet collective bargaining is the means through which the interests of workers can be articulated. While there are two main unions in this sector, the United Domestic Workers of South Africa (UDWOSA) and the South African Domestic Service and Allied Workers Union (SADSAWU), neither of them has been registered by the Department of Labour. Furthermore, only 0.5 per cent of domestic workers in South Africa were unionised in 2017.[37] WEIGO sums up the organisational challenge in the domestic work sector as follows:

> Most domestic worker are not organised into trade unions and have no representative voice. In some countries they are not allowed to join trade unions. Even where they have the legal right to organise, because they are isolated and vulnerable, it is not easy for them to do so. Where they do organise into unions these organisations struggle to

[33] Department of Labour, *Adequacy of resources for effective inspections to be conducted within the South African labour market* (March 2017) www.labour.gov.za/DocumentCenter/Research%20Documents/2017/Adequacy%20of%20resources%20for%20effective%20inspections%20to%20be%20conducted%20%20within%20the%20South%20African%20labour%20market.pdf.

[34] ibid.

[35] Section 65 (2&3) of the BCEA.

[36] Section 65(3) of the BCEA; Social Law Project. 2014. Domestic Workers' Laws and Legal Issues in South Africa. WIEGO Law and Informality Resources. Cambridge, MA, USA: WIEGO.

[37] ILAW, *Mapping Domestic Work and Discrimination in Africa: A study of Global and African Regional Norms with case studies on Ethiopia, Kenya, Nigeria, Malawi, Ghana, South Africa, Uganda, Mauritius and Lesotho* (March 2023) 64.

> grow and sustain themselves. Generally, established unions and national centres have not prioritised organising domestic workers precisely because they are invisible, are women in 'low status' jobs, seemingly without collective power, difficult to organise using traditional approaches and a challenge for financial sustainability.[38]

The above challenges imply that the post-apartheid regulatory framework has failed to achieve transformative change for domestic workers in South Africa, leading to the persistence of indecent work deficits in this sector.

These indecent working conditions continue to be perpetuated in the platform economy. The emergence of digital labour platforms has given rise to new forms of work. As previously stated, in South Africa, digital platforms offer income-generating opportunities, particularly given the context of income inequality and rising unemployment levels in the country. However, platform work also raises several challenges and concerns.[39]

Contracts in the platform economy assume equality between the parties and are typically outside the scope of the employment relationship.[40] Platform workers do not have access to social security benefits, as these are typically tied to employment status. Their classification as independent contractors means they cannot engage in collective bargaining, as this would violate competition laws and principles. Despite being portrayed as independent contractors, many workers exhibit clear characteristics of employment. However, the business model of platforms 'relies on the precariousness and flexibility of labour conditions'.[41] These issues call for even more attention in the domestic work sector, where the legacy of apartheid means that digital domestic platforms are reinforcing pre-existing inequalities. Research shows that while workers on digital domestic platforms earn the minimum wage after the deduction of work-related costs, the wages are inadequate to cover the basic needs of these workers.[42] Furthermore, difficulty with obtaining consistent bookings from clients means that the earnings of workers were irregular 'as the remuneration model across the platforms

[38] Women in Informal Employment: Globalizing and Organizing (WIEGO) 'Informal Workers In focus: Domestic Workers' (September 2008) www.wiego.org/sites/default/files/resources/files/WIEGO_Domestic_Workers_0.pdf 1, 3.

[39] M Graham, I Hjorth and V Lehdonvirta, 'Digital Labour and Development: Impacts of Global Digital Labour Platforms and the Gig Economy on Worker Livelihoods' (2017) 23 *Transfer: European Review of Labour and Research* 135.

[40] While it appears that platform workers and digital labour platforms transact on equal terms, a survey of contracts adopted in the platform economy show the contrary. Indeed, unequal bargaining positions between platforms and platform workers is reflected in the fact that contractual terms are decided and can be changed unilaterally by platforms without prior notification or provision of reasons to workers, power of termination or suspension of the contract lies solely with platforms and platforms more often than not, solely control the whole work processes, at the same time, portraying themselves as mere intermediaries. See S Guido, 'The Protection of the weaker parties in the platform economy' in *N Davidson, M Finck and J Infranca (eds), Cambridge Handbook of the Law of the Sharing Economy* (Cambridge, Cambridge University Press, 2018).

[41] D Kasparian et al, 'Socio-Labour Inclusion of Low-Income Women in the Digital Economy: A Comparison between Corporate and Cooperative Domestic Work Platforms' (2023) 12 *Social Sciences* 1.

[42] W Sibiya and D du Toit, 'Sweeping Up Decent Work'; Fairwork, *Fairwork South Africa Ratings 2023* 24.

is no work, no pay'.[43] Thus, while relative ease of entry is one of the characteristics of platform work, oversupply of workers and limited bookings mean access to regular work is at times limited and this impacts income security.

Violence and harassment in the workplace are part of the daily experience of many domestic workers in South Africa.[44] This is linked to the country's history, its present-day socio-political landscape and the invisibility of domestic work. In addition to this, digital domestic work comes with unique safety risks, as workers have to provide services to different, unknown clients. Some platforms offer minimal protection against workplace violence to their workers. For example, SweepSouth provides workers with guidance on handling emergencies, has SOS helplines in place, and workers still receive payment in cases where they leave houses because of safety concerns.[45] Nonetheless, the risks and responsibilities for safety remain disproportionately on workers.

One other key aspect of the working conditions of digital domestic workers is the role of algorithms to organise work, allocate tasks and assess their performance. Through this, platforms exert surveillance and control over domestic workers.[46] However, this limits the autonomy and flexibility of workers, as rejecting work affects their ratings, which in turn impacts their access to future work. Moreover, the use of algorithms to assess the performance of workers has significant implications for the deactivation of workers, job allocation and dispute resolution, potentially reinforcing pre-existing biases in the sector.

Given the need to facilitate decent work for digital domestic workers while improving their livelihoods, platform cooperatives offer an alternative to the prevailing capitalist platforms.

III. PLATFORM COOPERATIVES

The International Cooperative Alliance (ICA) defines cooperatives to mean 'an autonomous association of persons united voluntarily to meet their common economic, social and cultural needs and aspirations through a jointly-owned and democratically-controlled enterprise'.[47] The guiding principles of cooperatives are voluntary and open membership; democratic member control; member economic participation; autonomy and independence; education, training and

[43] A Shamira, T Chinembiri, M Moyo and A Gillwald, 'Future of Work in the Global South (FOWIGS): digital labour, new opportunities and challenges' (2021) *Working Paper: Research ICT Africa*.

[44] MA Anwar and K Brukwe, '"We Endure Because We Need Money": Everyday Violence, COVID-19 and Domestic Workers in South Africa' (2023) 44 *Canadian Journal of Development Studies / Revue canadienne d'études du développement* 575.

[45] Fairwork, *Fairwork South Africa Ratings 2023* 24.

[46] U Rani and M Furrer, 'Digital Labour Platforms and New Forms of Flexible Work in Developing Countries: Algorithmic Management of Work and Workers' (2020) 25 *Competition & Change* 212.

[47] International Cooperative Alliance (ICA), *Cooperative identity, values & principles* (1995) www.ica.coop/en/cooperatives/cooperative-identity.

information; cooperation among cooperatives; and concern for the community.[48] Cooperatives have been argued to 'empower people by enabling even the poorest segments of the population to participate in economic progress; they create opportunities for those who have skills but little or no capital; and they provide protection by organising mutual help in communities'.[49] Cooperatives have also been recognised as necessary for facilitating access to social protection, promoting social dialogue and gaining legal recognition, particularly for informal workers who are typically not covered in law and/or in practice by labour and social security laws.[50] It is within this context that the cooperative model has been innovatively transformed into digital cooperatives as an intervention to address some of the challenges of platform work.[51]

A platform cooperative is a digital enterprise that is owned and managed by workers.[52] Platform cooperatives maximise the benefits of technology while having a structure that is geared towards equitable outcomes and participatory governance for producers of labour. In other words, they offer similar services as capitalist platforms, while their members (who are both owners and users) have control and participate in the development of the platform. Just like in traditional worker cooperatives, management decisions are collectively made, creating a sense of solidarity.

Platform cooperatives have the potential to address many of the decent work challenges of typical platform work. In respect to earnings, workers can gain a larger share of the revenue generated because, depending on the bylaws of the cooperatives, surplus earnings can be allocated to members.[53] For example, members can allocate surplus resources to training and skills development which is one of the principles of the ICA. For representation, given that one of the guiding principles of cooperatives is democratic member control, workers can articulate their interests and participate in the decision-making process. In this way, the right to organise and collectively express their interest, which is typically low among platform workers, is realised. This increases the likelihood of instituting fair and equitable rules and policies especially in relation to algorithmic management which could reinforce existing biases particularly in the domestic work sector.[54] Furthermore, a crucial function of platform

[48] ICA, *Cooperative identity, values & principles*; See also, *The Guidance Notes on the Cooperative Principles www.ica.coop/en/media/library/the-guidance-notes-on-the-co-operative-principles.*

[49] ILO, *Promoting cooperatives: An information guide to ILO recommendation no. 193* (2014) Geneva.

[50] A Osiki, 'Esusu Cooperative as a Means of Extending Social Protection to the Nigerian Informal Economy' (2020) 15 *Contemporary Social Science* 461.

[51] Bronowicka et al, ch 8, in this book.

[52] N Schneider, 'An Internet of Ownership: Democratic Design for the Online Economy' (2018) 66 *The Sociological Review* 320; T Scholz et al, *Policies for Cooperative Ownership in the Digital Economy* (2021) www.platform.coop/blog/policies-for-cooperative-ownership-in-the-digital-economy/.

[53] T Scholz, *How to coop the digital economy* (2017) www.diktio-kapa.dos.gr/keimena/18-treborscholz.pdf; F Martinelli et al, 'Innovative Models of Cooperative of Independent Workers for Decent Work in Europe' (2022) 13 *Revista Nacional de Administración* 11.

[54] JB Schor and S Eddy, 'The Just and Democratic Platform? Possibilities of Platform Cooperativism' in *A Political Economy of Justice* (Chicago, University of Chicago Press, 2022) 263.

cooperatives is the creation of better working conditions and flexibility for workers. Within this context, the work process is democratised and perceived as a tool for social change, leading to working environments that are more inclusive and equitable.[55] Compliance with ICA principles means platform cooperatives will be accountable and transparent in all their activities.

A platform cooperative is a pathway to professionalise economic activities such as domestic work, which is typically undervalued.[56] Research shows that worker-owned cooperatives invest in the professional development and training of their workers.[57] By participating in these development and training programmes, domestic workers acquire skills that they leverage to secure better working conditions, ultimately enhancing the occupational value of domestic work. Finally, a platform cooperative serves as a pathway to facilitate an inclusive feminist platform economy.[58] This is particularly imperative in the context of South Africa, where domestic work intersects with various oppressions based on race, gender, social status and class, which the fragmented nature of platform work has exacerbated.

Platform cooperatives are gaining traction in many countries through numerous initiatives by researchers, civil organisations and public agencies to promote their development.[59] One such initiative is the DPCP which is based at the CENTROW, Faculty of Law, UWC, South Africa.

IV. DIGITAL PLATFORM COOPERATIVE PROJECT AS AN ACADEMIC RESEARCH PROJECT: HISTORY AND CONTEXT

In the last few decades, the growth in the knowledge economy, globalisation as well as socio-economic and environmental crises have prompted the emergence of service as the third mission of universities.[60] In this context, the role

[55] J Rothschild, 'Workers' Cooperatives and Social Enterprise: A Forgotten Route to Social Equity and Democracy' (2009) 52 *American Behavioral Scientist* 1023; J Battilana et al, 'Democratizing Work: Redistributing Power in Organizations for a Democratic and Sustainable Future' (2022) 3 *Organization Theory* 1.

[56] OECD (2022), 'From Informal to Formal Jobs: The contribution of Cooperatives in Colombia', OECD Local Economic and Employment Development (LEED) Papers, No. 2022/07, OECD Publishing, Paris.

[57] See M Lenore, *Providing Care through Cooperatives 2: Literature Review and Case Studies* (Geneva, ILO, 2017); ILO, *Care Work and Care Jobs for the Future of Decent Work* (Geneva, ILO, 2018)

[58] J Salvagni, R Grohmann and E Matos, 'Gendering Platform Co-operativism: The Rise of Women-owned Rider Co-operatives in Brazil and Spain' (2022) 30 *Gender & Development* 710.

[59] See www.platform.coop. Examples of platform cooperatives include: The Drivers Cooperative (www.drivers.coop/); Homecare Thailand (homecarethailand.com); Autonomía Switzerland: Bronowicka, Orth and Schumacher (ch 8) in this book.

[60] G Trencher, M Yarime, K McCormick, CNH Doll and SB Kraines, 'Beyond the Third Mission: Exploring the Emerging University Function of Co-creation for Sustainability' (2014) 41 *Science and Public Policy* 151; HE Hadidi and DA Kirby, 'Universities and Innovation in a Factor-driven Economy: The Performance of Universities in Egypt' (2016) 30 *Industry and Higher Education* 140.

of universities has expanded to include becoming engines that contribute to the socio-economic development of the communities in which they operate.[61] This is achieved through applying and transferring mainly research expertise and technologies to industry and to society at large, as well as 'to promote entrepreneurial skills, innovation, social welfare and the formation of human capital'.[62]

This contribution to societal socio-economic development is commonly known as community engagement in South Africa and is recognised as the third pillar of the core responsibilities of universities.[63] In partnership with communities and cities, issues like engineering design and construction,[64] urban crisis and spatial justice,[65] and enhancing the rights of marginalised workers are some of the problem-based challenges South African universities have co-resolved.[66] This is the basis for the DPCP, a research initiative located at the UWC.

In 2009, the Domestic Workers Research Project (DWRP) was launched under the auspices of the Social Law Project (SLP), which is now incorporated under CENTROW. The aim of the project, which was conducted from 2009 to 2012, was to assess the effectiveness of SD7 and other relevant labour legislation on the rights of domestic workers in South Africa.[67] The research project showed that the provisions of the SD7 were largely not complied with by employers.[68] Domestic workers' lack of awareness of their rights in terms of SD7 and structural problems with the Department of Labour contributed to this widespread non-compliance.[69] This remains the state of the domestic work sector.

At the same time, the standard-setting process for what eventually became the Domestic Workers Convention, 2011 (No. 189) was ongoing at the ILO. The DWRP contributed to this process by providing research support to South

[61] A Tommaso, C Barra and R Zotti, 'Research, Knowledge Transfer, and Innovation: The Effect of Italian Universities' Efficiency on Local Economic Development 2006–2012' (2019) 59 *Journal of Regional Science* 819; S Giustina et al, 'Mobilising Intellectual Capital to Improve European Universities' Competitiveness: The Technology Transfer Offices' Role' (20017) 18 *Journal of Intellectual Capital* 607.

[62] L Compagnucci and F Spigarelli, 'The Third Mission of the University: A Systematic Literature Review on Potentials and Constraints' (2020) 161 *Technological Forecasting and Social Change* 1.

[63] Department of Higher Education and Training *National Plan for the Post-School Education and Training 2021–2030* (Pretoria, DHET, 2023).

[64] See J Scott and RF Vaz, 'Understanding Impacts: Community Engagement Programs and Their Implications for Communities, Campuses and Societies' in W Leal Filho and S Nesbit (eds) *New Developments in Engineering Education for Sustainable Development* (Cham, Springer, 2016).

[65] LM Brown, 'Community-university Engagement: The Philippi CityLab in Cape Town and the Challenge of Collaboration Across Boundaries (2013) 65 *Higher Education* 309.

[66] F Bidandi, AN Ambe and C Mukong, 'Collaboration and Partnerships Between South African Higher Education Institutions and Stakeholders: Case Study of a Post-apartheid University' (2022) 1 *Discover Education* 2.

[67] R Mungoshi, 'Domestic Work Neglected Heart of Global Economy' (2010) 34 *South African Labour Bulletin* *www.southafricanlabourbulletin.org.za/wp-content/uploads/2021/11/Domestic-work.-Neglected-heart-of-global-economy_0.pdf;* D Du Toit, 'Extending the Frontiers of Employment Regulation: The Case of Domestic Employment in South Africa' (2010) 14 *Law, Democracy & Development* 1.

[68] The research findings from the DWRP led to the publication of Du Toit (ed) (n 13).

[69] ibid.

African domestic workers, which helped in articulating their contribution at the International Labour Conference in 2010 and 2011. A major outcome of the DWRP, apart from highlighting the need for continued research in the domestic work sector, was the recognition of advocacy to facilitate the implementation of domestic workers' existing rights. In subsequent years, this became one of the main objectives of SLP.[70] In this regard, over the last decade, SLP has focused on advocacy, capacity building, outreach and other related activities for South African domestic workers.[71]

One main conclusion that emerged from the work conducted by SLP was the inappropriateness of the model of industrial trade unionism in the domestic work sector. For example, there were failed experiments with organisational strategies, such as meeting domestic workers in neighbourhood parks and malls, which aimed to emulate the industrial trade union model. Furthermore, the SADSAWU — which was arguably similar to other industrial trade unions- was later deregistered by the Department of Labour because it lacked the resources to maintain an organisational framework. This means till date there is no organisational structure in the domestic work sector which can hold employers and the government accountable for the implementation of the existing statutory rights of domestic workers. To address this gap, SLP began to work towards building a cooperative of domestic workers. This led to the establishment of the DPCP.

The DPCP involves the co-creation of a worker-owned social enterprise, based on the ICA cooperative principles, to facilitate the achievement of decent work in the domestic work sector. The aim of the project is:

> to promote human development and equip a vulnerable category of workers in the labour market (domestic workers experience intersectional forms of discrimination in the workplace) to benefit from digital transformation and make use of widely accessible technology as a means to access decent work and opportunities for organising and learning.[72]

This project has three phases. The first phase, which was the research phase entailed preparation for the co-creation of the social enterprise start-up in the domestic work sector. This phase, which was executed from 2020 to 2022, also included equipping domestic workers with digital skills and knowledge of the platform economy, as well as developing technology for the platform cooperative. Phase two is the transition and current phase of the DPCP. During this phase, DPCP is transitioning from an academic project to the pilot phase of a

[70] D du Toit, 'Introduction' in du Toit (ed) (n 13).

[71] See *Annual Report:2021/2022* CENTROW, www.centrow.org/wp-content/uploads/2023/06/Draft-Annual-Report-21-22.pdf; 'Domestic workers demand better access to social protection' www.lrs.org.za/2022/08/18/domestic-workers-demand-better-access-to-social-protection/; *Report of the Portfolio Committee on Labour on the workshops and public hearings held on the national minimum wage* (8 March 2017) www.parliament.gov.za/storage/app/media/BusinessPubs/National_Minimum_Wage_Report/CONSOLIDATED_REPORT_ON_NMW-adopted_8_March_2017.pdf.

[72] *Annual Report:2021/2022* CENTROW, www.centrow.org/wp-content/uploads/2023/06/Draft-Annual-Report-21-22.pdf.

digital platform called WeCare. So far, the Constitution of WeCare has been developed and signed off by founding members; the business plan, including the vision and mission of WeCare, has been developed; the testing of the website and mobile application is ongoing, and the market research survey is underway. The third phase is the implementation phase, where the members will be fully capacitated to run their own, and will commence in the fourth quarter of 2025.

The next section discusses some of the challenges of transitioning DPCP to WeCare.

V. TOWARDS HAVING THE WECARE DIGITAL COOPERATIVE: SOME TRANSITIONAL CHALLENGES

A. Legal Form

One of the biggest challenges in the transition process was determining the legal form the digital cooperative should take. In this regard, whether WeCare should take shape as a traditional legal model cooperative, as defined by the regulatory framework, a limited liability company or some other legal entity.

Cooperatives in South Africa are regulated by the Co-operatives Act 14 of 2005 and Regulations of 2019. A key question was to what extent the provisions of the Act enable the flourishing of a digital domestic workers' cooperative. Although the Act lacks a definition of platform cooperatives, the purposes of the Act are enabling to the development and survival of a digital cooperative. In terms of section 2, the purposes of the Act include:

a) Promoting the development of sustainable cooperatives that comply with cooperative principles as means to increase the economic enterprises operating in the formal economy.
b) Encouraging persons and groups who subscribe to the values of self-reliance and self-help, who choose to work together in democratically controlled enterprises to register as cooperatives.
c) Enabling the above-mentioned enterprises to register and acquire a legal status which is distinct from their members.
d) Promoting equity and greater participation in the formation and management of cooperatives by persons from previously disadvantaged communities.
e) Ensuring the implementation of cooperative development support programmes and measures by all agencies of national departments.

The above purposes are broad enough to include the objective and needs of WeCare. The objective of WeCare is to facilitate community development for South African domestic workers by promoting community-based projects relating to self-help, empowerment, skills development, capacity-building or anti-poverty initiatives through the provision of decent livelihoods and working conditions for domestic workers on the platform, among other pathways.

In reality, WeCare, taking on the legal form of a cooperative, will be constrained by the administrative requirements provided in the Co-operatives Act. Section 14(1) of the Act outlines the mandatory matters that must be included in the constitution of a cooperative. Section 14(2) provides 10+ optional matters that may be addressed in a cooperative's constitution. However, the flexibility in subsection two is superseded by the obligatory requirements mandated in the Act.[73] For example, requirements such as the maintenance of the registered office,[74] contribution of members to the capital of the cooperative[75] and liability of members,[76] among others. These minimum requirements are not suitable for the unique context of WeCare. Also, the dispersed nature of the workplaces of domestic workers makes it challenging to have a central place of administration to serve as their registered office. The virtual context of the platform economy as well contributes to this. In terms of capital, the Act envisages that financing for cooperatives will be raised from membership fees, shares and members' funds, such as loans. However, the income of digital domestic workers is irregular and insufficient, making it unrealistic to expect these workers to contribute financially to the set-up of the platform cooperative. In addition, this prevents crowdfunding for seed capital and decentralised equity participation, which were necessary to create the WeCare platform.

Relatedly, governance is a significant obstacle to the cooperative legal form. Sections 78 and 79 of the Act grant the Department of Trade and Industry oversight powers over cooperatives. This is exercised by the Companies and Intellectual Property Commission (CIPC) which monitors compliance of the Cooperative Act including administrative requirements. However, 'the [oversight] system is highly formal and appears to have been designed with relatively sophisticated enterprises in mind rather than organisations of marginalised workers' such as WeCare.[77] The opposite seems to be true in countries like Switzerland, where the minimal statutory requirements for establishing cooperatives allowed the creation of the Autonomía platform cooperative.[78]

Furthermore, members of WeCare, as both members of the cooperative and workers performing the services of the cooperative are a challenge to the protection of these workers under the LRA. This is because Schedule 1 and section 1 of the Co-operatives Act do not consider a member of a cooperative as an employee within the context of the LRA. This could potentially hinder access to protection under the LRA and BCEA for domestic workers who are both co-owners and workers in WeCare. Taking the above into consideration, we concluded that South Africa's cooperative law is not conducive to the registration of WeCare as a cooperative.

[73] See chapters 2 to 6 of the Co-operatives Act 14 of 2005.

[74] See 14(1) &20 (1) of the Co-operatives Act 14 of 2005 read with regulation 16 of GNR.593 of 18 April 2019: Co-operatives Administrative Regulations, 2016.

[75] Section 40 of the Co-operatives Act 14 of 2005.

[76] Section 23 of the Co-operatives Act 14 of 2005.

[77] D Du Toit and TG Tiemeni, 'Do Cooperatives Offer a Basis for Worker Organisation in the Domestic Sector-An Exploratory Study' (2015) 36 *Indus LJ* 686.

[78] Bronowicka, Orth and Schumacher, ch 8, in this book.

An alternative regulatory framework, open to the collective ownership basis of WeCare, was explored. In 2023, WeCare was registered as a public non-profit organisation – in other words, a social enterprise. Apart from bypassing some of the onerous administrative requirements of the Co-operative Act, this legal form ensures that perpetual membership is guaranteed even when the current founding members leave WeCare. The assets and liabilities of WeCare are separate from those of its members, thereby removing unforeseen liabilities from the domestic workers. This legal form provides WeCare with the opportunity to establish itself in the hyper-competitive platform economy while implementing ICA's cooperative principles and fulfilling its public benefit objective for domestic workers in South Africa.

B. Operations/Administrative Change

Related to the issue of the legal form is the determination of how the operations and administration of WeCare should change to reflect its business identity outside of the academic project from which it emerged. In other words, it had to be decided whether WeCare would remain as a research and development initiative or a business.

The domestic workers largely spearheaded this push to have a distinct business identity. South Africa's regulatory framework has been criticised for being paternalistic and a vehicle for the disempowerment of domestic workers.[79] This is because it fosters the perception that domestic workers are too vulnerable to act in their own interests. Thus, there was a need to ensure DPCP's origin as a research project does not become a tool for the disempowerment of WeCare members. This required imagining how the daily operations and administration of WeCare will be carried out according to the guiding principles of cooperatives.

As part of the transition process, some researchers from DPCP have been fully seconded to WeCare to provide business support services, such as marketing support and technical assistance, to address some of the operational and scalability challenges of the cooperative. In the meantime, the governing board of WeCare are currently undergoing specialised management and business trainings in preparation to run the cooperative entirely.

C. Upskilling and Reskilling

To successfully operate a platform cooperative, there is a need for a diverse skill set. Domestic workers often possess vocational skills (such as cleaning techniques, ability to manage budgets and to care for the elderly, children and persons with disabilities, among others) and transversal skills (such as trustworthiness, proficiency in a common language and communication skills, among

[79] SA Ally, *From Servants to Workers: South African Domestic Workers and the Democratic State* (Ithaca, NY, Cornell University Press, 2010).

others). However, entrepreneurial and management skills, which are required to run a platform cooperative, are outside the skill set of the founding members of WeCare. None of these workers has ever run a business, small or otherwise. Thus, to bridge this skills gap to ensure the effective operation of WeCare, DPCP has been conducting specialised skills training and workshops since 2022 for workers who are part of the governing board. Before this time, participating domestic workers had been introduced to the digital economy and taught basic digital/computer literacy skills.

As the transition to WeCare began in 2022, content around basic business models was introduced. Through the collaborative efforts of experts from academia, researchers in DPCP and the private sector, structured training sessions focusing on business development and sustainability, cooperative governance, technology management, ownership and data processing have been conducted. These collaborative efforts were vital as academics and researchers provided theoretical knowledge while experts from the private sector offered practical insights. These workshops are still ongoing.

D. Financing

Financing mechanisms were another obstacle we encountered during the transition process, as the unique co-ownership model of WeCare made it challenging to secure seed funding. Businesses require a source of capital to build and sustain the business.[80] Traditional cooperatives often rely on the collective pooling of members' resources to start and grow. The irregular and poor earnings of domestic workers mean they cannot contribute to the financial resources needed to start up a digital platform. Furthermore, the pre-existing disadvantaged socio-economic background of WeCare members means these domestic workers cannot afford to be unpaid or underpaid for any work performed while waiting for the platform to become financially self-sustaining.

Moreover, platforms are capital-intensive businesses and cannot be financed this way. Capitalist platforms have financial security from venture funding, which allows them to operate at a loss for an extended period. This situation was also complicated by the cooperative's inability to access the government's financial support for cooperatives, as WeCare could not meet the necessary bureaucratic requirements. Hence, we needed sufficient and patient capital, as well as other forms of financial resources, to build and sustain WeCare. This required exploring alternative sources of capital.

In this regard, we leveraged multi-stakeholder collaboration and partnership to gain the required capital. First, we applied for and received external funding from the Deutsche Gewerkschaftsbund (DGB), the principal trade union

[80] D McCann and E Yazici, *Disrupting Together: The Challenges and Opportunities for Platform Cooperatives* (London, New Economics Foundation, 2018) 24.

federation of Germany. To develop the WeCare app, we received additional funding from UWC. Finally, to support the research activities of DPCP, we received funding from within the law faculty at UWC.

These forms of financing are attached with varying conditions on WeCare particularly, with respect to intellectual property rights such as trademarks, patents and copyright embedded in the software. Intellectual property rights as part of research outputs from South African universities are regulated by the Intellectual Property Rights from Publicly Financed Research and Development Act 51 of 2008. Section 4 of this Act stipulates that intellectual property emanating from publicly financed research shall be owned by the institution that undertakes the research and development, in this case, UWC. In addition, the long-standing principle for donor-supported projects in South Africa is that the intellectual property rights be shared. Consequently, DGB and its trade union affiliates are entitled to the intellectual property rights from WeCare, subject to the approval of the South African Reserve Bank and the National Intellectual Property Management Office. This intellectual property can only be used for non-commercial, developmental and academic purposes. However, the practical implementation of this sharing intellectual property structure remained uncertain. Ultimately, following consultations with all stakeholders, including domestic workers, it was decided that the data generated by WeCare would become part of the commons.

VI. CONCLUSION

Platform cooperatives have emerged as one of the responses to the decent work challenges in the platform economy. However, despite the widespread support for platform cooperatives, there exist few promising examples as many platform co-ops are not operational yet. Two of such are the WeCare digital cooperative based in South Africa and Autonomía based in Switzerland. Like any complex social organisation, platform cooperatives are multifaceted. This chapter has not tried to highlight all the challenges, ambiguities and potentials of platform cooperatives but rather documented the specific challenges of WeCare as it transitions towards full operation by the end of 2025. In this regard, there is need for regulatory reform to foster the growth and sustainability of platform cooperatives in South Africa. Finally, although in its infancy, research is needed to assess the success or failure of platform cooperatives, particularly as a pathway to achieving decent work for domestic workers.

8

Autonomía: Exploring the Potential of Platform Cooperatives to Revalue Cleaning Work

JOANNA BRONOWICKA, BARBARA ORTH AND SABRI SCHUMACHER

I. INTRODUCTION

AUTONOMÍA IS SWITZERLAND'S first platform cooperative for cleaners. A group of committed women started this pioneering initiative to improve the working conditions of predominantly female migrant cleaning workers in Zurich. The cooperative employs about 40 female workers and offers a wage of CHF 30 per hour, which is well above the legal minimum of CHF 19.95 per hour. In addition to paying a living wage, the cooperative supports worker autonomy, well-being and solidarity. Within weeks of its launch in December 2021, *Autonomía* garnered the interest of hundreds of potential clients, quickly scaling up its operations to match the unexpectedly high demand. Three years later, the organisation became financially sustainable, and the women behind it were eager to develop the cooperative further and inspire similar initiatives in other locations.

The success story of *Autonomía* is intriguing because the organisation succeeded in the domestic cleaning sector, where employers are known to pay low wages, operate informally and engage in exploitative or abusive practices. Moreover, domestic cleaners are often women who society marginalises due to their race, ethnicity or migration status.[1] *Autonomía* is notable among companies that digitally intermediate cleaning jobs, as such companies typically fail

[1] H Lutz, 'Care as a Fictitious Commodity: Reflections on the Intersections of Migration, Gender and Care Regimes' (2017) 5 *Migration Studies* 356; K Shinozaki, *Migrant Citizenship from Below: Family, Domestic Work, and Social Activism in Irregular Migration* (London, Palgrave Macmillan, 2015).

to offer stable employment contracts, fair wages or access to social rights and protections.

While *Autonomía* is already exceptional as a fair employer, the ambition of its initiators goes much further. As stated on its website, the cooperative unites women from different cultures with different professional backgrounds with 'the vision to give cleaning the financial and social appreciation it deserves'. *Autonomía* chose the organisational model of a platform cooperative for two reasons. First, the organisation pursues a social mission of providing fair working conditions, rather than maximising profit. Second, it strives for self-determination as 'every additional cleaner who joins us benefits from a decent income, good social security, and can have a say in the cooperative'.[2] Moreover, *Autonomía*'s initiators hope to inspire similar initiatives in the future, both in Switzerland and beyond, while offering information about how to apply this novel organisational model to cleaning work.

This chapter examines the case study of *Autonomía* and the successes and challenges this platform cooperative encountered during its first three years of operation. Based on interviews we conducted in the autumn of 2024 with three key members of *Autonomía*, as well as an analysis of its website and coverage in the Swiss media, this study aims to answer two research questions: What advantages do platform cooperatives offer compared to for-profit platforms in cleaning work? What unique challenges arise when applying this new organisational model in this particularly undervalued type of work? This study contributes to research on the diversification of digital intermediaries in care and domestic work, as well as research about the potential of platform cooperatives to advance fair work and self-determination in cleaning work.

The first section outlines the context of cleaning work in Switzerland, reviews recent literature on for-profit cleaning platforms, and highlights the existing gap in empirical research on platform cooperatives in this type of work. The second section presents findings from interviews we conducted with three people who helped found *Autonomía*, including one of its initiators and two members of its Board of Directors. Drawing on their insights, this section explores how *Autonomía* intermediates between cleaners and clients, detailing the strengths and weaknesses of its operational model. Moreover, the section examines the challenges of developing *Autonomía*'s organisational structure and governance to enable workers' participation in democratic decision-making. The third section evaluates the advantages platform cooperatives offer in comparison to for-profit platforms. This section also discusses the challenges of designing organisational structures to fit the needs of a predominantly migrant workforce. The conclusion explores whether *Autonomía*'s model can serve in other socioeconomic contexts and considers the broader potential of platform cooperatives to raise the visibility and recognition of cleaning work.

[2] *Autonomía*, en.autonomia-kooperative.ch/team.

II. CLEANING WORK AS A PLAYING FIELD FOR DIGITAL INTERMEDIARIES

A. Cleaning Work in Switzerland

In industrialised societies, employers typically pay low wages for cleaning work, create precarious working conditions and mostly rely on women, particularly in private households.[3] Cleaning work generally requires minimal qualifications or language skills, which makes it accessible to migrants without recognised credentials. At the same time, it has low social value, is often invisible and offers limited opportunities for upward mobility.[4]

In Switzerland, individuals engaged in cleaning work within private households are largely invisible in official statistics and academic research. In 2018, a market research institute estimated that one in seven of Switzerland's four million households engages a cleaning worker, and that these workers are often not registered for social security.[5] There is no reliable quantitative data on the number and sociodemographic profile of cleaning workers in Switzerland, but qualitative studies suggest that a significant part of the workforce comprises women who migrated from various countries in South America, Africa and Europe.[6] Undocumented migrants likely make up a significant number of informal arrangements – for example, the estimated number of *sans-papiers* domestic cleaners in the canton of Zurich was around 8,000.[7] In sum, migrant women appear to meet a large share of the demand for cleaning work.

Legally speaking, cleaners working in private households fall under the Standard Employment Contract for Housekeeping. This means that a household officially registering its cleaners ought to pay them a minimum wage of CHF 19.95 per hour.[8] However, statutory provisions on health and safety, such as regulations on working hours, breaks and rest periods, do not apply to domestic cleaners. Most households (72 per cent) report contracting self-employed cleaners.[9] A recent qualitative study highlights a widespread financial instability

[3] C Avril and M Cartier, 'Subordination in Home Service Jobs: Comparing Providers of Home-Based Child Care, Elder Care, and Cleaning in France' (2014) 28 *Gender & Society* 609.

[4] A Gonon and A John, 'Der Ungleiche Wert Geringqualifizierter Arbeit: Erwerbschancen in Der Bau- und Reinigungsbranche' (2022) 28 *Industrielle Beziehungen. Zeitschrift für Arbeit, Organisation und Management* 260.

[5] Comparis, 'Medienmitteilung: Comparis-Umfrage zeigt Unwissen bezüglich Anstellung von Haushaltshilfe' (2018) www.comparis.ch/-/media/files/mediencorner/medienmitteilungen/2018/immobilien/haushaltshilfe/mm-haushaltshilfe-comparis-20180524.pdf.

[6] A Borges, M Greve and K Massoudi, 'An Investigation of Work Precarity Among Paid Domestic Cleaning Workers in Switzerland' (2024) 33 *Journal of Career Assessment* 569; K Ettarfi, 'Professionalization from above in Domestic Work: Accessing Work on Marketplace Platforms' (2024) 0 *Critical Sociology* 1.

[7] A Knoll, S Schilliger and B Schwager, *Wisch und Weg!: Sans-Papiers Hausarbeiterinnen Zwischen Prekarität und Selbstbestimmung* (Zurich, Seismo, 2012).

[8] Staatssekretariat für Wirtschaft SECO, www.seco.admin.ch/seco/de/home/Arbeit/Personenfreizugigkeit_Arbeitsbeziehungen/normalarbeitsvertraege/Normalarbeitsvertraege_Bund.html.

[9] Comparis (n 5).

among cleaning workers in Switzerland, describing their situation as a 'state of permanent uncertainty' regarding both their immediate and long-term financial security.[10]

B. Platform's Broken Promises

The rise of digital intermediaries is both shaped by and shaping the social dynamics of cleaning work in Switzerland. Despite recurring promises of 'smart homes', the full automation of household tasks is unlikely in the foreseeable future; instead, digital technologies mainly facilitate their gradual streamlining.[11] In recent years, digital labour platforms have positioned themselves as solutions to the crisis of social reproduction.[12] These platforms cater to middle-class clients by offering gig workers who collect groceries, transport children or clean homes, effectively giving clients more time for their paid work. Moreover, investor-backed for-profit platforms show interest in the speculative value of the data generated through service provision.[13]

Platforms like Care.com offer a variety of domestic services, Aupair.com and Babysitting24 provide childcare and elderly care, while Batmaid offers cleaning services.[14] Despite the advent of care and domestic work platforms in Switzerland, research into the working conditions on these platforms is scant.[15] Insights from other countries can, however, help to illuminate the main features of the for-profit digital labour platforms and their impact on conditions in cleaning work.

Domestic platforms present themselves as safer, more efficient ways to hire cleaners, formalising interactions that once relied on word-of-mouth.[16] Many for-profit platforms frame themselves as fighting the 'black market' while offering flexible arrangements.[17] By classifying workers as independent contractors, they cut costs and avoid traditional employer responsibilities, sometimes overlooking occupational insurance or immigration requirements – occasionally opening rare

[10] Borges et al (n 6) 15.

[11] H Hester and N Srnicek, *After Work: A History of the Home and the Fight for Free Time* (London, Verso, 2023).

[12] U Huws, 'The Hassle of Housework: Digitalisation and the Commodification of Domestic Labour' (2019) 123 *Feminist Review* 8; M Altenried, J Dück and M Wallis, *Plattformkapitalismus und die Krise der sozialen Reproduktion* (Münster, Verlag Westfälisches Dampfboot, 2021); Rodríguez-Modroño, ch 1, in this book.

[13] N van Doorn and A Badger, 'Platform Capitalism's Hidden Abode: Producing Data Assets in the Gig Economy' (2020) 52 *Antipode* 1475.

[14] S Schumacher, 'Die Wirkungsanalyse von Autonomía, der Plattformkooperative von Reinigerinnen in Zürich' (unpublished MA thesis, Center for Philanthropy Studies, Universität Basel 2024).

[15] Ettarfi (n 5); M Keller, 'Getting the First Gig: Exploring the Affective Relations of Accessing Place-Based Platform Labour' (2023) 5 *Digital Geography and Society* 100067.

[16] JM Lentz et al, 'From Exceptionalism to Normalisation: How Narratives of Platform Companies Legitimise Precarious Work and Commodified Care' (2025) 0 *Critical Sociology* 1.

[17] Teke-Laurent, ch 2, and Starčević, ch 4, in this book.

income opportunities for those without legal work authorisation.[18] By navigating regulatory frameworks, labour markets and cultural norms, these platforms position themselves between formal and informal work, creating new forms of labour intermediation that largely replicate existing informal arrangements.[19]

Moreover, for-profit digital platforms mediate interactions through digital infrastructure, which, despite being able to match the needs of potential clients, may restrict the autonomy and flexibility of workers.[20] The use of automated decision-making systems by care and domestic work platforms depends on their operational model – marketplace platforms automatically sort workers' profiles akin to social media networking sites,[21] while on-demand platforms can automate sanctions for behaviours they see as undesirable.[22] However, digital placement agencies do not typically use automated tools to match or rank their workers and cater to clients seeking to establish employment contracts.[23] Some have argued that the use of algorithmic management in the cleaning sector is comparatively limited to other types of platform work and that it is the restricted social and legal status of workers that serves as a management device.[24]

In sum, non-profit platforms do little to improve the value of domestic work, working conditions, or the status of cleaning workers, and while domestic workers might be compelled to become visible online, they remain largely invisible in the material world.[25]

[18] B Orth, 'Stratified Pathways into Platform Work: Migration Trajectories and Skills in Berlin's Gig Economy' (2024) 56 *Environment and Planning A: Economy and Space* 476; I Stingl and B Orth, 'Becoming "Platform Workers": A Biographical Exploration of Temporary Visa and Worker Subjectivities in the Gig Economy' (2024) *International Migration Review* 01979183241299717; N van Doorn, 'Liminal Precarity and Compromised Agency: Migrant Experiences of Gig Work in Amsterdam, Berlin, and New York City' in D Das Acevedo (ed), *The Routledge Handbook of the Gig Economy* (London, Routledge, 2022).

[19] Teke-Laurent, ch 2, and Starčević, ch 4, in this book.

[20] Aloisi and Potocka-Sionek, ch 11, in this book.

[21] F Flanagan, 'Theorising the Gig Economy and Home-Based Service Work' (2019) 61 *Journal of Industrial Relations* 57; M Piña, M-J Establés and M Guerrero-Pico, 'Double the Tasks, Double the Control: An Analysis of Workers' Practices to Increase Visibility in Cleaning, Care, and Accommodation Platforms in Spain' (2024) 0 *Critical Sociology* 1; A Mateescu and J Ticona, 'Invisible Work, Visible Workers: Visibility Regimes in Online Platforms for Domestic Work' in D Das Acevedo (ed), *Beyond the Algorithm: Qualitative Insights for Gig Work Regulation* (Cambridge, Cambridge University Press, 2020)

[22] V Pulignano, C Marà, M Franke and K Muszyński K, 'Informality of Employment in Digital Domestic Care Platforms: A Study on the Individualization of Risk and Unpaid Labour in Mature Market Contexts' (2023) 29 *Transfer: European Review of Labour and Research* 323; P Rodríguez-Modroño, 'A Taxonomy of Business Models of Digital Care Platforms in Spain' (2024) 18 *Sociology Compass* 1.

[23] Rodríguez-Modroño, ch 1, in this book.

[24] V Niebler and S Animento, 'Organising Fragmented Labour: The Case of Migrant Workers at Helpling in Berlin' (2023) 34 *The Economic and Labour Relations Review* 689; K Floros, 'Rethinking Algorithmic Management in Minor Key: The Case of Housecleaning Platform Labour in Denmark' (2024) 1 *Platforms & Society* 29768624241273468; B Orth and F Baum, 'Researching Care Platforms: Methodological and Ethical Considerations in the Broad Field of Domestic Platform Labour' (2024) 0 *Critical Sociology* 1.

[25] K Gruszka and M Böhm, 'Out of Sight, out of Mind? (In)Visibility of/in Platform-Mediated Work' (2022) 24 *New Media & Society* 1852.

C. Platform Cooperatives as an Alternative?

Worker-owned platform cooperatives prioritising worker well-being appear as a promising alternative to the exploitative labour dynamics of for-profit platforms.[26] Platform cooperatives operate primarily through digital infrastructures, such as websites or mobile applications, and adhere to principles of communal ownership, democratic governance and transparent data practices.[27] Thus, their potential lies in combining technological innovation with social and economic justice.[28] Research on platform cooperatives suggests that just like traditional cooperatives, they face trade-offs between their business goals and social missions, but they also have to engage in intense competition with well-funded multinational platforms.[29]

Platform cooperatives for domestic cleaners aim to improve the working conditions of cleaners and offer them a collective voice.[30] To date, however, there has been little research about platform cooperatives in cleaning work specifically, with only a few exceptions, such as Up & Go in New York,[31] Clean Coop in Vancouver, Canada[32] and WeCare in South Africa.[33] Research on similar platform cooperatives in South Korea highlights challenges including high marketing and platform maintenance costs, and the difficulty of balancing growth with democratic engagement.[34] However, these studies offer little discussion of platform cooperatives' business strategies or organisational models and rarely situate their success within broader socioeconomic contexts or the dynamics of migrant labour.

[26] T Scholz, 'Platform Cooperativism vs. the Sharing Economy' (10 July 2015) *Medium* medium.com/@trebors/platform-cooperativism-vs-the-sharing-economy-2ea737f1b5ad.

[27] AB Da Silveira, D Wegner and J M Monticelli, 'Platform Cooperativism as an Alternative to Post-Covid-19 Economic Development: Evidence from Brazil' (2024) 10 Revista de Gestão e Organizações Cooperativas 1; T Scholz, 'Platform Cooperativism: Challenging the Corporate Sharing Economy' (1970) 84 *The Quarterly Journal of Economics* 488.

[28] OECD, 'Platform Cooperatives and Employment: An Alternative for Platform Work' (2023) 16 OECD Local Economic and Employment Development (LEED) www.oecd.org/en/publications/platform-cooperatives-and-employment_3eab339f-en.html.

[29] DJ Bunders and T De Moor, 'Paradoxical Tensions as a Double-Edged Sword: Analysing the Development of Platform Cooperatives in the European Gig Economy' (2024) 33 *Journal of Management Inquiry* 366; DJ Bunders et al, 'The Feasibility of Platform Cooperatives in the Gig Economy' (2022) 10 *Journal of Co-operative Organization and Management* 100167; M Mannan and S Pek, 'Platform Cooperatives and the Dilemmas of Platform Worker-Member Participation' (2024) 39 *New Technology, Work and Employment* 219.

[30] International Labour Organisation, 'Cooperating out of Isolation: Domestic Workers' Cooperatives' (2014) 2 Cooperatives and the World of Work Series www.ilo.org/publications/cooperating-out-isolation-domestic-workers%E2%80%99-cooperatives.

[31] M Cannon, J Thorpe and S Emili, *Up & Go: A Platform for Fair Work and Liveable Wages* (2020) The Institute of Development Studies and Partner Organisations opendocs.ids.ac.uk/articles/report/Up_Go_A_Platform_for_Fair_Work_and_Liveable_Wages/26432989?file=48082726.

[32] Mannan and Pek (n 29).

[33] Osiki, ch 7, in this book.

[34] SM Kim, BG Jeong and H Eum, 'Aligning Cooperative Principles with Platform Cooperatives: Challenges and Insights from South Korea's Domestic Service Sector' (2024) 21 *Social Enterprise Journal* 689.

This chapter addresses gaps in two closely related fields of research and strengthens connections between these two areas. First, the chapter examines the diversity of digital intermediaries in care and domestic cleaning work by posing the question: What advantages do platform cooperatives offer compared to for-profit platforms in the cleaning sector? Second, it explores the potential of platform cooperatives by asking: What are the unique challenges of applying this organisational model to cleaning work? Furthermore, the chapter sheds light on the effect of socioeconomic context and workforce composition on the successes and challenges of platform cooperatives in cleaning work.

III. AUTONOMÍA IN PRACTICE: SUCCESSES AND CHALLENGES

A. Introducing *Autonomía* and Its Migrant Workforce

Autonomía began as a project to provide better working conditions to women in the cleaning sector in Switzerland. The project's initiator was Sabri Schumacher, who had previously worked on gender equity and youth projects for the second-largest Swiss trade union Syna, and Jael Bueno, who had founded an association for migrant women over the age of 50 facing discrimination in the Swiss labour market (FRAUEN 50Plus). Owing to their prior professional experiences, engagement with the community of migrants from Latin America, and participation in feminist movements, the initiators were well aware of the challenges that women in cleaning work experience. Inspired by Up & Go in New York, the two women decided to explore the possibility of starting a platform cooperative for cleaners in Zurich.

The project began with a six-month course supported by a grant from the city of Zurich. The initiators recruited ten women, who were primarily from Spanish-speaking Latin American countries, to collaboratively develop the model of a platform cooperative. External experts covered aspects related to labour law, human resources management, communication, entrepreneurship and marketing. The initiators presented the legal requirements for setting up a cooperative compliant with Swiss law, as well as principles of the corporativism movement according to the International Cooperative Alliance, which include voluntary membership, democratic control, equitable economic participation, autonomy, education and training for members, cooperation among cooperatives and a commitment to community development.[35]

Participants in the six-month preparation course collaboratively defined *Autonomía*'s social mission and business model. The initiative aimed to provide good working conditions, offering stable employment, fair wages and flexibility in setting one's working schedule and workload. The name *Autonomía*, the Spanish word for 'autonomy', was to reflect the social mission

[35] International Cooperative Alliance, ica.coop/en/cooperatives/cooperative-identity.

of the platform cooperative and promote the autonomy and self-determination of its workers.

Autonomía decided to cooperate closely with the Centre for Care Cooperatives (Zentrum für Care Kooperativen, formerly FRAUEN 50Plus). The Centre pursues a dual mission: advancing fair working conditions in the care sector through cooperative structures and strengthening worker participation in Swiss society. Central to the shared vision of *Autonomía* and the Centre is a commitment to challenge the devaluation of cleaning work – reframing it as a dignified profession and making domestic cleaners more visible and valued in both the economy and society.

Seven course participants became the organisation's founding members, and the cooperative was registered with the court in December 2021. The Swiss media featured the launch of *Autonomía*, contrasting the organisation with for-profit platforms.[36] Following this positive media coverage, within a couple of weeks, as many as 500 potential clients expressed their interest in working with an *Autonomía* cleaner. This unexpectedly high demand accelerated the cooperative's efforts to develop the operational model and recruit its first workers.

Autonomía's workforce quickly grew to about 40 women. The workers represent diverse sociodemographic backgrounds and range in age from their early twenties to their mid-sixties. While a small minority are naturalised Swiss citizens, the vast majority are migrants to Switzerland who speak little or no German. Considering the initiators' ties to Spanish-speaking communities in Switzerland, three-quarters of *Autonomía*'s workers come from South America, while the remaining workers come from South and Eastern Europe, Africa and the Middle East. All hold a stable immigration status in Switzerland as resident foreign nationals (B permit) or settled foreign nationals (C permit).

The people interviewed for this study describe attitudes towards cleaning work as falling into two main groups, which vary according to their sociodemographic background. The first group consists of women who arrived in Switzerland with little or no formal education, faced challenges when learning German, and viewed cleaning as a necessity due to limited professional opportunities. The second group comprises women with secondary education and experience in other sectors. The second group often considers cleaning as a temporary job, which they plan to leave once they improve their German language skills, have their foreign qualifications recognised in Switzerland, or acquire new skills and networks for future career development. The tension between viewing cleaning as a long-term profession and as a temporary fix contributes to the challenges we will discuss in the following section.

[36] S Serafini, 'Wie diese Frauen den schlechten Bedingungen in der Gig Economy trotzen' (20 December 2021) *Watson* www.watson.ch/!628954898; K Kynd, 'Zürcher Reiniger:innen gründen Genossenschaft "Autonomía"' (20 December 2021) *Das Lamm* daslamm.ch/autonomia-reinigerinnen/; N Keusch, 'Reinigungskräfte gründen Plattform für faire Arbeitsbedingungen' (26 December 2021) *Neue Zürcher Zeitung* www.nzz.ch/wirtschaft/fuer-fairere-arbeitsbedingungen-zuercher-reinigungskraefte-gruenden-ihre-eigene-vermittlungsplattform-ld.1661509.

B. Aligning Business Strategy with Social Mission

In the course of the organisation's development of its business strategy during the first six months, its initiators had to contend with the lack of initial funding, which required them to work on a voluntary basis until the cooperative began generating revenue. To understand the local market, the organisation analysed competitor information available on websites and by posing as potential workers. Initially, the price for clients was set at CHF 40 per hour, and the wage for workers was set at CHF 30 per hour, which was above the legally required minimum wage of CHF 19.95 per hour. The gross margin was used to cover operational expenses and social security contributions for the workers.

To ensure good working conditions, *Autonomía* acts as an employer and offers employment contracts, granting employees access to the full range of labour and social rights. Additionally, employees can determine their own working schedules and workload, which allows them to work part-time and balance their employment with other paid jobs or unpaid care responsibilities. Unlike some companies that limit working hours to avoid paying contributions to the Swiss pension system, *Autonomía* provides sufficient working hours for those who want to qualify for pension contributions.

Lacking a marketing budget, *Autonomía* relied on media coverage and the assumption that customers who aligned with its social mission would be willing to pay more for ethical employment practices. However, the scale of demand surprised even *Autonomía*'s initiators, as it suggested that this segment of the consumer market might be larger than they had previously assumed. A business strategy aimed at customers who were willing to pay fair wages also had a positive effect on interactions between clients and workers. Many workers reported that clients genuinely appreciated their work, often expressing gratitude through kind words and small gestures, which further reinforced their sense of dignity and recognition.

As *Autonomía* developed, the management duties, including customer care, personnel and financial accounting, as well as marketing and communication, transformed from volunteer roles into part-time jobs at the cooperative's office. To cover staff costs, the initial price for clients grew from CHF 40 to CHF 43 per hour. As a cost-cutting measure, *Autonomía* developed its digital infrastructure based on generic digital tools without support from technical experts. During its first three years, the cooperative operated at a modest deficit, but closed 2024 with a balanced budget. Looking ahead, the Migros Pioneer Fund will support the development of *Autonomía* with a three-year grant.

Autonomía aligns its business goals with two interrelated social goals: to challenge the widespread devaluation of cleaning work by promoting it as dignified and valuable employment and to support workers in their active participation in Swiss society. To this end, *Autonomía* collaborates with the Centre for Care Cooperatives through a social franchise model. The Centre plays a key role in offering education and professional development opportunities tailored to the needs of a predominantly migrant workforce, including digital skills training, cleaning certification and German language courses.

As they reflected on the cooperative's role in providing education and training to its workers, *Autonomía*'s initiators recognised how their assumptions differed from the realities of the migrant experience. While some considered speaking German as necessary for participating in Swiss society, they also acknowledged that German was not required to perform cleaning work. Workers only interact with clients minimally and can communicate in other languages, such as English or Spanish, or use translation apps. Additionally, workers perform most of their tasks in isolation, which requires them to use few communication skills. Workers consider attending German classes without the opportunity to practice the language regularly as insufficient for making progress. In addition to the lack of opportunities to practice their language skills outside the classroom, they also have to balance language learning with paid work and unpaid caregiving responsibilities. Those who lack formal education or have low self-esteem face additional barriers. Additionally, some workers face financial pressures, needing to work long hours to support families both in Switzerland and abroad, which leaves them little time for learning German or pursuing professional development. Combined, these challenges meant that the social goal to help workers achieve fluency in German proved difficult to achieve.

Educational and training activities also brought to the fore the differences in attitudes towards cleaning work: workers who planned to remain in the cleaning sector saw little professional value in learning the language, while others were eager to learn German to leave their cleaning posts. However, this attitude contradicts the view that cleaning jobs are considered decent work, which workers would be willing to do long-term if the conditions were suitable.

This tension also illustrates the challenge of low social recognition of cleaning work, which *Autonomía* and the Centre for Care Cooperatives hope to address through media presence and collaboration with other actors committed to improving the working conditions and visibility of cleaners. Their efforts saw the establishment of the Network for Fair Cleaning (Netzwerk Faire Reinigung) alongside two Swiss non-profit organisations: Crescenda, a Basel-based association dedicated to empowering migrant women through training programmes, and Proper Job, an initiative of Fairness at Work, a Bern-based consulting and service company that ensures fair employment conditions for over 300 domestic workers and cleaning personnel across Switzerland. While all these organisations share the common goal of promoting fair working conditions for cleaners, they follow different organisational models. Among them, only *Autonomía* is a platform cooperative. This distinct organisational model brings both advantages and challenges that the sections below will explore.

C. Prioritising Human Decision-Making over Automation

Autonomía serves as an intermediary between clients and workers, leveraging digital tools to streamline internal processes and foster communication and trust. However, unlike for-profit platforms, *Autonomía* limits its use of technology in its operational model, ensuring that key decisions belong to staff members rather than automated systems.

Autonomía offers clients a convenient way of finding a cleaner – they complete an online form specifying their needs. Clients can choose from weekly, bi-weekly or monthly cleaning services, with a minimum booking requirement of 2.5 hours. Staff members conduct the process of client-worker matching by comparing the data collected from the online form with the cleaner availability according to their calendars. To minimise workers' travel time, the matching process also considers the client's location.

In its effort to be accessible for migrant workers, *Autonomía* does not require formal training or proficiency in German. Instead, a staff member conducts an interview in German or Spanish, while a trial cleaning session evaluates the applicant's skills. Workers must be willing to use digital tools to enter their availability in a digital calendar, track their hours and communicate with the office via Telegram. While some workers have limited digital skills, most successfully navigate these tools with support from family members or *Autonomía* staff.

Once *Autonomía* matches a client with a worker, the organisation negotiates the terms and schedules for the first cleaning session. At this stage, both the client and the worker receive each other's phone numbers, allowing direct communication in urgent matters. After the initial session, the cleaner is solely responsible for handling ongoing communication, with this cost-cutting measure also benefitting the workers. Many cleaners, having previously worked for intermediaries that restricted direct contact, appreciate this approach as it helps prevent unnecessary misunderstandings. *Autonomía*'s staff intervene only in the event of problems or complaints, prioritising its social mission in how issues are resolved. For instance, if a client reports damage, the organisation contacts the cleaner and assesses the claim carefully for plausibility before taking further action.

Overall, *Autonomía* limits its use of automated systems to essential administrative tasks, such as generating invoices based on inputs from time-tracking software, which both clients and workers use. Even this automated task is always under the control of a staff member to ensure accuracy. Unlike for-profit platforms, *Autonomía* does not implement automated feedback mechanisms based on client reviews, but instead actively mediates the client-worker relationship. Moreover, the cooperative neither collects nor processes workers' data for any purposes beyond operational necessity and remains fully transparent in its technological design. Looking ahead, *Autonomía* plans to further develop its digital infrastructure and explore automation for tasks that are particularly tedious and repetitive. The goal of these optimisations is to reduce administrative costs and, ultimately, increase the cleaners' wages.

Despite adopting digital tools, *Autonomía* prioritises its social mission over profit maximisation. Technology enhances efficiency while ensuring fair working conditions, worker autonomy and transparent processes. At the same time, human employees remain essential for internal processes, such as quality assurance, client-worker matching, conflict resolution and the verification of reported hours. Rather than replacing human oversight, technology supports trust, respect and fair employment. By balancing automation with staff involvement, *Autonomía* ensures efficiency while upholding its cooperative values.

D. Empowering Workers to Govern the Cooperative

Autonomía embraces the cooperative model to empower its worker-members, actively involving them in key governance decisions. In contrast to for-profit platforms, which exclude workers from democratic decision-making, *Autonomía* fosters participation that enhances decision quality, builds members' skills and amplifies the voices of those facing exploitation, marginalisation and oppression, which remains a vital issue for the cleaning sector.[37] Beyond improving governance, worker participation cultivates mutual trust, solidarity and a strong sense of belonging.[38] However, in striving towards these goals, *Autonomía* has encountered challenges that have prompted reflection on ways to further strengthen its cooperative model in the future.

The first challenge stems from the fact that, during its initial three years of operation, *Autonomía*'s organisational structure remained underdeveloped. Swiss law sets minimal requirements for registering a cooperative,[39] and *Autonomía*'s statute includes only basic provisions: all members have the right to participate in the annual General Assembly and can submit a vote in the Board of Directors' elections every four years. However, in its early years, Autonomía prioritised operational and financial stability over defining key aspects of governance, such as membership criteria, hierarchical structures and leadership roles.

Another challenge revolves around fostering member participation, but the fact that most of *Autonomía*'s workers are not cooperative members has hindered this effort. Only about 25 per cent have chosen to join, with the rest citing a lack of time or interest in governance. While allowing workers to opt out of membership enabled the cooperative to rapidly expand its workforce during periods of unexpectedly high demand, it also created a structural divide between members and non-members. Researchers have noted that platform cooperatives often struggle to encourage participation because they tend to be tolerant of 'multihoming'. This simultaneous or sequential use of multiple job platforms can reduce workers' incentive to engage in governance.[40] This situation is particularly relevant for *Autonomía*, where workers are free to take

[37] Mannan and Pek (n 29).

[38] P Bernstein, 'Necessary Elements for Effective Worker Participation in Decision Making' (1976) 10 *Journal of Economic Issues* 490.

[39] Federal Act on the Amendment of the Swiss Civil Code (Part Five: The Code of Obligations), 30 March 1911 (Status as of 1 January 2025), Title 29 (Arts 828–926 CO).

[40] Mannan and Pek (n 29).

jobs from other clients or intermediaries. Additionally, the nature of the work presents further obstacles: cleaners work in isolation, function in geographically dispersed households, and have few opportunities to meet and socialise at the office. The linguistic and cultural diversity of workers adds another layer of complexity, potentially complicating communication and collective decision-making. These factors can limit participation in the cooperative or make it uneven, reinforcing an asymmetry between members and non-members and challenging *Autonomía*'s ability to foster feelings of trust and solidarity.

The lack of clarity surrounding hierarchy and leadership roles at *Autonomía* further complicated the democratic governance within the organisation. In the cooperative's early stages, some members noted that the benefits of joining were framed using terms like 'owners' or 'bosses'. This language may have led some to believe that leadership roles would provide financial or professional advantages, creating misaligned expectations about participation in governance. As the organisation failed to formalise its day-to-day decision-making procedures, leadership duties concentrated within the Board of Directors, initially composed of five members. While the cooperative's statute defines the Board's role as overseeing strategic governance, the urgency of setting up operations led some members of the Board to additionally take on management duties – first voluntarily, and later as paid part-time roles. As a result, strategic governance became intertwined with day-to-day management, leading to a power imbalance between a core leadership group and regular members. This conflation of roles made it harder to establish a clear and democratic decision-making structure within the cooperative.

To address these tensions and support the professionalisation of management roles, the Board decided to outsource management duties to the Centre for Care Cooperatives. The majority agreed that this approach would promote long-term good working conditions by enhancing efficiency, reducing costs and fostering professionalism as a foundation for sustained economic success. However, this decision encountered opposition from a single Board member, leading to internal conflict and the departure of several workers in the fall of 2023. In response, the remaining Board members took steps to further develop and formalise *Autonomía*'s democratic governance structure. One key clarification was that the Board of Directors' positions would remain unpaid and focused solely on strategic governance, preventing future conflation with management roles. Additionally, the organisation made efforts to establish clearer rules regarding its membership, members' rights and responsibilities, and adjust the cooperative's communication patterns to better reflect its collaborative and non-profit nature.

The experience of *Autonomía* illustrates the complex balancing act that platform cooperatives must perform between building a sustainable business model and fostering democratic governance. Moving forward, *Autonomía*'s ability to formalise its governance processes, create more accessible avenues for member participation, and reinforce its cooperative identity will be critical in strengthening its democratic foundations and long-term resilience.

IV. DISCUSSING THE POTENTIAL OF PLATFORM COOPERATIVES IN CLEANING WORK

A. Platform Cooperatives as an Alternative to For-Profit Platforms

The case of *Autonomía* provides valuable information about the growing diversity of digital intermediaries in the cleaning sector. Its example demonstrates how the platform model can serve the interests of both clients and workers. For clients, using an intermediary offers the convenience of finding a verified cleaner with ease, removes the burden of handling administrative formalities, and ensures that workers enjoy formal employment with fair working conditions. For cleaners, the platform provides access to a broader client base while giving them the flexibility to choose their working hours and workload.

What distinguishes *Autonomía* from the vast majority of digital intermediaries in the cleaning work sector is its commitment to offering employment rather than reliance on self-employment. This approach ensures that workers have access to the full range of social and labour rights. While for-profit digital platforms often assert to promote formalisation, they usually assume that cleaners are self-employed and registered with authorities, without actually verifying this fact.[41] In contrast, *Autonomía* competes successfully on the market while providing formal employment contracts, offering wages higher than the legal minimum, allowing workers to reject jobs that do not fit their schedule, and enabling them to work enough hours to qualify for pension funds.

Importantly, *Autonomía* fosters a supportive working environment where both staff and clients value the cleaners and their work. The key element of *Autonomía*'s mission involves using the platform model not to maximise profit, but to improve the working conditions and the social standing of cleaning workers. *Autonomía*'s success demonstrates that this business model can be financially viable with the markup on wages limited to covering essential overhead costs.

The case of *Autonomía* also deepens our understanding of what it means to be a digital intermediary in the cleaning sector. In contrast to for-profit platforms, *Autonomía*'s digital infrastructure employs a range of generic, free or paid digital tools, rather than proprietary software or custom mobile apps. Moreover, it does not rely on automated feedback mechanisms, such as ratings or rankings found on for-profit platforms, which often grant clients disproportionate power over workers. Additionally, *Autonomía* does not use its digital tools to collect data for the purpose of controlling the workers' labour or commercialising data by selling it to third parties – a practice typical for digital labour platforms. In contrast to for-profit platforms, which often lack transparency about the extent of their technology use and decision-making processes, *Autonomía*'s digital infrastructure is open and allows workers to participate in decisions about its implementation. This example highlights that investing in technology might

[41] Teke-Laurent, ch 2, and Starčević, ch 4, in this book.

be less critical for platform development when the primary goal is to connect clients with workers in a fair and transparent way.

Indeed, the case highlights an ongoing debate about the prevalence and relevance of algorithmic management in domestic and care work platforms. Floros argues that 'applying algorithmic management as a blanket term to describe all work environments where algorithms assume managerial tasks weakens its effectiveness as an analytical tool'.[42] In domestic and care work platforms, the use of algorithmic management depends on the platform's operational models, which in turn creates differentiated impacts on working conditions in terms of access to tasks, remuneration, flexibility and means of control.[43] The fact that *Autonomía* relies on manual matching rather than algorithmic management, and aims to foster long-term relationships between clients and workers, positions it more closely to the model that digital placement agencies employ. So far, these agencies have focused on care services such as childcare or elderly care, rather than domestic cleaning work. In cleaning work, the prevalent operational models have included matching and on-demand platforms, where algorithmic management sorts and ranks workers' profiles based on client reviews. In the latter case, the platform applies algorithmic management most extensively, encouraging cleaners to remain with the platform and restricting client communication to prevent off-platform earnings.[44] In contrast, *Autonomía* does not require the workers to maintain an online presence, shares their contact information only with matched clients, and enables direct communication to foster working relationships. This solution reduces the incentive to take the relationship off the platform because the cooperative pays the cleaner's social dues as an employer and the overhead costs for staff who help with formalities and mediate in cases of misunderstandings.

In sum, *Autonomía* offers benefits comparable to those of for-profit platforms, while aligning more closely with the digital placement agency model that fosters long-term relationships between clients and workers. At the same time, it avoids the common pitfalls of for-profit platforms, such as reliance on self-employment and the use of algorithmic management. *Autonomía* demonstrates that digital intermediaries can effectively fulfil their responsibilities as employers while remaining financially viable, proving that a cooperative model can indeed provide fair working conditions in cleaning work.

B. Challenges of the Platform Cooperative Model in Cleaning Work

The case of *Autonomía* contributes to research on platform cooperatives by enhancing our understanding of how such organisations adapt to the unique

[42] Floros (n 24) 12.

[43] Rodríguez-Modroño, ch 1, in this book; Rodríguez-Modroño et al (n 22).

[44] Floros (n 24); Niebler and Animento (n 24); Orth (n 18).

challenges of domestic cleaning work. While *Autonomía* accomplishes its goal of being a fair employer, it must reconcile its mission to provide education and training and to enable democratic governance with the diverse needs and limitations of its predominantly migrant workforce. Not all workers can enjoy full access to the benefits *Autonomía* offers, such as free German language classes, professional training opportunities and a supportive network, as numerous workers face challenges stemming from their positionality as transnational migrants.[45]

Many workers are compelled to work long hours to support themselves and their families in their country of origin or to meet income thresholds resulting from immigration regulations. *Autonomía* cannot alleviate the financial and mental burden of being a 'target earner',[46] which significantly hinders certain workers' ability to invest time in learning German or participating in the cooperative's governance. In other words, while *Autonomía* provides good working conditions, it cannot resolve the existing inequality between those who are 'time-wealthy' and those who are 'time-poor' and unable to engage in education and community work. Amplified by the fact that workers perform cleaning work in isolation, the goal of building trust, solidarity and a feeling of belonging among cleaners is arguably more difficult than in other types of work.

An associated challenge is the fact that *Autonomía*'s workforce displays diverse attitudes towards the value of cleaning work, with these attitudes complying with the workers' diverse sociodemographic backgrounds. The primary concern of certain workers, particularly those committed to cleaning work in the long term – whether due to limited professional opportunities or because they find the work fulfilling – is that society respects, recognises and values their work. On the other hand, some educated migrant women, who may perceive cleaning work as downward social mobility, might be reluctant to identify with this profession in the long term and may seek other professional opportunities.[47] It appears that in *Autonomía*'s case, the desire for upward mobility might have motivated some women to seek leadership roles in the cooperative. Further research should explore if and how differences in workers' attitudes towards cleaning work might affect their interests in education and training opportunities, as well as governance activities.

The fact that *Autonomía*'s workers and members are predominantly migrant women has had a significant impact on the development of its organisational structure. Recognising that some workers may lack the resources, time or interest

[45] R Parrenas, 'The Mobility Pathways of Migrant Domestic Workers' (2021) 47 *Journal of Ethnic and Migration Studies* 3.

[46] H Bauder, *Labor Movement: How Migration Regulates Labor Markets* (Oxford, Oxford University Press, 2006).

[47] For non-platform work, see AP Gutiérrez Garza, 'Performing Race, Class, and Status: Identity Strategies Among Latin American Women Migrants in London' (2024) 50 *Journal of Ethnic and Migration Studies* 3472; Shinozaki (n 1); for platform domestic and care work, see Orth and Baum (n 24); Stingl and Orth (n 18).

to engage in governance activities, *Autonomía* made cooperative membership optional. Nevertheless, it ensured that all workers – regardless of their membership status – had access to fair working conditions, as well as education and training opportunities. While this approach may have introduced power asymmetries between members and non-members, it also enabled the cooperative to build a smaller but more committed core of engaged members. Further research involving perspectives from both groups would allow a better understanding of how platform cooperatives design and adapt membership rules over time, and how they navigate the tension between democratic participation and organisational growth.

While democratic governance and the ability to co-determine working conditions are the core principles of the cooperative model, *Autonomía* initially postponed the development of participatory decision-making structures to focus on building a financially viable business. This tension between economic sustainability and democratic participation is common across cooperatives. [48] In *Autonomía*'s case, prioritising growth led to the establishment of paid staff roles, which accelerated growth but also blurred the boundaries between strategic and operational responsibilities. This conflation of roles within the Board created conditions for misunderstandings and conflict concerning leadership and hierarchy. The organisation addressed this problem by outsourcing management tasks to a third party while also clarifying governance structures and member participation. Despite these measures, *Autonomía* failed to avoid an internal conflict.

Autonomía and *WeCare*, the South African platform cooperative discussed in this book, faced different yet overlapping challenges in their development.[49] *WeCare* found the cooperative legal form under South African law unsuitable and struggled with financing, while *Autonomía* could adopt the cooperative form under Swiss law and launch without seed funding. Both, however, required upskilling and reskilling to manage operational and administrative demands. *WeCare*'s experience highlights the importance of legal and socioeconomic context, a factor crucial for platform cooperatives as well as for-profit platforms.[50] Future research should examine the role of legal form in shaping cooperative feasibility and sustainability, track the emergence of cleaning-sector cooperatives over time, and explore how they formalise decision-making, adapt structures to the needs of predominantly migrant members, navigate domestic cleaning dynamics and sustain their operations over the long term.

Finally, further studies should analyse the potential of platform cooperatives to address the problem of exploitation among domestic cleaners. The case of

[48] D C Jones and P Kalmi, 'Economies of Scale Versus Participation: A Co-Operative Dilemma?' (2012) 1 *Journal of Entrepreneurial and Organizational Diversity* 37.

[49] Osiki, ch 7, in this book.

[50] N Koutsimpogiorgos, K Frenken and AM Herrmann, 'Platform Adaptation to Regulation: The Case of Domestic Cleaning in Europe' (2023) 65 *Journal of Industrial Relations* 156.

Autonomía is interesting because it shows that it is possible for a digital intermediary to promote long-term employment in cleaning work. To date, this type of relationship has been typical for elderly care work. However, we should also note that some people might have no access to the benefits *Autonomía* offers – including short-term residents in Switzerland, cross-border commuters, people without legal right to work, or those with undocumented immigration status. Workers belonging to these categories might be attracted to for-profit platforms solely because they do not verify their immigration status or their registration as self-employed.[51] In other words, the impact of initiatives like *Autonomía* may only apply to those who already have a relatively privileged social and legal status.

In sum, the platform cooperative model may offer a viable solution for a subset of the migrant workforce in the cleaning sector, but it cannot address the wider exploitative dynamics of the sector at large. Improving access to social and labour rights through employment status is a viable solution for those who face no immigration-related restrictions in respect of their work. The forthcoming debates on the implementation of the Platform Work Directive by the European Union should consider that such platforms might not be the best tool to improve the conditions of migrant women who work in care.[52] Furthermore, given that some platforms may adjust their operational models to avoid employer responsibilities, policymakers and regulators must pay greater attention to the rights and safeguards of genuinely self-employed cleaning workers, as well as those whose immigration status reflects the constraints of restrictive or exclusionary welfare and migration regimes.[53]

V. CONCLUSION: LESSONS FROM AUTONOMÍA

Autonomía's example shows that platform cooperatives can enhance working conditions and increase the social recognition of cleaners, particularly migrant workers. Platform cooperatives in the cleaning sector could further amplify their transformative potential through strategic coalitions with other cooperatives, unions, NGOs and ethical tech developers, as well as thanks to public funding for other worker-led pilot projects in diverse socioeconomic contexts.

Autonomía's experience offers compelling evidence that platform cooperatives can operate successfully within competitive markets. The organisation's ability to thrive without initial funding underscores the significance of supportive local conditions, including Zurich's high wages and customer demand for ethical services. However, understanding the model's scalability and adaptability

[51] Niebler and Animento (n 24); Orth (n 18); Stingl and Orth (n 18).

[52] Hießl (ch 9), Ratti (ch 10), Sedacca and Atkinson (ch 12) in this book.

[53] E Kocher E and J Bronowicka, 'A Blunt Tool for Women in Platform Work? A Feminist Perspective on the Platform Work Directive' (2025) 16 *European Labour Law Journal* 565.

beyond this specific context requires careful attention to local economic and labour dynamics, legal frameworks, and, critically, customer preferences. High demand for *Autonomía*'s services prompts a reflection that the consumer market for ethical services may be larger than many scholars and policymakers acknowledge.[54] *Autonomía*'s success demonstrates that clients might be willing to prioritise fair working conditions and ethical practices over low prices, especially when these values align with their own expectations.

Further research into potential platform cooperatives in the cleaning sector should include comparative analyses across diverse socioeconomic contexts, since factors such as national labour laws and workforce composition play a crucial role in the platforms' operation. Researchers should also examine platforms that promote fair employment – such as *Asoclim* (Ecuador), *AseoYa* (Colombia) and *Domestico24* (Spain)—without cooperative ownership, as well as traditional cooperatives like *Brightly* (UK) that use digital tools but do not identify as platforms. By analysing the distinctions and overlaps among these models, researchers can gain valuable insights into how digitalisation, governance and ownership affect cleaners' working conditions and the social recognition of cleaning work.

[54] J Pentzien, 'Building Platforms Differently: Collective Action and Legitimation Dynamics in the Field of Platform Cooperativism' (2023) 1 *Journal of Political Sociology* 104.

Part IV

Regulating Digital Intermediaries in Europe

9

Domestic Platform Work as a Multiparty Relationship: Regulatory Loopholes and Ways to Address Them

CHRISTINA HIESSL

I. INTRODUCTION

THERE IS PROBABLY no form of work that is even nearly as difficult to reach by legal protections, notably social security and labour law, as domestic work. The prevalence of informality, lack of regulatory supervision, lack of awareness among all parties, and the resulting lack of respect for even the most basic protective rights and principles have been widely documented and discussed.[1] Informal domestic work is widespread in effectively every single country, and estimated to constitute the majority of arrangements in many of them.[2] Attempts to achieve a certain formalisation of a sector which is growing steadily[3] have frequently included regulation meant to ease the financial and/or administrative burden for the employing households – with the frequent side effect of lowering the level of protection of domestic workers considerably in relation to those working for public or private undertakings (see section IV.C).

[1] See M Fischl, 'Serving in the Master's House: Legal Protection for In-Home Care Workers in the United States' (2016) *Faculty Articles and Papers* 491; E Chieregato, 'The House as a Workplace: Challenging the Speciality of Domestic Work in Labour Law' (2021) PhD Thesis (University of Verona).

[2] See S Razavi and S Silke, 'Underpaid and Overworked: A Cross-national Perspective on Care Workers' (2010) 149 *International Labour Review* 422; M Blofield and M Jokela, 'Paid Domestic Work and the Struggles of Care Workers in Latin America' (2018) 66 *Current Sociology Monograph* 531.

[3] ILO estimates of 2021 put the overall number of domestic workers worldwide at 75.6 million in 2019, up from 53 million in 2010, indicating that those numbers had more than doubled since 1995. Of them, 76.2 per cent were women. ILO, *Making Decent Work a Reality for Domestic Workers: Progress and Prospects Ten Years after the Adoption of the Domestic Workers Convention, 2011 (No. 189)* (Geneva, ILO, 2021) 10 et seqq. For ongoing trends in the further development, see Blofield and Jokela (n 2) 532.

In this context, agencies and intermediaries have long come to play a key role. Called upon primarily to match supply and demand, they can offer a range of services for those supplying and demanding domestic work, including administrative assistance, processing of payments, insurance cover, dispute settlement, guidelines, training and so on. The resulting presence of a professional actor in the contractual relationship basically presents a key opportunity to 're-normalise' the application of legal standards, as the agency might reasonably be expected to understand and manage the administrative burden of a commercial employer. At the same time, the price tag attached to its services may weaken its attractiveness vis-à-vis informal arrangements. In this regard, the digitalisation of intermediation offers not only the benefits of increased matching efficiency, allowing for more flexible short-term decisions on individual agreements, their modification and cancellation, but also potentially lower costs due to the partial automation of the service.

No form of domestic work would potentially stand as much to gain from digital intermediation as long-term care (LTC) provision in case of extensive or continuous care needs. Dependence on care is a phenomenon of rapidly mounting importance in societies characterised by rising life expectancy, pushes to de-institutionalise LTC and a dwindling likelihood of informal care by family members to be an option. In this context, the drastic increase of recourse to live-in care as a highly problematic form of labour[4] is frequently motivated by the sheer impossibility to manage and coordinate care among a larger group of individuals to ensure a form of permanent availability in case of need.[5][6] Particularly a combination of intermittent physical presence with periods of remote stand-by availability in case of need could be a pathway towards allowing also individuals with significant care needs to continue living at home without requiring unreasonable sacrifices from either family members or paid carers. This is, arguably, precisely what digital platforms specialise in.

[4] Live-in domestic work has not only expanded in those regions of the world where economic development took place in a context of particularly pronounced inequality, but has also very much returned to many of the 'most developed' countries in the context of care for the frail and disabled. The pertinent literature (eg, K Christensen and J Manthorpe 'Personalised Risk: New Risk Encounters Facing Migrant Care Workers' (2016) 18 *Health, Risk & Society* 137; Fischl (n 1) 23, 36 speaks of 'tremendous' or 'dramatic' growth, and numbers which double within just 15 years.

[5] In practice, a large share of live-in agreements are reported to be arranged for demented beneficiaries – see eg M Leiblfinger et al, 'Impact of COVID-19 Policy Responses on Live-in Care Workers in Austria, Germany, and Switzerland. Journal of Long-Term Care' (2020) *Special Collection: COVID-19 and Long-Term Care Policy* 144, 147. Notably in cases where no mobility restrictions or comparable conditions exist which would necessitate around-the-clock availability of physical support, it would seem plausible that beneficiaries could be served by a system that effectively coordinates the intermittent presence of individuals involved in care provision (health or nursing professionals, family members, volunteer helpers etc.). See C Hießl, 'Labour Rights for Live-In Care Workers: The Long and Bumpy Road Ahead' (2022) 11 *Social Sciences* 547.

[6] See the approach taken in South Korea, as described eg in 염지혜 (2013), 노노케어의 시행과정과 향후 정책적 과제. 한국노년학 [Implementation Process and Prospects of the Elderly-Care-for-the-Elderly], 33(2), 221–38, and recent and planned developments reported by 안병준 (2021), 실시간 도움요청앱 애니맨, 대한노인회와 시니어전문 앱 `실버맨` 론칭 제휴 [Real-time help request app Animan, Korea Senior Citizens Association and senior professional app 'Silver Man' launch partnership]. 매일경제 2021/3/22, www.mk.co.kr/news/business/9797929.

In principle, thus, all stakeholders, including workers, might benefit from a well-regulated system of digital care intermediation as a viable alternative to the informal and/or legally dubious constructions that have historically dominated all forms of domestic work, including care work.[7] At the same time, the current legal landscape across countries features numerous difficulties and uncertainties as concerns the classification of the contractual relations between the parties in such a context, as well as the resulting rights and duties.

The present chapter aims to contribute to this debate by giving an insight into the decisions that have evaluated the legal status of domestic work platforms in Europe so far (Section II) and the reasoning applied for construing the contractual relationships involved in a particular way (Section III). Based on the circumstances of and considerations raised in these cases, Section IV discusses a number of legal issues that merit consideration in respect of the allocation of rights and responsibilities in the at times highly complex contractual relationships involved. Section V offers some tentative conclusions on how current uncertainties and legal loopholes could be addressed in order to turn domestic platform work into an opportunity for decent work for a traditionally overlooked group of workers.

II. THE STATUS OF PLATFORMS AND THEIR WORKERS: A CASE LAW OVERVIEW

Within barely a decade, more than 1,500 decisions on the status of platforms and their workers have been handed down by courts and administrative institutions across Europe.[8] This sheer number indicates the difficulties that these types of relationships pose in terms of classification under the existing categories of legal relationships. The fact that, despite such extensive litigation, legal certainty about status questions is still not nearly in sight for most platform workers has much to do with the 'cat-and-mouse-game' emerging between platforms and decision-making bodies in many countries. Note that, on the one hand, national case law in several countries evolves over time – often specifically with a view to including platform workers under a legal regime that offers better protection than that formally chosen by the contracting parties. As a result, among all decisions handed down so far, about two-thirds (and even four-fifths of last-instance decisions) have seen platform workers as employees; barely more than a quarter (11 per cent of last-instance decisions) have considered them self-employed.[9] Vice versa, platforms are adapting their business models

[7] See ILO, *The road to decent work for domestic workers* (Geneva, ILO, 2023) 10.

[8] For a detailed overview see C Hießl, 'Case Law on the Classification of Platform Workers: Cross-European Comparative Analysis and Tentative Conclusions (2024) Updated to February 2024, https://papers.ssrn.com/sol3/papers.cfm?abstract_id=3839603. Note that the numbers indicated below refer to an updated version that has not yet been published.

[9] The remaining decisions have either viewed platform workers as a tertium genus ('workers' in the UK and 'lavoro eteroorganizzato' in Italy) or as employees of another undertaking – an intermediary /subcontractor or a customer of the platform. For details, see Hießl (n 8).

even much faster and much more often than courts get the opportunity to adjust their assessment – and frequently a platform's terms and conditions are changed as a direct reaction to a judgment which views certain elements of the previous model as an indication of their status as an employer, a user undertaking or any similar responsible position.

While the case law across Europe is thus voluminous and dynamic, litigation has so far been strongly concentrated on particular types of platforms – notably delivery and ride-hailing platforms. Decisions on platforms offering services in private households stand out not only by their very low overall number, but also the fact that, in several of these few cases, the very courts that confirm employee status for delivery riders are not necessarily confirming it for domestic platform workers as well. To illustrate, Table 9.1 provides an overview of all last-instance judgments with definite findings on platform workers' status, by category of platform work.

As can be seen, only one (very recent) last-instance decision has dealt with the status of domestic platform workers – and has considered them employees of the platform.

To illustrate that this does not necessarily represent a general trend, Table 9.2 zooms in on the – generally very scarce – decisions concerning platform work in private households, including administrative and lower-level court rulings. As can be seen, there is a remarkable variety including rulings determining platform workers' status as self-employed, employed or a third genus; and those assuming an employment relationship diverge when allocating the role of employer – including those seeing the customer (ie the household) as the employer, those

Table 9.1 Categorisation of platform workers by last-instance courts in European countries, 2024

	Platform's employee	**Self-employed**	**Employee of another**	**Tertium genus**	**Total**
Food delivery	CH, ES, FI, FR, IE, NL, PT, SE	HU, UK	ES	IT	**20**
Ride-hailing	CH, FR	FR		UK	**12**
Other delivery	ES		ES		**2**
Mystery shopping	DE	FR			**2**
Cleaning	NL				**1**
Total[1]	**29**	**4**	**2**	**2**	**37**

[1] Note the several last-instance decisions on the same platform type exist in some countries, hence the number here is not necessarily the sum of the countries enumerated in the table.

Table 9.2 Decisions on platform work in private households, 2024 (last-instance cases in bold)

	DK	ES	NL	NO	SE	UK
Administrative decisions						
1st	2 self-employed	2 platform's employee		platform's employee	2 self-employed	
2nd				customer's employee		
Judicial decisions						
1st			customer's employee		2 self-employed	worker[2]
2nd		2 platform's employee	TAW		2 self-employed	worker
3rd		2 platform's employee	TAW			worker
4th		Pending				worker

[2] The tertium genus of (limb (b)) workers is defined in Section 230(3)(b) Employment Rights Act; it essentially ensures protection under minimum wage and working time law, but not other aspects of employment law such as dismissal protection. These decisions relate to the Pimlico Plumbers case, which did not involve a digital platform, but a similar gig economy model for organising the work of formally self-employed plumbers in private households. For the last-instance decision see UK Supreme Court of 13 June 2018, [2018] UKSC 29.

assuming a 'simple' bilateral employment relationship with the platform and those categorising the situation as temporary agency work (TAW).

The following section goes into some more detail on how the decision-making bodies came up with the conclusions on classification as indicated in Table 9.2.

III. EXAMPLES: CLASSIFICATION OF DOMESTIC PLATFORM WORKERS AS . . .

A. Self-employed

Domestic platform workers have been viewed as self-employed in two cases each in Denmark[10] and Sweden. The latter case, in which the third-instance decision

[10] Konkurrencerådet of 26 August 2020, Konkurrencerådsafgørelse (on cleaning platforms Hilfr and Happy Helpers). These decisions were the only ones in the entire collection presented in Table 1 where the platforms wanted to categorise themselves as employers, but were found to work with self-employed cleaners by a competition authority.

was made final for lack of an appeal to the Swedish Supreme Administrative Court, was initiated by investigations of the Work Environment Authority, which considered the platforms TaskRunner and Tiptapp (which offer various services such as assembly of furniture, gardening, transport of goods, repair work, painting etc) as employers in two reasoned decisions of October 2020.[11] Both have been overturned in court,[12] a decision which was confirmed on appeal.[13]

To arrive at their decision, the courts weighed the elements that indicated the platforms' employer status against those characterising the workers as self-employed. The first included mainly the fact that the platforms contract workers who generally work personally, subject workers to a skills/quality assessment, prohibit any circumvention of the platform by directly contracting with the customer (subject to sanction by suspension), operate a sanctioning regime (monitoring of 'small', 'medium' and 'large' mistakes as basis for temporary or permanent suspension), and process payments. In case of TaskRunner, the decisions additionally point to a form of career development (possibility of promotion to 'Business runner'), in case of Tiptapp, to a strict control system involving constant GPS tracking and workers' obligation to take and submit pictures as proof. All of this was eventually found insufficient to outweigh the indicators of self-employment, notably as the workers effectively arrange all aspects of work and remuneration by agreement with the customer, are not directed nor required to perform a minimum of activities nor to coordinate them with others, are not provided with materials nor guaranteed a salary by the platform, do not appear as platform's employees, and are not prevented from exercising competing activities.

In light of all these elements, the courts found that the platform did not exercise a form of direction and control that could justify responsibility for the workers' health and safety.

B. Employed by the Household

Basically very similar arguments are brought forward in the cases that considered cleaners working through a platform employees of the client household. This was the case in the first-instance decision in the Helpling case (see below Section III.D) as well as a Norwegian case decided in second and last instance by the appeals board of the Labour Inspection Directorate.[14] Similar as in the Swedish case just described, it upheld an appeal by the platform against a reclassification

[11] Arbetsmiljöverket of 9 and 13 October 2020, 2019/062973 and 2020/000125.

[12] Förvaltningsrätten i Malmö of 22 June and 14 November 2021, Mål nr 13356-20 and Mål nr 1332-21.

[13] Kamarrätten i Göteborg of 19 November 2021 and 9 December 2022, Mål nr 4120-21 and Mål nr 6394-21.

[14] Direktoratet for arbeidstilsynet of 16 July 2015, 2016/2078.

of its employees by the labour inspectorate[15] and restored the contractual setup chosen by the platform – which in this case was that series of very short fixed-term employment contracts were concluded between the cleaners and each individual household requesting their services.

The decision effectively compares the 'employer-like' traits of the platform Vaskerhvitt to those of the household. It took into account that the former assigns cleaners to customers (including a change of cleaners at the customer's request within one week), provides a template for the employment contracts with the customers, prohibits separate agreements between cleaner and customer, manages the administration of contracts and payments, ensures holiday pay on top of the salary and determines a notice period of one week. The customer in turn is in charge of guiding and controlling all aspect of the concrete cleaning work, provides tools and equipment, is in control of the work environment, negotiates the fee with the cleaner (whereby the platform commission is calculated independently), and cannot hold Vaskerhvitt liable for outcome of the cleaning or potential damage. Thus, it appeared to the Directorate that the customer was better placed than Vaskerhvitt to ensure health and safety at work and should therefore be seen as the employer.

C. Employed by the Platform

A very different outcome was reached in the two Spanish cases – including a very recent one on cleaning,[16] as well as the hitherto only case involving a caregiving platform. The latter has been upheld in second instance. In May 2023 by the Catalonian Appeals Court[17] and is currently pending before the Spanish Supreme Court. It confirms an assessment by the labour inspection dating back to 2018,[18] in which the platform Joyners was reclassified as an employer in respect of 104 of its caregivers. The case is to move on despite the platform's insolvency in 2021.[19]

To arrive at the conclusion that the caregivers were not self-employed but had an employment relationship with the platform, the courts argued in essence that Joyners established concrete preconditions for working via the platform

[15] Arbeidstilsynet Sør-Norge of 25 February 2014, 2014/58106.

[16] Tribunal Superior de Justicia de Cataluña (Catalonia Appeals Court) of 13 February 2025 (on cleaning platform Clintu).

[17] Tribunal Superior de Justicia de Cataluña of 4 May 2023, 2789/2023.

[18] Unpublished, but summed up by de Heredia Ruiz, Ignasi Beltran (2018), Nueva intervención de la Inspección de Trabajo en los servicios de la economía de las plataformas: el caso Joyners. Blog de Derecho del Trabajo y de la Seguridad Social, https://ignasibeltran.com/2018/05/26/nueva-intervencion-de-la-inspeccion-de-trabajo-en-los-servicios-de-la-economia-de-las-plataformas-el-caso-joyners.

[19] A Salas, 'El TSJC condena a la extinta Joyners por emplear a 104 cuidadoras como falsas autónomas' (2023) Cravegravy News of 21/6/2023, https://cravegravy.com/el-tsjc-condena-a-la-extinta-joyners-por-emplear-a-104-cuidadoras-como-falsas-autonomas.

(relating to age, training and experience), which were validated and controlled, that it conducted job interviews, supervised performance, including through unannounced inspections, offered standard take-it-or-leave-it offers of work tasks, determined and processed the payment for those tasks and used customer ratings for evaluating the caregivers' performance. Although the carers were always free to accept or reject individual assignments, they were obliged to indicate their preferred times in advance and report absences as soon as possible, to follow guidelines (on clothing, hygiene, safety, the performance of specific tasks, and limits to their competences eg in respect of medical tasks), and generally had no genuine own business infrastructure.

D. Hired Out (TAW)

The only major judicial reclassification of a platform that has been confirmed through a final decision by the country's highest court concerns the cleaning platform Helpling in the Netherlands. Whereas the first-instance court[20] upheld the platform's construction of contractual relations, which designated the client household as the employer, the Amsterdam Appeals Court agreed with the claimant trade union that the platform needed to be seen as a temporary work agency. Just like Joyners, the platform company has in the meantime been declared insolvent. The Dutch Supreme Court declared the question continuously relevant nonetheless[21] and eventually upheld the classification as TAW.[22]

The second-instance decision thus upheld[23] starts by underlining that the classification of the cleaners as employees, who provided work for remuneration subject to instructions, was not disputed; the question was merely whether this can legitimately be set up as a series of exclusively bilateral fixed-term contracts with the client households. The key reasons for the court to eventually view Helpling as a temporary work agency are that the platform used standardised recruitment procedures, including qualifications assessment and initial training, that it provided customers with profiles, including the cleaners' experience and hourly pay rate, and influenced pay rates by allowing only for a range between the minimum wage and EUR 45 (which could be waived on request, though) and by issuing recommendations, which effectively led to largely uniform price levels. The platform also processed the payment and managed a rating system, which the court also saw as a control mechanism serving the platform's own interests. The court also took into account that the assignment of cleaners was Helpling's core business, and concluded from the suggestions provided to clients that the platform itself did not really view the latter as employers, as the suggestions

[20] Juzgado de lo Social de Barcelona (Barcelona Social Court) of 1 July 2021, 738/2018.
[21] Hoge Raad (Supreme Court) of 12 January 2024, 21/05264.
[22] Hoge Raad (Supreme Court) of 11 April 2025, 21/05264.
[23] Gerechtshof Amsterdam, 21 September 2021, 200.268.510/01.

were incompatible with employer duties (regarding sick pay, the cancellation of assignments, or dismissal protection).

E. Hired Out . . . and Out Again?

Finally, it seems worth mentioning that the Joyners decision described at section III.C featured a group of caregivers who had originally been registered with a service cooperative that managed their invoices, payments, taxes and contributions etc. In its appeal against the lower-instance decisions, the company behind Joyners included also that cooperative as a defendant, arguing that *if* the caregivers concerned were found to be employees, the cooperative should be seen as the employer. Such argumentation has in the past been accepted in other countries, notably in a Swedish decision on Foodora,[24] which found that the service company that had administratively managed a part of the riders (those using a motorcycle) was the contractual employer of the workers that Foodora was hiring out in a clandestine TAW relationship. Combined with the Dutch court's finding that the *platform* might be a temporary work agency, it seems that a constellations such as in case of Joyners could be found to constitute a chain agency work construction, in which the platform is a user and agency at the same time.

IV. SELECTED LEGAL ISSUES

The previous section has illustrated that the relationship between the parties involved in a domestic platform work relationship – the worker, the platform, the customer and potentially other actors as described at section III.E – makes it difficult for courts to come up with a balanced classification. Apart from the question whether the contractual freedoms enjoyed by workers (notably the choice whether and when to work) might be contrary to a classification as employee, which is at issue in all gig economy cases, there is the problem of identification of one entity as the employer, when in reality several entities may exercise employer-like functions. This section will discuss the options and difficulties of approaching these questions in current legal systems.

A. A Functional Concept of the Employer?

Among the decisions mentioned in the previous subsection, notably the Norwegian and Swedish second-instance decisions on Vaskerhvitt, Tiptapp and TaskRunner stress that they are limited to questions of responsibility for

[24] Arbetsdomstolen of 16 November 2022, Mål nr A 154/21.

workplace health and safety. The Norwegian decision even states expressly that, while the customer has to be seen as the employer in relation to health and safety, the platform might still be considered an employer in respect of other areas of law. This indicates that national law in some states basically enables courts to develop a 'functional approach' to the concept of employer,[25] testing the personal scope of different pieces of legislation separately and with a view to identifying the person or entity best suited to fulfil employer functions in relation to each of them.

While this would seem an alluring concept, one may also note that it is bound to come with significant uncertainties. Notably in relation to health and safety, which was at issue in all the Norwegian and Swedish cases, one might also argue that private households cannot be expected to bear the responsibility which the law generally imposes on an employer (cf below regarding the exclusion of private employees from health and safety provisions in many legal orders), but that the employee should also not be deprived of the protections offered by occupational health and safety legislation.

In this regard, it seems worthwhile exploring whether existing models of 'sharing' employer responsibilities – notably the concept of TAW – could achieve an adequate allocation of rights and duties.

B. TAW

i. Relevance for Present and Future Platform Models

As can be concluded from the examples above, the classification as a temporary work relationship appears to be of special relevance for platform workers working in private households.

Unlike with ride-hailing or delivery platforms, which are characterised by a high degree of standardisation of the service provided and the price charged, the level of direction exercised by the platforms in question vis-à-vis their workforce is often limited. Depending on the business model,[26] platforms often enable customers to pick an individual (rather than assigning a worker based on an algorithm) and to negotiate the task specifications and price. As a result, decision-making bodies may find it impossible to see any substantial indications of direction and control – which is part of the definition of the employment relationship in all countries.[27]

Notably, as could be seen, most of the cleaning platforms figuring in case law so far had a pronounced hands-off approach when it comes to the determination of the exact tasks desired by the household and the price charged in return. Generally, they offered only voluntary guidance regarding work performance and the handling of specific situations encountered by cleaners. Particular

[25] See J Adams-Prassl, *The Concept of Employer* (Oxford, Oxford University Press, 2015) 155–94.
[26] P. Rodríguez Modroño, ch 1, in this book.
[27] Hießl (n 8) section 2.1.6.

importance is attributed in the pertinent rulings to the individual agreement of prices between the cleaner and customer – even though many did establish minima[28] or maxima.[29] Platforms like Taskrunner or Tiptapp grant even more autonomy to their workers than the ones specialising in cleaning, as they do not even specify the type of service but enable various tasks to be agreed with customers. Such considerations (determination of tasks and prices by agreement between worker and customer) were a key reason for the Swedish courts to overturn the Labour Authority's classification of these two platforms as employers.

The fact that the decision-making bodies in the Spanish cases have so far seen an essentially bilateral relationship between the platform and the workers seems to be crucially relying on the feature that – unlike for the platforms mentioned in the last paragraph – these platforms always agreed the main parameters of the service with the client in advance. In the case of Joyners, the client needed to indicate certain details on the kind and extent of the care services required, based on which the platform set an indicative price for it in advance. Later price changes depended on the circumstances and actual duration of the service, not on individual negotiations between caregiver and client. Thereby, even though the platform did not normally interfere in the work performance itself, the combination of relatively extensive general rules (on clothing, hygiene, safety, performance of specific tasks, limits of competences), which could be controlled by inspections, and the individually pre-defined care package gave the platform sufficient dominance over the work performed. In this way, its role was expressly found comparable to that of food delivery platforms, which in Spain have long been unanimously classified as employers.[30]

However, none of these features is necessarily associated with the nature of a platform offering caregiving services, and counter-examples can already be found in today's care platform landscape. If the development of business models of ride-hailing and delivery platforms can be seen as a precedent, one may expect also domestic platforms, including care platforms, to be prepared to eliminate or reduce elements pointing to their caregivers' subordination, even if that requires a rather substantial change of their business model.[31]

This is why the most recent ruling (by the Dutch Supreme Court on Helpling, above at section III.D) could mark a new pathway for this category of workers to be recognised as employees of their platforms *despite* a very limited or even virtually non-existent intervention in the individual work. Indeed, a temporary work agency is generally characterised by its organisational role and responsibility, whereas concrete instructions are given by the user undertaking. And at least potentially, this could have great advantages for an employee compared to an employment relationship with a private household, notably in terms of

[28] Hilfr and Happy Helper required compliance with their minimum hourly rates, partly in accordance with a collective agreement.

[29] Helpling required the prices to lie between the minimum wage and a maximum determined by the platform by region.

[30] Hießl (n 8) section 1.14.2.

[31] Hießl (n 8) section 2.2.

the stability of contractual relations, the application of collective labour law or the non-applicability of any exemptions from protective provisions for private households.

At the same time, even if courts find that a categorisation as TAW may best represent the practical reality of the contractual relationship at hand, there are a number of legal considerations that deserve mention. The following subsections will touch on some of the key issues and uncertainties arising in this context.

ii. Private Households as User 'Undertakings'?

The question the Amsterdam Appeals Court was clearly struggling with most when finding in favour of TAW was the idea that, in line with the *ratio legis* of laws on TAW, the concept has traditionally been understood as covering a business relationship between two *undertakings*. Paragraph 3.16.4 of the judgment notes that the Dutch Civil Code simply denotes the user a *derde*, that is, a third (party), yet a memorandum to a legislative proposal clearly indicated that this third party should be a company. The court eventually decided to ignore that memorandum, stressing that the law in question had been changed several times, so had the legislator actually wanted to restrict the concept of TAW to business relationships between undertakings then it would have had ample opportunity to do so.

At EU level, things are not quite as simple, as virtually all language versions of the Temporary Agency Work Directive 2008/104 (TAWD[32]) use terms whose ordinary meaning does not necessarily include private households, with the English version speaking of a user 'undertaking'. Similarly, Article 1(2) of Directive 91/383/EEC on health and safety for temporary workers[33] refers to an assignment to work in 'an undertaking and/or establishment'. While Article 3(1)(d) TAWD clarifies that the user undertaking can also be a natural person,[34] Article 1(2) stipulates that '[t]his Directive applies to public and private undertakings which are temporary-work agencies or user undertakings *engaged in economic activities* whether or not they are operating for gain' (emphasis added). This makes it rather clear that, while one might argue that a household making use of services for pay is engaging in economic activities, the use of the term *undertaking* certainly indicates that the provisions at issue were not written with private household users in mind[35] – certainly when considering the meaning given to the equivalent term in EU internal market law.[36]

[32] Directive 2008/104/EC of the European Parliament and of the Council of 19 November 2008 on temporary agency work.

[33] Council Directive 91/383/EEC of 25 June 1991 supplementing the measures to encourage improvements in the safety and health at work of workers with a fixed-duration employment relationship or a temporary employment relationship.

[34] Stipulating that 'any natural or legal person for whom and under the supervision and direction of whom a temporary agency worker works temporarily'.

[35] N Zekić, 'Commentary on the Temporary Agency Work Directive', in C Hießl (ed), *EU Labour Law: A Commentary* (Alphen aan den Rijn, Kluwer, 2025) 680.

[36] Eg CJEU of 23 April 1991, C-41/90 (Höfner and Elser), para 21.

Needless to say, these European standards are expressly formulated as minimum standards (cf Article 9 TAWD and Article 9 of Directive 91/383/EEC), so that the Member States are not prevented from applying the same protections also to situations that are outside their scope as defined. Nonetheless, it may be assumed that the national law in most countries is using the same or similar terms, so that an extension to private households may be considered to be impossible or at least to require very strong teleological arguments – which may also be difficult, as set out in the next subsection.

iii. Relevance/Adequacy of Existing Rules on TAW for Households?

An extension of the rules of TAW to work in private households may also be seen as contrary to the underlying rationale of these rules. Certainly at EU level, and by extension in many national legal systems, this rationale primarily revolves around the aim of equal treatment between temporary agency workers and the user undertaking's own staff. Accordingly, the core provisions require equal treatment in relation to basic working conditions (Article 5 TAWD) as well as access to facilities (Article 6(4)) and the right to health and safety protection in line with the level granted to the user's employees (Article 2(2) Directive 91/383/EEC). Needless to say, none of these equal treatment provisions will have any effect if the user is a private household, which will in the vast majority of cases not have any direct employees. Similar concerns could be raised in relation to workers' representation (Article 7 TAWD): if a national legislator makes use of the choice option given in Article 7(3) and requires temporary agency workers to be represented in the user undertaking instead of the agency, this could effectively deprive platform workers of the right to elect a body to represent them in the platform undertaking.

In this sense, the case for a teleological extension of rules on TAW to work in private households may be put into question by the fact that the possibly most important aims of these rules would not be achieved for domestic workers anyway.

Yet, it should be stressed that the TAWD also includes certain obligations for temporary work agencies, notably in its Article 6. One of those is the stipulation in Article 6(3) that the agency 'shall not charge workers any fees in exchange for arranging for them to be recruited by a user undertaking, or for concluding a contract of employment'. This idea that workers should never be charged was in fact immediately relevant to the Dutch Helpling case. To be precise, due to the extension of this protection to other types of 'intermediaries' under national law,[37] Helpling was found to have violated this principle already by the first-instance court (which did *not* see the contractual construct at issue as a TAW relationship).

Equally interesting seems the provision in Article 6(2), according to which 'clauses prohibiting or having the effect of preventing the conclusion of a

[37] Art 9 of the Law on the allocation of workers through intermediaries (Wet allocatie arbeidskrachten door intermediairs, Waadi).

contract of employment or an employment relationship between the user undertaking and the temporary agency worker' are null and void. In this respect, it is evident from the decisions described above that every single one of the platforms analysed envisaged a strict prohibition of any arrangements between workers and households to circumvent the platform and sanctions (incl. deregistration) in case of violation. In the TaskRunner case, the Malmö Administrative Court even argues – not without reason – that running this type of platform model without strong protections against circumvention would be almost unthinkable. Accordingly, the Dutch courts up to the Supreme Court found that Helpling's particularly strict policy, which prohibited the conclusion of an employment contract in the two years following the last assignment of the cleaner to the client via Helpling, constituted a violation of the rules on TAW.

Considering the lack of EU-level case law on the interpretation of Article 6(2), it seems uncertain whether any form of absolute prohibition could be justified here. The rather clear formulation makes this seem unlikely, even in the likely case that the worker may still wish to remain on the platform for additional work tasks while working for one or several individual clients directly. This might indicate that the platforms would need to offer the option for clients to transparently take over individual platform workers – obviously in return for a 'reasonable level of recompense', as it is expressly allowed by Article 6(2).

All in all, elements such as those discussed in the last three paragraphs could constitute a basis for courts to find in favour of a teleological extension of legal rules for TAW to domestic work, even if not all provisions will be relevant for work in private households. This conclusion would however, be put into question if a qualification as TAW would lead to an unacceptable burden on private households.

iv. Unacceptable Burden for User Households?

While, as illustrated in the preceding subsection, *EU law* does not contain any noteworthy duties for users of TAW which, like private households, do not have any significant own staff, the same cannot necessarily be said about national law.

This starts with the fact that, unlike the Netherlands, where the first decision reclassifying a platform focusing on household tasks as a temporary work agency was handed down, most countries seem to require agencies to obtain a licence to operate their business legally. Illegal TAW (without a licence, and/or without living up to other legal requirements) can have serious consequences not only for the agency (platform), but notably for the user undertaking. The latter may be subject to (heavy) fines,[38] subsidiary[39] or even joint and

[38] As demonstrated inter alia in cases where platform have been reclassified as user undertakings of their subcontractors e.g. in France and Spain. Cf the sums mentioned eg in Tribunal correctionnel de Paris of 12 January 2023 (on Stuart) or Tribunal Superior de Justicia de Cataluña of 11 December 2023, 11121/2023 (which annuls a penalty imposed on Just Eat).

[39] See an Austrian decision considering this applicable to Uber: Oberlandesgericht Wien of 23 November 2020, 10 Ra 59/20z.

several[40] liability for wages and/or social security contributions, or a reclassification as direct employer of the illegally hired-out employee.[41] All of these consequences would arguably seem disproportionate for a private household making use of a platform service which is retroactively qualified as TAW.

To the degree that such consequences are mandatory and do not allow for a judge to waive them with a view to the position of the household, one may arguable expect decision-making bodies to be very hesitant to reclassify platform workers as temporary agency workers. Consequently, if existing strict rules for user undertakings are to be preserved, it would seem that the regulation of TAW could at best be applied in a modified form to situations in which the user is a private household. This could barely be achieved by a court decision in the individual case, and would thus require legislative intervention.

v. A Stable Relationship with the Platform as an Agency?

Finally, it also does not necessarily seem a given that a categorisation of the contractual relationship as TAW would provide the worker with the benefits of a stable employment relationship, including rights that may be subject to a waiting period (as tends to be the case for various forms of leave rights – annual leave, sick leave, family-related leave, training leave etc) and rights the generosity of which depends on seniority (eg wages, dismissal protection etc).

Note that many countries' law permits temporary work agencies to conclude successive fixed-term contracts with a worker each time the latter is hired out to an individual user.[42] As far as the law allows this, despite it being clear that the platform retains their former employee's details in order to match them for further assignments,[43] the same would seem to apply to platforms. And whereas employees in 'regular' temporary work agencies may be hired out at least for several months or weeks per user, the individual 'placements' in domestic platform work may only last a couple of hours. How such work patterns are taken into account when each assignment is considered to constitute a separate fixed-term contract with the platform will depend on the intricacies of national calculation rules for waiting periods and seniority. Note that, if the platform is seen as a temporary work agency, the Fixed-term Work Directive does not apply,[44] so that no violation of EU law could be claimed if the seniority of a platform worker is negatively affected by the fact that, for them, daily and weekly rest periods are periods without a contract.

[40] As applied eg in a Spanish decision on Cabify: Tribunal Superior de Justicia de Cataluña [Catalonia Appeals Court] of 25/5/2023, No. 3378/2023.

[41] See Section 10(1) of the German Law on Temporary Agency Work (Arbeitnehmerüberlassungsgesetz).

[42] C Hießl, Comparative VUP Groups Report. Deliverable 3.4. for Horizon 2020 project 'Working, Yet Poor', section 3.2.4.2 (2023).

[43] See M Kaufmann, 'Eine Krise im Zeitraffertempo. Leiharbeit unter Druck' (2020) Der Spiegel of 23/8/2020, www.spiegel.de/wirtschaft/leiharbeit-in-der-corona-krise-das-schlaegt-voll-auf-die-arbeitnehmer-durch-a-5860683b-790d-4590-a9fd-df9c8c8bc7e1.

[44] See CJEU of 11 April 2013, C-290/12 (Della Rocca).

C. Special Regimes for Employer-Households

Irrespective of whether a worker is considered to be employed in a bilateral relationship with the platform or a temporary agency relationship, the question may arise whether special regimes for private households acting as employers as mentioned in the introduction apply – and whether they should apply.

Such schemes have been put in place in various countries with the aim of minimising the administrative and financial burden for households and thus incentivise a formalisation of domestic work relationships. Some of them, notably those focusing on an exemption from or reduction of tax and/or social security contributions, can work as a public subsidy and need not necessarily reduce workers' rights.

Note that in both of the above examples of platforms designating the household as the employer in their standard business model (ie Vaskerhvitt and Helpling), this was clearly based on considerations of provisions that exempted private employers from taxes and social security contributions in the Netherlands[45] and Norway.[46] The Dutch courts, as well as the union federation that brought the Helpling case before them, have in fact been the subject of some harsh criticism, as Helpling's bankruptcy in early 2023 was linked to the reclassification of the contractual relationship.[47] And indeed, the prospects to have to raise prices for cleaning substantially due to the sudden applicability of taxes and contributions had been a major factor in the platform's decisions that led eventually led to its insolvency. Consequently, there is merit in the criticism that the proceedings have eventually hurt workers rather than benefitting them, as domestic work is likely to move back to the informal sector if the only legal way of performing it via a platform such as Helpling would be prohibitively more expensive. At the same time, the solution cannot be to criticise unions for bringing a case which self-evidently did not have the aim of increasing tax revenue, but to achieve the applicability of a sectoral collective agreement to the cleaners. Much rather, a regulatory debate would seem warranted on the necessity to extend special regime for employer-households to domestic work provided by employees of a commercial provider (be it a platform, agency or other) – to avoid the perverse effect of making precisely those forms that could offer better protection to the workers financially unviable for households.

Another question is how to deal with the widespread forms of exemptions of domestic work from labour rights, often including health and safety and/or working time provisions, which is partly mirrored at supra- and/or international

[45] The regulation of *dienstverlening aan huis* is spread over several legal acts. For an overview see Belastingdienst, Handboek Loonheffingen 2024, 270 et seqq.

[46] As explained prominently on Vaskerhvitt's website – see www.vaskerhvitt.no/om-oss.

[47] See eg M Arets, 'Hoe het faillissement Helpling de weeffouten van het debat blootlegt' 16 Jnuary 2023, www.martijnarets.com/nieuwsbrief/hoe-het-faillissement-helpling-de-weeffouten-van-het-debat-blootlegt-2/.

level – including in EU Directives and International Labour Organization (ILO) conventions.[48] Regulation entailing a waiver or reduction of financial entitlements (minimum wage and/or social security rights) are often limited to rather small-scale activities,[49] yet some legislators have chosen to legalise even the provision of live-in care in return for wages that do not nearly reflect the quasi-permanent availability of the caregiver.[50] This can involve forms of condoned (mis-)classification of workers as self-employed, the determination of minimum wages exclusively on a monthly (not hourly) basis, or the simple exemption from the relevant protective provisions. Where such specific provisions are missing, basically illegal practices may be societally 'normalised' to the degree that authorities may find it difficult to intervene.

Specifically with regard to health and safety obligations, the considerations of the Norwegian and Swedish rulings described above at sections III.A and III.B are certainly justified in the sense that platforms regularly have no way of immediately influencing the health and safety conditions in their workers' work environment. At the same time, subjecting private households to strict sanctions and/or liability for work-related health and safety issues may not seem warranted either. Whether this is a problem may depend significantly on national law. For instance, if the law ensures comprehensive coverage by industrial injury insurance, coupled with a limitation of employer's direct liability to cases of gross negligence or intent,[51] its applicability to private households would seem less problematic. By contrast, notably systems without mandatory social insurance for workplace injury and instead strict concepts of employer liability[52] generally exempt private households, leaving employees without protection. Notably in the latter case, it may be worth serious consideration whether any professional provider involved in the provision of the service (platform, agency or other) should be subject to obligations in line with their position – such as a duty to take out insurance for the workers,[53] and provide safety training to the workers and/or appropriate guidance to the clients.

[48] M Oelz, 'The ILO's Domestic Workers Convention and Recommendation: A Window of Opportunity for Social Justice' (2014) 153 *International Labour Review* 143, provides an overview of the remarkable number of ILO instruments that allow for the exclusion of domestic workers. For the EU, one might point to the express exclusion of domestic workers from the scope of the Health and Safety Framework Directive 89/391/EEC (see section IV.C) – which may also have an impact on their coverage under the Maternity Directive 92/85/EEC and the Working Time Directive 2003/88/EC – just as the Employer Insolvency Directive 2008/94/EC. Labour law directives passed since 2019 have generally contained a recital stating that domestic workers 'could fall within the[ir] scope', whereby notably the Transparent and Predictable Working Conditions Directive 2019/1152/EU expressly states that domestic workers can be excluded from some of its provisions. For details see C Hießl, 'General Concepts: Worker/Employee' in C Hießl (ed), *EU Labour Law: A Commentary* (Alphen aan den Rijn, Kluwer, 2025) 18–19.

[49] See examples for Belgium, Germany and Italy in Hießl (n 44), sections 4.2.2, 4.2.4 and 4.2.5.

[50] See eg the Austrian legislation on live-in carers in the 2007 Hausbetreuungsgesetz.

[51] See eg Section 104(1) of the Seventh Book of the German Social Security Code (SGB VII).

[52] As in the Netherlands: see Art 7:658(4) of the Civil Code (BW).

[53] As many platforms are already doing – as obvious inter alia from the decisions in Joyners and Helpling.

To a certain degree, the most appropriate solution may thus be a shift of responsibility to the platform/agency. Other aspects, and most notably social security, may require a certain financial commitment from the state – specifically by letting domestic and care workers accrue rights to social benefits despite exempting these relationships fully or partly from contributions in order to promote formalisation.

D. Use by Formal Care Institutions

One striking feature mentioned about the caregiving platform Joyners (see sections III.D and III.E) is that its professional carers had been booked not only for work in private households, but also for example in residential care homes. This illustrates that 'domestic work platforms' may in reality often have a mixed clientele. This is notably likely in the care sector, where acute staff shortages are increasingly forcing care institutions to source their workforce via external providers,[54] but may certainly also apply for example to cleaning tasks.[55] As a result, it might be important to keep in mind that decisions on classification and mutual rights and duties should also appear fair in a context where the client is *not* a private household.

Such considerations might underline the necessity to take a more serious look at the viability of a classification as TAW. The latter arguably appears the most appropriate way to look at the assignment of cleaners or carers to business clients which determine the individual work performance in their undertaking in the way that is typical for a user undertaking. For non-platform agencies, there have already been cases reclassifying purportedly self-employed caregivers hired in via an agency as temporary agency workers.[56] To ensure a coherent classification, it may be worth exploring ways to keep workers that are assigned to both households and institutions or companies within a single status, albeit special rules may be necessary to avoid that undue responsibilities or costs are placed on private households, as set out at section IV.B.iv.

E. Chain Agency Work?

Finally, some thoughts may need to be dedicated to whether 'chain agency work' should be a valid classification in cases that involve a separate service company or cooperation that is in charge of administrative tasks relating to the platform worker's payment, insurance, tax, social security contributions and so on. The

[54] Cf eg A Leuxner and M von Schwanenflügel, 'Reform der Pflegeberufe. Mehr Qualität und Attraktivität im zukünftig größten Ausbildungsberuf' (2018) *Neue Zeitschrift für Sozialrecht* 202.

[55] Helpling is an example of a platform which also offered cleaning in business premises.

[56] See eg a German last-instance decision in Bundessozialgericht of 7 June 2018, B 12 R 6/18 R.

more extensive services are provided by such a player, and the more certain platforms might indeed limit their role to little more than an intermediary for matching demand and supply, the more it might seem appropriate to discuss the presence of shared employer functions between the companies involved. As described for Joyners supra at III.E, this may come down to viewing the platform as the middle link in a chain of TAW – a user undertaking in relation to the service company as the worker's direct employer, and an agency in relation to the household as the 'end user'.

Whether or not chain agency work should be considered as a valuable concept in case of complex responsibilities might also depend on what the consequences would be in terms of the rights and responsibilities of individual actors. Notably, if platforms were to be seen as agencies and users at the same time, would that imply their joint and several liability for all duties, or would it be exempted from all duties which the legislator clearly allocates with only one of the parties (agency or user)? The answer would seem unclear in many legal systems at presence.

V. CONCLUSION

With a view to the scarcity of cases in which any particular platform model has been scrutinised in detail by an administrative or judicial body so far, any attempt at drawing conclusions needs to be approached with caution. This is notably true at a point in time when the highest courts of the countries in which the cases studied occurred have not yet pronounced themselves on their merits, so that any conclusions at this point are necessarily temporary. It should also be noted that there has not been a single case in which the workers concerned were a party themselves, as all of the litigation so far has been initiated by a public institution or – exceptionally – a trade union. Consequently, the voice of the individuals whose protection is at stake is largely absent from the decision-making bodies' reasoning, on which much of the above discussion is based.

What has become clear, though, is that the complexity of the relation between the different actors involved in platform work in private households makes it difficult to identify a single entity as the employer – a difficulty which, for lack of other options, may result in the workers' classification as self-employed despite clear indications of subordination and organisation integration in relation to the different entities. In the current legal landscape, TAW would seem the most promising concept to achieve a balanced outcome – as it is designed to attach structural employers' duties to the agency as the entity with the organisational responsibility for the workers' employment, while direction and control are exercised by a user undertaking. At least potentially, a construction which sees the platform (or another business entity, as discussed at section IV.E) as the agency and the household as the user could thus enable a solid classification as an employment relationship, which could entail a certain stability beyond the individual assignment, ensure the application of collective labour rights for domestic workers vis-à-vis the commercial entities that organise their work, and avoid the applicability of any exemptions from protective provisions.

At the same time, the above discussion has made it clear that, in many (probably most) legal systems, the reliance on the concept of TAW would currently be either impossible (notably due to a clear restriction to user 'undertakings' and a legal design that makes a teleological extension to private households unconvincing) or lead to adverse consequences for household. This notably includes the penalisation of user undertakings in case of illegal TAW, and/or their responsibility in case of the agency's failure to pay wages and social security contributions in many countries. Both are based on the assumption that a user *undertaking* could be reasonably expected to verify the trustworthiness of an agency before hiring in workers from it – which obviously does not apply to private households. What's more, if using an agency means that domestic and care work becomes prohibitively more expensive (notably in terms of taxes and contribution) than direct employment or work with (bogus) self-employed workers, it may also be unrealistic to expect households to embrace a construction as TAW. As for workers' rights, it has been shown that all three above-mentioned possible advantages of being employed by the agency rather than the household (stability of relationship, collective labour rights, non-applicability of exemptions from protection) are actually dependent on national law in the different legal systems.

As a result, in most countries, targeted legislative interventions would be needed to ensure that TAW or similar concepts could be a realistic option for domestic platform workers and provide adequate protections. As has been discussed, this should notably involve the avoidance of an unreasonable burden or deterrent costs for private households, while the responsibility of intermediaries (and, for social security, the state) would need to be enhanced to gradually assimilate these workers' level of protection to that which would be considered self-evident for any other group of workers.

10

Legal Models of Labour Intermediaries and Digital Care Platforms

LUCA RATTI

I. INTRODUCTION

THE PLATFORM ECONOMY is increasingly dominating the domestic work and home care sectors, especially in countries of the so-called global North, where more and more clusters of the population still lack accessible, high-quality care services at affordable rates. Platform work typically features at least three actors: the ultimate client, the online platform and the worker. In legal terms, this triggers the question whether the empirical understanding of digital care platforms as intermediaries in the labour market should bear regulatory consequences and, in case, how can the EU legal framework be accommodated to such empirical reality.

Over the past decade, several hypotheses have been advanced concerning the nature of online platforms, which are frequently conceptualised as intermediaries. These have been described either as *linear* intermediaries – that is, entities or institutions that position themselves between workers and firms for the purpose of facilitating their matching – or as *triangular* intermediaries, in which the intermediary assumes an active role in shaping the manner in which work activities are organised and performed. This latter model took the name of temporary agency work and was regulated at EU level with Directive 2008/104. The EU directive on platform work adopted in 2024 (the Platform Work Directive) opens new conceptual and interpretative avenues, in that it refers to intermediaries and to some extent acknowledges the triangularity of work intermediated via platforms.

This chapter looks at digital care platforms as labour market intermediaries and advocates that on this basis they should be legally treated. The chapter will first address the main characteristics of the services provided by Digital Care Platforms (DCP) and focus on the main risks associated therewith, as resulting from empirical assessments. It will then try to match the regulatory model emerging from the EU Temporary Agency Work Directive with the concept of intermediary expressed by international sources. It will conclude by examining the EU Platform Work Directive's approach to cases when the service is provided through intermediaries, and highlight what are the main legal issues remained unaddressed after the enactment of the directive.

II. STRUCTURE AND RISKS OF DIGITAL CARE PLATFORMS

Empirical studies on the main characteristics of DCP started to emerge in parallel with the advent of the platform business model on the 'market' of long-term home care. As recalled by the Organisation for Economic Co-operation and Development (OECD), a range of 'medical, personal care and assistance services' are typically associated with long-term care needs, 'with the primary goal of alleviating pain and reducing or managing the deterioration in health status for people with a degree of long-term dependency'.[1] While DCP had the merit to break 'down the physical barriers and aggregate[d] workers',[2] their business model needs to be investigated in order to assess its ability to grant adequate labour rights and social protection to those – often migrant women from the Global South – who perform care tasks via such platforms. This leads, on the one hand, to acknowledge that platforms contribute to a 'selective formalisation' of certain aspects of domestic work relations;[3] but, on the other hand, that platforms remain immune from liability regimes both as employers and as intermediaries, thus leading to a possible 'erosion of workers' rights to benefits like social protection, medical insurance and minimum wage, with poor working conditions offered in exchange for a job opportunity'.[4]

DCP can be analysed from very different perspectives. Some detailed studies have tried to outline a typology of DCP at regional[5] or national[6] levels. Based

[1] OECD, *OECD Health Statistics 2023. Definitions, Sources and Methods* www.oecd.org/health/health-data.htm.

[2] E Smiley, 'Domestic Workers Are Using the Gig Economy Against Itself' (June 2021) *The Nation* www.thenation.com/article/society/domestic-workers-handy-labor/.

[3] N van Doorn, 'Stepping Stone or Dead End? The Ambiguities of Platform-Mediated Domestic Work under Conditions of Austerity Urbanism' in D Baines and I Cunningham (eds), *Working in the Context of Austerity: Challenges and Struggles* (Bristol, Bristol University Press, 2020) 49.

[4] N van Doorn, F Ferrari and M Graham, 'Migration and Migrant Labour in the Gig Economy: An Intervention' (2023) 37 *Work, Employment and Society* 1099.

[5] A Friedrich Ebert Stiftung report on South and Southeast Asia considers the position of care platform workers particularly instable and precarious, as a consequence of 'challenges in determining the legal and social status of such workers'. A Tandon and A Rathi, *Fault Lines at the Front Lines: Care Work and Digital Platforms in South and Southeast Asia* (Singapore, Friedrich Ebert Stiftung, 2021).

[6] Willard et al identify at least three main models in the Netherlands: a) community care platforms, designed to support local communities by enhancing social cohesion, operating as 'social marketplaces' thus matching offer and demand for care-related services; b) system integrator platforms, aimed at integrating existing services related to well-being in general (food, mobility, housing, care, social contacts, etc.) into one dedicated platform; c) care network platforms 'designed to support (informal) caregivers who wished to coordinate assorted collaborations and (health) care issues for an older person'. See S Willard, E van Rossum, M Spreeuwenberg and L de Witte, 'A Typology of Online Care Platforms for Community-Dwelling Older Adults in the Netherlands: A Scoping Review' (2019) 18 *Gerontechnology* 122.

on empirical studies conducted in Spain by Blanchard et al,[7] a 2024 report by the Friedric Ebert Stiftung[8] outlines two main types of DCP: a) digital placement agencies that operate in a way similar to typical employment agencies: the services offered include an assessment of client's needs, exact matching with specific carers, and administrative management of the working arrangement; b) on-demand DCP that operate similarly to on-demand labour platforms operating in other sectors such as food delivery and ride hailing. This second type of DCP tends to specialise in short-term services and not to create long-term relationships between the carer and the family. The workers set their own schedule, and the platform takes a percentage of the service as commission.[9]

This dual model partly reflects what another Friedric Ebert Stiftung Report found to happen in South and South-East Asia, where three main types of DCP operating in the care work sector have been identified: a) on-demand platforms that place workers in short-term gigs, similar to the uberisation model of organising services; b) digital placement agencies that find workers for employers, that are charged a one-time fee for the placement service received; c) marketplaces that result in online job boards, wherein workers create profiles and add their skills, and employers pay a fee to access workers' profiles.[10]

Judy Fudge and Claire Hobden conceptualise the typology of domestic work intermediaries in broader terms,[11] including not only private recruitment and employment agencies, but also public authorities, public or private enterprises, cooperatives and trade unions. Specifically focusing on online intermediaries, they recognise that some platforms 'simply match domestic workers with private households, and are not involved with directing the work and setting the working conditions', while other digital platforms 'establish the payments that the domestic workers receive, ensure a certain quality of service, or a branding of their services'.[12]

Notwithstanding some minor differences, the aforementioned typology of DCP allows to identify three commonalities between platforms established in different regional contexts. First, individuals (ie, workers and/or self-employed) dealing with DCP typically belong to socio-ethnical minorities and/or have a migrant background. Second, DCP promote a type of domestic work which generates low-incomes and tends to be remunerated below minimum wage standards. Third, both when DCP serve as mere intermediaries matching jobseekers with

[7] O Blanchard et al, *Home Care and Digital Platforms in Spain* (Berlin, Friedrich Ebert Stiftung, 2021). On Spain, see P Rodríguez-Modroño, ch 1, in this book; R Martinez-Buján and P Moré, 'Home Care for Profit: Intermediary Agencies and Digital Platforms Brokering Migrant Women's Labour in Spain' (2024) 76 *Current Sociology* 1036.

[8] C Murphy, I Pais and T Gibbons, *Care Platforms: Impacts and Challenges from a Trade Union Perspective* (Berlin, Friedrich Ebert Stiftung & EPSU, 2024).

[9] ibid 8.

[10] Tandon and Rathi (n 5).

[11] J Fudge and C Hobden, *Conceptualizing the Role of Intermediaries in Formalizing Domestic Work* (Geneva, ILO, 2018).

[12] ibid 5–6.

employers and when their role is more 'intrusive' and continues along the entire duration of the work relation between the two parties, platforms are able to set labour and employment conditions and extract their added value from 'commissions', that is fees that one or both parties involved in a domestic work relation are required to pay. Vulnerability on the labour market, poor working conditions, and a disproportionally inferior position of domestic workers vis-à-vis DCP are thus features that deserve attention from a legal standpoint.[13] The specific issue of the use of algorithms by digital labour platforms in managing work relations is addressed elsewhere in this book.[14]

As far as the position of the platform vis-à-vis working individuals is concerned, a distinction may therefore be drawn between, on the one hand, DCP operating as mere labour market intermediaries in the form of placement service provides; and, on the other hand, DCP acting as proper employment agencies. These two models will serve as guidance to set out the main legal principles and obligations related to one or the other model,[15] both corresponding to the broad notion of labour market intermediaries famously elaborated by David Autor.[16]

III. INTERNATIONAL STANDARDS ON INTERMEDIARIES AT WORK: LESSONS TO BE LEARNT FOR DCP?

The International Labour Organization (ILO) defines a digital labour platform as 'a company that mediates and facilitates labour exchange between different users, such as businesses, workers and consumers'.[17] Current narratives on work performed through digital platforms, however, conceptualise the position of these latter either in terms of employers having platform workers at their dependence or, at the opposite, as simple clients of individual service providers. Particularly for what concerns DCP, such narratives fail to correctly address the division of competences and employer's prerogatives amongst the parties involved therein. While domestic platform work is not exclusively performed in the care sector, it is also clearly recognised by international documents that domestic workers provide direct and indirect care services, and as such are key members of the care economy.

[13] *Amplius* see Hießl, ch 9, in this book.

[14] Aloisi and Potocka-Sionek, ch 11, in this book.

[15] The following paragraphs partly build on L Ratti, 'Online Platforms as Labour Market Intermediaries' in A Lo Faro (ed), *New Technology and Labour Law. Selected Topics* (Torino, Giappichelli, 2023) 89.

[16] DH Autor, 'Studies of Labor Market Intermediation: Introduction' in DH Autor (ed), *Studies of Labor Market Intermediation* (Chicago, University of Chicago Press, 2009), where labour market intermediaries are defined as 'entities or institutions that interpose themselves between workers and firms to facilitate, inform, or regulate how workers are matched to firms, how work is accomplished, and how conflicts are resolved'.

[17] ILO, *World Employment and Social Outlook 2021: The Role of Digital Labour Platforms in Transforming the World of Work* (Geneva, ILO, 2021).

As written in the Preamble to the ILO Domestic Workers Convention no. 189 (2011),[18] domestic work deals primarily with 'caring for ageing populations, children and persons with a disability', therefore its regulation needs to be tailored to the specific needs of people performing domestic tasks.[19] Since the 1970s, care work has been labelled as 'reproductive labour', in that it involves tasks that are essential to the household but lacks legal and economic recognition.[20]

From an ILO perspective, the main aspect to be considered when assessing the concrete operation of DCP concerns the free-of-charge principle. With ILO Convention no. 96 (1949), the ILO allowed Member States to choose between a policy of prohibition of fee-charging and profit-seeking employment agencies, and a more liberal policy of regulation. Since 1997, the ILO abandoned the option of a progressive abolition of private employment agencies and introduced specific substantive safeguards. Convention no. 181 (1997) on Private Employment Agencies and the relevant Recommendation no. 188, despite their relatively scarce ratifications,[21] have played an important role in steering international and EU-level regulatory initiatives.[22]

In the ILO Convention no. 189 on domestic work, the free-of-charge principle is expressed by Article 15(1)(e), which requires Member States to 'take measures to ensure that fees charged by private employment agencies are not deducted from the remuneration of domestic workers'. In turn, Article 7 of the ILO Convention no. 181 on Private employment agencies prohibits agencies from charging 'directly or indirectly, in whole or in part, any fees or costs to workers'.

As clarified in the 2019 non-binding 'ILO general principles and operational guidelines for fair recruitment', it derives from the free-of-charge principle that Member States are required to adopt measures to eliminate the charging of recruitment fees and related costs to workers and jobseekers, aiming in particular at 'preventing fraudulent practices by labour recruiters, abuse of workers, debt bondage and other forms of economic coercion'. As a consequence, 'prospective employers, public or private, or their intermediaries, and not the workers, should bear the cost of recruitment. The full extent and nature of costs, for instance costs paid by employers to labour recruiters, should be transparent to those who pay them'.[23]

[18] So far ratified by only nine EU Member States: Italy, Ireland, Portugal, Belgium, Sweden, Spain, Germany, Malta and Finland.

[19] For a contextualisation of domestic work see V Pavlou, *Migrant Domestic Workers in Europe: Law and the Construction of Vulnerability* (Oxford, Hart Publishing, 2021) 6.

[20] *Ex multis* U Huws, 'The Hassle of Housework: Digitalisation and the Commodification of Domestic Labour' (2019) 123 *Feminist Review* 8.

[21] To date, Convention no. 181 (1997) counts 34 ratifications by Member States. Notable non-ratifying Member States include Austria, Brazil, Canada, China, Cyprus, Denmark, Germany, Greece, Indonesia, India, Luxembourg, Malta, Romania, Slovenia, Sweden, Switzerland, the UK and the US.

[22] ACL Davies, 'ILO Convention 181 Private Employment Agencies Convention, 1997 (No. 181)' in E Ales et al (eds), *International and European Labour Law* (Oxford, Hart/Beck/Nomos, 2018) 911.

[23] ILO, *General Principles and Operational Guidelines for Fair Recruitment & Definition of Recruitment Fees and Related Costs* (Geneva, ILO, 2019) 16.

ILO Convention no. 189 on domestic workers recommends the regulation of recruitment agencies as intermediaries rather than employers. Its Article 15 provides that Member States shall: (a) 'determine the conditions governing the operation of private employment agencies recruiting or placing domestic workers, in accordance with national laws, regulations and practice' with a view to 'effectively protect domestic workers, including migrant domestic workers, recruited or placed by private employment agencies, against abusive practices'.

According to Article 1, ILO Convention no. 181 (1997), three types of labour market intermediaries fall within its scope: a) The first type provides services for matching offers of and applications for employment, without the private employment agency becoming a party to the employment relationships which may arise therefrom. b) The second type provides services by employing workers with a view to making them available to a third party. This party may be a natural or legal person (referred to as a 'user enterprise') which assigns their tasks and supervises the execution of these tasks. c) The third type of intermediary provides other services relating to job-seeking, determined by the competent authority after consulting the most representative employers' and workers' organisations, such as the provision of information, which do not set out to match specific offers of and applications for employment.

As such, all three models contemplated by ILO Convention no. 181 (1997) are used in the digital care sector, with most DCP being either mere intermediaries (type a) or becoming party to a triangular work arrangement (type b). Less frequent is the use of DCP as mere points of information for jobseekers (type c).

The core principle on which ILO Convention no. 181 is based – the free-of-charge principle enshrined in Article 7 – is complemented by the requirement that agencies should not prevent workers from concluding direct employment relationships with the end user or with another enterprise. Of specific interest for the DCP sector are two additional obligations imposed to Member States by Article 8 of the Convention. The first one relates to the duty to 'provide adequate protection for and prevent abuses of migrant workers recruited or placed in its territory by private employment agencies', which duty applies 'both within its jurisdiction and, where appropriate, in collaboration with other Members'. The second relates to the situation in which workers are recruited in one country to work in another. In such case, the Members concerned shall consider concluding bilateral agreements to prevent abuses and fraudulent practices in recruitment, placement and employment.

At the time of writing, ILO is discussing on a possible standard setting on decent work in the platform economy. Based on a decision by the ILO Governing body dated March 2023, the 113th and 114th Sessions of the International Labour Conference are devoted to discuss on a possible Convention, which is based on several guiding principles, including that whenever the use of intermediaries is permitted by national legislation, States should determine and allocate the respective responsibilities of digital labour platforms and intermediaries to ensure compliance with the provisions of the proposed Convention. Particularly concerning aspects such as occupational safety and health, the payment of remuneration and social security contributions, the proposed ILO Convention raised issues on the role of platforms as intermediaries and how to adequately allocate legal accountability.[24]

IV. EU LAW AND 'LINEAR' INTERMEDIARIES

At the EU level, the function of labour market intermediaries has been the focus of two important cases decided by the Court of Justice of the European Union (CJEU).

The first case *Höfner and Elser*[25] concerned a private employment agency which was active in the head-hunting (placement) of business executives. Germany had ratified ILO Convention no. 96 (1949), which implied a gradual abolition of fee-charging in the job matching done by employment agencies. At that time, German law entrusted the attainment of the general aim to achieve and maintain a high level of employment to the *Bundesanstalt für Arbeit* (Federal Office for Employment). German authorities argued their compliance with Article 5 of ILO Convention no. 96 since it allowed exceptions

> in respect of categories of persons, exactly defined by national laws or regulations, for whom appropriate placing arrangements cannot conveniently be made within the framework of the public employment service, but only after consultation, by appropriate methods, with the organisations of employers and workers concerned.

In *Höfner and Elser*, the CJEU first considered the question whether a public employment agency such as the Bundesanstalt may be regarded as an undertaking within the meaning of the relevant EU principles on internal market competition. In particular, the fact that employment procurement activities are normally entrusted to public agencies does not contradict the economic nature of such activities. As a consequence, employment procurement is not an exclusive activity of public entities. From this derives that Member States cannot maintain in force legal provisions that create 'a situation in which a public employment agency cannot avoid infringing Article 86'. The conclusion of the *Höfner and Elser* case is that every monopoly of employment intermediation activities is contrary to EU law provided that four conditions are satisfied: a) the exclusive right extends to executive recruitment activities; b) the public employment agency is manifestly incapable of satisfying demand prevailing on the market for such activities; c) the actual pursuit of those activities by private recruitment consultants is rendered impossible by the maintenance in force of a statutory provision under which such activities are prohibited and non-observance of that

[24] See ILO, Realizing decent work in the platform economy. International Labour Conference 113th Session, 2025 (2025).

[25] CJEU, C-41/90 *Klaus Höfner and Fritz Elser v Macrotron* [1991] ECLI:EU:C:1991:161.

prohibition renders the contracts concerned void; and d) the activities in question may extend to the nationals or to the territory of other Member States. In the specific case decided by the Court of Justice, such a monopoly was indeed a violation of competition rules provided that it was capable of affecting transnational trade.

A second important case before the CJEU originated from Italy. The *Job Centre* case[26] concerned a private cooperative company which, without any prior licensing from the Italian State, requested to be registered under the public register of employment agencies, exercising its freedom of establishment and freedom to conduct a business. Against the refusal from the Italian authorities to allow its registration, the company argued that Italian law was infringing EU primary principles. The CJEU held that Member States breach Article 90(1) TFEU whenever they prohibit any activity as an intermediary between supply and demand on the employment market, be it an employment agency or an employment business, since as such this situation infringes Article 86 of the Treaty. Similarly to the previous case, the CJEU made its findings conditional to the occurrence of specific circumstances: a) the public placement offices are manifestly unable to satisfy demand on the market for all types of activity; b) the actual placement of employees by private companies is rendered impossible by the maintenance in force of statutory provisions under which such activities are prohibited and non-observance of that prohibition gives rise to penal and administrative sanctions; and c) the placement activities in question could extend to the nationals or to the territory of other Member States.

The result of the two aforementioned cases was that across the EU, Member States started opening their doors to private entities, which saw their role progressively enhanced in the subsequent decades. It also kicked off the possible liberalisation of temporary work agencies, which since then started to be at the centre of the process of European social dialogue and was expected to be regulated through a 'negotiated directive' similarly to what had happened with part-time and fixed-term work.[27]

V. TRIANGULAR WORK ARRANGEMENTS IN THE EU DIRECTIVE ON TEMPORARY AGENCY WORK: A BLUEPRINT FOR PLATFORM WORK?

For decades, and notably even after the 1997 CJEU case *Job Center II*, EU Member States have individually regulated temporary agency work arrangements without

[26] CJEU, C-111/94 *Job Centre Coop* [1995] ECLI:EU:C:1995:340.

[27] *Amplius* cf ACL Davies, 'Regulating Atypical Work: Beyond Equality' in N Countouris and M Freedland (eds), *Resocialising Europe in a Time of Crisis* (Cambridge, Cambridge University Press, 2013) 230.

co-ordination or harmonisation, leading to a progressively intricate array of diverse legislations throughout Europe.[28]

In response to the pressure exerted by the temporary work agencies industry on the EU legislature, and given the inability of EU social partners to reach an agreement at EU level similar to those concluded in the late 1990s on part-time and fixed-term work, a Directive on temporary agency work was enacted only in 2008. In fact, Directive 2008/104 accommodates a broad variety of temporary agency work arrangements, ranging from a model where temporary work agencies are deemed to be the employer (Germany) from other systems where they are just intermediaries and thus facilitate job matching instead of taking an active part in the employment relation. This reveals therefore that the Eurofound typology may not be up-to-date.

In analysing the regulatory approach deriving from Directive 2008/104, Feldman distinguishes between ex ante and ex post legal measures.[29] It is argued that the Directive governs ex ante the prerequisites that temporary agencies must satisfy to engage in domestic labour markets, while it also regulates ex post the procedures following the establishment and operation of contracts between the intermediary and the worker, and between the intermediary and the user firm. Specifically on ex ante requirements, Directive 2008/104 expresses a rather liberalising attitude prompted by the so-called flexicurity agenda. With its Article 4, the Directive requires Member States to remove restrictions in the use of temporary agency work except those that may conflict with fundamental rights of workers.[30]

The emergence of online platforms as labour market intermediaries raised the question whether Directive 2008/104 could be used as blueprint to conceptualise platform work.

A. Platform Work as a Form of Work Intermediation

Similar to temporary agency work, platform work typically features at least three parties: the ultimate client, the online intermediary and the worker. As remarked

[28] A 2016 Eurofound report identified at least four distinct legal environments within Europe where agency work was developed: a) A market-driven environment characterised by minimal formal regulation, as seen in the United Kingdom (UK); b) A social dialogue-based environment, exemplified by countries such as Denmark or Germany, where a balance exists between legislation and agreements established through collective bargaining; c) A legislator-driven environment, such as Italy or Belgium, where temporary agency work is subject to substantial regulation imposed by legislative bodies; d) Emerging markets characterised by a legislative framework yielding mixed impact results, as observed in Poland. Cf. Eurofound, *Regulation of Labour Market Intermediaries and the Role of Social Partners in Preventing Trafficking of Labour* (Luxemburg, Publications Office of the European Union, 2016) 20.

[29] Y Feldman, 'Ex Ante vs Ex-Post: Optimizing State Intervention in Exploitative Triangular Employment Relationships' (2009) 30 *Comparative Labor Law & Policy Journal* 751.

[30] ACL Davies, 'The Legal Nature of the Duty to Review Prohibitions or Restrictions on the Use of Temporary Agency Work' (2016) 53 *Common Market Law Review* 493.

by an EU-OSHA report, 'in the case of platforms matching professional freelancers with clients, the self-employed status of the freelancer is generally clear (though there may be borderline cases where there is some doubt). The most contentious cases are those involving the online co-ordination of low-skill online work and of offline work',[31] care work performed via platforms belonging certainly to this latter group.

The broad definitions of a temporary work agency (Article 3(1)(b), Directive 2008/104) and of temporary agency worker (Article 3(1)(c), Directive 2008/104) have led the CJEU to interpret extensively the personal scope of application of the directive. In the *Betriebsrat der Ruhrlandklinik* case,[32] the CJEU was confronted with a not-for-profit association of nurses acting as intermediary and a number of nurses supplied to an end user (a hospital) on the basis of a specific licence. Despite lacking proper employment contracts with the association, nurses were sent to work for user undertakings under the latter's functional and organisational instructions. Under the agreement concluded by the association with its clients, the former received, in return for each secondment, a payment covering the gross personnel costs plus a three per cent flat-rate administrative charge. In turn, nurses were granted the same remuneration as workers directly employed by the end user and were subject to virtually comparable employment conditions. The legal issue at stake concerned the refusal by the hospital's works council (*Betriebsrat*) to the use of the association's nurses, based on the fact that the secondment was not temporary, thus contrary to the German implementing legislation (*Arbeitnehmerüberlassungsgesetz* – AÜG). In order to judge on that issue, the CJEU had to correctly qualify the legal arrangement concluded by the parties of the case.

As suggested by its Advocate General,[33] the CJEU determined that the exclusion of a particular group of individuals from being designated as 'workers' solely due to their lack of engagement in an employment contract governed by private law should not be permissible. The Court identified the risk associated with adopting too narrow definitions of 'temporary agency worker' and 'temporary work agency', emphasising that regulatory disparities among Member States may risk undermining the achievement of the Directive's objectives, contravening the principle of *effet utile*.[34]

In the specific sector of domestic workers performing care work, when the platform arranges legal and practical matters with a view to supply one or more care workers to a household, this latter can be considered as an end user. Within such household, DCP are generally prevented from exercising coercive powers

[31] European Agency for Safety and Health at Work, 'Online Labour Exchanges, or "Crowdsourcing": Implications for Occupational Health and Safety' (Discussion Paper presented at the Bilbao Seminar, June 2015).

[32] CJEU, C-216/15 *Betriebsrat der Ruhrlandklinik* [2016] ECLI:EU:C:2016:883.

[33] Advocate General Saugmandsgaard Øe, Opinion in Case C-216/15, *Betriebsrat der Ruhrlandklinik gGmbH v Ruhrlandklinik gGmbH*, delivered on 6 July 2016.

[34] CJEU, C-216/15 *Betriebsrat der Ruhrlandklinik* [2016] ECLI:EU:C:2016:883.

vis-à-vis domestic care workers, as instructions, monitoring and (eventually) sanctions are exercised directly by the household members themselves. There could also be, however, platforms exercising some of the employer's prerogatives directly over of domestic care workers' performance. At times, DCP may retain the power to terminate the assignment or delete individuals' profile in case of dislike or non-compliance with the rules of the engagement. The platform's prerogatives suggest that the intermediary keeps fragments of managerial control, which must, therefore, be coordinated with those of the final user. The outcome is one according to which the individual's reputation is essential for the evaluation of the single performance and also for future assignments, both in terms of frequency and rates. In the legal qualification of DCP, therefore, concepts used for digital platforms in general can be borrowed, such as that of online marketplaces[35] or brokers.[36] In the light of this triangular structure, the question is whether the empirical understanding of DCP as labour market intermediaries should bear legal consequences.

Some scholars picked up the idea of applying temporary agency work rules to the field of platform work and, more precisely, of considering platforms as temporary work agencies. Rosin looked closer at the many implications of Directive 2008/104, including the concrete application of the principle of equal treatment (enshrined in Article 5 of the Directive) and of the removal of restrictions (Article 4). Her conclusions are in the sense that the directive 'would appear to be applicable to platform workers, as long as they are classified as "workers", and the work is performed under the user's supervision and direction'. The application of equal treatment, however, 'may not be as expected', especially for the difficulty to find a suitable comparator in the field of crowdwork.[37]

Zekić acknowledges marked organisational similarities between online platforms and temporary work agencies, and reports a Dutch case decided in 2021 where the Amsterdam Appeals Court seems to agree with classifying the provision of work through a digital platform as a form of temporary agency work.[38]

Potocka-Sionek convincingly argues that digital labour platforms 'do much more than providing a mere match between providers and suppliers', which denotes 'a fundamental shift in the model of labour intermediation and calls for a reconsideration of the ways of regulating the indirect model of the employment

[35] SC Kingsley, ML Gray and S Suri, 'Monopsony and the Crowd: Labor for Lemons?' (2014) https://papers.ssrn.com/sol3/papers.cfm?abstract_id=3257857.

[36] R Smith and S Leberstein, *Rights on Demand: Ensuring Workplace Standards and Worker Security in the On-Demand Economy* (National Employment Law Project, 2015); B Bergvall-Kåreborn and D Howcroft, 'Amazon Mechanical Turk and the Commodification of Labour' (2014) 29 *New Technology, Work and Employment* 213.

[37] A Rosin, 'Applying the Temporary Agency Work Directive to Platform Workers: Mission Impossible?' (2020) 36 *International Journal of Comparative Labour Law and Industrial Relations* 166.

[38] The Dutch case is *Helpling*, Appeal Court of Amsterdam, 21 September 2021, ECLI:NL:GHAMS:2021:2741. For a more contextualised analysis, see N Zekić, 'Possible Avenues for a More Effective Temporary Agency Work Directive' (2024) 15 *European Labour Law Journal* 68, 72–73.

relationship'.[39] This seems to result in the conclusion that the legal status of online platforms is in between the one of direct and indirect employers.[40]

Kocher's monograph on digital work platforms represents a seminal contribution to the legal scholarship on the subject.[41] Kocher offers a wide range of comparative examples while calling for regulatory changes which ensure protection of platform workers' labour rights. While rejecting the possible use of Directive 2008/104 as proxy to regulate platform work, Kocher argues that digital labour platforms are in fact market organisers. They exploit transaction cost benefits by drawing on contingent labour and create external markets by replacing existing ones.[42] More specifically, according to Kocher, digital labour platforms act as 'partial' market organisers in that they facilitate and aggregate contingent workforce while pursuing also side goals such as gathering data from users.[43]

I have elsewhere argued that a certain contiguity exists between the core functions of temporary work agencies and those of crowdwork platforms. Both categories of intermediaries self-regulate a wholly virtual labour market and, rather than merely facilitating contact between jobseekers and potential employers, take an active role in shaping the contractual arrangements between them, even retaining certain prerogatives traditionally associated with the employer.[44]

De Stefano and Wouters observed that online platforms in reality act as mere bridges between platform workers and the final recipient of the service, so that only ILO Convention no. 181 should be considered.[45] This option would require Member States to enforce the application of the free-of-charge principle, put at the core of the ILO Convention and adequately mirrored by the same Directive 2008/104 (Article 6(3)).[46] Further attention should be given to transparency and data protection for platform workers, directly deriving from Article 6, ILO Convention no. 181.[47]

[39] N Potocka-Sionek, *Platformisation of work: Challenges beyond employment classification* (PhD Thesis, EUI, 2023), at: https://cadmus.eui.eu/handle/1814/75755, 142–43.

[40] ibid 135.

[41] E Kocher, *Digital Work Platforms at the Interface of Labour Law. Regulating Market Organisers* (Oxford, Hart Publishing, 2022).

[42] ibid. 147.

[43] ibid. 152.

[44] L Ratti, 'Online Platforms and Crowdwork in Europe: A Two-Step Approach to Expanding Agency Work Provisions' (2017) 38 *Comparative Labor Law & Policy Journal* 477.

[45] V De Stefano and M Wouters, *Should Digital Labour Platforms Be Treated as Private Employment Agencies?*, ETUI Foresight Brief No. 07 (2019); M Wouters, 'Directing Labour Market Outcomes: Why Are Digital Labour Platforms Not Deemed Private Employment Agencies?' in G Casale and T Treu (eds), *Transformations of Work: Challenges for the National Systems of Labour Law and Social Security* (Torino, Giappichelli, 2018) 1431.

[46] Article 6(3), Directive 2008/104 provides that 'Temporary-work agencies shall not charge workers any fees in exchange for arranging for them to be recruited by a user undertaking, or for concluding a contract of employment or an employment relationship with a user undertaking after carrying out an assignment in that undertaking'.

[47] Article 6, ILO Convention no. 181 provides that 'the processing of personal data of workers by private employment agencies shall be: (a) done in a manner that protects this data and ensures respect for workers privacy in accordance with national law and practice; (b) limited to matters related to the qualifications and professional experience of the workers concerned and any other directly relevant information'.

Wouters further pointed out that intermediaries are free to change the terms of the contractual agreement with the workers.[48] That element can be attributed to the lack of domestic safeguards and the absence of international instruments. Even if a unilateral change of contract can be outlawed in domestic jurisdictions, intermediaries are still not included in this restriction.

It is undeniable that categorising platform work as intermediaries, particularly akin to temporary agency work, does not serve as a universal solution for safeguarding platform workers,[49] being understood that 'only workers under a contract of employment or who are in an employment relationship with a temporary work agency fall under the scope of the Directive on TAW (Art. 3(1))'.[50] Yet, certain insights into managing litigation concerning platform work[51] may suggest that, in specific instances, rules on temporary agency work could offer a framework for interpreting the proposed EU directive on the working conditions of platform workers.

As noted by some scholars,[52] the main challenge would be the application of the principle of equal treatment as per Article 5(1), Directive 2008/104. This may prove difficult, in particular when no 'direct ordinary employee' (ie, the comparator) is actually hired by the end user. Some help in this regard may come from the fact that Article 5(1) itself is based on a hypothetical comparison, not an actual one, between the temporary agency worker's working conditions and 'those that would apply if they had been recruited directly by that undertaking to occupy the same job'.[53] This may fit with the specific situation of platform workers in general, and of care and domestic workers in particular.

How this relates to the specific case of DCP is far from being established. In fact, the abovementioned typology of DCP does not allow to go as far as *sic et simpliciter* applying the TAW Directive to DCP. In particular, the underlying assumption of the Directive is that the intermediary (the agency) is in fact the employer (Article 2, Directive 2008/104). This would certainly not fit well with the normality of DCP, which either limit themselves to the mere intermediation of domestic care activities or at best follow-up the activity during the entire duration of the assignment, foregoing their employer functions vis-à-vis care workers. However, when DCP operate as intermediaries between the worker and the household – as it is often the case – and provided that care work is regulated by national law, the intermediation by a DCP may therefore not escape such regulatory framework.

[48] M Wouters, *International Labour Standards and Platform Work: An Analysis of Digital Labour Platforms Based on the Instruments on Private Employment Agencies Home Work and Domestic Work* (Alphen aan den Rijn, Wolters Kluwer, 2022) 289.

[49] N Potocka-Sionek, 'The Changing Nature of Labour Intermediation. Do Algorithms Redefine Temporary Agency Work?' in J Wratny and A Ludera-Ruszel (eds), *New Forms of Employment: Current Problems and Future Challenges* (Wiesbaden, Springer VS, 2020) 169.

[50] A Aloisi, 'Platform Work in Europe: Lessons Learned, Legal Developments and Challenges Ahead' (2022) 13 *European Labour Law Journal* 17.

[51] See C Hießl, 'Multiparty Relationships in Platform Work: Cross-European Case Law Developments and Points of Departure for (Supranational) Regulation' (2023) 14 *European Labour Law Journal* 514.

[52] A Rosin, 'Applying the Temporary Agency Work Directive to Platform Workers: Mission Impossible?' (2020) 36 *International Journal of Comparative Labour Law and Industrial Relations* 166.

[53] N Countouris and R Horton, 'The Temporary Agency Work Directive: Another Broken Promise?' (2009) 38 *Industrial Law Journal* 329 ff.

VI. THE ROLE OF INTERMEDIARIES IN THE EU DIRECTIVE ON PLATFORM WORK

Before the 2024 Platform Work Directive's agreement was reached, discussions on digital platforms as intermediaries were confined to academic debates. Nothing specific on that point could be inferred from the text initially tabled by the EU Commission in December 2021,[54] except a reference in its explanatory memorandum.[55] The long and uncertain legislative process has seen the initial text radically revised by the European Parliament, whose plenary assembly approved a new text in February 2023 and allowed rapporteurs to enter into negotiations with the Council. In the Parliament's text, a particular emphasis was put on the role of intermediaries in platform work arrangements, but from the point of view of the subcontracting chain.[56] The Council's general approach preliminary agreed in June 2023 had watered down the Parliamentary provisions but still contained interesting considerations on tripartite work arrangements realised through online platforms.[57]

The text finally agreed within the Council in March 2024 and further refined in October 2024 deals with intermediaries several times.

[54] European Commission, *Proposal for a Directive on Improving Working Conditions in Platform Work* COM (2021) 762 final.

[55] The directive proposal's explanatory memorandum recalled that 'due to the typically triangular contractual relationship of platform work, this Directive [ie, Directive 2008/104] can be of relevance for platform work. Depending on the business model of a digital labour platform and on whether its customers are private consumers or businesses, it might qualify as a temporary-work agency assigning its workers to user companies. In some cases, the platform might be the user company making use of the services of workers assigned by temporary-work agencies'.

[56] The proposed Article 12, in fact, expressly provided that 'in order to tackle fraud and abuse, Member States may, after consulting the relevant social partners in accordance with national law and/or practice, take additional measures on a non-discriminatory and proportionate basis in order to ensure that in subcontracting chains the contractor of which the employer (service provider) is a direct subcontractor can, in addition to or in place of the employer, be held liable by the platform worker with respect to any outstanding net remuneration corresponding to the minimum rates of pay and/or contributions due to common funds or institutions of social partners'.

[57] Council of the EU, Interinstitutional File: 2021/0414(COD), at https://data.consilium.europa.eu/doc/document/ST-10107-2023-INIT/en/pdf. See proposed Recital 18a (also reflected in proposed Article 2(4)(a), which provided: 'In some cases, persons performing platform work do not have a direct contractual relationship with the digital labour platform, but are in a relationship with an intermediary through which they perform platform work through digital labour platform. Such a way to organise platform work often results in a vast array of different and complex triangular relationships, as well as in blurred responsibilities between the digital labour platform and the intermediaries concerning platform work. Persons performing platform work through intermediaries are exposed to the same risks in terms of misclassification of their employment status and automated monitoring or decision-making systems as persons performing platform work directly for the digital labour platform. Member States should therefore lay down adequate measures, including by establishing systems of joint responsibility, if appropriate, in order to ensure that, under this Directive, they enjoy the same level of protection as persons performing platform work who have a direct contractual relationship with the digital labour platform'.

(a) First of all, references to intermediaries can be found in the body of the Directive. Article 3 titled 'Intermediaries', provides that:

> Member States shall take appropriate measures to ensure that, where a digital labour platform makes use of intermediaries, persons performing platform work who have a contractual relationship with an intermediary enjoy the same level of protection pursuant to this Directive as those who have a direct contractual relationship with a digital labour platform. To that end, Member States shall take measures, in accordance with national law and practice, to establish appropriate mechanisms, which shall include, where appropriate, joint and several liability systems.

Furthermore, Article 2(1)(2) defines 'platform work' as 'any work organised through a digital labour platform and performed in the Union by an individual on the basis of a contractual relationship between the digital labour platform *or an intermediary* and the individual, irrespective of whether a contractual relationship exists between the individual or an intermediary and the recipient of the service' (emphasis added). Article 17(1)(d) further provides that

> Member States shall ensure that digital labour platforms make the following information available to competent authorities, as well as to representatives of persons performing platform work: . . . (d) the intermediaries the digital labour platform has a contractual relationship with.

(b) A second locus where the conceptualisation of digital labour platforms as intermediaries may be relevant concerns the Directive's preamble. In particular, Recital 26 expressly creates a link between the Platform Work Directive and the Temporary Agency Work Directive, where it provides that 'Where a party is found to be an employer and fulfils the conditions of being a temporary work agency in accordance with Directive 2008/104/EC, the obligations under that Directive apply'.

(c) One last mention must be made concerning the periodic revision of the directive's effects on EU and domestic legislation. Article 30 provides that

> By [5 years from the date of entry into force of this Directive], the Commission shall, after consulting the Member States, the social partners at Union level and key stakeholders, and taking into account the impact on SMEs, including microenterprises, review the implementation of this Directive and propose, where appropriate, legislative amendments. In its review, the Commission *shall pay particular attention to the impact of the use of intermediaries on the overall implementation of this Directive as well as to the effectiveness of the legal presumption.* (emphasis added)

The conceptualisation of platform work as a form of work intermediation seems therefore not alien to the spirit and text of the 2024 Platform Work Directive. Of the three *loci* where intermediaries are contemplated by the Directive, the second one deserves specific consideration.

The assertion contained in Recital 26 – for which the obligations under Directive 2008/104 apply whenever 'a party is found to be an employer and fulfils the conditions of being a temporary work agency' – is particularly important. It helps excluding an interpretation of the two directives as distinctive and non-interfering silos, as it has been the case, in the past, between same Directive 2008/104 and Directive 99/70 on Fixed-Term Work.[58]

Contrary to that jurisprudence, here the Platform Work Directive seems to imply that, as far as a digital platform may be identified as a temporary work agency, the provisions of Directive 2008/104 would apply. This involves a two-step assessment. First, relying on the expansive interpretation of the concept of temporary work agency proposed by the CJEU in the aforementioned *Betriebsrat* case,[59] it cannot be excluded that platforms concluding 'contracts of employment or employment relationships' (as per Article 3(1)(b), Directive 2008/104) with platform workers in order to assign them to the platform's clients to work there under their supervision and direction, will not be required to comply with national legislation on the operation of temporary work agencies, including licensing and other forms of public control. Second, considering digital labour platforms as agencies will determine that the working conditions of platform workers must respect inter alia the principle of equal treatment dictated by Article 5(1), Directive 2008/104.

The first step might be facilitated by the operation of the subordination presumption as per Articles 4, 5 and 6 of the 2024 Platform Work Directive. Once classified as platform workers, individuals operating through DCP may not only have access to labour law's typical protections, but also to the additional provisions laid down by that same Directive, in particular those addressed to workers (eg, Article 12 on safety and health), to public authorities (eg, Article 16 on the declaration of platform work and Article 17 on access to relevant information) and to workers' representatives (eg, Article 10(1) on human oversight of automated monitoring and decision-making systems, and Articles 13 and 14 on information and consultation).

VII. CONCLUSION: DOES THE REGULATORY MODEL EMERGING FROM THE PLATFORM WORK DIRECTIVE MATCH WITH THE CONCEPT OF INTERMEDIARY EXPRESSED BY DCP?

The platform economy's growing role in the domestic work and home care sectors has prompted a reconsideration of the legal status of DCP within the EU. Empirical studies highlight the dual nature of DCP as either intermediaries facilitating worker-client matches or as active agents shaping the terms and conditions of employment. Despite DCP's role in formalising aspects

[58] Cf eg, CJEU, C-290/12, *Della Rocca*, ECLI:EU:C:2013:235.
[59] CJEU, 17 November 2016, C-216/15, *Betriebsrat der Ruhrlandklinik*.

of domestic work, concerns persist about worker protections, especially for vulnerable groups. These platforms often evade employer liabilities, leading to precarious work conditions, low wages and limited access to social protections. International frameworks, like ILO conventions, stress the importance of regulating intermediaries to protect workers, particularly emphasising the principle that recruitment fees should not be borne by workers.

EU law has grappled with the regulation of intermediaries through key rulings, opening the door for private employment agencies while maintaining competition and worker protection principles. However, challenges remain in ensuring that platforms operating under diverse legal models provide adequate safeguards for domestic workers.

The discussion on triangular work arrangements under the EU Directive on Temporary Agency Work provides a useful framework for conceptualising platform work in the care sector performed through DCP. With both forms involving intermediaries between the worker and the final service recipient, parallels can be drawn, especially in terms of how workers are supervised and directed by end-users. This appears particularly promising when the platform provides nothing 'but the infrastructure to allow a legal relationship in the above sense to be formed' between the worker and the platform.[60]

The expansive interpretation of the Temporary Agency Work Directive – following CJEU rulings like *Betriebsrat der Ruhrlandklinik* – opens up the possibility of applying its principles to platform work and specifically to DCP. However, while some scholars support this approach, others argue that platforms function as more complex market organisers, which may demand distinct regulations beyond the temporary agency work framework.

The 2024 Platform Work Directive recognises the role of platforms as intermediaries, signalling that, in cases where they fulfil the criteria of temporary work agencies, the obligations of Directive 2008/104 may apply. This includes respecting the principle of equal treatment for platform workers.

The diverse and evolving nature of DCP precludes the possibility of drawing generalised conclusions applicable to all their typologies. Yet DCP operating on a business model centred on intermediation – where the platform formally employs care workers and provides their services to households – appear to align with the definition of an intermediary under both Directive 2008/104 and the 2024 Platform Work Directive. From a regulatory standpoint, the 2024 Directive's Recital 26, which serves as a conceptual bridge between the two frameworks, may facilitate the classification of certain instances as constituting 'digital' temporary agency work.

[60] J Prassl and M Risak, 'Uber, Task Rabbit & Co.: Platforms as Employers?' (2016) 37 *Comparative Labor Law & Policy Journal* 619.

11

*House of Gigs: Domestic Workers, Algorithmic Management and the EU Platform Work Directive**

ANTONIO ALOISI AND NASTAZJA POTOCKA-SIONEK

I. INVISIBILITY OF (PLATFORMISED) DOMESTIC WORKERS: CAUSES AND CONSEQUENCES

ABBY (PLAYED BY Debbie Honeywood), a care assistant who works with the elderly and disabled, is the co-protagonist in the 2019 drama *Sorry We Missed You*. In the film, the British director Ken Loach grippingly depicts her working and living conditions. Abby often feels frustrated about the limited time she is able to spend with her patients because her employer sets strict time limits for each visit and only pays her for those hours, omitting breaks and travel time. As a result, Abby regularly spends more time caring for her patients than she is actually paid for. This is because she (over)works for a subcontractor with no 'evident concern for her humanity, let alone that of the clients whom she treats with maximal warmth and heroic empathy'.[1] While she could decline visits and any additional effort – given that she has a zero-hour contract[2] – her dedication prevents her from refusing them, as doing so would mean leaving the patients without care. Loach also portrays Abby's determination when dealing

* Antonio Aloisi's contribution to this chapter forms part of the project PID2023-149184OB-C43 granted by MCIU/AEI/10.13039/501100011033 and the FSE+. The authors express their gratitude to Eva Kocher, Lorena Poblete and all of the participants at the Oñati Workshop on Digital Intermediaries in Domestic and Care Work, which was held in May 2024 at the International Institute for the Sociology of Law, Spain, for their helpful feedback and insightful comments on an earlier version of this chapter. Thanks are also due to Lara Šimić and Sara Kabiri for their invaluable research assistance.

[1] W Morris, '"Sorry We Missed You" Review: The Human Toll of That One-Click Buy' *New York Times* (New York, 4 March 2020) www.nytimes.com/2020/03/04/movies/sorry-we-missed-you-review.html.

[2] A Adams-Prassl, M Freedland and J Adams-Prassl, 'Zero-Hours Contracts in the United Kingdom: Regulating Casualwork, or Legitimating Precarity?' (2016) *Giornale di diritto del lavoro e di relazioni industriali* 148.

with the exhausting cycle of 'second shifts' that mothers have to perform,[3] showcasing the correlation between (under)paid care work, unpaid emotional labour and the constant struggle to make ends meet.[4]

Abby's story is, however, secondary to the vicissitudes of her husband Ricky (played by Kris Hitchen), who works as an allegedly self-employed parcel delivery driver. The film's plot reflects the commonplace portrayal of the platform economy, which is predominantly associated with food delivery and urban transport apps, relegating (platformised) domestic work to the margins of the debate.[5]

Domestic or care work,[6] which typically involves performing household chores such as babysitting, cooking, cleaning and caring for the elderly or disabled,[7] can manifest in various forms of employment, in a 'twilight zone' of legal opacity and ineffective enforcement of applicable regulations. The walls of a domestic residence often create a veil of invisibility, concealing the realities of the work performed inside. Hence, a primary objective of this chapter is to illuminate the state-of-the-art situation, offering an analysis of whether and, if so, how digital intermediaries have transformed work in the domestic sector.

The 'platformisation' of domestic work – that is, its intermediation and organisation through digital labour platforms – has various faces. The terms and conditions vary significantly across platforms, and evidence suggests that an individual platform may adopt different formats and features depending on the regulatory contexts of the countries in which it operates.[8] A common denominator is the introduction of organisational practices supported by technological tools – namely, (semi)-automated monitoring, recruiting and decision-making – that have a profound impact on domestic workers' experiences.

Multiple classifications of digital intermediaries have been proposed, depending on the local contexts, legal structures and specific natures of the services provided. For instance, according to the taxonomy developed by Rodríguez-Modroño, platforms in this sector can be divided into three

[3] C Umphress, 'Revealing the Gendered Experience: The Complexity of Care Work in Loach's Sorry We Missed You and I, Daniel Blake' (2022) 4 *Tracks* 28; A Hochschild and A Machung, *The Second Shift: Working Families and the Revolution at Home* (NY, Penguin, 2012).

[4] Z Goodall and K Cook, 'Paid, Domestic, and Emotional Work in the Precariat: Ken Loach's Sorry We Missed You' (2022) 22 *Feminist Media Studies* 1195.

[5] There are a few notable exceptions, however. For an overview of the specific issues related to platformised domestic work, see generally, U Huws, 'The Hassle of Housework: Digitalisation and the Commodification of Domestic Labour' (2019) 123 *Feminist Review* 8; F Flanagan, 'Theorising the Gig Economy and Home-Based Service Work' (2019) 61 *Journal of Industrial Relations* 57; P Rodríguez-Modroño, A Agenjo-Calderón and P López-Igual, 'Platform Work in the Domestic and Home Care Sector: New Mechanisms of Invisibility and Exploitation of Women Migrant Workers' (2022) 30 *Gender & Development* 619.

[6] The two terms are used interchangeably and are almost synonymous; however, domestic work emphasises the location, adopting a neutral approach to encompass various formats, whereas care work highlights the ultimate purpose or function of the roles.

[7] L Salter, L Vonk, Center for Culture-Centered Approach to Research & Evaluation and A Fromm, Public Service Association, *Experiences of Digital Technology for Home Support Workers – The Need for a Human Centered Approach* (PAS and CARE 2023).

[8] N Koutsimpogiorgos, K Frenken and AM Herrmann, 'Platform Adaptation to Regulation: The Case of Domestic Cleaning in Europe' (2023) 65 *Journal of Industrial Relations* 156.

categories: i) marketplaces, ii) on-demand platforms and iii) digital placement agencies.[9] At the same time, the business models of intermediaries vary widely. Some resemble a search engine or 'digital bulletin board', where workers and clients are connected with minimal oversight, while others operate as 'Uber-like' digital platforms, offering more structured intermediation and a higher degree of control over the labour process. Finally, some platforms adopt a model that is closer to a 'traditional' temporary work agency, directly managing placements and worker–client relationships.

In general terms, while marketplaces are 'mere intermediaries' and digital placement agencies can be analysed through the lens of the temporary agency work regulations at the EU and national levels,[10] the on-demand domestic platform model is more nebulous. Platform-related work arrangements have proven difficult to classify, particularly when control over domestic workers is shared by clients and the platform. Cases where care workers, who are often contractually described as self-employed, are managed by both the platform and clients (households) evidence the complexity of assigning responsibility to a single entity.

At the outset, one might wonder whether the emergence of digital intermediaries represents a significant break from the past or a continuation – and perhaps even an exacerbation – of the longstanding challenges in the domestic work sector, such as precariousness, income instability, in-work poverty and heightened exposure to health and safety risks, including harassment. A significant body of research argues that the emergence of new players has intensified, reshaped and perpetuated the deep-seated structural problems in the sector. This perspective illustrates the 'historical continuities'[11] between digital platforms and their pre-digital counterparts,[12] showcasing how many issues observed today mirror those associated with traditional intermediaries in the domestic sector. Triangular or even more complex multi-party arrangements have long been the norm rather than the exception, as has undeclared work. Working conditions have regularly been shaped by the pressure to deliver services while subject to exploitative practices, and this has occurred against a backdrop of intersecting inequalities and unbalanced bargaining powers. From a demographic perspective, the data reveal the disproportionate representation of women, who account for three-quarters of the workforce, and migrants, who constitute one in four workers in this sector.[13] Additionally, domestic workers have historically relied

[9] P Rodríguez-Modroño, ch 1, in this volume.

[10] L Ratti, ch 10, in this volume.

[11] Flanagan (n 5).

[12] F Ustek Spilda, A Bertolini, O Alyanak, K Howson and M Graham, 'Gender and Care Work Platform Operational Models: Setting a Research Agenda' in O Blanchard and A Hunt (eds), *Global Perspectives on Women, Work, and Digital Labour Platforms: A Collection of Articles from Around the World on Women's Experiences of Digital Labour Platforms* (Barcelona, Digital Future Society, 2022).

[13] C Murphy, I Pais and T Gibbons, *Care Platforms: Impacts and Challenges from a Trade Union Perspective* (Brussels, Friedrich-Ebert-Stiftung, 2024). See also European Commission, *Communication from the Commission to the European Parliament, the Council, the European Economic and Social Committee and the Committee of the Regions on the European Care Strategy* (COM/2022/440 final).

on juggling multiple jobs due to the inherently discontinuous nature of their engagements, particularly when their clients are private households. In terms of the time arrangements, the sector has long embodied a contradictory reality, where the excessively long hours worked by some workers are compounded by instances of underemployment.[14]

Against this background, the present chapter revisits the legal debate surrounding domestic work platforms, focusing on the persistence and change between platformised and non-platformised domestic work. In so doing, it examines the implications of adopting algorithmic management (AM) systems in the sector and discusses the parallels and divergences between the digital tools that exercise managerial functions and the peculiar forms of management that can be found in domestic work. Furthermore, it discusses some of the main challenges in relation to domestic work, which predate the emergence of digital intermediaries considerably, such as temporal precariousness. The Working Time Directive (WTD)[15] and the Transparent and Predictable Working Conditions Directive (TPWCD)[16] are used as case studies to demonstrate how certain areas of labour law have failed to adequately respond to the systemic challenges inherent in domestic work arrangements, in the platform economy and beyond. Finally, this chapter examines whether the Platform Work Directive (PfWD),[17] with its key provisions concerning the presumption of employment and protection against AM-related risks, can bring about meaningful change in the domestic sector. We conclude that, despite significant advances having been made, the PfWD's design fails to fully capture the complexity and specific challenges of domestic work.

II. ALGORITHMIC MANAGEMENT COMES HOME: HOW DIGITAL SYSTEMS SHAPE DOMESTIC WORK IN THE AGE OF INTERMEDIARIES

AM systems, which can be broadly defined as a set of 'software to automate organisational functions traditionally carried out by human managers',[18] have predominantly been examined through the lens of platforms in the delivery and

[14] K Scheiwe, 'Domestic Workers, EU Working Time Law and Implementation Deficits in National Law – Change in Sight?' (2021) *EUI Department of Law Research Paper* 2021/03.

[15] Directive 2003/88/EC of the European Parliament and of the Council of 4 November 2003 concerning certain aspects of the organisation of working time.

[16] Directive (EU) 2019/1152 of the European Parliament and of the Council of 20 June 2019 on transparent and predictable working conditions in the European Union.

[17] Directive (EU) 2024/2831 of the European Parliament and of the Council of 23 October 2024 on improving working conditions in platform work.

[18] AJ Wood, 'Algorithmic Management Consequences for Work Organisation and Working Conditions' (2021) *JRC Working Papers Series 2021/07*; S Baiocco, E Fernández-Macías, U Rani and A Pesole, 'The Algorithmic Management of Work and Its Implications in Different Contexts' (2022) *JRC Working Papers Series on Labour, Education and Technology 2022/02*.

transport sector and, to a lesser extent, freelance and crowdwork platforms.[19] By contrast, AM systems in the context of domestic work remain under-researched. As discussed above, this lack of research perpetuates the invisibility of domestic workers, leading to the absence of their stories and experiences in the media and scholarly spheres,[20] reinforcing longstanding gender divides.[21] Fortunately, an emerging body of literature is starting to gradually shed light on the fact that AM enables the management of domestic workers' relationships across the full lifecycle of the work relationship, much as it does in other 'gigified' sectors.

The extent of platforms' command and control over domestic workers varies considerably, although AM is a feature that permeates all categories of digital platforms in this sector – whether marketplaces, digital placement agencies or on-demand platforms – influencing organisational practices and worker experiences. AM tools enable the exercise of managerial prerogatives over workers both directly (using GPS, time-reporting widgets and monitoring devices) and indirectly (most notably, using clients' ratings). As documented in the literature,[22] control via rating systems is instrumental in the exercise of disciplinary powers in the form of warnings and consequential sanctions, including exclusion from the relevant platform.[23]

Algorithms play a pivotal role not only during the recruitment and onboarding phases but also in matching workers to clients. On some platforms, electronic monitoring is used to shorten visit durations due to the pressure of 'call cramming' – that is, back-to-back visits with inadequate time between them for the care worker to reach the next client.[24] The introduction of AM has also given rise to the challenge of accurately recording working hours through apps, particularly in terms of logging the inception and completion of tasks. This process often involves a time-consuming login procedure or interaction with user support services in the case of discrepancies or infrastructural glitches.[25] Moreover, some AM tools nudge workers to extend their availability[26] or to

[19] See generally, N Potocka-Sionek and A Aloisi, 'The Spillover Effect of Algorithmic Management and How (Not) to Tame It' in K Vandaele and S Rainone (eds), *The Elgar Companion to Regulating Platform Work. Insights from the Food Delivery Sector* (Cheltenham, Edward Elgar Publishing, 2025).

[20] Koutsimpogiorgos, Frenken and Herrmann (n 8).

[21] D McCann, 'Temporal Casualisation and "Availability Time": Mencap, Uber and the Framed Flexibility Model' (2020) *DWR Research Paper 01/2020*.

[22] K Floros, 'Rethinking Algorithmic Management in Minor Key: The Case of Housecleaning Platform Labour in Denmark' (2024) 1 *Platforms & Society* 29768624241273468.

[23] A Asher-Schapiro, 'Uber for Nurses. US Health Workers Turn to Gig Work' (*Context*, 13 December 2023) www.context.news/digital-rights/uber-for-nurses-us-health-workers-turn-to-gig-work

[24] S Moore and LJB Hayes, 'Taking Worker Productivity to a New Level? Electronic Monitoring in Homecare – The (Re)production of Unpaid Labour' (2017) 32 *New Technology, Work and Employment* 101.

[25] Salter, Vonk, Center for Culture-Centered Approach to Research & Evaluation and Fromm, Public Service Association (n 7).

[26] A Piasna, 'Algorithms of Time: How Algorithmic Management Changes the Temporalities of Work and Prospects for Working Time Reduction' (2024) 48 *Cambridge Journal of Economics* 115.

work long and/or antisocial hours.[27] For example, workers with greater availability may have a higher assessment score and access to more rewarding tasks. Failure to accept these nudges and predetermined goals might have negative consequences for workers.

Given their awareness of the potential repercussions of failing to adhere to platform rules – whether explicit or not fully transparent – concerning aspects such as availability and punctuality,[28] domestic workers habitually engage in 'anticipatory compliance' practices.[29] These behaviours reflect workers' attempts to pre-emptively align themselves with corporate expectations while facing pressure to maintain their positions or secure favourable ratings and client reviews,[30] which operate as a feedback loop that influences workers' access to future tasks and their overall standing on the platform.

Thus, there are clear parallels between AM mechanisms introduced by digital platforms in relation to domestic work and those applied in other sectors. However, notable differences also exist due to the unique characteristics of domestic work. Workers often experience a greater degree of latitude, even when detailed instructions are delivered via digital tools. This flexibility is largely due to the nature of tasks such as caregiving and cleaning, which are more labour-intensive and difficult to measure when compared with discrete, one-off tasks such as delivering packages or driving. This distinctiveness also explains why domestic work is less prone to automation.[31] Additionally, direct surveillance by platforms is inherently limited in the domestic context, as related activities take place within private spaces, which are impenetrable for privacy reasons and often remain inaccessible to competent authorities such as labour inspectorates. On a sour note, this circumstance makes it more difficult to conduct fieldwork and assess working conditions.

Based on these factors, Floros conceptualises AM in the domestic sector as 'minor algorithmic management'.[32] The word 'minor' has a twofold meaning in this context. First and foremost, analysing the impact of AM in terms of domestic work provides a fresh and complementary perspective on areas that are often

[27] AJ Wood, M Graham, V Lehdonvirta and I Hjorth, 'Good Gig, Bad Gig: Autonomy and Algorithmic Control in the Global Gig Economy' (2019) 33 *Work, Employment and Society* 56.

[28] C Haldrup, A Ilsøe and T Pernilla Larsen, 'With or Without Algorithms: Managing the Self-Employed in the Danish Platform Economy' in W Conen and E Reuter (eds), *Research Handbook on Self-Employment and Public Policy* (Cheltenham, Edward Elgar Publishing, 2024).

[29] EL Bucher, P Kalum Schou and M Waldkirch, 'Pacifying the Algorithm–Anticipatory Compliance in the Face of Algorithmic Management in the Gig Economy' (2021) 28 *Organization* 44.

[30] K Uysal and C Boyraz, 'Autonomy and Control in the Gig Economy and Platform Work: Domestic and Home Repair Workers in Turkey' (2024) 26 *Journal of Balkan and Near Eastern Studies* 23.

[31] Cleaning and caring remain within the domain of work that cannot be fully automated. Such tasks demand physical presence, dexterity and emotional intelligence – that is, qualities machines are unable to replicate. Mark Bergfeld, 'Between Viability and Social Acceptance: Technologies in Cleaning' (2024) *European Cleaning Journal* www.europeancleaningjournal.com/blog/2024/09/26/between-viability-and-social-acceptance-technologies-in-cleaning.

[32] Floros (n 22).

overlooked in mainstream research on the platform economy.[33] Second, this characterisation captures the 'subtleties' of the interplay between human and non-human management. In the domestic context, AM exerts a more nuanced and less dominant influence on the labour process when compared with its application in other sectors, such as delivery or transportation.[34]

In a nutshell, a specific characteristic of the domestic work sector is the 'entanglement' between human and non-human management practices rather than the full assumption of managerial functions by algorithms. Domestic workers and their clients retain greater agency over platform-mediated work performance than, for example, Deliveroo couriers or Uber drivers. Hence, caution is required when extrapolating the findings of the AM literature and applying them to domestic work.

On a less positive note, however, the hybrid model of human and automated management not only fails to enhance transparency but also often heightens the arbitrariness of decision-making processes. Nonetheless, scholars highlight how, particularly in highly informal contexts in the Global South, the presence of AM can facilitate more accurate recording of working hours, contributing to a certain degree of institutionalisation in these labour markets.[35] AM systems could address critical aspects of domestic work. For instance, algorithms can be programmed in a way that considers both clients' needs and workers' preferences,[36] and this can improve workers' occupational safety and health (OSH). By way of the positive prospects, AM could be used to reduce unpredictability and better allocate both shifts and clients, enhancing workers' opportunities for leisure and family time.[37] Moreover, AM could increase workers' autonomy, thereby improving their well-being.[38]

Despite such prospects, robust evidence of the positive impacts of AM on the domestic work sector is currently lacking. Notably, the vast majority of examples found in the literature highlight a streamlining of processes that primarily benefits managers in the case of on-demand platforms or clients in the context of marketplaces and digital placement agencies, while largely sidelining workers' interests. To consider but one aspect, it has been shown that algorithmic

[33] C Katz, 'Revisiting Minor Theory' (2017) 35 *Environment and Planning D: Society and Space* 596; C Katz, 'Towards Minor Theory' (1996) 14 *Environment and Planning D: Society and Space* 487.

[34] K Floros, 'Imperfect Presents, Uncertain Futures' (PhD thesis, IT Univeristy of Copenhagen 2024) ch 7 https://pure.itu.dk/ws/portalfiles/portal/105389367/Phd_Thesis_Final_version_Konstantinos_Flores.pdf.

[35] L Poblete, F Pereyra and A Tizziani, 'Digital Intermediation in Paid Domestic Work in Argentina: An Analysis of Ambivalent Effects on Working Conditions' (2024) 0 *Critical Sociology* 1.

[36] X Parent-Rocheleau and SK Parker, 'Algorithms as Work Designers: How Algorithmic Management Influences the Design of Jobs' (2022) 32 *Human Resources Management Review* 100838.

[37] B Burchell, S Deakin, J Rubery and DA Spencer, 'The Future of Work and Working Time: Introduction to Special Issue (2024) 48 *Cambridge Journal of Economics* 1.

[38] H Kinowska and L Jakub Sienkiewicz, 'Influence of Algorithmic Management Practices on Workplace Well-Being – Evidence from European Organisations' (2023) 36 *Information Technology & People* 21.

dynamic pricing significantly influences the determination of hourly rates. Some on-demand or marketplace platforms caution workers that their fees may be too high when compared with the average,[39] fostering implicit competition and driving workers to underbid their peers. Moreover, algorithm-based reputation mechanisms such as ratings, which increase workers' dependence on platforms, have been identified as a significant driver of unpaid labour in the domestic sector.[40] In short, the surplus of data collected and generated by platforms is predominantly leveraged to benefit the end clients, not to address issues such as unpredictability, health and safety risks[41] or inadequate compensation. While ostensibly intended to enhance productivity, AM systems primarily serve to track working hours and exert control over task allocation for the benefit of intermediaries. Still, these monitoring systems are often far from precise.[42] The power and information asymmetries are further reflected in the design of the app, where the clients can receive detailed information on workers, whereas workers are not given much information about clients.[43] As a result, workers often have to rely on informal methods, such as Facebook groups, to identify bad payers or abusive customers.

III. WORKING CONDITIONS IN THE DOMESTIC SECTOR, CONTINUITIES IN TEMPORAL PRECARIOUSNESS AND LIMITATIONS OF THE LAW

Having examined the 'minor' impact of AM systems, this section addresses a range of major challenges in relation to domestic work that predate the emergence of digital intermediaries quite considerably. It also examines the legal framework addressing some of these issues – namely, the WTD and the TPWCD. We contextualise the analysis of platform-mediated domestic work, revealing that pre-existing problems have been exacerbated, rather than mitigated, by digital intermediaries.

Undeniably, task-based work models, irregular schedules that result in income instability, fragmented hours, excessively long working arrangements or, conversely, lack of consistent work guarantees all contribute to the precarious working conditions often experienced by domestic workers. Kountouris's notion

[39] Ustek Spilda, Bertolini, Alyanak, Howson and Graham (n 12).

[40] V Pulignano, C Marà, M Franke and K Muszynski, 'Informal Employment on Domestic Care Platforms: A Study on the Individualisation of Risk and Unpaid Labour in Mature Market Contexts (2023) 29 *Transfer: European Review of Labour and Research* 323.

[41] Salter, Vonk, Center for Culture-Centered Approach to Research & Evaluation and Fromm, Public Service Association (n 7).

[42] J Rubery, D Grimshaw, G Hebson and SM Ugarte, '"It's All About Time": Time as Contested Terrain in the Management and Experience of Domiciliary Care Work in England' (2015) 54 *Human Resource Management* 757.

[43] L Wiesböck, J Radlherr and ML Angelique Vo, 'Domestic Cleaners in the Informal Labour Market: New Working Realities Shaped by the Gig Economy?' (2023) 11 *Social Inclusion* 262.

of 'temporal precariousness',[44] which denotes the instability and unpredictability of working time arrangements, remains particularly relevant in this context. Despite the promises of enhanced transparency, there is no evidence to suggest that AM reduces the volatility and erraticism that are characteristic of human managers or intermediaries in this sector. Instead, it can be observed that the adoption of AM systems further aggravates such issues by imposing schedules shaped by fluctuating client and platform demands, often leaving workers with little (f)actual control over the organisation of their time.

The domestic work sector is among those sectors where non-conventional working time patterns have long been the norm. For instance, cleaners often enter work premises at antisocial hours, such as in the early morning or late evening. Similarly, as illustrated by the film character introduced earlier in this chapter, care workers frequently encounter demands for extended working hours in an irregular and unpredictable manner. Overtime is often mandated by the employer or client, with workers facing explicit or implicit consequences for refusing it, ranging from less desirable tasks or shifts to missed opportunities for better timeslots.[45] Additionally, workers' ability to push back is often limited by their vulnerable legal status or, in the case of migrant workers, the potential risk of losing their work visas, compounding their precarious situation. Emotional guilt can also be used as a tactic to pressure workers into taking on more than the agreed workload.[46]

Another troubling aspect is the prevalence of non-voluntary part-time jobs and overly short working hours, which compel domestic workers to navigate multiple gigs in an effort to combat 'time-related underemployment'.[47] To secure sufficient income, workers are compelled to prolong their availability or to accept as many gigs as possible, sometimes commuting long distances between different clients. In this vicious circle, income instability is closely tied to work intensification, and this 'multi-homing' exposes the dilemma of uncompensated travel times between engagements.[48]

Moreover, as rest time is not compensated or remains difficult to measure when workers operate via multiple entities, some workers engaged in task-based

[44] N Kountouris, 'The Legal Determinants of Precariousness in Personal Work Relations: A European Perspective' (2012) 34 *Comparative Labor Law & Policy Journal* 21.

[45] D McCann, *Decent Working Hours as a Human Right: Intersections in the Regulation of Working Time* (Oxford, Hart Publishing, 2010).

[46] S Nogues and DG Tremblay, 'From Chosen to Forced: A Qualitative Exploration of Nurses' Experiences With Overtime' (2023) *Employee Responsibilities and Rights Journal* 1; Bucher, Kalum Schou and Waldkirch (n 29).

[47] A Bogg, 'The Regulation of Working Time in Europe' in A Bogg, C Costello and ACL Davies (eds), *Research Handbook on EU Labour Law* (Cheltenham, Edward Elgar Publishing, 2016).

[48] The CJEU ruled that travel time counts as working time insofar as the worker is required to be physically present at a place determined by the employer and to be available to carry out work. When there is no fixed or habitual place of work, the journey is deemed technically indispensable for providing the service and, therefore, must count as working time. D Mangan, K Muszyński and V Pulignano, 'The Platform Discount: Addressing Unpaid Work as a Structural Feature of Labour Platforms' (2023) 14 *European Labour Law Journal* 541.

models of domestic work are unlikely to seek enforcement of the rules. Similarly, they may overlook the application of work–life balance provisions because such provisions may diminish their volatile earning opportunities, further entrenching the gendered dynamics in the sector, where women are disproportionately affected by the burden of unpaid care work.[49] Domestic work also epitomises the prevalence of on-call or stand-by models,[50] whereby workers are expected to remain available either on or in proximity to the client's premises to attend to their needs, despite not actively working. These arrangements often involve ambiguity regarding how 'non-active' working time should be compensated. Furthermore, a large portion of domestic workers lack flexibility and autonomy when it comes to selecting their work hours, having little agency over their terms and fees.[51]

In the context of the unpredictability of working hours, workers cannot freely modify their schedules or rosters, while some clients or intermediaries can unilaterally introduce last-minute changes without workers' consent. This dynamic creates a significant power imbalance between the parties, making it difficult for workers to reconcile their work and personal life.

A. The Working Time Directive

The Working Time Directive (WTD) sets minimum standards for the organisation of working time in an attempt to protect workers' health and safety. Its provisions are premised on the dichotomy between 'working time' and 'rest periods',[52] which may prove ineffective when 'snippets of time' are semi-algorithmically determined and allocated.[53] Indeed, the WTD is based on the assumption of a regular unfolding of standard working patterns – that is, a characteristic seldom found in relation to domestic work. This mismatch may jeopardise the overarching OSH rationale of the WTD. For instance, if rest periods and breaks are allocated haphazardly, it is doubtful that they can adequately fulfil the intended purpose of allowing workers to rest meaningfully and recover from work. One could argue that this approach shifts the costs of extreme and one-sided organisational flexibility onto workers, who are expected to function

[49] J Fudge, 'A New Gender Contract? Work/Life Balance and Working-Time Flexibility' in J Conaghan and K Rittich (eds), *Labour Law, Work, and Family: Critical and Comparative Perspectives* (Oxford, Oxford University Press, 2000).

[50] A Aloisi, S Rainone and N Countouris, 'An Unfinished Task? Matching the Platform Work Directive with the EU and International "Social Acquis"' (2023) ILO Working Paper 101.

[51] Rubery, Grimshaw, Hebson and Ugarte (n 42).

[52] The WTD defines working time as 'any period during which the worker is working, at the employer's disposal and carrying out his activity or duties, in accordance with national laws and/or practice' (Art 2(1)). Conversely, the term 'rest period' is defined as any period that is not working time (Art 2(2)).

[53] ACL Davies, 'Working Time' in G Davidov, B Langille and G Lester (eds), *The Oxford Handbook of the Law of Work* (Oxford, Oxford Academic, 2024).

in a mode characterised by constant multi-tasking and permanent availability, adapting to unpredictable schedules and fragmented tasks without adequate compensation or support. Furthermore, as working time is directly linked to pay, workers may be discouraged from enforcing the WTD's limits and guarantees, instead opting to trade leisure time for additional income to counterbalance their precarious earnings.[54]

Resolving the dilemma of distinguishing between working hours and rest periods is thus essential for health and safety purposes; however, paradoxically, health and safety regulation is precisely the area in which protections at the EU level are notably limited or, at least, contentious. In fact, the OSH Framework Directive[55] explicitly excludes 'domestic servants' from its personal scope (Article 3(a)),[56] arguably to avoid placing undue burdens on private households, which may struggle to comply with such legislation. Analysing the extensive debate concerning the inclusion of domestic workers in the scope of working time or OSH legislation is beyond the remit of this chapter.[57] Still, even assuming their inclusion, several critical aspects of the material scope of the WTD remain misaligned with the realities of how working time is organised in both standard (analogue) and algorithmic domestic work settings.

Additionally, in many jurisdictions, the WTD operates by regulating the actions of individual employers. As a result, it is possible for a worker who has reached the working time threshold with one employer to take on additional hours with another employer – an issue particularly relevant in the context of domestic work, whether platformised or not. This makes it challenging to effectively intervene, as no individual employer bears responsibility for enforcing the cumulative limits on working time, leaving workers vulnerable to overwork and the associated risks.

According to Article 17 WTD, workers engaged in 'unmeasured' work are excluded from many of the rights granted by the Directive.[58] Given the nature of domestic tasks, which often lack clear boundaries or standardised measures of working time, some domestic workers may fall into this excluded category at the national level, leaving them without the protections afforded to workers who operate based on defined schedules.

[54] ibid.

[55] Council Directive of 12 June 1989 on the introduction of measures to encourage improvements in the safety and health of workers at work (89/391/EEC).

[56] ibid.

[57] T Novitz and P Syrpis, 'The Place of Domestic Work in Europe: An Analysis of Current Policy in the Light of the Council Decision Authorising Member States to Ratify ILO Convention No. 189' (2015) 6 *European Labour Law Journal* 104; Scheiwe, 'Domestic Workers' (2021); V Pavlou, 'Domestic Work in EU Law: The Relevance of EU Employment Law in Challenging Domestic Workers' Vulnerability' (2016) 3 *European Law Review* 379.

[58] This exclusion, however, was originally intended for managers and senior employees with greater leeway and autonomy in terms of organising their work, not for domestic workers whose flexibility often stems from necessity rather than choice.

Moreover, the WTD does not expressly[59] regulate the issue of remuneration for working time, including aspects such as stability, regularity and quantity, nor does it require additional compensation for overtime. This gap becomes even more pressing in the context of AM systems, which are designed to optimise efficiency by minimising the time actively spent on individual tasks. As a consequence, questions surrounding payment for 'non-active' working time become all the more pertinent, highlighting the inadequacy of existing provisions when it comes to addressing this conundrum.[60] In hyper-casual work arrangements, workers' availability and on-call time do not constitute genuine rest time but remain uncompensated.

To conclude, as argued by Davies,[61] two main problems persist in the domestic work sector. First, workers may often be tempted to work excessive hours to compensate for periods with little or no work, leading to significant physical and mental strain. Second, in terms of platformised domestic work, the boundaries between distinct time units – such as active working time, availability time and rest periods – are increasingly blurred, making it difficult to delineate, regulate and remunerate them effectively.

B. The Directive on Transparent and Predictable Working Conditions

The limitations of the WTD in addressing the irregular distribution of working time have been, to some extent, regulated by the Transparent and Predictable Working Conditions Directive (TPWCD). Unlike the WTD, which was conceived over three decades ago for a paradigmatic worker engaged in a standard employment relationship, the goal of the TPWCD is to update the existing legal acquis[62] and address the problems faced by workers in atypical, casual work arrangements. Hence, domestic workers are expressly mentioned in the Preamble to the TPWCD, along with on-demand, intermittent, voucher-based and platform workers.[63]

The TPWCD provides workers with a set of important safeguards in the context of (platformised) domestic work.[64] It sets out an extensive catalogue of *essential* aspects of the employment relationship about which workers should be informed in writing. These aspects include the identities of the parties to the employment relationship, the place of work, the category of work or a brief

[59] Case C-55/18, *Federación de Servicios de Comisiones Obreras (CCOO) v Deutsche Bank SAE*, ECLI:EU:C:2019:402.

[60] Piasna (n 26).

[61] Davies (n 53).

[62] The TPWCD repealed the previous instrument dating back to 1991 – that is, the Written Statement Directive.

[63] Recital 8.

[64] I Durri, *Casual Work Arrangements and Platform-based Work: The Casual Work Agenda as a Way to Enhance the Labour Protection of Platform Workers* (Vol 115, Alphen aan den Rijn, Kluwer Law International BV, 2023).

description of it, the starting date and the remuneration, among other issues (Article 4).

For workers whose work patterns are 'entirely or mostly unpredictable', as in the case of many (platformised) domestic workers, the TPWCD provides additional information rights. Aside from information about the very fact that their work schedule is variable, such workers should know the number of guaranteed paid hours and the remuneration for any additionally performed work, the reference hours and days the worker may be required to work, the minimum notice period before the start of the assignment and the deadline for cancellation of a work assignment (Article 4(2)(m)). Moreover, such workers shall not be required to work unless the work takes place within the predetermined reference hours and days, and they must be notified 'within a reasonable notice period'. If these conditions are not cumulatively fulfilled, the worker has the right to refuse a work assignment without any negative consequences (Article 10). The TPWCD also foresees a provision addressing a specific aspect of income instability – namely, if a work assignment is cancelled after a specified deadline, the worker has the right to the previously agreed compensation.

Additional attention is devoted to 'on-demand or similar' employment contracts. Article 11 TPWCD requires Member States to introduce measures to limit the abuse and duration of such contracts, such as limitation of their use or duration, or a rebuttable presumption of an employment contract, including a minimum number of paid hours calculated based on the average hours worked during a given period.

Hence, the TPWCD provides a set of safeguards addressing some aspects of 'temporal precariousness' that can be meaningful for domestic workers, whether it be in the platform economy or elsewhere. However, some personal and material exceptions in terms of the scope of the TPWCD undermine its effectiveness in this context. First, only if domestic workers are considered to be in an employment relationship – that is, according to the national definition of worker with consideration of the Court of Justice of the European Union (CJEU) – does the TPWCD apply. Some casual workers, including platformised domestic workers, may fail to comply with these requirements, falling through the cracks in the Directive. Moreover, workers who work, on average, three or fewer hours per week in a reference period of four consecutive weeks may be excluded from the TPWCD's scope of application by Member States. Finally, the TPWCD allows Member States to establish specific rules to exclude individuals who are acting as employers of domestic workers in households from the requirements laid down in it (Article 1(7)). The opt-outs can concern i) the right to transition to a more predictable and secure form of employment after at least six months of service for an individual employer (Article 12), ii) the right to obtain mandatory training that is free of cost and calculated as working time (Article 13) and iii) the right to redress mechanisms based on favourable presumptions in the case of information missing from the documentation workers should receive (Article 15(1)).

In short, while the TPWCD marks a clear step forward in tackling temporal precariousness in domestic work, its reliance on employment status and its fairly generous scope for national opt-outs mean that many of the workers most in need of protection are precisely those left standing outside the Directive's shelter.

IV. WILL THE PLATFORM WORK DIRECTIVE CLOSE THE GAPS IN WORKERS' PROTECTION?

October 2024 marked the end of a roughly three-year-long negotiation process concerning an instrument intended to address the working conditions of platform workers, including domestic platform workers – that is, the EU Platform Work Directive (PfWD). This Directive has three primary objectives that contribute to achievement of its overarching goal of improving platform workers' working conditions: i) facilitating the establishment of the correct employment status, ii) protecting workers' personal data in relation to platform work and iii) improving transparency concerning platform work, including in cross-border situations (Article 1(1)). The following analysis focuses on the provisions that contribute to achieving the first two objectives, reflecting on their effectiveness in the domestic work sector.

A. Employment Presumption

The first objective of the PfWD is pursued via a set of provisions that establish an employment presumption, accompanied by supporting measures (Articles 4–6). First, the PfWD reaffirms the primacy of facts principle, according to which it is the actual work performance, rather than the contractual description of the relationship between the parties, that is decisive when it comes to the employment classification. AM is explicitly mentioned as a factor that should be taken into account when determining employment status. This wording is a clear sign that the use of AM systems in the organisation of work, even though not decisive per se for the distinction between employment and self-employment, plays an important role in shaping work dynamics and needs to be factored into the equation.

Second, Article 4(3) provides that if an employment relationship is established, 'the party *or parties* assuming the obligations of the employer' must be clearly identified (emphasis added). Such a provision recognises the problems associated with assigning legal responsibilities when employment prerogatives are dispersed among various parties. This complex scenario is prevalent in the platformised domestic sector, where platforms typically undertake only some employer prerogatives, leaving much to the discretion of clients.

Third, and most crucially, workers who perform their services through digital platforms are covered by the presumption of an employment relationship with the relevant platforms, provided that the facts indicating both direction and control are presented in a legal proceeding before local courts (Article 5(1) PfWD). This presumption is a procedural facilitation intended to benefit those who perform platform work, which should by no means increase the burden of proving their employment status. This prevents Member States from setting a higher threshold for employment classification than that stemming from their national laws and CJEU case law. Platform workers and their representatives are able to initiate administrative or judicial proceedings when the determination of the correct employment status is at issue.[65] Protection against adverse consequences resulting from initiating such proceedings to enforce workers' rights under the PfWD is ensured by Article 22. Moreover, national authorities are obligated to initiate proceedings when they consider a person who performs platform work to have been misclassified.

The PfWD also sets out supporting measures to ensure the effectiveness of the employment presumption, such as the development of guidance on its interpretation in the national context and the establishment of guidelines facilitating non-compliance tracking by authorities and ensuring effective control of platforms that act as employers (Article 6).

Getting to the core of the question, the effectiveness of the employment presumption ultimately hinges on how both direction and control are defined and demonstrated in practice. The employment presumption is not absolute: it can be rebutted when a platform succeeds in proving that its relationship with platform workers does not constitute an employment relationship. This could be the case if the platform shows that the direction and control over the domestic worker is exerted solely by the client, for example, the household, or if it demonstrates that the domestic worker is genuinely independent, when the burden of proof is shifted.

All things considered, the above-described measures have great potential to increase workers' awareness of the legal situation and encourage them to realise their rights. This could lead to an upsurge in litigation, which has, to date, been marginal in the area of domestic work.

However, achieving the classification of domestic workers as platforms' employees may be an uphill battle. Indeed, the exercise of 'direction and control' by domestic platforms tends to be more tenuous than in other sectors, meaning that it is unclear whether the employment presumption will be applicable. Even if that does prove to be the case, it could be expected that a platform may relatively easily rebut the presumption by demonstrating that it does not effectively direct and control domestic workers, including via algorithmic means. This brings us back to the concept of 'minor' AM, where human agency and algorithmic decision-making are strictly interwoven and the impact of algorithms is less tangible than in other sectors. Employment prerogatives can be shared between the platform and the client, and the line between the authority of these two actors is, in some cases, extremely thin. For instance, this issue is visible in the realm of working time, where the exact schedule is set by the client and the

[65] S Rainone and A Aloisi, '*The EU Platform Work Directive. What's New, What's Missing, What's Next?' (2024) ETUI Policy Brief 2024.06.*

worker, although the platform can sanction the worker for non-compliance with the schedule or for changing it with too little notice. It should be noted that the PfWD's employment presumption seems to have been designed with the ideal type of courier or delivery worker in mind – an archetype that fails to capture the diversity and complexity of domestic and care work.

This is not to say that the reclassification of care workers as platforms' employees based on current employment tests is excluded. Even before the adoption of the procedural facilitations within the PfWD, the Spanish Tribunal Superior de Justicia held that the care work platform Cuideo has a direct relationship with the carers who work through it.[66] In that decision, the Tribunal held that clients have a direct relationship with the platform. Despite the existence of subordination being, in the Tribunal's words, 'certainly tenuous',[67] consideration was given to workers' dependence, which was understood as integration into the scope of organisation and management of the employer. In particular, the conditions of the care service provided, such as the schedule, place, duration, nature of the service and fees, are indicated by the client or Cuideo, without the caregiver being able to determine them. Moreover, the platform has a designated coordinator (or trainer) who explains to the caregivers the tasks to be performed in the client's home. The client pays the price of the service to the platform and the latter transmits it to the caregivers, deducting a commission of 25 per cent. By contrast, other judgments have classified domestic workers as workers employed by the client or as independent contractors.[68]

It is difficult to predict the future tendency of case law in this regard. The effectiveness of the presumption will ultimately depend on the implementation of the PfWD in EU Member States by December 2026. Another key question that remains open concerns how the 'hybrid' formula of worker, which relies on the national definition(s) *with consideration* of the CJEU case law, will be interpreted and applied. While this wording has been interpreted as an attempt to broaden the scope of the notion of a worker, it is not clear whether the *Lawrie-Blum*-shaped[69] understanding of a 'worker' will be able to cover the highly ambiguous cases of platformised domestic workers.[70]

[66] STSJ CAT 2522/2022.

[67] Workers were free to accept or reject orders, while there was no control by means of performance reports, no requirement of exclusivity, the possibility of working for third parties, autonomous organisation of the provision of services and contribution of material means for the provision of services.

[68] C Hießl, ch 9, in this volume.

[69] In this case, the CJEU set out the criteria for the EU's notion of a worker, stating that 'the essential feature of an employment relationship is that, for a certain period of time, a person performs services for and under the direction of another in return for which he receives remuneration' (para 17). Three criteria have thus emerged as relevant to the assessment: (a) the performance of effective and genuine economic activities, (b) remuneration and (c) subordination. See the Judgment of the Court of 3 July 1986, *Deborah Lawrie-Blum v Land Baden-Württemberg*, Case 66/85.

[70] On the application of the 'hybrid' worker formula to casual workers (in the context of the TPWCD), see D Georgiou, 'The New EU Directive on Transparent and Predictable Working Conditions in the Context of New Forms of Employment' (2022) 28 *European Journal of Industrial Relations* 193.

B. Algorithmic Management

The second 'pillar' of workers' rights according to the PfWD, irrespective of the employment classification, relates to protection against risks stemming from the use of AM.[71] First, all people who perform platform work, including domestic workers, will benefit from the extended catalogue of grounds for the processing of personal data under Article 7. This involves a ban on certain automated systems, including systems used to make predictions about the exercise of fundamental rights and systems applied to infer certain characteristics, such as migration status or racial and ethnic origin. Such a provision represents an important red line, which is crucial for ensuring that migrant domestic workers (who constitute the majority of platform workers in this sector) are not discriminated against. It must be stressed that Article 7 PfWD has remarkably broad scope, given that it applies to all 'automated systems supporting or taking decisions that affect persons performing platform work *in any manner*' (emphasis added). This implies that systems that do not affect workers 'significantly', but only to a 'minor' extent, are also covered (Article 7(3)). As argued above, the extensive substantive scope of this provision may be particularly important in the domestic work sector, which is characterised by the prevalence of 'minor' AM systems.

Second, Article 9 PfWD provides a long list of ex ante transparency rights, ensuring stronger protection when compared with the right under the General Data Protection Regulation (GDPR).[72] Digital platforms have to disclose information about the use of algorithmic systems and all types of decisions supported or made by such systems, even when the algorithmically driven decisions do not have a significant impact on persons who perform platform work.[73] Apart from information about the fact that such systems are in use or are being introduced, the information provided shall cover the categories of automated or semi-automated decisions, categories of data and main parameters that the systems take into account, as well as their 'relative importance'. Based on this provision, domestic workers will be provided with information about how their conduct influences (semi-)automated decisions. The grounds for certain decisions concerning account restriction, suspension or termination, payment refusal after work performance and contractual status will be made available to

[71] For a comprehensive overview of the PfWD provisions in this regard, see generally, N Potocka-Sionek, 'Gestión de algoritmos. El caso del trabajo en plataformas' [Algorithm Management: The Case of Platform Work] (2024) 5 *LABOS Revista de Derecho del Trabajo y Protección Social* 47.

[72] Regulation (EU) 2016/679 of the European Parliament and of the Council of 27 April 2016 on the protection of natural persons with regard to the processing of personal data and on the free movement of such data, and repealing Directive 95/46/EC (General Data Protection Regulation) (Text with EEA relevance).

[73] This fills an important gap in the GDPR, whereby data controllers are not obligated to inform data subjects about the existence of algorithms that, according to them, are not covered by Art 22(1) GDPR, provided they comply with the information obligations under Arts 13–15 GDPR. For a detailed discussion of the GDPR limitations in this context, see generally, H Abraha, 'Regulating Algorithmic Employment Decisions Through Data Protection Law' (2023) 14 *European Labour Law Journal* 172.

workers. They will also be informed about the use of automated monitoring, the categories of data and the actions subject to this kind of monitoring, including evaluation by the user, the aim and the means of monitoring, among others.

The PfWD guarantees not only ex ante transparency measures concerning automated systems but also their human oversight. It states that platforms must oversee and evaluate the impact of decisions made or supported by AM. This control should consider the impact of platforms on domestic workers' working conditions and their right to equal treatment at work. Here, suppose that a high risk of discrimination or infringement of rights by such systems is identified. In that case, the platform must implement the steps necessary to avoid such decisions in the future, including modification or discontinuation of the operation of AM systems. It is vitally important that the PfWD draws attention to the risk of algorithmic discrimination, not least in the domestic work sector, where gender and racial stereotypes are reinforced. Human overview can provide insights into the ways certain patterns are replicated in the digital sphere.

Additional important safeguards are enshrined in Article 11 PfWD, which provides for the right to human review, sometimes referred to as 'ex post transparency'.[74] Persons who perform platform work have the right to be informed about any decision made or supported by an automated decision-making system and to obtain access to a designated contact person. Besides information about automated decisions, persons who perform platform work shall be able to request a review of such decisions, including decisions that do not concern essential aspects of their contracts.

Finally, a crucial set of protections are detailed in Article 12 PfWD, which concerns the impact of AM on workers' OSH. According to this provision, platforms shall carry out a risk assessment regarding the impact of their systems on workers' health and safety, considering both psychosocial and ergonomic risks. Moreover, platforms shall introduce appropriate preventive and protective measures and evaluate whether the implemented safeguards are adequate to address the identified risks. These safeguards can certainly protect domestic workers from algorithmically driven overload, whereby the instructions surpass their abilities. This represents an important step towards the responsibilisation of platforms in terms of the health and safety of persons working through them and towards recognition of AM-driven psychosocial risks. Moreover, Article 12(5) requires that Member States ensure platforms adopt preventive measures to ensure the health and safety of platform workers, including with regard to violence and harassment. This is the only PfWD provision that seeks to address the duties of the platform in light of the risk posed by the other party – that is, the client. We find that this addition is especially salient in view of the complex multi-partite constellations prevalent in domestic work.While the OSH-related duties imposed on platforms by the PfWD represent a welcome advance, it

[74] M Vaele, MS Silberman and R Binns, 'Fortifying the Algorithmic Management Provisions in the Proposed Platform Work Directive' (2023) 14 *European Labour Law Journal* 308.

should be recalled that health and safety risks are multi-layered.[75] Some may stem not (only) from the platform but (also) be attributable to the client. This may be the case with the provision of cleaning equipment that does not meet safety standards or exertion of extra pressure to work beyond the agreed schedule. Article 12 PfWD does not go so far as to require platforms to 'programme' OSH compliance into their algorithms, which could have been the case. It is conceivable to require platforms to implement mechanisms ensuring respect for working time regulations, among others. This represents a missed opportunity for the full realisation of the fundamental right to healthy and safe working conditions, as enshrined in Article 31 of the Charter of Fundamental Rights of the EU. Another fundamental limitation of Article 12 is its narrow scope, which does not cover people who perform platform work as self-employed workers.

C. The Remaining Gaps

By contributing to the improvement of working conditions in this area, the PfWD partially addresses some gaps in the protection of domestic platform workers, but it does not fully resolve them. In fact, platform-mediated domestic work will continue to have many faces, as the PfWD is not set to bring uniformity to platform business models.

Crucially, the PfWD does not contain any provisions on working time or the transparency of the working conditions of platform workers per se. However, it applies without prejudice to existing legislation, meaning that it must be read in conjunction with other applicable laws that address these issues, as discussed above. Moreover, the PfWD does address such issues indirectly via the employment presumption: should platform workers be classified as employees, they will be unmistakably brought within the protective scope of labour and social law, including the working time organisation and working condition predictability provisions.

In addition, the reclassification of domestic platform workers would address some of the issues analysed above, not least by ensuring the applicability of other relevant tools, such as the TPWCD and the WTD. This would curtail the possibility of platforms assigning shifts with limited or no notice, increasing the transparency not only of the functioning of algorithms but also of working conditions. Yet, this will not overcome other issues stemming from working time 'atomisation' and income instability. Among these issues, the applicability of the TPWCD and the WTD remains status-dependent. Against this background, legislators' approach to the improvement of platform workers' working conditions appears fragmented and incomplete.

[75] European Agency for Safety and Health at Work, *Digital Platform Work and Occupational Safety and Health: A Review* (European Agency for Safety and Health at Work 2021) https://osha.europa.eu/en/publications/digital-platform-work-and-occupational-safety-and-health-review.

In summary, the platform-specific PfWD cannot address all the sector-specific issues associated with domestic work. As argued above, even before the emergence of platforms, the sector was characterised by 'gigified' non-standard work arrangements. The examples provided of the temporal and spatial 'divergences' of domestic work from the standard employment relations model illustrate the complexity of this issue. Despite the limitations, however, it is worth noting that platformised domestic workers may now enjoy stronger protections under the PfWD when compared with traditional domestic workers. This could be seen as a significant step forward, if not for the fact that these rules may be difficult to 'activate' at the individual level due to the unbalanced power dynamics, information asymmetries, economic dependence and fear of retaliation discussed earlier.

It can be contended that the PfWD offers some relief in certain circumstances without addressing the underlying issues for at least three reasons. First, domestic work encompasses highly heterogeneous cases, which do not always fit neatly into the scheme of subordinate employment. Second, even in cases where workers manage to secure reclassification, the structural limitations of instruments such as the WTD and the TPWCD hinder concrete improvement of their experiences. Third, to truly ensure fair working conditions, the rules on the transparency of automated monitoring and decision-making must be intricately connected with working time organisation provisions. This implies that any automated systems used to monitor workers' activities or make decisions about either task allocation or performance should operate within clearly defined parameters that respect workers' right to 'human-centred' working hours.[76] For example, platforms must ensure that workers are not subject to excessive on-call demands, fragmented shifts or schedules that disregard rest periods, and the algorithms must not impose unrealistic expectations on workers. Integrating these rules into a technology-neutral framework would help to address the intersecting challenges of algorithmic control, time unpredictability and worker well-being.

V. CONCLUSION

Domestic and care work is difficult to study, capture and regulate. Above all, this complexity can be attributed to the sector's distinctive character.[77] Historically, the intermediation of domestic workers plays a problematic role, as it is often facilitated by agencies and other 'middlemen', which may lead to exploitation,

[76] Bogg (n 47).

[77] C Marzo, 'The New Challenges of Care Work in Light of Digitalisation and Platformisation' in Laeticia Thissen and A Mach (eds), *The European Care Strategy: A Chance to Ensure Inclusive Care for All?* (Brussels, FEPS, 2023).

particularly among migrant and undocumented workers.[78] Structurally, domestic work represents an idiosyncratic form of employment, requiring a level of dedication that often exceeds conventional time limits[79] and fostering deep personal attachment to the recipient of the service. From a contractual perspective, the sector has long been characterised by the proliferation of tailor-made legal schemes,[80] which were intended to reduce informality but instead often legitimised suboptimal regulation of working conditions.

As evidenced by the comparative research on national legal frameworks,[81] given its 'ambivalent' features,[82] domestic work is difficult to fit within existing legislative frameworks, and its platformised version only exemplifies these problems and introduces extra strain. For instance, the way domestic work is organised challenges the assumptions of linear working time settings in existing regulations. The risks typically include working time fragmentation, excessively long or short hours, on-call scheduling, unpredictable work patterns and poor work–life balance.

When domestic work platforms first entered the labour market roughly a decade ago,[83] it was hoped that their shiny technological infrastructure would elucidate the informal corners of the economy. Simultaneously, there was an expectation that the availability of presumably reliable, digital channels for work mediation could render labour intermediation fairer.[84] This optimism was particularly pronounced in the context of domestic work.

However, it remains unclear whether this decade-old promise has actually been fulfilled. While traditional word-of-mouth recommendation systems have increasingly been replaced by more efficient digital intermediation, reflecting the

[78] J Fudge and C Hobden, *Conceptualizing the Role of Intermediaries in Formalizing Domestic Work* (Geneva, ILO, 2018). See also N Van Doorn, 'Platform Labor: On the Gendered and Racialized Exploitation of Low-Income Service Work in the "On-Demand" Economy' (2017) 20 *Information, Communication & Society* 898; N Van Doorn, 'Stepping Stone or Dead End? The Ambiguities of Platform-Mediated Domestic Work Under Conditions of Austerity. Comparative Landscapes of Austerity and the Gig Economy: New York and Berlin' in D Baines and I Cunningham (eds), *Working in the Context of Austerity: Challenges and Struggles* (Bristol, Bristol University Press, 2020).

[79] D McCann and J Murray, 'The Legal Regulation of Working Time in Domestic Work' (2010) International Labour Office Conditions of Work and Employment Series 27.

[80] LJB Hayes, *Stories of Care: A Labour of Law. Gender and Class at Work* (Basingstoke, Palgrave, 2017).

[81] D McCann, 'New Frontiers of Regulation: Domestic Work, Working Conditions, and the Holistic Assessment of Nonstandard Work Norms' (2012) 34 *Comparative Labor Law and Policy Journal* 167; International Labour Office, *Making Decent Work a Reality for Domestic Workers: Progress and Prospects Ten Years After the Adoption of the Domestic Workers Convention 2011* (Geneva, ILO, 2021).

[82] L De Vita and A Bertolini, 'Underpaid or Uberpaid? The Platformisation of the Domestic and Care Work' (2025) 0 *Critical Sociology* 1.

[83] The no longer operating platform Homejoy, which started operations in Silicon Valley in 2010 and expanded to Europe in 2014, is considered a precursor of domestic work platforms. See Koutsimpogiorgos, Frenken and Herrmann (n 8).

[84] T Elrick and E Lewandowska, 'Matching and Making Labour Demand and Supply: Agents in Polish Migrant Networks of Domestic Elderly Care in Germany and Italy' (2008) 34 *Journal of Ethnic and Migration Studies* 717.

broader transformation of societal interactions, the structural power imbalances entrenched in the domestic sector persist. Restrictive immigration and labour policies, the segmented labour market and inadequate regulation of private employment agencies[85] continue to hinder efforts to draw domestic workers fully out of the shadows.

As this chapter has demonstrated, in those segments of the labour market that often escape policy attention, algorithms entrusted with managerial prerogatives can exacerbate the erratic nature of work organisation, particularly affecting workers who engage in sensitive tasks. Instead of addressing these systemic issues, digital intermediaries often replicate or even exacerbate existing inequalities, leaving many workers in a precarious position.

The challenges faced by domestic workers highlight a systemic issue within the existing legislation – namely, domestic work is consistently treated as a 'special' case, one that is often excluded from or inadequately covered by labour provisions. Both the WTD and the TPWCD include carve-outs, opt-outs and exceptions that primarily benefit users – whether employers, principals or clients – based on the justification of accommodating the unique traits of domestic work. While certain exclusions may be justified for specific facets of domestic work (for example, work performed in private households,) these exceptions have the broader effect of perpetuating the second-class employment status of domestic workers, reinforcing systemic inequities.

By contrast, the PfWD's redress mechanism, which aims to secure the correct classification of workers and to provide new information rights and transparency safeguards in terms of AM, may offer benefits to platformised domestic workers. However, it may not resolve all of the pressing issues, overlooking working time atomisation and income instability concerns. Moreover, the effectiveness of the PfWD in such a heterogeneous sector will depend on how Member States formulate the rebuttable employment presumption and supporting measures.

Hence, the lessons learned from the realm of domestic work should prompt policy makers and regulation to deploy interventions aimed at re-humanising working conditions. Such legislative measures should prioritise empowering workers to exercise control over their schedules and methods, especially in an era in which technology may be employed to diminish autonomy, intensify control and restrict flexibility. Granting workers greater latitude over the organisation of their work is a prerequisite for promoting job quality and formalising domestic work, removing it from the grey zone, particularly in the context of the increasing importance of the silver economy[86] and the widespread 'social-care crisis' affecting many countries due to deregulation, public welfare spending cuts and the disintegration of both family and community support networks.[87]

[85] Rodríguez-Modroño, Agenjo-Calderón and López-Igual (n 5).

[86] V Pavlou, 'Whose Equality? Paid Domestic Work and EU Gender Equality Law' (2020) 1 *European Equality Law Review* 36.

[87] Rodríguez-Modroño, Agenjo-Calderón and López-Igual (n 5).

12

*Platform Domestic and Childcare Work: Centring Labour Rights in the Formalisation Debate**

NATALIE SEDACCA AND JOE ATKINSON

I. INTRODUCTION

THE RAPID GROWTH of platform work has been a feature of labour markets around the world in the past decade[1] and has attracted significant scholarly attention. While earlier literature primarily focused on the most visible sectors such as delivery and ride hailing,[2] recent studies have begun to explore the specificities of platform domestic work, including by engaging with the concept of 'formalisation' to help understand its impacts and implications. There remains a need, however, for greater conceptual clarification of this term's meaning. Against an understanding of formalisation that focuses on the registration of businesses with taxation and other relevant authorities, this chapter argues for a 'thicker' and more normative conceptualisation that centres the implementation of labour regulation and social protection.

The chapter begins by outlining the regulatory challenges of domestic and platform work, identifying distinct issues raised by the intersection of these two forms of atypical working arrangement. Next, we examine various conceptions of formalisation in academic literature and policy documents, putting forward our normative understanding and justifying engagement with the concept despite its potential ambiguities. These distinct conceptions of formalisation in

* The authors are grateful to Lorena Poblete and Eva Kocher for detailed comments on the draft chapter, and to participants of the workshop on 'Digital Intermediaries in the Domestic and Care Work Sector' at the Oñati International Institute for the Sociology of Law in May 2024, particularly Matthew Johnson who acted as discussant.

[1] J Haidar and M Keune (eds), *Work and Labour Relations in Global Platform Capitalism* (Oxford, Edward Elgar Publishing, 2021); S Riso, 'Mapping the Contours of the Platform Economy - Working Paper' (Eurofound 2019).

[2] R Dukes, 'On Demand Work as a Legal Framework to Understand the Gig Economy' in Valerio De Stefano and others (eds) *A Research Agenda for the Gig Economy and Society* (Oxford, Edward Elgar Publishing, 2022) 140.

turn lead to different conclusions about the formalising effects of digital platforms, which we analyse in section IV. The workings and impacts of domestic work platforms are far from homogenous, so it is difficult to draw generalised conclusions. Contrary to the claims of platform companies themselves, however, we argue that they do not meaningfully progress formalisation for domestic workers, except in cases where platforms either provide employment contracts or take proactive steps to encourage labour law and social security compliance.

The chapter then examines how meaningful formalisation of platform domestic work can be achieved, putting the growing empirical and analytical literature on platform domestic work in conversation with recent legal developments. Since many platform workers are likely to fall outside notions of 'control' required to show employment status, we criticise approaches to the formalisation of platform domestic work that are entirely contingent on the classification of workers as employees, which is likely to continue to exclude many platform domestic workers. We argue instead for a universalist approach to formalisation, which aims to provide adequate and effective protections to all those involved in the personal performance of work, including the solo self-employed. Finally, we assess the impact of the EU Directive on Platforms agreed in March 2024 towards these goals, arguing that it represents only partial progress towards a universalistic approach.

II. DOMESTIC WORK AND PLATFORM WORK: DISTINCT BUT OVERLAPPING REGULATORY CHALLENGES

Shortcomings in regulation of domestic work long predate the use of platform intermediaries. The sector is highly feminised,[3] with a prevalence of migrant and ethnic minority women,[4] and devalued because of its association with the private sphere of the home and the family, viewed as separate from 'real' or productive work.[5] Through a combination of cultural ideologies, legal exclusions and its spatial location in the home, domestic work is a classic 'invisible' form of labour.[6] This is manifested in the widespread exclusion of domestic workers from labour law protections, both in terms of the formal coverage and enforcement of standards.[7] Domestic workers may therefore struggle to

[3] ILO, *Making Decent Work a Reality for Domestic Workers - Progress and Prospects Ten Years after the Adoption of the Domestic Workers Convention, 2011 (No. 189)* (Geneva, ILO, 2021) 12.

[4] ILO, 'Report IV(1) - Decent Work for Domestic Workers - 99th Session of the International Labour Conference' (2010) 5.

[5] M Duffy, 'Doing the Dirty Work: Gender, Race, and Reproductive Labor in Historical Perspective' (2007) 21 *Gender & Society* 313.

[6] E Hatton, 'Mechanisms of Invisibility: Rethinking the Concept of Invisible Work' (2017) 31 *Work, Employment and Society* 336.

[7] ILO, 'Report IV(1) 99th Session'; V Mantouvalou, 'Human Rights for Precarious Workers: The Legislative Precariousness of Domestic Labor' (2012) 34 *Comparative Labor Law & Policy Journal* 133; A Blackett, *Everyday Transgressions: Domestic Workers' Transnational Challenge to International Labor Law* (Ithaca, ILR Press, 2019).

enforce rights and organise collectively due to compounding disadvantages such as precarious migration status, lack of time and awareness, the decentralised nature of their work, and the difficulty of establishing effective bargaining structures in an isolated workplace.[8]

Following concerted campaigning by domestic workers and their organisations, the ILO adopted Convention 189 on domestic work ('C-189') in 2011, providing a comprehensive scheme for protection of domestic workers' rights on matters including payment, hours of work and rest times, collective bargaining, social security and health and safety.[9] The adoption of a hard law instrument represented a breakthrough and signified the importance placed on regulating domestic work.[10] In some respects, the years since then have seen significant progress, including a 16 per cent decrease in the proportion of domestic workers wholly excluded from employment rights and social protections.[11] This is subject to significant regional variation, however, with ILO statistics suggesting 'virtually all' domestic workers in Europe and Central Asia are now covered by some form of labour law whereas in 'the Arab States, 94 per cent of domestic workers are excluded from the scope of national labour laws and covered only by subordinate regulations'.[12] There are also ongoing challenges in making rights effective. The ILO identifies enforcement issues, rather than legal scope, as accounting for a third of failures to adequately protect domestic workers, and as the main cause of such failures in Europe.[13] This de facto lack of labour rights for domestic workers even where legal protections exist is pronounced because of the invisibility of domestic work in private homes, the non-applicability of labour inspection, and the prominence of non-legal norms in home workplaces.[14]

The appropriate regulation of platform work is a more recent challenge, which remains unresolved and has been hotly contested over approximately the past decade. The rise of platform work tends to be viewed as part of a broader ongoing trend away from 'more stable and rewarded standard employment' in many labour markets.[15] Platform work shares characteristics with other 'atypical'

[8] L Delap, *Knowing Their Place: Domestic Service in Twentieth-Century Britain* (Oxford, OUP, 2011) 83; E Albin and V Mantouvalou, 'Active Industrial Citizenship of Domestic Workers: Lessons Learned from Unionizing Attempts in Israel and the United Kingdom' (2016) 17 *Theoretical Inquiries in Law* 321; R Dukes, 'Regulating Gigs' (2020) 83 *Modern Law Review* 217.

[9] M Blofield and M Jokela, 'Paid Domestic Work and the Struggles of Care Workers in Latin America' (2018) 66 *Current Sociology* 531; D Cherubini, G Garofalo Geymonat and S Marchetti, 'Global Rights and Local Struggles. The Case of the ILO Convention n.189 on Domestic Work' (2019) 11 *Partecipazione e Conflitto* 717.

[10] E Albin and V Mantouvalou, 'The ILO Convention on Domestic Workers: From the Shadows to the Light' (2012) 41 *Industrial Law Journal* 67.

[11] ILO (n 3) 61, 65.

[12] ibid.

[13] ibid.

[14] A Blackett, 'Introduction: Regulating Decent Work for Domestic Workers' (2011) 23 *Canadian Journal of Women and the Law* 1; ILO, *Labour Inspection and Other Compliance Mechanisms in the Domestic Work Sector: Introductory Guide* (Geneva, ILO, 2016).

[15] G Bhattacharyya, *The Futures of Racial Capitalism* (Cambridge, Polity Press, 2024) 136.

work forms such as casual and zero hours work, piecework, and remote work,[16] with common hurdles to securing decent conditions including precarity, instability and lack of control over one's time and income due to the casual nature of the work. As with agency work, there is also the challenge of determining who should be responsible for employment standards in a tripartite relationship.[17]

Despite these considerable overlaps, platform work does present some genuinely new regulatory challenges, such as the extensive use of monitoring and algorithmic technologies to collect data and allocate, manage, monitor and evaluate work. Tracking workers' location and performance on a minute-by-minute basis and combining this with other data sources to make decisions or recommendations presents an unprecedented threat to privacy, freedom of association and expression.[18] The close oversight enabled by algorithmic systems can reduce autonomy at work, heighten the level of subordination experienced by workers,[19] perpetuate discrimination[20] and have negative implications for worker health.[21] There are also significant legal and practical obstacles to platform workers exercising collective labour rights, as the remote and individualistic nature of much platform work hinders the formation of social relationships and solidarity. Key concepts found in collective bargaining law are difficult to translate to dispersed platform workers who lack any central hub.[22] Furthermore, workers do not normally know how algorithmic systems used by platforms to make decisions about their work or understand their inner functioning,[23] making it difficult to bargain and exercise voice over these matters.

Considering the intersection of the marginalisation of domestic work and risks of the platform model leads to an understanding of platform domestic work as exemplifying 'compound non-standard work', which combines many dimensions of atypical work.[24] It therefore fares poorly under the dominant

[16] M Finkin, 'Beclouded Work in Historical Perspective' (2016) 37 *Comparative Labor Law & Policy Journal* 16; J Prassl, *Humans as a Service: The Promise and Perils of Work in the Gig Economy* (Oxford, OUP, 2018); N Srnicek, *Platform Capitalism* (Cambridge, Polity Press, 2017).

[17] For discussion of the potential, and legal challenges, of treating platform work as temporary agency work see Hießl, ch 9 and Ratti, ch 10, in this book.

[18] J Atkinson and P Collins, 'Artificial Intelligence and Human Rights at Work' in Jeroen Temperman and Alberto Quintavalla (eds), *Artificial Intelligence and Human Rights* (Oxford, OUP, 2023).

[19] V De Stefano, '"Masters and Servers": Collective Labour Rights and Private Government in the Contemporary World of Work' (2020) 36 *International Journal of Comparative Labour Law and Industrial Relations* 425.

[20] J Buolamwini and T Gebru, 'Gender Shades: Intersectional Accuracy Disparities in Commercial Gender Classification', *Conference on fairness, accountability and transparency* (PMLR 2018); I Ajunwa, 'The Paradox of Automation as Anti-Bias Intervention' (2019) 41 *Cardozo Law Review* 1671.

[21] A Todolí-Signes, 'Making Algorithms Safe for Workers: Occupational Risks Associated with Work Managed by Artificial Intelligence' (2021) 27 *Transfer: European Review of Labour and Research* 433.

[22] A Aloisi, S Rainone and N Countouris, 'An Unfinished Task? Matching the Platform Work Directive with the EU and International "Social Acquis" - ILO Working Paper 101' (ILO 2023).

[23] Trade Union Congress, 'Technology Managing People - The Worker Experience' (2020).

[24] Eurofound, 'Labour Market Change: Trends and Policy Approaches towards Flexibilisation' (Publications Office of the European Union 2020) 18.

regulatory model of labour law, which was developed in the twentieth century to protect workers in more 'standard' forms of employment. It is based on assumptions that do not hold true for domestic platform work: namely, that work is being contracted for on an ongoing and bilateral basis, with stable hours and pay, to be performed at a single place alongside other workers performing similar tasks. Legal frameworks designed to address workers' inequality of power and vulnerabilities under these conditions may therefore be inadequate or ineffective. For example, regulations of working time and wages aimed at standard employment relationships have traditionally been focused on rights such as maximum hours, breaks and minimum hourly rates.[25] Yet platform workers will often have distinct concerns such as securing guaranteed minimum hours, remuneration for preliminary work to secure jobs on the platform, predictable schedules and payments for late notice cancellations.[26]

Recent studies have underscored that platform domestic work does not necessarily follow patterns observed in commonly discussed sectors such as ride hailing (e.g. Uber) and delivery (e.g. Deliveroo), which are based on automatically 'matching' workers and service users via an algorithm. The more diverse forms of domestic work platform can broadly be categorised into four 'models': 'on-demand' in which workers are algorithmically matched with or allocated work; 'marketplace', where platforms provide data and contact details for potential workers, allowing end users to contact them and reach their own agreements over work performance; 'digital placement agencies', which focus on selecting and matching workers; and 'digital labour agencies' where the intermediary hires workers to work at several households.[27] Some of these, such as the marketplace model, can diverge significantly from the 'intense, multidimensional control over all aspects of work' that is present in other types of platform work,[28] because of the degree of choice left to end users and the potential for workers to communicate and negotiate directly with them.

Nonetheless, platforms can still constrain and influence workers' behaviour by more indirect means. Workers frequently feel under pressure to respond quickly to messages, as even short delays can lead to poor reviews or loss of

[25] For discussion of the Working Time Directive and Directive on Transparent and Predictable Working Conditions in the context of domestic platform work see A Aloisi and N Potocka-Sionek, ch 9, in this book.

[26] Aloisi, Rainone and Countouris (n 22); T Katsabian and G Davidov, 'Flexibility, Choice, and Labour Law: The Challenge of on-Demand Platforms' (2023) 73 *University of Toronto Law Journal* 348; V Pulignano and others, '"Digital Tournaments": The Colonisation of Freelancers' 'Free' Time and Unpaid Labour in the Online Platform Economy' (2024) 48 *Cambridge Journal of Economics* 133.

[27] P Rodríguez-Modroño, A Agenjo-Calderón and P López-Igual, 'A Social Reproduction Analysis of Digital Care Platform Work' (2024) 29 *New Political Economy* 616; L Poblete, F Pereyra and A Tizziani, 'Digital Intermediation in Paid Domestic Work in Argentina: An Analysis of Ambivalent Effects on Working Conditions' (2024) 0 *Critical Sociology* 1. On the implications of these distinct models, see further Rodríguez-Modroño, ch 1, in this book. The discussion here is limited to capital-owned platforms. On the distinct question of worker cooperatives, see Osiki, ch 7, and Bronowicka et al, ch 8, in this book.

[28] Prassl (n 16) 69.

work opportunities,[29] and work is arranged at the convenience of potential clients, with workers expected to adapt their time accordingly.[30] An oversupply of workers increases competition and therefore pressure to accept low pay and undertake significant unpaid work both when marketing themselves on the platform,[31] and communicating with potential clients.[32] Platform domestic workers are also subjected to indirect forms of control by through algorithmic 'nudges' that dis/incentivise certain behaviours. Worker profiles may be downgraded or promoted to customers based on criteria such as past reviews, regular acceptance of work, response times to customer messages, or the completion of optional background checks.[33]

Any discussion of regulating platform *domestic* work must therefore be mindful that its compound non-standard nature means legal frameworks suitable for other sectors of the platform economy may fall short of securing effective labour rights for this sub-group. It must be sensitive to the long-term issues of informality and rights violations in the domestic work sector, as well as the varied forms taken by platform intermediaries as compared with other forms of the platform economy.

III. THE MEANING OF 'FORMALISATION'

A prominent framework that is commonly adopted to consider the rise of atypical work and appropriate regulatory responses is to ask how they relate to 'formalisation'.[34] Various understandings of the concept of formalisation can be identified in academic literature and policy documents, however, with differing

[29] L Wiesböck, J Radlherr and ML Angelique Vo, 'Domestic Cleaners in the Informal Labour Market: New Working Realities Shaped by the Gig Economy?' (2023) 11 *Social Inclusion* 262; J Muldoon, N Sedacca and P Apostolidis, 'Matchmakers: Placement Agencies and Digital Platforms in the UK Childcare Market' (2025) 5 *Work in the Global Economy* 6. See also Johnson et al, ch 3, in this book.

[30] M Keller, '"When Clean Angels Calls, I Run": Working Conditions of a Gigified Care-Worker' in A Strüver and Sybille Bauriedl (eds), *Platformization of Urban Life: Towards a Technocapitalist Transformation of European Cities* (Bielefeld, transcript Verlag, 2022) 141.

[31] A Mateescu and J Ticona, 'Invisible Work, Visible Workers - Visibility Regimes in Online Platforms for Domestic Work' in Deepa Das Acevedo (ed), *Beyond the Algorithm: Qualitative Insights for Gig Work Regulation* (Cambridge, CUP, 2020) 63; Muldoon et al (n 29).

[32] P Rodríguez-Modroño, A Agenjo-Calderón and P López-Igual, 'Platform Work in the Domestic and Home Care Sector: New Mechanisms of Invisibility and Exploitation of Women Migrant Workers' (2022) 30 *Gender and Development* 619; Wiesböck, Radlherr and Vo (n 29); P McDonald et al, 'Income Generation on Care Work Digital Labour Platforms' (2024) 62 *British Journal of Industrial Relations* 358.

[33] J Ticona and A Mateescu, 'Trusted Strangers: Carework Platforms' Cultural Entrepreneurship in the on-Demand Economy' (2018) 20 *New Media & Society* 4384.

[34] A Hunt and E Samman, '(Re)Conceptualizing Gendered Structures of Informality for Domestic Workers in the Platform Economy' in A Surie and U Huws (eds), *Platformization and Informality: Pathways of Change, Alteration, and Transformation* (Cham, Springer, 2023); A Tandon and A Rathi, 'Sustaining Urban Labour Markets: Situating Migration and Domestic Work in India's "Gig" Economy' (2024) 56 *Environment and Planning A: Economy and Space* 1245.

implications for the relationship between platforms and formalisation. In this section we consider how the formalisation of work should be best defined and understood and why it is important to engage with the concept despite ambiguities in its definition.

One understanding of 'formalisation' focuses on the registration of businesses with taxation and other relevant authorities, with workers performing services for unregistered businesses classed as 'informal' and those working for registered companies as 'formalised'. The first international standard for the statistical measurement of labour market informality was addressed at work in the informal sector (ie unregistered businesses),[35] and, while later statistical measures introduced the important distinction between the *informal sector* and *informal employment*, business registration remains a key factor for identifying employment in the informal sector.[36] In turn, some studies exploring the impacts and characteristics of informal work have utilised a definition of informality that emphasises the employing organisation's formal status or visibility of the work to state authorities.[37]

The International Conference of Labour Statisticians (ILCS) has subsequently adopted an approach to informality aligning with the ILO's description of informal work,[38] which encompasses all employment not 'in law or in practice, subject to national labour legislation, income tax, social protection or entitlement to certain employment benefits (such as advance notice of dismissal, severance pay, paid annual or sick leave)'.[39] On this view, informality can result from workers' exclusion from social security and labour law frameworks, a lack of compliance and enforcement of these frameworks, or inadequate substantive levels of rights and protections.[40] This definition also makes an important distinction between different understandings of formalisation. While the *informal sector* describes unincorporated or unregistered enterprises, the more comprehensive concept of *informal employment* includes all employment that lacks adequate legal and social protection.[41]

[35] ILCS, 'Resolution Concerning Statistics of Employment in the Informal Sector, Adopted by the Fifteenth International Conference of Labour Statisticians' (1993).

[36] ILO, 'Women and Men in the Informal Economy: A Statistical Picture (Third Edition)' (International Labour Office 2018) 8.

[37] J Shapland and J Heyes, 'How Close Are Formal and Informal Work?' (2017) 37 *International Journal of Sociology and Social Policy* 374; CE Weber et al, 'Steering the Transition from Informal to Formal Service Provision: Labor Platforms in Emerging-Market Countries' (2021) 19 *Socio-Economic Review* 1315.

[38] ILCS, 'Resolution Concerning Statistics of Employment in the Informal Sector, 21st International Conference of Labour Statisticians' (2023). On the evolution of these definitions see K Sankaran, 'Informality at Work—Towards a Law on Livelihoods?' in G Davidov, B Langille and G Lester (eds), *The Oxford Handbook of the Law of Work* (Oxford, OUP, 2024).

[39] ILO, 'Promoting Employment and Decent Work in a Changing Landscape - 109th Session of the International Labour Conference' (2020) 155; ILCS (n 38) 55–63.

[40] ILO (n 3) 199.

[41] ILO (n 36) 7–12; Michael Rogan and Laura Alfers, 'Gendered Inequalities in the South African Informal Economy' (2019) 33 *Agenda (Durban)* 91, 91.

Crucially, whether a worker is in the formal *sector* does not automatically determine whether they are in formal *employment* with adequate protection. Employers in the formal sector, registered for tax purposes, may be more likely to create formal employment relationships, but the connection is by no means automatic. Informal work can exist within a formal enterprise,[42] or the formal *sector*, where there is a move away from standard employment relationships that can be described as 'informalization'.[43] Workers in the formal sector are not automatically better paid than those in informal enterprises.[44] Conversely, in some cases, workers may have a valid employment contract and legally enforceable employment rights even where the employer is not registered for tax and other business purposes.[45]

A conception of formalisation based on whether an enterprise is incorporated or registered with relevant authorities for social security and tax purposes can therefore be contrasted with understandings that focus on entitlement to labour rights and social protection.[46] We favour the latter conception, advocating a view of formalisation as a 'thick' concept that is inherently normative, which prioritises the implementation of labour regulation and social protection and seeks to advance the goal of decent work for all. The proposed conceptualisation of formalisation is somewhat similar to what Unni has termed a 'labour view' and contrasted with a 'capital view' entailing simply incorporation of enterprises within tax regimes and financial systems that arguably amounts simply to 'normalization'.[47]

Despite the importance of institutional visibility and business registration in other contexts, such as tax law, formalisation must require additional steps beyond this if it is to provide a valuable conceptual framework for labour lawyers. Our approach aligns with a 'central case' method, where the true nature of concepts is understood by reference to 'a prototype that provides a meaningful reference point' and aligns with its underlying moral purposes.[48] The concept of formalisation should therefore be understood purposively, in a way that reflects and advances the underlying normativity and protective goals of labour law. Reducing formalisation to business registration or visibility falls short of this, as workers who are registered with relevant authorities but excluded from adequate legal protections cannot be said to be in formalised employment in the sense we propose.

[42] K Sankaran, 'Labour Law in South Asia: The Need for an Inclusive Approach' in T Tzehainesh (ed), *Labour Law and Worker Protection in Developing Countries* (Geneva, ILO, 2010) 229.

[43] Sankaran (n 38) 234.

[44] Rogan and Alfers (n 41) 94.

[45] Entitlement to social security protections will generally be more problematic, however, as non-registered enterprises will not have made the necessary tax or insurance contributions.

[46] Hunt and Samman (n 34) 239.

[47] J Unni, 'Formalization of the Informal Economy: Perspectives of Capital and Labour' (2018) 61 *Indian Journal of Labour Economics* 87.

[48] S Atrey, 'On the Central Case Methodology in Discrimination Law' (2021) 41 *Oxford Journal of Legal Studies* 776.

This overarching understanding of formalisation holds even though the substantive rights and protections required for formalisation will vary across sectors and circumstances.[49] In domestic work, for instance, formalisation must entail rights that are responsive to power relations that structure work within a private household in highly unequal ways.[50] Importantly, this conceptualisation of formalisation recognises that work may be formalised to different degrees. Properly understood, formalisation is a continuum rather than binary,[51] and the process of formalisation is an ongoing and incremental rather than a one-off activity.[52] At the 'top' end, fully formalised work comprises labour rights and social security coverage as well as registration with public authorities, formal contracts and payment records.[53] Many intermediate positions exist between fully informal and fully formalised work, such as where workers are covered by existing employment law but the substantive content of these protections is inadequate or enforcement is lacking. The extent of progress along the continuum depends on a range of factors, including socio-economic and institutional contexts, labour market trends and historical specificities of the domestic work sector.[54] Furthermore, employers may grant some but not all labour rights to domestic workers, even viewing this incomplete adherence as a 'courtesy.'[55]

Given the disparity in understandings of formalisation, the value of the term from a labour regulation perspective can be questioned. Davidov has criticised the definitions of informality previously used by the ILO and the ILCS for being too broad, and for downplaying the distinction between the legal scope of particular regulations and a failure to apply regulations in practice.[56] He views the label of informality as inappropriate for both these categories, as the non-application of a law due to the definition of its scope is not a question of its formality, and compliance failures should be understood as 'legal disobedience' rather than 'informality' since the latter term downplays the seriousness of the situation and the harm it causes to workers.[57] We agree on the need for conceptual clarity, and on the important differences between questions of appropriate

[49] MA Chen Martha, 'The Informal Economy: Definitions, Theories and Policies - WIEGO Working Paper No. 1' (WIEGO 2012) 15.

[50] A Blackett, 'Domestic Workers and Informality - Challenging Invisibility, Regulating Inclusion' in M Chen and F Carré (eds), *The Informal Economy Revisited: Examining the Past, Envisioning the Future* (Abingdon, Taylor & Francis, 2020) 110.

[51] J Fudge and C Hobden, 'Conceptualizing the Role of Intermediaries in Formalizing Domestic Work' (Geneva, ILO, 2018); ILO, 'Formalizing Domestic Work' (International Labour Office 2016) 12–13.

[52] M Chen, 'Recognizing Domestic Workers, Regulating Domestic Work: Conceptual, Measurement, and Regulatory Challenges' (2011) 23 *Canadian Journal of Women and the Law* 167.

[53] ILO (n 51) 13.

[54] K Jaehrling, F Pereyra and L Poblete, 'Introduction: The Formalization of Paid Domestic Work – Current Trajectories and Challenges Ahead' (2024) 163 *International Labour Review* 359.

[55] F Pereyra and L Poblete, 'The Persistence of Informality in Paid Domestic Work in Argentina' (2024) 163 *International Labour Review* 435.

[56] G Davidov, 'Enforcement Problems in "Informal" Labor Markets: A View from Israel' (2005) 27 *Comparative Labor Law & Policy Journal* 3.

[57] ibid.

coverage and enforcement. But this does not mean that an overarching concept of formalisation encompassing both, as well as the additional category of informality not discussed by Davidov where the substantive level of employment standards is inadequate, cannot be a useful organising framework and platform for legal reforms and policy interventions.

Furthermore, the label of informality does not imply that these are not harmful arrangements. On the contrary, under our proposed normative understanding of the concept the existence of informality is, by definition, a significant problem, whereas describing the widespread and systematic exclusion of marginalised workers, particularly women, from employment protections as simply a 'coverage' issue might also be seen as trivialising. Additionally, to discard the term in favour of focusing on questions of 'legal disobedience' arguably goes too far in exceptionalising the informal sector. In much of the Global South, including larger emerging economies such as South Africa and India, the informal sector constitutes a large proportion – even a majority – of the workforce.[58] Furthermore, irregular migrants and asylum seekers lacking a right to work may be pushed towards jobs in the informal sector to avoid destitution, as in the UK.[59]

It is also important to engage with and understand formalisation given it is frequently adopted as a central concept as regards the regulation of paid domestic work. C189 is based on an 'assumption that formalization . . . is a necessary condition for decent work' although the two terms are not synonymous.[60] The concept of 'formalisation' is also prevalent in academic and policy literature on platforms, as well as the way platforms present themselves. For example, Helpling has presented itself as having a formalising effect in Germany, by acting as an alternative to the dominance of informal labour in the domestic cleaning sector,[61] with similar claims made by platforms in France.[62] These claims of formalisation are based on the thin understanding of formalisation rejected above, with the platform claiming to allow the regular employment of reliable cleaners 'without having to go through the bureaucratic process of registering the cleaner oneself'.[63] Weber et al also use a thin definition of informal work as 'economic activity that is not registered with formal authorities' to argue that platforms have a formalising effect in emerging market countries because they require workers to register, report income and pay taxes, as well as creating a

[58] S van Eck, 'Constitutionalisation of South African Labour Law: An Experiment in the Making' in CF Fenwick and T Novitz (eds), *Human Rights at Work: Perspectives on Law and Regulation* (Oxford, Hart Publishing, 2010); S Routh, *Labour Justice: A Constitutional Evaluation of Labour Law* (Cambridge, CUP, 2024) xiv.

[59] H Lewis, L Waite and SN Hodkinson, '"Hostile" UK Immigration Policy and Asylum Seekers' Susceptibility to Forced Labour' in F Vecchio and A Gerard (eds), *Entrapping Asylum Seekers: Social, Legal and Economic Precariousness* (Basingstoke, Palgrave Macmillan, 2017).

[60] Jaehrling et al (n 54) 360–63.

[61] N Koutsimpogiorgos, K Frenken and AM Herrmann, 'Platform Adaptation to Regulation: The Case of Domestic Cleaning in Europe' (2023) 65 *Journal of Industrial Relations* 156,.

[62] Teke-Laurent, ch 2, in this book.

[63] Koutsimpogiorgos et al (n 61) 169.

record of services and transactions.[64] Similar claims that the platform economy supports formalisation are contained in the employer group responses to an ILO questionnaire on the platform economy.[65]

However, it is problematic from a labour law perspective to present platforms as having a formalising effect without any assessment of their impact on working conditions. Failing to clarify and advance the best understanding of formalisation therefore risks allowing the concept to be deployed to depict changes in labour relations as positive even when they do little to improve – or even hinder – access to labour rights and social security.

IV. FORMALISATION AND DOMESTIC WORK: PLATFORMS AS CATALYST OR CONSTRAINT?

As a starting point, a relationship between an individual domestic worker and an individual private employer is generally in the informal *sector*, in the sense that the employer is not a corporate body that is registered for tax purposes. However, that relationship can be 'formalised' (in a sectoral sense) by the employer registering with the appropriate bodies to arrange deductions. In the UK, for example, an employer can use 'Nannytax' to set up deductions for tax and national insurance. A self-employed domestic worker registering to pay their own tax would also move them into the formal *sector*; in some countries schemes also exist to facilitate self-employed workers paying social security contributions such as the Microempreendedor Individual (MEI) in Brazil.[66]

If a domestic worker is working for a labour intermediary, then their work may be viewed as within the formal *sector* if the platform is appropriately registered. This is one way that platforms have been able to present themselves as having a 'formalising' effect; at the most basic level, work via a platform generally creates some record of each job undertaken. Yet platforms vary even in the extent to which they require or encourage workers to be registered for tax. In the US context, Ticona and Mateescu assess platforms as having some degree of formalising effect based on providing payment interfaces that record hours and pay, giving information on relevant employment and immigration laws, and encouraging and facilitating registration with tax authorities.[67] In the UK, by contrast content analysis suggests most childcare platforms do not actively encourage self-employed workers to report taxable earnings on a tax

[64] Weber et al (n 37) 1316.

[65] ILO, 'Report V(2) - Realizing Decent Work in the Platform Economy - International Labour Conference 113th Session, 2025' (2025) 26, 38. The employers also emphasised the role of platforms in progressing decent work.

[66] R Fragale Filho and M dos Santos Lima, 'Alguém se meteu no meio: modelos de intermediação digital do trabalho doméstico no Brasil' (2024) 89 *Revista de Estudios Sociales* 81.

[67] Ticona and Mateescu (n 33) 4385. See also Johnson et al, ch 3, in this book on the situation in Belgium.

return.[68] Even in the US, where platforms may be more active on tax, Ticona and Mateescu go on to note that formalisation efforts are 'mainly aspirational' since institutional visibility, while encouraged, is not actually required and the platforms do not take a stance on workers' employment status with end users.[69]

More fundamentally, even where platforms facilitate registration for taxation, there is a significant gap between moving domestic workers into the formal *sector* through such means and formalisation of work in the 'thick' sense we advocate. Clearly, registration for tax purposes and visibility to authorities is not necessarily enough to mean formality in terms of labour rights, for example ensuring limitations to working hours, health and safety and so on. Most claims of formalisation by platforms thus rely on an impoverished conception of formalisation. At most, their impact might be characterised as '*selective formalisation*' – 'a set of business and management practices that formalise some aspects of gig work while perpetuating the precarity associated with informal labour markets'.[70] For example, the Bubble platform for 'on-demand' childcare in the UK provides digital payment processes and relevant insurance for workers, but does not entail those aspects of formalisation that would increase the work's security, such as creating a contract.[71]

Of the various models adopted by domestic work platforms outlined above, a recent Spanish study found only the 'digital placement agency' model to be associated with formalisation. This solely related to care work and resulted in households hiring workers directly, rather than the platform acting as an employee.[72] Interestingly, this model is similar to more traditional placement agencies, which predate and exist independently of digital platforms, calling into question whether any formalising effect of platforms is novel. While the role of employment agencies varies, they can play a positive role in formalisation where there is appropriate regulation in place.[73] If a worker moves from formal work mediated by an agency to an 'on-demand' or 'marketplace' model of platform work, this is likely to amount to a process of *informalisation*,[74] particularly given the acceleration of hiring without a formal contract that platforms often encourage.[75] 'Informalisation' can also arise from features of platforms that militate against the applicability of rights that have been introduced to protect domestic workers

[68] Muldoon et al (n 29) 14–15.

[69] Ticona and Mateescu (n 33) 4385.

[70] N van Doorn, F Ferrari and M Graham, 'Migration and Migrant Labour in the Gig Economy: An Intervention' (2023) 37 *Work, Employment and Society* 1099, 1102.

[71] D Gebrial and P Bettington, 'The Insecure Economy: Measuring and Understanding the Contemporary Labour Market' (Autonomy 2022) 48–49, available at https://autonomy.work/wp-content/uploads/2022/03/insecure_economy-v1.pdf

[72] Rodríguez-Modroño et al (n 27) 620–21.

[73] DH Autor (ed), *Studies of Labor Market Intermediation* (Chicago, University of Chicago Press, 2009); Fudge and Hobden (n 51) 3–9.

[74] On the comparison between agencies and platforms, see Muldoon et al (n 29).

[75] Paula Rodríguez-Modroño, 'The Platformization and Marketization of Care: Business Models and Competitive Strategies of Care Platforms' (2025) 29 *Competition & Change* 554.

more generally, thus undermining movement towards greater formalisation.[76] In South Africa, for example, it is rarely possible for those working via platforms to meet the 24 hours per week of working for a single employer that triggers entitlement to social security registration, because of the platforms' 'insistence on being merely a technology provider' rather than an employer.[77]

Conversely, formalisation may be promoted where platforms encourage an employment relationship with the end user and provide information on applicable labour regulations, although this is contingent on active steps to enforce such measures.[78] The Zolvers platform in Argentina had been viewed as a relatively positive example for disseminating labour regulations to employers and workers and offering technical support to employers wishing to register workers for social security.[79] However, a more recent study found that of the range of hiring models it offers, it is only the jobs managed by the platform on behalf of employers – amounting to around 37 per cent of total jobs on the platform – that clearly contribute to formalisation.[80] More direct support for formalisation is seen in the 'Batmaid' platform, examined in an Italian study, which employs cleaners directly, providing employment contracts and associated labour provisions such as maternity protection, occupational safety and related insurance and trade union rights.[81] Outstanding issues with working conditions remain – in particular, a guarantee of at least 15 hours of work weekly can be undermined by short notice cancellations.[82] Despite this, the platform undoubtedly has a formalising effect compared to alternate models such as the Helping platform to which the study compares it. The latter acts as an intermediary leaving workers without social protection, and arguably intensifies informality even compared with work arranged by word of mouth because it obscures the fact that employment contracts are lacking.[83]

It is therefore evident that, rather than having a generalising effect of formalisation, the impact of platforms varies subject to their features and characteristics.[84] Our understanding of formalisation, which centres compliance with labour and social rights, is only directly met by those platforms that directly employ workers on terms that comply with labour laws, or that actively and

[76] Filho and Lima (n 66) 68.

[77] Hunt and Samman (n 34) 252–53.

[78] Ticona and Mateescu (n 33).

[79] S Filipetto et al, 'Platform Labour in Contexts of High Informality: Any Improvement for Workers? A Critical Assessment Based on the Case of Argentina' (2024) 39 *New Technology, Work and Employment* 259.

[80] Poblete et al (n 27).

[81] I Pais and A Marcolin, 'Digital Platforms in the Italian Domestic Care Sector: The Emergence of an Unprecedented Corporate Logic and Its Implications for Workers' Social Protection' (2024) 163 *International Labour Review* 397.

[82] ibid, 397.

[83] ibid, 397, 401, 408.

[84] Rodríguez-Modroño et al (n 27) 620; A Micha, M Trombetta and F Pereyra, 'Digital Labor Platforms, Domestic Work and Formalization: Evidence from Argentina' (Red Nacional de Investigadores en Economía (RedNIE) - Working Papers 330, 28 June 2024). See also Teke-Laurent, ch 2, in this book.

effectively promote compliance with labour rights and social security, and not through the limited steps taken by many other platforms. Working arrangements may be partially formalised to the extent that transactions are recorded, and the work is for a registered entity. But from the perspective argued in this chapter, workers' inclusion within employment law and social security protections are the more significant factors. The goal of labour law and market regulation in this context should be to move platform domestic work along the continuum from informality to formalised employment, in the thick sense advanced here.

V. STRATEGIES FOR FORMALISATION: BEYOND EMPLOYMENT STATUS

The formalisation of work necessarily involves the provision of effective employment rights and social protections. While platforms seek to avoid such requirements by arguing that they are simply labour market intermediaries rather than employers,[85] workers have increasingly challenged this by bringing cases seeking reclassification as employees. There are many examples of success, particularly in the transport and delivery sectors.[86] However, we contend that formalisation should not be limited to those able to meet the stringent tests for classification as an employee, because these decisions are highly contingent on the specific features of each platform and may be more difficult for domestic workers to meet given the range of models in this sector. Accordingly, the distinctive attributes of many domestic work platforms mean that otherwise positive developments in the law on employment status may still result in this sector's exclusion from protections.

National courts have often had to develop or depart from the existing legal tests used to determine employment status to conclude that platform workers are employed by the platform.[87] The techniques commonly used to bring platform workers within the scope of employment rights include adopting a broader understanding of control; a more relaxed approach to obligations of personal performance; and placing greater emphasis on the reality of workers' position and level of organisational integration rather than the written documentation.[88] Nonetheless, platform workers generally still need to show subordination in

[85] Prassl (n 16) 4.

[86] C Hießl, 'The Legal Status of Platform Workers: Regulatory Approaches and Prospects of a European Solution' (2022) 15 *Italian Labour Law e-Journal* 13; V De Stefano and M Wouters, 'Embedding Platforms in Contemporary Labour Law' in Jan Drahokoupil and Kurt Vandaele (eds), *A Modern Guide To Labour and the Platform Economy* (Cheltenham, Edward Elgar, 2021).

[87] E Kocher, 'Reshaping the Legal Categories of Work: Digital Labor Platforms at the Borders of Labor Law' (2021) 1 *Weizenbaum Journal of the Digital Society* w1. 1.2, 7–9; C Hießl, 'Jurisprudence of National Courts Confronted with Cases of Alleged Misclassification of Platform Workers: Comparative Analysis and Tentative Conclusions - Updated to 31 August 2022' (European Commission 2022).

[88] Hießl (n 86) 64.

order to enjoy full employment rights.[89] Although courts appear to be adapting traditional understandings of subordination to accommodate platform work, a threshold level of control is still required. This threshold may be more difficult to establish in domestic and care work than other sectors, as the most intense forms of 'hitherto unthinkable control'[90] over workers via algorithmic technologies and ratings systems are not always present. While the nudges that platform domestic workers are subjected to will often have an indirectly coercive effect, this may not reach the requisite level of control. In many cases where platforms adopt a marketplace model, for instance, they will not directly allocate or oversee tasks, or determine the conditions of work, with these matters instead determined between workers and the platform end users. While some platform domestic workers do report significant detrimental effects or view ratings as important for visibility, others feel confident securing work without them or view them as separate to the key concern of securing a regular job.[91] In particular, the characteristics of the childcare sector seem to relate to some workers viewing their qualifications and previous experience to have more weight than ratings on the platform.[92]

There are far fewer cases involving domestic platform workers seeking to establish employee status than in the delivery and ride-hailing sectors.[93] Hießl's comparative analysis of nearly 1,000 European decisions on the employment status of platform workers contains just one case specifically involving a caregiving platform, with only a total of 29 concerned with the delivery of services in private households. Of these, eight found that the workers were employees of the platform, five that they were employees of another (ie the end user), and seven categorised them as self-employed. This contrasts sharply with the food delivery sector, where the overwhelming majority of workers have been found to be employees of the platform.[94] Importantly for the purpose of understanding how these results may affect platform workers more broadly, the successful claims exhibited distinctive features that are not generalised among domestic work platforms. For example, a Barcelona court found workers to be in a labour relationship with the cleaning platform Clintu, because, inter alia, cleaners were not allowed to contact clients directly, prices were set between the platform and client, and the platform provided insurance and played a role in resolving delays in service delivery.[95] By contrast, some other domestic work platforms do permit

[89] Aloisi, Rainone and Countouris (n 22) 7.

[90] J Adams-Prassl, 'Employment Law and AI' in Ernest Lim and Phillip Morgan (eds), *The Cambridge Handbook of Private Law and Artificial Intelligence* (Cambridge, CUP, 2024).

[91] Wiesböck, Radlherr and Vo (n 29) 267; McDonald et al (n 32) 375; Muldoon et al (n 29) 17.

[92] Muldoon et al (n 29) 17.

[93] N Potocka-Sionek, 'Easier Done than Said? An Empirical Analysis of Case Law on Platform Work in the EU' (2023) 2023(1) *Hungarian Labour Law E-Journal* 46.

[94] Hießl, ch 7, in this book

[95] Juzgado de lo Social nº 15 de Barcelona - 26.06.2023. See also Eurofound, 'The Social Court in Barcelona, Spain, Rules Clintu Online and the Workers Are in an Employment Relationship (Court Ruling), Record Number 4276' (*Platform Economy Database, Dublin*, 2023) https://apps.eurofound.europa.eu/platformeconomydb/the-social-court-in-barcelona-spain-rules-clintu-online-and-the-workers-are-in-an-employment-relationship-110039.

workers to communicate directly with potential end users.[96] It is therefore far from certain that most platform domestic workers would be able to show the levels of control and subordination needed for employee status.

A further concern about over-reliance on status classification is that platforms may tweak their terms to fit an independent contracting model.[97] For example, the cleaning platform Helpling has adjusted to regulations in various European countries by avoiding initial involvement in price setting, as well as changing its business model in the Netherlands to circumvent classification as temporary agency, and removing control over workers to remain within the independent contracting model in France and Germany.[98] The 'primacy of facts' doctrine, whereby employment status is determined based on the reality of the relationship rather than any written documentation, may go some way to addressing the problem of any sham terms in platforms' documentation. But it does nothing to constrain platforms' ability to *genuinely change* their business practices in ways that avoid a finding of employment status, including the allocation of risks between the parties and levels of organisational integration and autonomy afforded to workers.

Taken together, these issues mean that there are real risks to an approach to formalisation of platform work based solely on employment status as the conduit for rights. Traditional understandings of employment provide an unsuitable vehicle for ensuring platform domestic workers are entitled to the rights and protections needed to ensure decent work. Even where a relationship lacks adequate indicators of direct control to meet the criteria for employee status, for example because the worker sets her own rates or retains discretion over aspects of the way tasks are performed, labour protections are still necessary to address insecurity, lack of job stability and competitive pressures to complete unpaid work and reduce fees.

Accordingly, we share critiques of the 'all or nothing' approach based on a total exclusion of those who lack status from labour rights,[99] and endorse the view that labour law protections should be reshaped to assist platform workers regardless of their formal status.[100] We therefore propose – as a 'more radical' means of supporting platform workers[101] – that the entitlement to labour rights, as a key element of substantive formalisation, needs to be decoupled from traditional understandings of employment status. Although not our focus here, we have argued elsewhere that human rights principles, as universal and equally held entitlements, provide a valuable normative basis for this proposed shift.

[96] Pais and Marcolin (n 81) 404; Muldoon et al (n 29).

[97] Sandra Fredman et al, 'Thinking Out of the Box: Fair Work for Platform Workers' (2020) 31 *King's Law Journal* 236.

[98] Koutsimpogiorgos et al (n 61) 166, 174.

[99] A Aloisi, 'J.K. v TP S.A. and the "Universal" Scope of EU Anti-Discrimination Law at Work: A Paradigm Shift?' (2023) 52 *Industrial Law Journal* 977, 978.

[100] Fredman et al (n 97) 236; E Kocher, *Digital Work Platforms at the Interface of Labour Law: Regulating Market Organisers* (Oxford, Hart Publishing, 2022) ch 7.

[101] Hunt and Samman (n 34) 262.

Consequently, the exclusion of platform workers from employment protections that secure aspects of human rights, such as freedom of association, private and family life, and decent work, are suspect and stand in need of justification.[102]

VI. FORMALISING PLATFORM DOMESTIC WORK: TOWARDS UNIVERSAL RIGHTS

Against our proposed inclusive framework, it is pertinent to consider the recently agreed EU Platform Work Directive (PWD), as a significant regulatory development aiming to develop platform-specific rights. The Directive appears to be a positive step towards alignment with an approach to formalisation based on universal rights but not to resolve all issues. Although requiring an effective legal presumption of employment status to be triggered by 'facts indicating control and direction',[103] states are left with substantial freedom to define the factual circumstances that demonstrate the appropriate level of control.[104] There is therefore a risk that the presumption will not apply where domestic platform workers are working under arrangements where less direct control is exerted by the platform. Moreover, the presumption can also be rebutted if a platform can prove the 'relationship in question is not an employment relationship' under national law.[105] As a result, many platform domestic workers are likely to continue to be excluded from employment status.

Notably, however, the PWD also contains some more universal rights and protections, which extend to all 'persons performing platform work' rather than 'platform workers', meaning those with or deemed to have an employment relationship under national law. This broader category encompasses all individuals working via a 'digital labour platform', meaning any entity using electronic means for the 'organisation of work performed by individuals in return for payment' which also uses automated monitoring or decision-making systems.[106] At the least, digital labour platforms play a significant role in matching demand for work with workers rather than simply advertising offers or requests.[107] This definition is therefore likely to capture many domestic platform workers even if they cannot be classed as employed, since it is less focused on questions of control and subordination. The rights conferred include limits on the collection or processing of some types of personal and private data, and the processing of data to infer some characteristics or predict the exercise of fundamental

[102] J Atkinson and N Sedacca, 'Realising Decent Work for Platform Workers: A Human Rights Approach' (2025) 16 Transnational Legal Theory 578.

[103] Council of the European Union, 'Proposal for the DIRECTIVE OF THE EUROPEAN PARLIAMENT AND OF THE COUNCIL on Improving Working Conditions in Platform Work - Analysis of the Final Compromise Text with a View to Agreement' (2024), para 32, Article 5(1) and (2).

[104] Article 4(2).

[105] Article 5 (1).

[106] Paras 20–21; Article 2(1).

[107] Para 21.

rights.[108] There are also rights to transparent information, including the grounds for any decisions to restrict, suspend or terminate accounts or refuse payment, and to the portability of data generated while working on the platform.[109] These provisions could benefit platform domestic workers by providing greater insight into any penalties being applied to them, for example for slower response times or other indirect forms of control, assisting challenges to decisions that potentially violate their employment or non-discrimination rights.

The Directive also contains important provisions on human oversight of automated systems,[110] communication channels for platform workers to contact each other and representatives regardless of status, [111] and representatives' rights to receive information on algorithmic systems.[112] The provision of certain entitlements to workers regardless of status is conceptually significant since it 'breaks the taboo of confining labour rights and protections to employees alone'[113] and is an important step forward from the status quo in which platforms can make arbitrary decisions without redress. However, the set of rights afforded to self-employed workers is more restrictive than for 'platform workers', excluding, for example, the health and safety provisions in Article 12, raising concerns that some platform domestic workers who cannot meet tests around subordination and control could also be excluded from these rights. In general, moreover, the universally applicable rights remain primarily procedural and focused on data protection matters, while more substantive labour rights are limited to those classed as 'platform workers' based on indications of employment status.

The PWD therefore represents only partial progress towards substantive formalisation, which requires decent conditions, collective bargaining and job security for all platform domestic workers. By contrast, it is promising that the Draft Convention on platform work published by the ILO in summer 2025 refers to a definition of 'digital platform workers' as being 'regardless of their classification of status in employment'.[114] It is to be hoped that this more universalistic approach is maintained in the final adopted text.

VII. CONCLUSION

Platform domestic work poses a unique set of regulatory challenges. As a compound non-standard form of work, it combines the concerns with casualisation of work

[108] Article 7.
[109] Article 9.
[110] Articles 10 and 11.
[111] Article 20.
[112] Articles 8(2); 9(1) and (4); 10(4); 11(2). Other information rights are restricted to representatives of 'platform workers', rather than all persons performing platform work.
[113] N Countouris, V De Stefano and J Hendy, 'Social Europe Needs a New Concept of "Worker"' (*Social Europe*, 10 April 2024) www.socialeurope.eu/social-europe-needs-a-new-concept-of-worker.
[114] ILO, 'Report V(3) - Decent Work in the Platform Economy - International Labour Conference, 114th Session, 2026' (2025) 32.

characteristic of the gig economy with the longstanding devaluation of feminised labour and the invisibility of work conducted in the private sphere to employment law. It raises distinct challenges from sectors like ride hailing, where automated matching and algorithmic control play a more direct and consistent role. Given widespread pre-existing informality in domestic work, platforms present themselves as 'formalising' the sector, but in many cases, this reflects an impoverished view of formalisation based on record keeping and registration with authorities. Against this, we have proposed pursuing a thick normative understanding of formalisation for platform domestic workers, which centres the goal of decent work for all and labour and social protections, both in line with other sectors and adapted to the specificities of domestic work.

Initiatives for regulation of platform work have primarily centred on fitting those performing it into employee status as a conduit to accessing rights. Courts in many jurisdictions have developed more flexible approaches to the scope of employment rights, including by looking beyond the written contractual terms to the true nature of the relationship. But these progressive decisions have still required indicators of control and subordination by the platform; factors which may be more difficult for some platform domestic workers to show given the possibilities for direct contact with clients, some choice over work organisation, variable impact of ratings and largely indirect forms of algorithmic control. Crucially, however, these workers still require protection given their exposure to competitive pressures, requirements for unpaid work, lack of job security and unpredictable hours and income.

We have therefore argued for a move away from reliance on employment status to allocate the rights and protections required for the formalisation of work, and assessed the EU's Platform Work Directive as a means for achieving this. While the Directive is significant for extending certain rights to self-employed workers on digital platforms, thus decoupling some rights at work from employment, these primarily data-related and procedural rights are insufficient on their own to advance meaningful formalisation of platform domestic workers, which also requires protection of decent working conditions and social security. Such measures may be ambitious, but without them, a move to platform work stands to intensify casualisation, insecurity and low paid work in a sector that has long been unjustifiably excluded from labour rights protection.

Index

www.ingramcontent.com/pod-product-compliance
Ingram Content Group UK Ltd.
Pitfield, Milton Keynes, MK11 3LW, UK
UKHW020245290926
15470UKWH00002B/746